Missions Impossible

Missions Impossible

Higher Education and Policymaking in the Arab World

John Waterbury

The American University in Cairo Press
Cairo New York

First published in 2020 by
The American University in Cairo Press
113 Sharia Kasr el Aini, Cairo, Egypt
One Rockefeller Plaza, New York, NY 10020
www.aucpress.com

An earlier version of Chapter 5 appeared as "Governance of Arab Universities: Why Does It Matter?,"
in Adnan Badran, Elias Baydoun, and John Hillman, eds., *Universities in Arab Countries: An Urgent
Need for Change* (Switzerland: Springer, 2018), 55–70. Reproduced by permission.

An earlier version of Chapter 6 appeared as "Reform of Higher Education in the Arab World," in
Elias Baydoun and John Hillman, eds., *Major Challenges Facing Higher Education in the Arab World:
Quality Assurance and Relevance* (Switzerland: Springer, 2019), 133–66. Reproduced by permission.

Dar el Kutub No. 11150/19
ISBN 978 977 416 963 2

Dar el Kutub Cataloging-in-Publication Data

Waterbury, John
    Missions Impossible: Higher Education and Policymaking in the Arab World / John Waterbury.—
Cairo: The American University in Cairo Press, 2020
    p.   cm.
    ISBN 978 977 416 963 2
    1.   Education, Higher—Arab countries
    2.   Universities and Colleges—Arab countries
    378

1 2 3 4 5   24 23 22 21 20

Designed by Sally Boylan
Printed in the United States of America

To Sarah, tqm

Contents

Figures and Tables

Figures

Tables

Preface:
Brainstorming Arab Higher Education

Higher education in the Middle East in general, and in the Arab world in particular, is not understudied but, as the references for this monograph show, a lot of the empirical work has been carried out by the international donor community, specialized United Nations and regional organizations, and nongovernmental organizations. Regional governments have undertaken periodic strategic plans, but how seriously they are taken is a matter of debate. The reference section of this book is also testimony to a burgeoning literature on education that is generated by scholars in the region.

My interest in this subject was nourished by my decade as president of the American University of Beirut (1998–2008), when I had to wrestle not only with the challenges of providing high-quality education in a relatively low-income region but also with those of being a player of sorts in the regional arena of higher education more generally. After the American University of Beirut (AUB) I was for a year advisor to the Government of Abu Dhabi on higher education (2011–2012). In that capacity I carried out an extensive survey of institutions of higher learning in the United Arab Emirates. To the best of my knowledge that survey was never released. I mention this merely to indicate that while I will pay little attention to higher education in the oil-rich countries of the Arab world, I am not unfamiliar with it.

In my academic career, I have been a student of politics and public policy in the Middle East since the early 1960s. I have also been part of some notable universities: Columbia, Michigan, Aix-Marseilles III, Princeton,

AUB, and New York University Abu Dhabi. Like many of my colleagues I lived in the academic environment without studying it. My fieldwork in several countries inevitably led me to local universities, but I went to them in search of expertise. I never studied them in their own right, which, in retrospect, seems embarrassingly short-sighted.

A premise of this study, so widely held that I doubt it would arouse any dissent, is that Arab higher education has been and remains in a state of structural crisis. This has been documented at fairly high altitude since 2002 in various *Arab Human Development Reports*, especially those of 2003 on "Building a Knowledge Society" and 2009 on "Toward Productive Intercommunication for Knowledge." Surveying all levels of education, the World Bank study of 2008, *The Road Not Traveled: Education Reform in the Middle East and North Africa*, is equally critical. Finally, the most focused study, although gentler in its critique, is Munir Bashshur's 2004 *Higher Education in the Arab States*.

As I shall examine in what follows, there may be nothing peculiarly 'Arab' about this crisis. I suspect that many developing countries that committed themselves to democratizing higher education find themselves in similar situations. Indeed, it came as something of a surprise to me that there are no problems in higher education unique to the Middle East and North Africa region or even to developing countries. The problems Arab universities face and the pathologies with which they grapple differ in degree but not in kind from those in other countries. Let me mention just a few here:

- Crises in public financing of higher education, as real for the United States (US) or the United Kingdom (UK) as for Egypt or Morocco.
- The erosion of the academic profession or what I call the myth of the full-time professor. Adjuncts in the US have become the indispensable cogs of higher education just as the nominally 'full-time' professor in the Arab world has had to seek employment outside academia to make ends meet.
- The tendency for universities to reinforce class privilege rather than overcome it is ubiquitous.
- Dropout rates are a universal problem. Argentina has been a world leader in this respect.

However, to the extent that these problems have their roots in the political institutions of the region, there may be something peculiarly Arab about the problem.

There are two broad levels that require examination. The first is national 'strategy' and goals, in the current instance, in the higher education sector. Strategies evolve, so we need to know where the sector has been in order to understand priorities for the future. The second level involves governance structures, including how leadership is selected and performance monitored (accountability), and the incentives that both principals and agents have to achieve any particular set of goals. Obviously, a big part of the governance picture is finances and resources. An equally big part is the effective degree of autonomy the institution enjoys.

It is safe to say that the 'crisis' has been created at both levels—national strategy and institutional governance—and to address it will require changes at both levels. Much of the policy literature mentioned above and to which we shall return is prescriptive. It says more about what *should* be done than *how* to do it, given the political context.

One way to understand what is possible is to select cases of successful reform, islands of excellence, or at least cases in which palpable progress is being made. For example, Cadi Ayyad University (CAU) in Morocco or Suez Canal University in Egypt may have been able to make progress where their older and more illustrious sisters, like Mohammed V University or Cairo University seem mired in inertial practices. The problem here is that outside the private sector there may be very few such success stories.

Or one could look at success in other regions altogether. One example might be the National University of Singapore (NUS) or perhaps the Indian Institutes of Technology. We shall look further on at the NUS and also at Sharif University of Technology (SUT) in the Islamic Republic of Iran.

Whether one selects for success or on the basis of some other criteria, I think we may best understand basic problems by hearing the agents themselves: the rectors and chancellors, the deans and vice presidents. We may understand effective governance, incentives, and accountability best through their eyes. It is also the medium of direct interviews with which I am most comfortable and experienced.

It is always difficult to identify one's audience. The general mission of this study is to help policymakers and third-party agents of change think about the main challenges facing higher education in the Middle East and North Africa. But that may be overambitious, and, as Lisa Anderson rightly warns, the kind of political science and policy analysis I present may not be in a format that is readily digestible:

Presenting the finished, polished, completed findings from research conducted in a political science department to policymakers today is rather like drawing a map of Europe on a blackboard: it is neither what today's policymakers need—it takes too long to produce, it is not interactive or mobile, it precludes questions; in short, it does not reflect the requirements of the audience, any audience, today—nor is it what a true political scientist is, or should be, really good at. Our contribution—to the lives of our students as to the work of our policymakers—should be more in the way of guides or coaches. As such, we support and test, encourage and question those who are confronting the challenges of living in and governing human communities. The joy of learning is a spirit that can be reflected and replicated elsewhere—the "campuses" of Google and Microsoft come to mind—but it should be the hallmark of university life, and it should be reflected in the interaction of the denizens of universities with their communities, whether policymakers, neighborhood communities or, not least, students. (Anderson, 2012: 392)[1]

As the post-independence model of publicly funded and administered higher education has faltered in the Arab world, out of expediency or surrender, the private sector, both local and international, has been allowed to enter the 'market.' A survey of private sector initiatives would be a worthy and complex undertaking in its own right (see Levy, forthcoming). No doubt some entrepreneurs have entered this market with the same profit expectations they might hold for investments in hotels or hospitals. Typically, the for-profit private ventures emphasize marketable skills, especially business and computer science, but they do not offer an integrated educational experience. Most enroll only a fraction of the total enrolled cohorts in any specific country. There are some exceptions, such as Islamic Azad University in Iran, which may have two million students across its many campuses. It is important to ask if this development can provide any long-term answers to dealing with the crisis or whether it will be only a short-term fix for the relatively well-off. Experiences in Latin America, for instance, suggest that private higher education offers structural solutions to the challenges facing that region. Over 50 percent of Latin American students in tertiary education are in private institutions. At the same time, the most prestigious institutions remain public.

We are joining an ongoing debate on the fundamental nature of education in society, who benefits from it, and who pays for it. One school argues that education at all levels enhances the individual earnings of its products and that they should therefore pay for it out of taxes on their enhanced incomes. In this view, education is a private good that generates an income stream (see Cooper, 2017).

At the opposite end of the spectrum are those who see education as a right, the violation of which will harm society as a whole. Education is a public good that provides benefits for all of society (even to those who drop out of high school or never go to university). The benefits are the provision of actors fit to be responsible, informed citizens as well as trained participants in a dynamic workforce and a healthy economy. Given that many educational institutions enjoy tax-free status and benefit from public land, and given that taxpayers fund public higher education from which, in most societies, many adults do not benefit, the preponderant view seems to be that education is a public good (see Anomaly, 2018).[2]

One final observation: the giant national universities will for many decades to come take on the heavy lifting of higher education in the Arab world. They educate in the hundreds of thousands, and their graduates often swamp the civil service and public enterprise sector. They are underfinanced (except in some of the petroleum-exporting states) but, at the same time, represent huge sunk investments that cannot be written off nor easily broken up into more manageable pieces. Is there any vision for the future either at the level of the principals or at the level of the agents? Are there 'disruptive innovations' on the horizon that might blow the old public ships out of the water? We will engage these questions throughout the chapters that follow.

A Note on Sources

The reader will find an extensive list of references at the end of this study. I do not cite all of these references in the text, but they have all informed my analysis and may be useful to others going down similar paths.

I also conducted several interviews and email exchanges in the course of my research. These were aimed at eliciting interpretations of events and policies. None of my interlocutors forbade me from quoting or citing them, but, given that many of the observations are politically sensitive, I have chosen, in many instances, not to cite them by name.

A Note on Organization

I have written each chapter in this study with the hope that it can stand alone. That means there is some repetition from chapter to chapter. I wanted chapters that told complete stories but a book that told an integrated story. Hubris, perhaps.

Acknowledgments

I began my academic involvement with the Middle East more than sixty years ago, in 1958, and made my first trip to Egypt in 1960. Much of my life since then has been spent in the region. I began a family there in Morocco in 1967 and have shamelessly abused the region's justifiably renowned hospitality ever since. Countless Middle Easterners have shared their experience and wisdom with me with no expectation of a quid pro quo. There was, in fact, no way I could compensate them, individually or collectively, for their generosity. They know who they are. Not a few are no longer with us. This may be my last opportunity to salute them all. It is a grossly inadequate gesture.

The research for this study was carried out over several years, beginning in 2008–2009. It was largely self-financed, but I do owe thanks to New York University Abu Dhabi, where I was visiting global professor from 2012 to 2014, for providing me with a research budget during those years. I also am obliged to the Issam Fares Institute for Public Policy and International Affairs at the AUB for supporting research assistance (provided by Tara Mahfoud) during one phase of the study. I extend belated thanks to Tara.

I am also deeply grateful to my former colleague at the AUB, Dr. Prem C. Sexena, where he was professor and chairman at the Department of Population Studies in the Faculty of Health Sciences. Prem Sexena went on to become the Garware chair professor at the Tata Institute of Social Sciences in Mumbai, India. Dr. Sexena is responsible for an analysis of existing and projected gross enrollment ratios for select Arab countries, referenced in Chapter 1 and Appendix 1.

I worked with a small team of Nadia Naqib, Miriam Fahmi, and Jonathan Boylan at the American University in Cairo Press. Nadia in particular was both meticulous and non-invasive in her editing. This is a very delicate balance to achieve, and I am in debt for her thoughtfulness and sensitivity. I owe the whole team sincere thanks for all they did.

There are some colleagues who merit special mention for their time, wisdom, and willingness to engage. Some are old friends, others I only know through email or telephone conversations: Adnan El-Amine, Elizabeth Buckner, Paul Lingenfelter, Ahmad Jammal, Hassan Diab, Sari Hanafi, Ragui Assaad, Dan Levy, Munir Bashshur, John Blackton, Nazli Choucri, Fred Moavenzadeh, Sheikh Nahayan, Ali al-Din Hilal Dessouki, Rasha Faek, the late Galal Amin, the late Sadiq al-Azm, Wail Benjelloun, Faissal Aziz, Azmi Mahafzah, and the late Clayton Christensen, whom I never met, but whose theory of disruptive innovation is central to parts of this book. I hope they will not be unhappy with this book, but if they are, it's all on me.

Abbreviations

AFESD	Arab Fund for Economic and Social Development (Kuwait)
AI	artificial intelligence
AKP	Justice and Development Party (Turkey)
AROQA	Arab Organization for Quality Assurance in Education
ASU	Arab Socialist Union (Egypt)
AUB	American University of Beirut
AUC	American University in Cairo
BAU	business as usual
CAU	Cadi Ayyad University (Morocco)
CBE	competency-based education
CMI	Center for Mediterranean Integration (World Bank)
CNRS-L	National Council for Scientific Research, Lebanon
EBRD	European Bank for Reconstruction and Development
ECOSOC	United Nations Economics and Social Council
ESCWA	Economic and Social Commission for Western Asia (United Nations)
EU	European Union
FTE	full-time equivalent
GCC	Gulf Cooperation Council
GDP	gross domestic product
GER	gross enrollment ratio
GERD	general expenditures on research and development
ICT	information and communications technology

IFI	international financial institution
IHL	institution of higher learning
IMF	International Monetary Fund
KAUST	King Abdullah University of Science and Technology (Saudi Arabia)
KPI	key performance indicator
LMD	*license, master, doctorat*
MENA	Middle East and North Africa
MOOC	massive open online course
MVU	Mohammed V University (Morocco)
MVUA	Mohammed V University, Agdal (Morocco)
MVUS	Mohammed V University, Souissi (Morocco)
NDP	National Democratic Party (Egypt)
NGO	nongovernmental organization
NUS	National University of Singapore
OAPEC	Organization of Arab Petroleum Exporting Countries
OCP	Office Chérifien des Phosphates (Morocco)
OECD	Organisation for Economic Co-operation and Development
OPEC	Organization of the Petroleum Exporting Countries
PKK	Kurdish Workers' Party
R&D	research and development
RORE	rate of return to education
SCU	Supreme Council of Universities (Egypt)
SME	small and medium enterprise
SOE	state-owned enterprise
SPC	Syrian Protestant College (Lebanon)
STEM	science, technology, engineering, and mathematics
SUT	Sharif University of Technology (Iran)
TÜBITAK	Scientific and Technological Research Council (Turkey)
UAE	United Arab Emirates
UAR	United Arab Republic
UK	United Kingdom
UN	United Nations
UNAM	Universidad Nacional Autónoma de México
UNDP	United Nations Development Programme
UNESCO	United Nations Educational, Scientific and Cultural Organization
US	United States

USAID	United States Agency for International Development
USJ	Université Saint-Joseph (Lebanon)
WHO	World Health Organization
YÖK	Council of Higher Education (Turkey)

Introduction

My approach to what many have called the 'crisis' of higher education in the Middle East is to understand the public policy options available to policymakers and their political masters and why some have been adopted and others rejected or neglected. I look both backward and forward: backward mainly in the sense of understanding institutional histories and pathologies; forward mainly in the sense of understanding politically feasible (non-regime threatening) reforms, highly destabilizing reforms, and disruptive or undisruptive innovations.

The period in which I researched and wrote this book bridges the years during which many of us focused on 'Arab exceptionalism,' the effective resistance of nearly all Arab regimes to any significant liberalization or democratization, the shorter period of the Arab uprisings of 2011–2012, and then what might be called the restoration of unmitigated authoritarianism everywhere but in Tunisia. In terms of public policy, a transition to greater accountability, direct lobbying for policy outcomes, and competition for public support of certain policies was aborted. There is accountability in authoritarian regimes, but it has its own logic and is very difficult for the outsider to observe.

Policy Innovation

The hypothetical I wish to explore is not so hypothetical. It in fact describes where I sit or stand. I am an outside observer who was once a marginal player in a regional and national system that had lost its sense of mission and defined goals. I am an advocate for change, but what kind of change? Is it what Clayton Christensen (Christensen et al., 2008) calls sustaining or supportive innovation that helps the existing system to survive, if not prosper? Or is it disruptive innovation that emerges outside the system and makes the status quo increasingly unviable?

If I enter into the logic of sustaining innovation, then my aim will be to persuade policymakers and university administrators that there are measures which can be taken that would measurably improve outcomes (I beg the question, what outcomes?) without destroying careers or so upsetting the distribution of resources that vested interests would bring any change to a halt. Most important, I cannot propose anything that would threaten the political stability of the regime. It does not matter if the threat is real or merely perceived. Obviously, this kind of change is incremental and reversible.

If I enter into the logic of disruptive innovation, then policymakers and administrators are merely obstacles to be got round (or under as Christensen suggests), not partners in change. My allies will be entrepreneurs who want to bring the disruptive innovation to market. According to Christensen this is always a market that is ill-defined or untested. It is a market in which existing educational institutions do not or cannot compete. As an outsider I need to find the entrepreneurs and the 'product,' or the entrepreneurs need to find me to develop the product, or perhaps they can ignore me altogether. Whatever my role, existing institutions are under threat and may not survive in their current form. Change that eliminates players is not reversible. That is why it is disruptive.

The nature of this study is to promote supportive innovation. I recognize the possibility that current systems are beyond repair or may not be able to serve their basic purposes given the structure of existing markets. But it is hard to imagine a scenario in which I go to policymakers and espouse change that would undermine existing structures with all their mature patronage and power relations in exchange for something that by its disruptive nature is unpredictable and destabilizing.

Is this the formula for having it both ways? What might this look like in universities? Companies such as Hewlett-Packard, Johnson & Johnson, and General Electric have managed to survive the last few decades by creating new, smaller, autonomous disruptive business units and shutting down or selling off mature ones that had reached the end of their sustaining-technology trajectories. Universities, I argue, can and do see disruptive innovations coming down the track, but in the environment of the Middle

East and North Africa (MENA) region they may face daunting hurdles in taking measures to meet or preempt them.

I will have several occasions, beginning now, to warn the reader of a trap which I would like to avoid but into which I am sure I have fallen. Let us say we have an observed policy outcome—for example, the introduction of tuition fees in public universities. This is our dependent variable. Then we surmise that the main beneficiaries are the ministries of education and finance, which collect the fees, and wealthier parents who can afford to pay them, while the great majority of the less privileged are 'screwed.' We may then conclude that the ministries and the wealthy engineered the new policy. Because we outsiders cannot directly observe the policymaking process (legislatures, the press, and formal lobbies are marginal actors in autocratic systems), the conclusion may be logical but simply wrong.[1]

Real situations about which I speculate in this study involve, among others, the informal sector and brain drain. In a number of Arab countries, the informal sector may account for 30–40 percent in value of all economic activity. This activity is beyond the fiscal reach of the state that foregoes tax revenues. At the same time many Arab states suffer from low national savings as compared to national investment levels. The gap between savings and investment is closed through increasingly unsustainable levels of borrowing. I surmise that the politicians and policymakers see the informal sector as the lesser of evils. It does not require state resources to function, it creates jobs, and it is adaptable and innovative, so let it be. That is not an unreasonable conclusion, but I have no direct evidence to sustain it.

Many Arab countries suffer high rates of brain drain whereby students in their higher education systems, in whom they have made large investments, take their skills to other economies. Why would this happen? Because politicians and policymakers see brain drain as exporting those most likely to challenge autocratic rule. In addition, the exportees remit earnings that help sustain the local economy. This again is a surmise, and except for some anecdotal evidence from Lebanon, I cannot cite documented decisions.

Similarly, one may try to identify the driver(s) of significant policy change. Leave aside the crucial issue of how we define significant, we may hypothesize that only crisis situations will bring about real policy change. That is, political leaders will have to deal with cumulative and profound damage to polities or economies, failing which the regime itself may be threatened. Again, the observer may argue backward from what s/he identifies as significant change to an explanation that assumes crisis. This is no more satisfying than the first gambit.[2] I posit that meaningful reform may be underway in the higher education sector in a number of Arab countries. I then try to establish what might have happened to push autocrats to sponsor change they might otherwise avoid. My answer is a crisis in youth employment with, as 2011 showed, existential threats for regime survival. I am not comfortable with this reverse engineering, but, *faute de mieux*, I have to go with what I can see.

Crisis

While the perception of educational crisis is widespread in the Arab world, and in the Middle East, different observers have different metrics in mind. From inside, the most severe critiques have come in the various *Arab Human Development Reports*, especially that of 2003 on "Building a Knowledge Society." From outside, the World Bank's 2008 study, *The Road Not Traveled*, has had significant regional impact. Occasionally heads of state weigh in. King Mohammed VI of Morocco, in a speech from the throne in August 2013, referred to parts of Morocco's universities as "factories of the unemployed."

The dimensions of the crisis are quite predictable and will concern us throughout the coming pages. In the broadest sense there has been a massive pedagogical failure. Jordan's former Foreign Minister Marwan Muasher (2014) singles out the prevalence of rote learning and the uncritical acceptance of the text, which yield obedience to power as well as intolerance (see also Cammack et al., 2017). The victims are pluralism, critical thinking, analytic thinking, embracing diversity, and demanding accountability of those in power.

The Arab world in relative terms does invest heavily in the educational sector (see Chapters 1 and 8). The crisis is more one of money poorly spent, with grossly inadequate returns to the investment. The region has made great progress in the numbers enrolled in higher education but has done poorly in terms of graduation rates and employment. Were public tertiary education not basically free, the low private returns to it might lead prospective students to shun it altogether.

The crisis has built over several decades. The end of colonial control, after the Second World War, ushered in an era of egalitarianism and populism. Colonial authorities were rightly regarded as having thwarted or discouraged tertiary education. Such education was regarded by colonized societies as critical to their own liberation and authentic independence. Making education available to all was proclaimed a right and not a privilege (let alone a personal investment in the future). Professedly socialist countries, such as Egypt, and more market-oriented countries, such as Jordan or Morocco, all implemented fairly populist educational policies.

Moreover, newly independent societies needed skilled personnel to staff new public bureaucracies designed to meet the neglected needs of poor populations. Nowhere were the needs more pressing than in the educational sector itself. Lebanese University, for example, grew out of Lebanon's normal school and was designed to provide high school teachers to the nation's burgeoning public *lycée* system.

Tertiary education was and is characterized by a 'trilemma' involving three variables: quantity, quality, and cost (see Chapter 8). Only two of the three can be achieved, while a third is always sacrificed. Quantity coupled with low cost will sacrifice quality. High cost and quality will sacrifice quantity. Quantity and quality will come at the expense of affordability (Kapur, 2011).

In the 1970s the trilemma was on the loose in the MENA like an angry beast. Rapid population growth meant that the entire educational system was swamped with new entrants while universities saw their enrollments rise several-fold. Some countries, like Egypt and Syria, implicitly or explicitly, guaranteed public sector jobs for all university graduates. New universities were established at a dizzying pace, and badly prepared and poorly paid faculty were recruited to teach (see Chapters 1 and 9). Little wonder that in many instances they turned to private lessons and group tutoring to supplement their incomes.

Before long, public bureaucracies were saturated and civil service hiring stalled. In the 1990s, Algeria, for instance, eliminated half a million public sector jobs. Egypt, as I write, is trying to reduce its civil service from six to four million (*Al-Araby Al-Jadeed*, 2018), with those furloughed probably migrating to the informal sector, which, in general, has become a sponge for overqualified university graduates. The more fortunate have emigrated abroad. This economic reckoning in the 1970s and 1980s corresponded to the first boom in petroleum prices (as a result of the 1973–74 Organization of Arab Petroleum Exporting Countries (OAPEC) embargo on oil sales to the US). The surge in oil prices led to a spurt of investment in infrastructure and services in the Gulf Cooperation Council (GCC) countries and Libya, which in turn created thousands of jobs for educated and unskilled Egyptians, Jordanians, Lebanese, Yemenis, and Sudanese. When the oil bust inevitably came, the oil-poor suffered as much economically as the oil-rich. Demand for labor contracted and remittance flows fell off.

The oil-poor, people-rich countries grappled with structural adjustment programs, frequently guided by the International Monetary Fund (IMF) and other creditors, to bring fiscal balance to public finances. Economies that had been dominated by state investment and centralized planning had to invent a new model. It was not, in most instances, pretty. The private sector, both domestic and foreign, was given incentives to invest and to buy up privatized state assets, including factories, banks, insurance companies, and transportation facilities. The domestic private sector was invited to invest in higher education, establishing in many instances for-profit universities. Many students of the region decried an era of 'crony capitalism' and 'neoliberal' economics (see Diwan et al., 2019). 'The Washington Consensus' became a dirty phrase.

There is solid empirical evidence that authoritarian redistributive social contracts sapped structural adjustment programs of their impact. Eric Rougier (2016), for example, constructed a score by multiplying the extent of redistribution in MENA countries by the degree of authoritarianism. He found that the MENA scores were twice those of any other region in the world. Ersatz neoliberal reforms did little to foster broad-based private sector development or sophistication in exports. What many have dubbed 'crony capitalism' left authoritarian regimes with high youth unemployment and, outside the informal sector, anemic private enterprises unable to absorb much labor at any skill level.

Rougier (2016) and Ragui Assaad and Caroline Krafft (2016a) in fact see reform of the private sector and reform of the training/educational sector as key to economic transformation. The agenda is designed to accommodate the authoritarian structures as much as possible, not to overthrow them.

Structural adjustment did not significantly alter the fundaments of autocratic controls of institutions of higher learning (IHLs). Universities were and are rightly perceived to be under the thumb of political authorities who meddle constantly in curricula, appointments, and promotions. Some use university employment as part of their patronage networks. Despite founding documents and charters that emphasize university autonomy, real autonomy is rare, if nonexistent (see Chapter 5).

Tertiary education fails in its two greatest duties toward society (and it is society, in that taxpayers pay for it): the formation of citizens who uphold the political order and the training of skilled participants in the nation's economy. One hears constantly about the mismatch between the skill sets of graduates and the needs of the job market (see Chapter 6). Some see the problem as one of universities mired in pedagogy designed to train public bureaucrats, while others see it as the result of private sectors oriented toward low skills and quick profits.

Universities have failed in their mission to produce new knowledge and carry out cutting-edge research. Key linkages are broken or have never existed. Universities do not interact with their own private sectors in terms of research and development (R&D) (see Chapter 7), and they do not directly serve the strategic goals of their governments. Governments may prefer to keep their research agendas within friendly and easily controlled public research centers, isolated from national universities. The private sector in the MENA has seldom entered high-tech areas of production. The tourism sector, for example, does not provide the same R&D opportunities as do information and communications technology (ICT) or biomedical research.

Arab universities interact among themselves very little. The fracturing of the Arab world is reflected in the lack of professional and research interaction. Many universities sign memoranda of understanding with sister institutions, but they seldom involve joint research or exchange of faculty or students. The same can be said of regional disciplinary associations. The organizations that normally set professional standards and apply ethical guidelines are at best atrophied, at worst totally absent.

Virtually regardless of the political orientation of particular regimes—from 'conservative' monarchies and emirates to populist republics—K–12 (kindergarten through twelfth grade) education and, increasingly, higher education have been touted as avenues of socioeconomic mobility. Yet everywhere class bias has come in through the back door and sometimes the front door. If we look at the region as a whole, on average about 30 percent of the age cohort eighteen to twenty-two is enrolled in tertiary education, the great bulk of it public (see Chapter 1). There is a distinct bias toward middle- and upper-income students in that share, yet society as a whole pays for the education. The well-off invest more heavily in private lessons, send their children to the best high schools, and frequently send them abroad for university education. A major facet of the crisis is, therefore, the absence of social equity (UNESCO, 2009, especially the chapter on "Main Challenges").

There are rare exceptions to the general gloom. Hana El-Ghali and her co-authors surveyed ninety institutions of higher learning and came away with some optimistic conclusions: "It is evident from an examination of the individual institutional survey results that these institutions clearly understood the needs of their societies in addition to their own specific institutional needs and that they were in the process of developing appropriate responses" (El-Ghali et al., 2010: 52).

Similarly, public opinion polls do not reflect a sense of crisis. Poll questions are very general, not specifying level of education, but by and large the scanty polling data we have indicate a public that ranges from indifferent to supportive of their educational systems (see next section). Quality of education does not appear to be a hot-button issue, at least in relative terms.

Attitudes

Those professionals closest to the education sector, including third-party experts and reformers, tend to be the most critical. They are most likely to write about declining standards, institutional atrophy, outdated pedagogy, and so forth. The actual consumers—Arab publics, parents, students—are far more charitable but hardly forgiving.

For instance, in their survey of nine thousand young Arabs in nine countries or populations, Jörg Gertel and Ralf Hexel (2018) found that trust in education systems was high, ranging from 64 percent to 90 percent, depending on the population. Other surveys reflect less positive assessments (Bollag, 2020).

Satisfaction is clearly limited. Nowhere does a majority of consumers express satisfaction with the system, and tellingly less than a third are happy with the relevance of skills learned.

By contrast, there is much more consistent concern for employment and job creation. The Arab Barometer (2014) shows that this concern dwarfs all others.

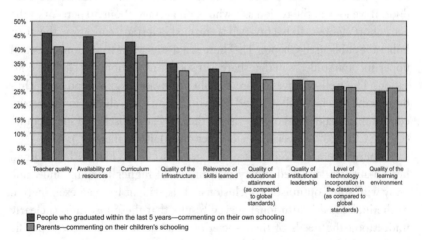

Figure I.1 Levels of Satisfaction with Aspects of Education: Students and Parents
Source: Dubai School of Government, 2013: 5

Table I.1 Arab Barometer Survey: What Are the Most Important Challenges Your Country is Facing Today?

Country	The economic situation (poverty, unemployment, and price increases)	Financial and administrative corruption	Enhancing (strengthening) democracy	Achieving stability and internal security	Other
Algeria	76.9	14.9	2.7	3.3	2.2
Egypt	87.6	6.5	1.4	1.3	3.1
Iraq	52.5	32.5	3.5	9.7	1.7
Jordan	81.0	14.0	1.1	0.7	3.3
Kuwait	56.5	25.3	9.4	0.9	8.0
Lebanon	60.6	24.4	3.5	7.1	4.3
Libya	23.1	32.3	2.3	0.7	41.6
Morocco	83.9	9.6	2.1	0.8	3.6
Palestine	50.3	8.7	1.3	3.0	36.6
Sudan	74.2	17.2	2.3	3.4	2.8
Tunisia	88.4	8.6	0.7	0.9	1.6
Yemen	74.6	17.1	3.9	2.8	1.6

Source: Arab Barometer, 2014

Assaad and Krafft (2016b) asked graduates how appropriate their studies were to their current work. Jordanian institutions performed the best, with only 16 percent of graduates saying that their education was either somewhat inappropriate or totally inappropriate. In Egypt, 34 percent of graduates deem their education totally inappropriate to the work they are currently doing, compared to 30 percent in Tunisia. The sum of those stating their education is either somewhat or totally inappropriate is 50 percent in Tunisia, as compared to 44 percent in Egypt.

Palestine provides a more detailed snapshot. The student assessments of various aspects of the tertiary course of study are strongly positive across all categories.

Elizabeth Buckner mentions that while people writing on the Middle East have said that young, unemployed men are the most vulnerable and dissatisfied in the region, her study in Syria shows that it is "specifically the *educated* unemployed that are the most discontent" (2013: 15, emphasis in original). In Chapter 4 we shall examine the evidence for the link between unemployment and political activism in the MENA.

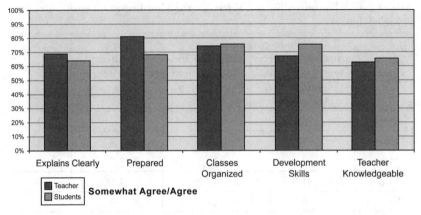

Figure I.2 National Study of Undergraduate Teaching in Palestine, Presented at An-Najah University, Nablus, July 23–24, 2009
Source: Cristillo, Jamal, and Said, 2009

Buckner goes on to pinpoint student grievances in Syria. Based on her 2010 survey, student dissatisfaction is due to government's sorting of educational trajectories in public universities based on results gained in *baccalauréat* exams. The state determines which career a person is to have based on grades alone, but no longer offers guarantees of employment after graduation as it did in years prior. According to Buckner, "the decoupling of the public university system from public sector employment means that higher education no longer promises the security it once did" (2013: 7). Young people believe they need to gain a higher education degree to make money but also that one must have money or family connections in order to find work after graduation. What is also frustrating to students in Syria is that for those who cannot afford private higher education, the state determines what they will study and hence what careers they can pursue based on their official examination results. This system also seems to be in place in Iran, whereby official examination results determine which universities and degrees students can pursue.

In Saudi Arabia, students who are able to choose, go to private universities, as they feel public universities lack practical training that links their degrees to work.

In another snapshot, a World Bank survey (Chauffour, 2017: 9) of Moroccans shows the high saliency of education (at all levels) among the major concerns of the country's citizens, far outstripping governance and fighting corruption, for example.

In 2016, five years after the Arab uprisings, a survey of some nine thousand young Arabs between the ages of sixteen and thirty was undertaken in Bahrain, Egypt, Jordan, Lebanon, Morocco, the Palestinian territories, among Syrian refugees, and Yemen (Gertel and Hexel, 2018). One thousand subjects were interviewed in each group, overweighting perhaps the unusual cases of Yemenis and Syrian refugees. Important countries were left out: Algeria, Iraq, Libya, Syria, Sudan, and Tunisia. It is not clear how their inclusion would have affected the study's results. The eight samples covered all socioeconomic strata and levels of education.

The entire region to varying degrees had been subjected to violence, civil war, political repression, economic restructuring, and stagnant or negative economic growth. Despite that, sampled youth were surprisingly positive about their current situations and the future. Only 50 percent of the most vulnerable populations—the Yemenis and Syrian refugees—felt insecure. When asked what they most trusted, family topped the chart by a good bit, followed by the military and education. Of the total sample, 42 percent expressed confidence in education. Two-thirds expressed guarded optimism about the future, and that proportion held steady across socioeconomic strata.

Legacies

As I shaped my own approach to the educational crisis, I was informed by research I carried out over two decades ago on state-owned enterprises (SOEs) in Egypt, India, Mexico, and Turkey. In that work I had expected that the different cultures and colonial histories of the four countries would significantly impact the way the public sector performed in each. The four countries had vastly different religions: Islam, Catholicism, Hinduism, and sometimes official *laïcité*, as in Turkey or Mexico. They also had different colonial histories, from Spanish and British to none (again, Turkey), and different ethnic compositions and political institutions, from Indian democracy, to Mexico's single-party *sexenio* (a single six-year term for the president of the republic), to Egypt's rulers for life.

In fact, it turned out that all these factors were swamped by the legal and policy regimes in which SOEs functioned: the nature of principals (owners) and agents (those who execute the owners' will), the relationship between principals and agents, the way in which missions were assigned to SOEs, and how managers read their incentive structures. Despite the great cultural, religious, and political-institutional disparities among the four, their SOEs shared many performance criteria and outcomes (Waterbury, 1993).

Having learned that lesson, I expected the same with respect to universities, above all in that I was focusing heavily on universities in Arab society and a few other neighboring predominantly Islamic countries (Turkey, Iran, Pakistan). I am not sure if I confirmed that hypothesis. Part of the problem lies in identifying significant performance criteria. Just as SOEs are burdened by multiple objectives—employment generation, regional development, strategic objectives, surplus or profit generation—so too are public universities asked to do a lot, including form citizens, train leaders, meet workplace demand, generate high-quality research, train new professors, and meet national strategic needs.[3] In both the SOE and university contexts, multiple objectives work at cross purposes. In both, outcomes have been distinctly suboptimal, although it is interesting to note that local commentary is much readier to evoke crisis and failure with respect to education than with respect to public enterprise. The educational enterprise plays a role in the daily lives of Middle Easterners that cannot be matched by SOEs.

There are historical legacies that count in comparing institutions of higher learning in the MENA, but I am not sure for how much. Private institutions prevail in Palestine and Lebanon, the French colonial legacy in North Africa has protected the overwhelming place of public universities, the British were skeptical that Egypt needed universities, while the French in Syria wanted the University of Damascus to be a beacon for the rest of the Arab world. Lebanon, meanwhile, did not have a public university until the 1950s (see Chapter 2).

Yet, as the discussion of crisis above indicates, the similarity in outcomes across the region outweighs the disparities. Outside the oil-rich countries of the GCC, no country has found a solution to the financial costs of the trilemma. Quality has been the victim. Although there has been some improvement in recent years, the only public universities to make it into the top two to three hundred in world rankings are in Saudi Arabia.[4] Most public universities have been factories for bureaucrats, if not for the unemployed. For at least three decades MENA countries have tried to foster their private sectors and reduce the budgetary burdens of the public sector. The public universities produce graduates that the private sector does not want or need. The residual employer becomes the informal sector, the gray economy that is unregulated, underfinanced, and characterized by low productivity and low skills.

The political science literature on the Middle East has stressed 'Arab exceptionalism'—the fact that the Arab world lags behind all other major regions on all measures of democratic practice. This holds despite a number of enabling variables, such as high levels of literacy, high rates of urbanization, growing middle classes, and substantial increases in per capita income over the last four decades. And as many have noted, the Arab world is plugged in, online, and social-media mad. The uprisings of 2011 offered hope that Arab exceptionalism was coming to an end, but, with the exception of Tunisia, those hopes have been dashed.

The absence of democracy in the Arab world has been attributed to the region's Islamic legacy, the prevalence of war(s), cultural patriarchy (or, put another way, the political, social, and economic subordination of women), and the prevalence of state systems dependent on rents, above all petroleum rents and rent-seeking (inter alia, see Elbadawi and Makdisi, 2017). All of these factors are probably in play, but none is exclusive to the Arab world. Less structural are analyses that stress alliances among regime reformers and hardliners and civil society moderates and radicals (Przeworski and Limongi 1997; Chaney, Akerloff, and Blaydes 2012). Each approach has its merits and seemingly explains some of the variance, but it is hard not to conclude that we really do not have a satisfactory explanation.[5]

Is there parallel exceptionalism in Arab higher education or in all levels of education? It came as something of a surprise to me that what we might call the pathologies of the educational crisis in the Arab world are reflected just about everywhere in the world. The trilemma is a powerful and ubiquitous conundrum. We may briefly review some of its component parts here:

- *Governance.* Everywhere countries tinker with the balance between university autonomy and accountability. Are democracies better at this than autocracies? We shall see (Chapter 6).
- *Sources of funding.* Who pays and how much? Is education a right or an investment? The debate is universal (Chapter 8).
- *Massification.* A terrible term but still graphic. South Korea extends higher education to approximately 90 percent of eligible cohorts. Organisation for Economic Co-operation and Development (OECD) averages are around 40 percent. The Arab world is not far behind. Free market systems, planned economies, autocracies, democracies, monarchies, republics are all headed in the same direction (Chapters 1 and 2).
- *R&D.* Globally, no one does enough, except, perhaps, Singapore, Israel, Finland, and a few others. Some countries do appear more adept than others at fostering productive interaction among universities, governments, and the private sector. The MENA region is notably weak in this domain (Chapter 7).

- *Class bias.* All educational systems, even the most nominally egalitarian, create back-door fixes that favor the well-to-do. Private lessons and tutoring are, in the Middle East, one of the notorious ways by which the better-off promote their offspring at the expense of the poorer sectors of society. But it is probably East Asia, led again by South Korea, where these upper-class outlays are the greatest.
- *Educated youth unemployment.* Until 2008 the MENA region was known for the highest rates of unemployment among educated youth and by far the highest rates of educated female youth unemployment. But with the 2008 economic collapse in more advanced economies like those of Greece, Spain, and Portugal, similarly high rates of educated youth unemployment emerged. Everywhere we hear of the mismatch between what universities produce and what the job market needs (Chapter 6).
- *Dropout rates.* University completion rates vary significantly across countries of the MENA but they are not exceptional. Argentina may have the worst university completion rates in the world. Reducing dropout rates could have huge implications for equity, financing tertiary education, and improving returns to investment in education. It is an area of reform that should not threaten incumbent autocrats (Chapter 8 and the Conclusion).

There are, then, differences in degree but not in kind in the pathologies of the crisis of higher education in the Middle East. Having said that, it is the case that there are no significant bright spots in the Arab landscape outside the oil-rich countries of the GCC. *I will argue that the combined weight of the pathologies of higher education in the Arab world constitutes a singular challenge of unusual proportions.*

I would go a step further. There is, it seems to me, one piece of the governance puzzle that does sharply distinguish the Arab university from its European and American peers. The Arab university is a particularly dangerous entity in the context of the prevailing autocracies of the Arab world. The concentration in universities of brain power, youth, energy, open debate, and daily engagement with big issues constitutes a threat for autocrats. There is, then, a direct link between the crisis in higher education and the region's democratic deficit. This is not the case, for example, in the European democracies of the southern Mediterranean.

The autocrats are schizophrenic when facing what they have created, hoping, on the one hand, that the university will produce the expertise needed to run the country without, on the other hand, constituting a constant source of threats and malevolent maneuvers. By the same token, the university sometimes sees itself as a vanguard, the bearer of the flame of speaking truth to power. It thereby confirms the ruler's worst fears. Formal governance structures mean little in such an environment of mutual suspicion.

Universities everywhere are engaged in and affected by politics with a lower-case 'p.' The politics are those of the purse strings and accountability. They result in political 'interference' in the academic enterprise. In the Arab world, by contrast, we have Politics with an upper-case 'P.' Universities may set precedents for the system as a whole. They may act as an 'estate,' acquiring institutional rights, carving out zones of autonomy, and offering protection to critics that contain the seeds of systemic change. Ironically, since the colonial period, Arab universities have seldom mounted systemic challenges,[6] but control-obsessed elites recognize the potential and act accordingly. Small-p educational politics are ubiquitous and healthy, as they set the bounds of accountability. Big-P politics are both exciting and dangerous for the university establishment and the regimes it serves.

It follows that real university excellence will depend more on an improved political environment than on money—that is, greater openness, decentralization, and institutional autonomy. Phrased differently, it would mean a retreat of the 'deep state' comprising the security and judicial apparatuses. That is a very tall order. It is easy to see that the political environment is well beyond the control of the university. To take but one example, if we were to see a public university in the Arab world granted true autonomy—the ability to recruit and promote its own faculty, set criteria for admissions, design its own curriculum, do its own financial planning—we would know that something profound had changed in the political system. Could the university itself be the source of that change? Under present circumstances, I very much doubt it.

Public Policy

Because many of the problems faced by tertiary education in the MENA are generic and not *sui generis*, we can learn from other countries about possible reforms. At the same time if big-P politics is unusually important in the MENA, then the reform process is likely to be unusually fraught.

The weak mechanisms of accountability that characterize the autocracies of the region might mean that leaders have unusual degrees of freedom to undertake bold initiatives and sweeping reforms. That, however, has not been the modus operandi of most autocrats. Saddam Hussein was foolishly bold in his foreign policies and paid a terrible price. More typical was the stodgy caution of Hosni Mubarak, who never saw an initiative he could love. There is, I argue, a strong bias for business as usual (BAU) in the MENA's autocracies. BAU is different from the status quo. BAU suggests a process, how one conducts the affairs of state. The status quo refers to situations and outcomes. In the MENA BAU leads to the status quo. To change the status quo, one needs to change BAU.

If that is the case, how does policy change come about? We all know the standard advice, "never let a good crisis go to waste." Crisis may be the only catalyst to reform. Informed foresight and analysis should drive policy change (think of global warming and greenhouse gas emissions) but seldom do. As I have noted, it is generally recognized in the region (as well as outside it) that MENA higher education is in crisis. Should we expect a policy response and, if so, what kind of response?

Just about everywhere in the world, fiscal crisis or crises in public finances have triggered fairly sweeping reforms that involve privatizing public assets, trimming bloated public-personnel rosters, slashing welfare entitlements and consumer subsidies, and enacting legislation to stimulate private economic activity. As noted above, in the 1980s and 1990s, the MENA engaged in this kind of crisis response. So-called 'social contracts' were shredded, some public sector assets unloaded, and defense budgets curtailed. Cost-of-living riots often ensued. Autocrats had to refashion their alliance bases, giving rise in many instances to crony capitalism. In the course of those reforms the sphere of higher education was opened to private investment. Some of the new cronies were educational entrepreneurs. The point is that crisis did drive policy change, and cautious autocrats reluctantly took big political risks as a result.[7]

It is also the case that the structural adjustment crises at the close of the twentieth century had far-reaching international ramifications, involving foreign creditors and trade partners. To do nothing was not an option. By contrast, crises in higher education are largely contained within the countries that gave rise to them in the first place. One might plausibly argue that there is spillover, in that poor-quality higher education feeds educated youth unemployment, which in turn fosters high out-migration and perhaps Islamist radicalism. It is plausible but a stretch. I have not heard any country threatened by radical Islamists demanding reform of higher education as a result.

A second driver of policy change is the leverage exerted by the donor and nongovernmental organization (NGO) community. The economic crises increased that leverage. Multilateral agencies such as the World Bank, the IMF, the United Nations Educational, Scientific and Cultural Organization (UNESCO), the United Nations Development Programme (UNDP), and the Economic and Social Commission for Western Asia (ESCWA) and bilateral agencies like the United States Agency for International Development (USAID), the German Technical Cooperation Agency (GTZ), the Swedish International Development Cooperation Agency, the Japanese International Cooperation Agency (JICA), and the UK's Department for International Development (DFID) all weighed in on the reform agenda and stimulated some action. As important, these agencies acted as conduits to the formation of 'communities of practice' (Haas 1992), whereby somewhat isolated and numerically small expert groups in countries undergoing reform were brought together with international expert groups that fully understood and understand best practice. Communities of practice provide validation for national pockets of expertise that often operate in a politically hostile environment. The combination of multilateral or bilateral funding and communities of practice can exert considerable pressure for reform.

The Reformer's Dilemma

The conviction that higher education in the Arab world is 'in crisis' and that there is a pressing need to launch bold reforms is widely shared. How to go about reform, however, does not generate uniform answers, let alone consensus. The analytic challenge is how to promote reform within autocracies. This is what we might call the 'reformer's dilemma.' By reformer I mean someone committed to process, transparency, accountability, and, ultimately, democracy. Some reformers will accept no compromise with autocrats and in essence postpone reforms until the political system as a whole opens up. Most reformers, however, accept the need to work with the existing autocrats. Their solution to the dilemma is, in effect, to hold their noses.

Their strategies depend on the policy area and its political salience and the resources they can mobilize. As we shall see in the chapters that follow, it is reformers in the external international financial institutions (IFIs) and NGOs who have the resources and who seek strategic allies within target countries. Together they can build communities of practice, assemble persuasive data, and use financial resources to make the political costs of reform more palatable.

NB: Reformers, if successful, mitigate crises that might otherwise bring about the collapse of regimes. The reformers may thereby rescue some truly bad actors. Revolutionaries may well say, "Let the crisis take its natural course; reform only shores up autocrats and their cronies." I fully recognize the dilemma but find myself among the reformers.

I will situate higher education reform among other policy areas with which I am most familiar: environmental policy and management of public assets.

Table I.2 Policy Parameters

Policy Area	Degree of Crisis	Political Saliency
Higher Education	Slow moving	Medium to high
Environment	Slow moving	low
Public Assets	Immediate	medium

For some time the crisis in higher education has been in the eyes of internal and external experts but not in the eyes of the policymakers. The crisis has been identified for decades; it is slow-moving rather than explosive. But higher education, like the entire education sector, is a critical part of the social contracts prevailing in the region since the 1960s. It touches virtually every family. Its costs and quality are matters of immediate concern. I argue that elites have come to recognize the critical links among mediocre education, youth unemployment and political instability. The awareness began to take hold in the 1990s and strengthened appreciably after the uprisings of 2011.

Despite this awareness, autocrats are not prepared to empower university leaders to spearhead the reform effort because they know instinctively that such empowerment could lead to real institutional autonomy in a sector rich in brains and political motivation. The policy solution to date has been to shift the financing burden to the private sector and to implement cosmetic reforms (for example, quality assurance) with the support of the donor community. It is a cat-and-mouse game: the donor community hopes that cosmetic reform will morph into institutional reform (see Mahmood and Slimane, 2018) while the autocrats take the money and eviscerate the reform process.

We may contrast this with the other two policy areas I mentioned. Environmental policy reform is in fact an integral part of other policy areas such as water management, agricultural development, and municipal waste water treatment. Multiple policy jurisdictions make coordination very difficult. Educational reform, by comparison, is to some extent contained within the education sector, although its role in feeding the labor force makes the sector directly relevant to the economy as a whole.

Finally, the issue of managing public assets (factories, banks, transportation systems, airlines, mines) was bound up in the fiscal crises of the 1970s and 1980s. These were crises with major external repercussions involving international credit ratings, investment flows, and possible defaults on external debt. The crises developed relatively quickly, required swift and convincing responses, and, like education, went to the heart of the region's social contracts, involving jobs, consumer subsidies, and public enterprise debt. The autocrats had no choice but to sign up for various forms of structural adjustment, often involving privatization, currency flotation, and the reduction of consumer subsidies and public employment. While some autocrats teetered (Anwar Sadat in 1977), none fell. As I write, several MENA countries are in the throes of yet another round of structural adjustment (Algeria, Egypt, Jordan, Sudan, Tunisia, Turkey),[8] provoking varying levels of social protest. Civil war and international sanctions in other countries (Iran, Syria, Libya, Yemen) make structural adjustment seem almost a luxury.

Incrementalism versus Big Bang Reform

There is a great deal of 'path dependency' involved in higher education. The universal model is one built on costly infrastructure (classrooms, labs, administrative facilities, recreational facilities, cafeterias, libraries, dormitories, and sometimes, faculty housing) and large personnel rosters of faculty, teaching assistants, and administrative and custodial staff. Could all that infrastructure, like the abandoned steel mills of the 'rust belt' in the US, be left to molder or be sold for other uses (see Chapter 7 on innovation)?

The university as we know it brings together in one place (not a virtual place!) students and teachers to produce synergies that are allegedly impossible otherwise. It lets the teachers stay at the frontier of their expertise by conducting research and creating knowledge, sometimes with the help of their students.

The infrastructure of the physical place, with all its attendant costs, is needed for the university to succeed. Proximity (again not virtual) is necessary for spontaneous learning. A big part of learning is from one's peers, not in the narrow sense of study groups but rather through broad social interactions that are occasionally unpleasant or unsettling.

Room, board, and tuition are supposed to pay for teaching and research. Over time new sources of revenue had to be found as only elite students could actually pay the full cost of their education, the infrastructure became more costly and sophisticated, and other professions lured talent away. The big but only partially disruptive innovations came in building endowments, in fundraising, and in the quest for federal funding or sponsored research funding more generally. North American universities were the leaders in these innovations.

In recent decades there has been explicit focus on the economic role of universities, especially in urban settings. One of the best documented is that of the University of Pennsylvania in what was once a blighted, violent, and drug-ridden neighborhood (Rodin, 2007), but just about any university could tell a similar tale. Rust belt cities such as Pittsburgh and Cleveland have been rescued by 'meds and eds': illustrious universities and associated medical centers such as the Cleveland Clinic.

Universities drive up property values, generate high demand for supplies and capital projects, and through students and faculty sustain robust rental markets as well as retail markets in restaurants, entertainment, and home goods. It is the physical, bricks-and-mortar university that does all of this, not its virtual competitor. Those in retirement love to live near these hubs of intellectual and cultural life. I know.

There are those who nonetheless foresee disruptive innovations in all levels of education that will destroy the old model just as surely as Asian steel killed Pittsburgh or digital technology maimed Kodak. Clayton Christensen has been the foremost (albeit contested: Lepore, 2014) analyst of disruptive innovation (Christensen, 1997; Christensen, Johnson, and Horn, 2008; Weise and Christensen, 2014; DeMillo, 2015). The basic proposition is that successful, well-established firms (or universities) do not see threats to their business model or value proposition until it is too late, until a new firm with a radically different model can deliver a similar although perhaps inferior product at much lower cost. The upstart may find a market that the established firm does not target, but once in the door the upstart goes after the established firm's customers. The irony that Christensen stresses is that the established firm may successfully engage in incremental improvements that lull it into a false sense of security. For Christensen my predilection for incrementalism will at best postpone the inevitable. My purpose here is not to explore the evidence for Christensen's conclusions (see Chapters 6 and 7 and the Conclusion), but I do recognize that what he proposes is well within the realm of possibility. If online education offers a disruptive business model (minimal infrastructure, maximum student–teacher ratios), it is unlikely that the public sector universities of the MENA will be the lead authors of it.

Suggesting that public education is similar to the markets for ICT or steel is simply in error. *Public* education is a public good, available to all, consumed by law in the first twelve years or so, and a quasi-state monopoly. The taxpayer foots a large part of the bill. Private providers of disruptive innovation will want to *sell* their innovation. Many customers of the existing paradigm cannot afford to switch. The only way for the disruptive innovation to become generalized is for the dominant system to buy it so that the taxpayer continues to foot the bill.

Finally, in Christensen's paradigm, incumbents have no real incentive to adopt the disruptive innovation until it is too late. Change will be driven from outside the BAU model, not from within. If that is the case the only policy lesson to be learned is how the incumbents deal with the debacle. But that may not be the case (as I shall explore in Chapter 7).

What if tertiary education had only one objective, similar to the firm's profit-and-loss bottom line? Let us imagine that the metrics are to achieve a graduation rate of 85 percent, to find appropriate employment for 80 percent of graduates within two years of graduation, and for those employed graduates to pay off the costs of their education within ten years of being employed. Programs would be assessed and ranked according to their success in meeting those three goals. Resources would flow according to relative performance.

All academic and non-academic staff would be hired and promoted with those three metrics in mind. Training for advanced work in science, technology, engineering, and mathematics (STEM) disciplines might look much as it does today. For those teaching in such fields, research would be a valuable asset. Otherwise, academic research would be virtually irrelevant, probably reserved to non-university specialized research units with full-time research personnel. They already exist throughout the MENA.

This model would not be driven primarily by technological change, although online learning would surely play a big part in it. It would be driven by a very different value proposition than the bricks-and-mortar model of today. It would deal with mass education (quantity), at a reasonable cost, and offer restricted quality. It would sacrifice the quality of life associated with some campuses, the training of citizens, the networking among classmates, and the extracurricular experiences that characterize 'good' universities. Anyone who has visited some of the behemoth public universities of the Arab world will know that those aspects of quality have long disappeared.

Is the Big Bang upon Us?

There is a real-world and profoundly disturbing natural experiment playing out before us. Since 2011 four Arab states have 'failed.' Their governments no longer monopolize the use of force, no longer fully control their territories, and therefore no longer make truly national policies. Those states are Syria, Iraq,* Yemen, and Libya. We could add to the list Lebanon, which, at the time of writing, is governed by two authorities, the official government of Lebanon and Hezbollah, which enjoys a preponderance of force. In the first four countries the destruction of physical infrastructure, including universities, has been extensive, and one university, Mosul in Iraq, was run by ISIS from June 2014 for three years. It was retaken in January 2017.[9]

One has to hope that these failed states will somehow be reinvented, and I use that term advisedly. They will have to reinvent themselves politically or they will shatter. That process may give them the opportunity to generate new models of higher education. At a minimum, it may be possible to convince their future leadership to establish some pilot projects that are out of the BAU box.

I am skeptical that we will see radical departures anywhere (Siira and Hill, 2016). Some kind of coalition of armed factions, still smoldering with unresolved grievances from the era of violence, will be in shaky control of the new policy arenas. Their first instinct may be to reestablish the deep state, not to foster zones of educational autonomy. Still, the possibility for new experiments in these damaged societies is there. They stand in sharp contrast to the undeniable costs of BAU.

---

*Since the collapse of the Islamic State of Iraq and Syria (ISIS) in early 2019, Iraq has regained control of most of its territory.

1
Orders of Magnitude

In this chapter I seek to define the educational universe under examination in broad statistical brush strokes. It is a large but moving target and risks being out of date within a few years. It moves also because there is no central database for education in the MENA and the Arab world. Tertiary-level institutions do not routinely contribute to and update data files on key indicators. For some, the data, such as graduation or retention rates, is distressingly incomplete. The Association of Arab Universities might logically be a data repository, but it is not, yet. Finally, definitions of data types are vague or inconsistent, starting with what is a tertiary-level institution.

Fortunately, UNESCO, ESCWA, the International Labour Organization (ILO), and the World Bank have developed over the years a broad range of statistical indicators covering the MENA and the rest of the world. They are supplemented by the various editions of the World Bank's *World Development Report*, the *Arab Human Development Report*, and a series of reports on education under the auspices of the Arab Thought Foundation, among others.

As a result, I am confident that we can describe systems of education in the MENA with a fair degree of accuracy, although also with a generous margin of error.

Demographics
The single most important independent variable driving the shape of education in the region is demography. The rate of population growth in specific age cohorts sets the parameters of demand for various levels of education. In labor-exporting countries of the region, out-migration of

school-age dependents can significantly modify basic demographic dynamics.[1] Likewise the massive in-migration of non-national labor in the oil-rich countries (above all, the GCC) boosts the demand for education far beyond the needs of the national population. Since the beginning of the civil war in Syria, something like four million refugees have poured into Turkey, Jordan, and Lebanon, placing enormous burdens on all forms of social infrastructure, including schools.

The total population of the Arab world in 2014 was about 370 million and is projected to rise to about 575 million by 2050. Because I will frequently pull two other countries in the neighborhood, Iran and Turkey, into comparative analysis, I note here that their populations in 2012 stood at about 76 million and 74 million, respectively. Along with Egypt at about 85 million in the same year, we have the three giants of the MENA. Egypt's population may reach 150 million by 2050.[2]

Fertility rates in the MENA have declined from their levels of two to three decades ago. Improved public health has led to reductions in infant mortality, while education and improved living standards have led to older ages at marriage and shorter child-bearing lifetimes. Today most countries in the MENA are at two to three live births per female in their child-bearing lives (Goujon and Barakat, 2010; Saxena, 2013).[3] A fertility rate of two represents replacement, that is, two children replacing their mother and father, resulting in no net population growth. This demographic transition has already altered the age pyramids of most MENA societies. Even as fertility declines, the number of women entering child-bearing age increases (because they were born in the era of higher fertility) so that the absolute number of births goes up. Nonetheless, as shown in Figure 1.1, there is now a youth bulge of young adults eligible to enter the workforce or to go on to tertiary education.

The youth bulge is a two-edged sword. It could constitute what has been dubbed the 'demographic dividend.' In East Asia the economic transformations of the 1970s, 1980s, and 1990s were based on the same demographic transition coupled with solid educational attainment K–12 and a massive shift of population from the countryside to the cities. This young, literate population became the backbone of the labor force in sectors such as textiles, automotives, and electronics, which led the Asian Tigers to prosperity. During the time the bulge dominates a country's demographics, the employed age cohorts are large relative to the cohorts in childhood and those over sixty to sixty-five and no longer working. The so-called 'dependency ratio' shrinks, while the tax base expands.

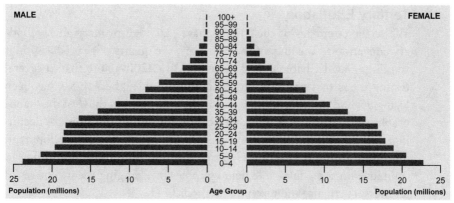

Figure 1.1 Youth Bulge among Arab League Member States, 2016
Source: Cammack et al., 2017

The youth bulge therefore opens a window of opportunity. That window is already partially open in the MENA, but it will not remain so indefinitely (Dhillon and Yousef, 2009). Perry Cammack and colleagues (2017: 19) see the opening lasting thirty years, while Prem Saxena (2013: 28) puts it more generously at fifty years. These are time frames sufficiently long to lull political leaders into inaction. The kinds of action that would be appropriate is the subject of most of the rest of this study.

To date in the MENA we are seeing the other edge of the sword: youth as a source of instability, frustration, and political menace. The spread of basic education has been near universal, the move to the cities substantial, but high rates of youth employment and high rates of gross domestic product (GDP) growth have not followed. The Asian model cannot be replicated, as the global economy has changed profoundly. The MENA faces stiff competition from earlier entrants in global trade, India, Pakistan, and Bangladesh among them. Private sectors in the MENA are anemic and risk averse. Robotics have reduced the need for assembly-line labor dramatically. The growth sectors of the future will need the products of the tertiary educational system or those with highly specialized vocational skills (Bishop, 2011).

The only effective safety net for youth in the MENA is the informal sector, which is a source of ingenuity far more than of innovation. Because it operates in a legal gray area, it cannot invest in capital goods or offer its employees training and sophisticated professional knowledge, or pensions and health insurance. It is a venue for deskilling. The public sector, by contrast, can offer all those perquisites, but it is saturated and trying to shed employees.[4]

If there is a solution to this riddle, education will be at its core.

Tertiary Education

While the countries of the MENA have extended primary and secondary education to the bulk of their citizens, the quality of that education is wanting. David Chapman and Suzanne Miric (2009) note that in several testing areas that are internationally comparable, the MENA has been losing ground to international peers. They note that because of the demographic transition, primary-school cohorts in some countries are declining, lowering the teacher–pupil ratio. Despite this favorable development, increased quality of outcomes has not followed. The MENA is failing to capitalize on some favorable demographics by changing the incentives of teachers, curricula, and teaching methods.[5]

Tertiary education has exploded in the last thirty years,[6] both in terms of the number of IHLs and in terms of students. Bashshur (2004) notes that in 2003 there were 233 Arab universities, of which 188 had been created in the preceding thirty years. Ninety-three were opened in the decade 1993–2003, of which 51 were private.[7] As we shall see going forward, this reflects the structural economic reforms underway in several Arab countries that curtailed public outlays and forced open the door for the private sector to enter the educational 'market.' By 2012 there were 206 public Arab universities and 193 private ones (Al Adwan, 2013). In 2001–2015 the numbers enrolled in Arab tertiary-level education rose from about five million to as many as nine million students (see Table 1.1). Despite the emergence of private institutions, the public sector still educated about 90 percent of all tertiary-level students until 2010 (Bhandari and El-Amine, 2011).

There can be a certain amount of false exactitude in statistical sources because the definitions of what is being measured are not always clear or consistent. Along with universities, tertiary institutions may include colleges, specialized institutes, and research centers, among others. Egypt in 2014 had 14 specialized government research centers, 219 centers under the auspices of ministries, and 114 centers at universities (ESCWA, 2014: 20). Student bodies may include distance learners. Faculty censuses may include double-counting, as many faculty members teach in more than one institution.

Turkey, Iran, and Israel are excluded from the totals for the Arab world. The Arab figures do not include four members of the League of Arab States: Comoros, Mauritania, Somalia, and Qatar. They would not significantly alter the totals. There is missing data, which, in the case of Iraq, could lower the totals appreciably.

Table 1.1 Higher Education Statistics in the Arab Region, 2011

Country	Number of Universities			Number of Students	Number of Faculty Members
	Public	Private	Total		
Tunisia	13	19	32	360,000	21,210
Iraq	25	8	33	397,784	31,990
Bahrain	2	8	10	35,848	3,100
Yemen	8	13	21	300,000	10,000
UAE	2	19	21	59,333	1,861
Morocco	14	4	18	419,885	12,085
Sudan	28	7	35	500,000	9,700
Lebanon	1	19	20	205,000	12,700
Oman	1	7	8	80,000	4,100
Kuwait	1	4	5	34,560	1,705
Saudi Arabia	23	8	31	667,000	21,320
Syria	5	10	15	282,484	9,500
Egypt	20	15	35	2,800,000	67,000
State of Palestine	2	13	15	196,625	5,900
Jordan	11	18	29	336,000	8,898
Libya	9	2	11	264,000	9,000
Somalia	3	11	14	4,147	195
Mauritania	1	–	1	25,000	1,175
Djibouti	1	–	1	15,000	580
Qatar	1	6	7	15,500	1,100
Algeria	34	2	36	1,149,899	19,500
Total	206	193	399	8,148,065	252,619

Source: MBRF and UNDP, 2014

In terms of sheer growth, the stars are Iran, Morocco, Palestine, Saudi Arabia, Sudan, and Turkey. They all more than tripled enrollments over the period. This could be pure 'massification,' meaning quantity at the expense of quality, but it is probably better than its opposite. On that score only Tunisia seems to be retreating, with a real decline in enrollments between 2006 and 2015. We shall return to that point further on.

Table 1.2 Tertiary Enrollments in the MENA, 2000–2015

Country	2000	2006	2015
Algeria	549,009	901,582	1,289,474
Egypt	2,118,675	2,402,860	2,544,107
Iran	1,404,880	2,398,811	4,685,386
Iraq	288,670	nd	nd
Israel	255,891	310,014	376,952
Jordan	142,190	217,823	306,630
Kuwait	34,799	nd	71,786
Lebanon	116,014	173,123	228,954
Libya	290,060	nd	nd
Morocco	295,634	385,953	877,404
Oman	nd	55,956	126,947
Palestine	71,207	150,128	221,018
Saudi Arabia	404,094	636,445	1,527,769
Sudan	182,012	420,369	632,377
Tunisia	180,044	339,363	322,625
Turkey	1,607,388	2,106,351	5,472,521
UAE	nd	nd	121,626
Yemen	164,166	200,853	nd
Total Arab	4,836,474	6,194,469	8,270,717

Source: data.uis.unesco.org

Gross Enrollment Ratio (GER)

UNESCO and the World Bank define the GER as the number of students enrolled at a given level of education, regardless of age, expressed as a percentage of the official school-age population corresponding to the same level of education. For the tertiary level, the population used is the five-year age group starting from the official high school graduation age. In practice, at the tertiary level, the GER covers the age cohort eighteen to twenty-three.

Everywhere in the world the GER is climbing. South Korea is the champion with over 90 percent of the eligible age cohort actually enrolled, while in the MENA, Yemen, before the regime collapse and civil war after 2011, had a GER of about 10 percent. Over two decades, from 1992 to 2012, the average world GER went from 14 percent to 32

Table 1.3. Gross Enrollment Ratios, MENA plus Turkey, 2005 and 2015

Country	2005	2015
Algeria	20	37
Egypt	35	36
Iran	24	72
Iraq	16	16
Jordan	40	45
Kuwait*	24	27
Lebanon	46	43
Libya	56	61
Morocco	11	28
Oman	18	nd
Saudi Arabia	29	63
Sudan	nd	16
Syria	14	44
Tunisia	30	35
Turkey	31	85
Yemen	9	10

Source: *A Decade of Higher Education in the Arab World* (2005) and on-line data bank World Bank EdStats (2015)
* The entries on Kuwait are inconsistent. UNESCO (2009) indicates a GER in 2005 of 49 percent. That is not consistent with its own database or with World Bank data. Given that civil wars have been raging in Libya and Syria since 2011, it is hard to give credence to their 2015 GERs.

percent (Duncan, 2015). While the world may not reach South Korea's near universal level of tertiary education (the US, for example, is at about 62 percent), the trend is clear, and over time most countries will exceed 50 percent.

The Arab world tracked that trajectory with a lag. In 1986, the average GER in the Arab world was 14.5 percent (Massialis and Jarrar, 1991: 30). By 2010, the average GER for nineteen Arab countries was 22 percent, with ten of the nineteen below 30 percent (inter alia, Buckner, 2011). The Arab region came in sixth out of eight regions (ahead only of Sub-Saharan Africa and South Asia; UNESCO, 2009: 41). Jaramillo (Jaramillo and Melonio, 2011) stresses the different positions of Arab countries in the demographic transition as crucial to understanding future GERs, but she may have underestimated the overwhelming impetus to massification even in countries where fertility has sharply declined. She projects a GER for the Arab world of 41 percent in 2030 (Jaramillo and Melonio, 2011: 23). Jaramillo wrote that before the Arab uprisings of 2011 and the subsequent civil wars that have presumably wreaked havoc with GERs in Syria, Libya, Yemen, and, to a lesser extent, Iraq.[8] A recent *Arab Human Development Report* joins in the lament of low GERs and surmises, "That colleges and universities have not significantly boosted their intake rates partly reflects the growing disenchantment of youth with the value of higher education amid the glut of unemployed graduates on the job market" (UNDP and AFESD, 2016: 31).

Let us review a few country cases to get a better sense of meaningful detail and variations.

Lebanon

Keeping in mind that in Lebanon tertiary education is split evenly between the one public university, Lebanese University, and dozens of private institutions, the evolution of the GER is similar to that of many other Arab states. Lebanon started, in 1970, at a higher level than most states: over 17 percent. By 2005, it had doubled that level, but has stagnated since. It made great progress (as did many other Arab states) in improving female GERs, such that they overtook those of males by 1996 and have maintained that edge ever since. Figure 1.2 shows Lebanon's progress, along with Jordan, the strongest in the Arab world.

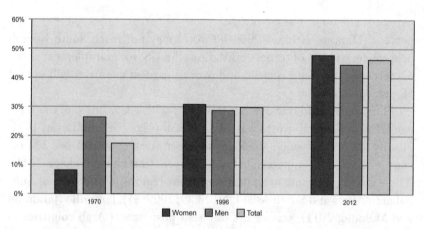

Figure 1.2. Net Enrollment Rates for Lebanon and Jordan in Tertiary Education (%)
Source: Chaaban, 2015

Egypt

During the presidency of Anwar Sadat in the 1970s, there was a major expansion of regional universities, but without adequate preparation of physical premises and teaching staff. Still, the effect was to raise Egypt's GER significantly.

Egypt's GER in 2013 was about 23 percent and grew to 26 percent in two years. The goal, according to Ashraf Hatem, secretary-general of the Supreme Council of Universities (SCU), is to reach 45 percent by 2023 (interview, 2013). Given what Iran and Turkey have achieved in recent years, that goal may be attainable, although it will require greater public outlays (see pages 41–44) and significant expansion of private IHLs.

Israel

While I do not pay systematic attention to Israel in this study, the question of Israeli GERs warrants mention. In 2011 the Israeli tertiary GER, according to the World Bank, was 62.5 percent—about the same as that of the US. But if we break out the Arab portion of Israeli citizens, we find that in 2006, 9.7 percent of eligible Arabs were enrolled in higher education. By 2016 that proportion had risen to 16 percent (Brummer, 2017). Israel is surely not alone in the region in discriminating against minorities in access to higher education, but the ratio of 62.5 to 16 is glaring. There has been improvement since 2016.

Iran

Despite an eight-year war with Iraq, a temporary shuttering of universities in 1980, and heavy economic sanctions applied by the US and the international community, Iran made prodigious progress in extending higher education to its citizens (see IIE, 2015; Faek, 2016; Harris, 2014)

Iran has over 4.5 million tertiary-level students. Sixty percent of them are women, according to government statistics. In 1999 Iran's tertiary GER was 19 percent, rising to 58 percent in 2013 and then 72 percent in 2015. In comparison to the rest of the Middle East, Iran's education system is academically competitive, and Iranian parents are spending $2.1 billion annually on their children.

Part of Iran's success is due to a private university, Islamic Azad University, founded in 1982 by Hashemi Rafsanjani, who had been close to the supreme leader, Ayatollah Khomeini. Azad University today may have as many as 1.5 million students throughout Iran (as well as branches abroad). It may be the world's largest university (Labi, 2008). Because of it and other private institutions, over 50 percent of tertiary-level students are enrolled in private institutions. In this explosion in private tertiary education, Iran may be the bellwether for the region as a whole.

The Maghreb

Algeria, Morocco, and Tunisia were colonized by France and to some extent mimicked the elitism of French higher education in the post–Second World War era (Vermeren, 2002). Algeria has been the most aggressive in moving toward massification, but all three are trending in the same direction.

In 2008 Morocco launched its educational emergency plan (Plan d'Urgence) that singled out low high school enrollments (about 50 percent of the eligible age cohort) and tertiary enrollments (a GER at that time of about 11 percent) as particularly egregious shortcomings in the system (see Kingdom of Morocco, 2008).

Tunisia is something of an anomaly. Its university population peaked in 2009 at 360,000, and then declined to 292,000 in 2014. It restored positive growth in 2015, but its progress appears to be slowing. High school enrollments peaked in 2004. The private tertiary sector grew from 1.1 percent of total enrollments in 2007–2008 to 9.4 percent in 2014–2015, adding about 30,000 students (Boughazala et al., 2016: 5; Assaad et al., 2017). The populations of Tunisia and Lebanon are the most rapidly aging in the Arab world, and they are further along the demographic transition. Their slowly growing tertiary GERs reflect that fact.

Libya demonstrates the variety typical of tertiary institutions. There are twelve public universities, five private universities, sixteen state technical faculties, and ninety-one higher technical and vocational institutes. Libya has half a million students in all fields of higher education, of which more than half (59 percent) are female. Most students (around 90 percent) are enrolled in public universities (Law, 2014). Libya's GER for 2015 is suspiciously high. It is hard to imagine 60 percent of eligible Libyans attending tertiary institutions in a country swamped by civil violence.

Syria

A few years before the beginning of the Syrian civil war, the country's tertiary GER stood at about 21 percent (Buckner and Saba, 2010). The World Bank generously recorded a GER in 2015 of 44 percent. Given over 500,000 war-related deaths (as of 2018), more than six million displaced persons and refugees, and horrendous destruction in major cities such as Aleppo, Homs, Deir ez-Zor, and, to a lesser extent, Damascus, some observers believe the real GER is more like 6 percent.

Sudan

Sudan is an extreme example of a fairly widespread phenomenon in regional higher education. Colonel Omar al-Bashir seized power in a coup in 1989, and, without thorough planning, created eighteen new universities by 1995. He doubled enrollments in existing universities. This came at a time when public expenditures on all levels of education fell from 4.8 percent of GDP to 0.8 percent (Elnur, 1998: 308; Bishai, 2008). The regime did not undertake the training of the teaching and other staff that the new universities and increased enrollments would require. Under Anwar Sadat, Egypt's president in the 1970s, something similar happened. Once again quality was sacrificed to quantity. Al-Bashir was driven from power by popular protests in 2019.

Turkey

Turkey's GER, at 85 percent, is by far the star performer in the MENA region, if we believe the World Bank and UNESCO figures for 2015. UNESCO's statistics below inflate Turkey's GER even further, showing it as 94.7 for 2015.[9]

What is not in dispute are the major quantitative strides made in higher education under the governments of the Justice and Development Party (AKP), which came to power in 2002.

Graduates and Dropouts

It is hard to know which group is the more significant, those who successfully complete their tertiary education or those who drop out. Both are likely to suffer frustration and disillusionment in the face of a public sector that no longer needs them and a private sector for which they are not appropriately educated. It is important to note that high dropout rates are

Table 1.4. Tertiary GERs for Turkey

Tertiary Education	2007	2008	2009	2010	2011	2012	2013	2014	2015	2016
Gross enrollment ratio (%)										
Total	38.48	39.93	46.21	56	60.73	69.3	78.98	86.31	94.73	...
Female	33.05	34.72	40.64	50.2	55.42	63.7	72.9	80.14	88.28	...
Male	43.82	45.04	51.69	61.69	65.92	74.78	84.91	92.32	101.01	...

Source: data.uis.unesco.org

a global norm. Over a third of tertiary students in better-off countries do not complete their degrees (*The Economist*, 2018a).

We begin our MENA story with the successful graduates.[10] Table 1.5 shows modest growth in graduates, reflecting basic demographics and a growing GER. Oman is the star performer. The United Arab Emirates (UAE) does very well, but it is important to note that the UAE, unlike the rest of the Arab world, may have enrollments of non-nationals outnumbering those of nationals. These are very much orders of magnitude, given missing data for a number of entries. To give a truer picture and to calculate totals, I estimated Lebanon's 2015 graduates to be 35,000. With that caveat in mind, the average annual growth rate in graduates over the eight-year period is a feeble 2.9 percent.

Table 1.5. Number of Tertiary-level Graduates, 2004–2015, Select Countries

Country	2007	2011	2015
Algeria	120,168	208,536	287,914
Egypt	nd	510,390	547,925
France	621,444	697,193	752,066
Iran	340,246	607,121	738,260
Iraq	87,849	nd	nd
Israel	nd	nd	nd
Jordan	49,574	60,686	69704
Kuwait	nd	nd	12,716
Lebanon	32,168	34,007	nd
Libya	nd	nd	nd
Morocco	88,137	82,346	135,732
Oman	9,129	13,734	18,462
Saudi Arabia	103,789	120,780	148,841
Sudan	nd	88,979	123,088
Syria	40,131	86,773	53,589
Tunisia	58,598	73,301	65,332
Turkey	415,329	534,055	733,237
UAE	13,060	19,366	28,533
Yemen	26,527	nd	nd
Total Arab	1,079,070	1,298,898	1,526,856

Source: data.uis.unesco.org

I know of no reliable source on MENA-wide retention rates, graduation rates, or dropout rates. They all reflect the proportion of students entering tertiary education who actually earn certification. If we look at the totals on Arab enrollments in Table 1.2 and the numbers graduating in Table 1.5, we see that in 2015 about 18 percent of the total enrolled actually graduated. One has to make some heroic assumptions to interpret these figures: first, that we are dealing mainly with four-year programs, and, second, that the four cohorts are of roughly equal size. On that basis there would appear to be an attrition rate of 7–8 percent over the four years.

This is not bad, but it is not credible. We know that in the US graduation rates on average are much worse. Only 61 percent of tertiary students complete their degrees within eight years of beginning them, and for those in two-year programs (community colleges) the rate is 21 percent (Koropeckyi, Lafakis, and Ozimek, 2017: 3). By some accounts Argentina wins the dubious accolade of the highest dropout rates in the world, stubbornly stuck at around 70 percent of those who begin tertiary programs (Kelly, 2013; Hurtado, 2015).

Morocco, which has moved to a three-year undergraduate degree (see Chapters 6 and 7), provides more detail than most Arab countries. In a survey of three universities' 'open-access' faculties, meaning faculties with no entry requirements other than the high school *baccalauréat*, "only a third, on average, of students in all [three] cohorts succeed in winning the basic *license*" (Kingdom of Morocco, 2018: 22). An online source in 2017 cites official figures: "58 percent of Moroccan Students Enrolled in Universities Do Not Graduate" (*Moroccan World News*, 2017). The report goes on to say that, beginning with the 2009–2010 cohort, the rate of credentialing in three to four years dropped continually: 26.4 percent for the 2009–2010 cohort, 25 percent for 2010–2011, and 20 percent for 2011–2012, reaching its lowest level ever in 2012–2013 at 19 percent (Kingdom of Morocco, 2018: 23). As we shall see, these were years of strenuous educational reform (Chapter 6).

Some sources indicate much more dramatic attrition. An internal assessment at Mohammed V University, Souissi (MVUS), noted an attrition rate in the Faculty of Letters and Human Sciences of 60 percent (Kingdom of Morocco, 2007: 122). Even highly selective schools such as the Institut Agronomique et Vétérinaire Hassan II in Morocco saw an attrition rate of 20 percent between first and second year (Ouattar, interview, 2014).

One of the obstacles facing new students in Morocco is the shift from Arabic to French in a range of courses. As Pierre Vermeren (2002) has chronicled, the rapid expansion of primary and secondary education in the Maghreb coupled with Arabization put many students at a disadvantage once they reached the tertiary level, which was and is taught mainly in French. Add to this the costs, other than tuition, associated with higher education—lodging, transportation, meals, books—and one has the mix of factors that produce dropout rates that are especially high among the less privileged (Aziz, interview, 2018).

Dropouts matter for a host of reasons, some of which we will explore in other chapters (especially Chapter 8). For the moment let us note that those who drop out come disproportionately from less privileged strata of society, so that there are major equity and distributional consequences. For example, completion of degree as opposed to beginning the program may boost earnings by as much as 40 percent for a bachelor's and 11 percent for an 'associate' degree (Koropeckyi, Lafakis, and Ozimek, 2017: 14).[11] Finally, depending on the true rate of attrition, IHLs may carry more faculty and non-academic staff than their actual enrollments require.

Other available sources on Arab/MENA retention rates are fragmented and anecdotal. Adriana Jaramillo summarized the situation some years ago:

> Although 70 percent of universities stated that they conducted tracking surveys, information that could be used to develop performance indicators, such as completion rates, number of years it takes to complete a degree, and data on graduate labor market insertion, was not readily available. This corroborates once again that even if institutions make the effort to collect information, they seldom make it available to the public. (Jaramillo et al., 2012: 44)

Lebanese University, Lebanon's only public university, has similar problems involving open admissions, poor preparation, and language of instruction. Out of 74,000 enrolled students, only about 7,000 graduate each year. Over four years that means that 28,000 graduate while 46,000 do not. That is financially and pedagogically crippling (Bitar, interview, 2012).

In general, nonselective majors disproportionately attract the least well-prepared students. They struggle with everything: skeptical parents, outlays on food, housing, and transport, sometimes coping with a poorly understood language of instruction (English or French), absentee instructors, and so forth. The underprivileged are given a chance, but the deck is stacked against them.[12]

The Corps of Instructors

Table 1.6 outlines the broad dimensions of active faculty in tertiary education in most of the countries of the MENA. It also shows instructor-to-student ratios by country. In that respect Lebanon and Tunisia are the regional leaders. The Lebanese ratio is suspiciously low.[13] The high Sudanese ratio reflects the under-resourced expansion of the university system mentioned above.

As of 2009 it was estimated that about one-third of all faculty members in the region were female (MBRF and UNDP, 2009).

On the whole these are respectable ratios, but they mask a couple of important phenomena. In some heavily enrolled, nonselective majors in the humanities, social sciences, religious studies, commerce, and teaching, enrollments are very large and teaching faculty relatively few. So the instructor to student ratio tends to be well above 1:30.[14] Second, the opening of new campuses gave rise to commuting faculty teaching at more than

Table 1.6. Number of Professors in Higher Education, MENA plus Turkey

Country	2006		
	No. of Profs	No. of Students	Ratio
Algeria	29,986	817,968	1:27.2
Egypt	99,478	2,477,159	1:24.9
Iran	122,068	2,398,811	1:19.6
Iraq	19,791	437,641	1:22.1
Jordan	8,513	220,103	1:25.8
Lebanon	21,434	146,961	1:6.8
Libya	19,212	394,801	1:20.5
Morocco	19,317	384,595	1:19.9
Oman	2,792	68,154	1:24.4
Sudan	7,106	318,520	1:33.6
Syria	9,090	307,953	1:33.8
Tunisia	18,642	321,838	1:17.2
Turkey	84,785	2,342,898	1:27.6
Yemen	6,246	210,434	1:33.6
Total Arab	261,607	6,105,767	1:23.3
Total with Turkey and Iran	468,460	10,847,476	1:23.1

Source: uis.unesco.org

one institution. I have not seen any systematic study of this phenomenon (some of it may be beneath the radar as it may be disallowed by the faculty member's primary employer). So, the gross figures of faculty numbers need to be treated cautiously because of double and even triple counting.[15]

Level and Type of Study

The IHLs of the MENA are overwhelmingly focused on undergraduate education (BAs, BScs, *license*). There are not yet research universities with large populations of PhD candidates and graduate students earning professional certification. One recent entrant in higher education, the King Abdullah University of Science and Technology (KAUST) in Saudi Arabia, is entirely graduate- and research-oriented. So far it is unique. So is its very large endowment. It will be hard to emulate.

In Chapter 6 on reform, we will revisit the issue of inappropriate training for the regional job market. In Figure 1.4, we see the distribution of students by broad disciplinary categories. Nearly two-thirds are in the humanities and social sciences, which reflects ease of entry and a reliance on Arabic, Turkish, or Persian. Given pedagogic styles and class sizes, these concentrations should not be confused with a 'liberal arts' education.

The experiences of Japan, Korea, and Taiwan suggest that if a country is to assimilate technology, one-third or more of its university graduates need to have studied science and engineering at the graduate level. Overall, MENA countries are far from this goal, with only 8 percent of students enrolled in engineering (Jaramillo and Melonio, 2011: 8).

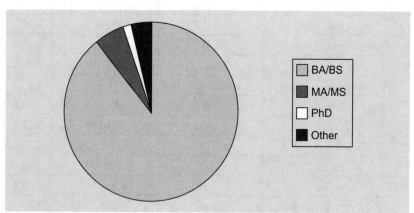

Figure 1.3. Distribution of Arab Students by Level, 2008
Source: UNESCO (2009: 45, Fig. 5-4)

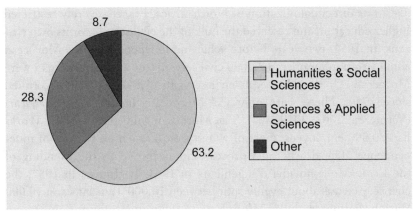

Figure 1.4. Distribution of Arab Students by Broad Disciplinary Categories
Source: UNESCO (2009: 44, Fig. 5-2)

The education systems of the MENA are dominated in terms of students by the public sector, the great majority of students pursue an undergraduate degree, and they avoid or cannot gain admission to the STEM disciplines. All these characteristics reflect the original mission of the education systems of the post-independence MENA: education for public employment. For some time that objective made good sense, but in the long, painful era of structural adjustment the governments of the region could not afford and did not need an expanding civil service. Nor was the timid private sector that emerged amid neoliberal reforms an aggressive employer.

The Civil Service Legacy

The Middle East shows a higher proportion of total employment in bureaucracies than any other region in the world. On average, about a third of all employment is in the public sector, where conditions are undemanding, wages relatively high, and benefits relatively good (ESCWA, 2012).

The oil-rich countries have the highest proportions of civil service employment (among nationals): 80 percent in Kuwait and 65 percent in Saudi Arabia. Egypt is about 30 percent, Lebanon 20 percent, and Morocco around 10 percent (*The Economist*, 2015a; World Bank, 2016; Springborg, 2018: 15–17). Elnur (1998: 323) estimates that in the 1990s about two-thirds of all Sudanese tertiary graduates joined the civil service. The outlays on civil service wages and government operations in the MENA are commensurately large.

In its direct colonization of North Africa, France severely restricted higher education and reserved the bulk of the civil service for its own citizens. In 1954, two years before achieving independence, the Moroccan administration numbered 22,000 civil servants, of whom only 2,635 were Moroccan. Of the Moroccan civil servants, 1,847 had been recruited since 1950. There were only 152 Moroccans in the *cadres supérieurs* (Vermeren, 2002: 2019, 303). The Moroccan Ministry of Public Works had 20,000 employees, most of whom were French on the eve of independence. The dearth of Moroccan engineers led to the founding of the Ecole Mohammadia d'Ingénieurs in 1963. In Tunisia in 1952, the civil service was about evenly split between 10,000 Tunisians and 10,000 French (Vermeren, 2002: 219, 303).

Contrast the Maghreb with Turkey, which inherited the Ottoman bureaucracy designed to run an empire. Even after triage for those who could not support the new republic, the Kemalist state did not lack for bureaucrats (Şevket Pamuk, email, December 30, 2014).

The educational sector alone is a major part of the civil service sector. In Egypt, as of 2006, there were 40,000 schools with 17 million students. Eighty-three percent of all schools were public. There were 821,000 teachers, 711,000 administrators, and 150,000 workers. It represented the biggest sector of employment outside the armed forces and over a quarter of total civil service employment (Farrag, 2010: 113; Assaad, Krafft, and Salehi-Isfahani, 2018).

The public sector is a safety net, a place to be secure rather than well-off. Work is rarely demanding, the salaries are reliable if inadequate, and the benefits package for health and retirement is decent. For women in particular the public sector is the preferred place and type of employment. Shrinkage of the civil service affects women disproportionately.

Assaad (1997) reports a moment in the 1990s when the Egyptian state tried to remove any candidate for public employment from the registry if s/he took a position in a formal private sector firm. What resulted was mass resignation of young Egyptians from these private firms.

Arab and MENA citizens will tolerate unemployment while waiting for a government job or eke by in the formal sector until the prize is available. Table 1.7 shows the strong residual preference for public employment despite poor wages and hiring freezes.

The government wage bill averages about 7 percent of GDP for middle-income countries, but in the Arab world it rises to 12 percent on average. Even more market-friendly countries, like Jordan or Morocco, exceed

Table 1.7. Desired Employment Sector, 2012–2013 (%)

		Egypt (%)	Jordan (%)	Palestine (%)	Tunisia (%)
Enrolled youth	Self-employment	6.0	7.0	11.0	10.0
	Public sector	76.0	64.0	51.0	66.0
	Private sector	18.0	29.0	36.0	24.0
	Family business/farm	0.3	0.2	0.3	0.1
Unemployed youth	Self-employment	1.0	6.0	8.0	11.0
	Public sector	81.0	64.0	33.0	49.0
	Private sector	18.0	30.0	54.0	40.0
	Family business/farm	0.2	0.0	0.5	0.4

Source: UNDP and AFESD (2016), based on International Labour Organization data

the average (World Bank, 2016). This use of scarce resources was and is targeted in most structural adjustment programs. After the Arab uprisings, it is estimated that Egypt cut its wage bill from over 8 percent of GDP to about 5 percent. But it was recalled that a similar effort, made in 1991, was rapidly eroded and that the wage bill crept back up (Momani, 2018).

Outlays on Tertiary Education

Table 1.8, although incomplete, highlights the impact of structural adjustment (aka, neoliberal reforms) on the higher education sector in the MENA.

Table 1.8. Index Numbers of Current Public Expenditures on Higher Education Per Capita, US Dollars, Constant Prices; 1980 = 100

Country	1980	1990	1993
Jordan	100	69	-
Tunisia	100	52	64
Syria	100	11	-
Iraq	100	44	-
Kuwait	100	61	
Egypt	100	45	24
Morocco	100	46	45
South Korea	100	203	288

Source: UNESCO Statistical Yearbook 1996

I cannot explain the drop-off in Syrian per capita expenditures. The Kuwaiti decline may be explained by collapsing oil prices. The consistent message is considerable belt-tightening, and, as we shall review below, the opening of the educational sphere to private actors and investment.

In 2000, when the Arab GER hovered around 20 percent, outlays on higher education were about 1 percent of GDP on average. If by 2030 the GER rises to 40 percent, it is estimated that outlays will rise to over 3 percent of GDP (Jaramillo and Melonio, 2011: 23).

By some measures the MENA has performed very well in educational outlays and investment. If we consider spending per pupil as a proportion of GDP per capita, we find that MENA countries spend more than any other group, including OECD countries. The difference is relatively modest at the primary and lower secondary levels, but it is substantial at the upper secondary and tertiary education levels. Indeed, MENA countries spend approximately 50 percent more than the middle-income countries chosen for comparison on upper secondary education and twice as much as OECD countries on tertiary education, in terms of GDP per capita (World Bank, 2008: 108; Jaramillo and Melonio, 2011: 16; Rizk, 2016).

The focus here is on *public* expenditures. The high outlays in the MENA reflect the fact that public education is entirely or mostly free and covers the great majority of tertiary students. Private outlays are substantial even where higher education is nominally free. We will return to this subject in Chapter 8.

To the best of my knowledge we do not have systematic data on the costs of education, per student, in the MENA/Arab world (but see El-Araby, 2010: 1–10). Sultan Abu-Orabi (2014), secretary-general of the Association of Arab Universities, presented some very summary figures: "The cost of a university student in the Arab world is about $2,700 a year, and it might be as little as $550 in some countries. In the Gulf countries, the student's cost is between $5,000 and $15,000."[16]

ESCWA (2014: 50) provides a bit more detail for 2008–2009 on public outlays:[17]

- Egypt: $757 per student per annum
- Syria: $814
- Morocco: $2,748
- Tunisia: $1,948
- Saudi Arabia: $8,186
- Jordan: $763
- Lebanon: $1,635

It is such disparities that define two universes of educational development in the MENA, the oil-rich and the people-rich, with Iran, Algeria, and Iraq straddling both. The trilemma for the countries of the GCC really does not exist. Table 1.9 gives a more dynamic rendering.

Table 1.9. Government Expenditure on Education as a Percentage of GDP and as a Percentage of Total Government Expenditures, Select MENA and Other Countries, 2005–2015

Country	2005		2008		2012–2015	
	% of GDP	% of Govt. Exp.	% of GDP	% of Govt. Exp.	% of GDP	% of Govt. Exp.
Algeria			4.35	11.4		
Egypt	4.8		3.8	10.5		
France	5.5	10.4	5.4	10.2	5.5	9.7
Iran	4.2	22.3	4.1	21	2.9	16.5
Iraq						
Israel	5.8	12.7	5.5	13.3	5.8	14.3
Jordan						
Kuwait	4.7	13.3				
Lebanon	2.7	8.4	2.03	5.9	2.57	8.6
Libya						
Morocco			5.3	17.5		
Oman	3.5			11	4.9	
Saudi Arabia	5.4	19.3	5.14	19.3		
Singapore	3.22	19.8	2.78	19.9	2.9	19.9
Sudan						
Syria		20	4.6	20		
Tunisia	6.4	27	6.3	25	6.2	21
Turkey	2.9	8.5			4.8	12.4
UAE						
Yemen			5.15	12.5		

Source: data.uis.unesco.org. Data for the last two columns are from any of the years 2012–2015, according to availability.

There is a story attached to each country entry. Some general features are that 2005 saw further and widespread programs of structural adjustment that required reducing public expenditures. The global crisis of 2008 impacted the region, but not as severely as, say, southern Europe. The region was significantly disrupted by the Arab uprisings of 2011. Turkey's unimpressive figures for 2005 may reflect the recent economic crisis from which it was emerging, followed by, in 2012–2015, the AKP's return to growth and social spending.

Since 1990 Egypt has spent between 4 and 5 percent of GDP on all stages of education. The 2014 constitution commits Egypt to spending not less than 4 percent of GDP on education and not less than 1 percent of GDP on scientific research. Article 238 of the constitution stipulates that the target level should be achieved no later than 2016–2017 and that secondary education will be universal by the same year.

We see overall, with a few exceptions, that over the decade 2005–2015 spending is flat or declining. This probably reflects the structural adjustment process but not demographic change. The real numbers of students at all levels was growing in this period. The countries bucking the downward expenditure trend were Saudi Arabia, Israel, and Turkey.

Some country characteristics to keep in mind are that in Lebanon the private sector takes on at least half the total financial burden of education, hence the relatively low levels of government expenditures (see Chapter 8). The downturn in Iran was influenced by the onerous sanctions regime applied to that country prior to the nuclear agreement concluded in 2015 (and partially resumed since 2018).

The UNESCO data does not cover the major petroleum exporters, aside from Saudi Arabia and Algeria. Saudi Arabia, along with Tunisia (not an oil exporter), shows the greatest effort in public expenditures on education as a percentage of both GDP and total government outlays.

Military Outlays

We can look at allocations of the public budget as indicative of government priorities. External and internal threats to order and stability are very real in the MENA. Wars and civil wars have been frequent. Outlays to shore up national security are hard to treat as discretionary. The figures from the MENA suggest that governments value military security as much as or more (Israel, Saudi Arabia, Oman) than an educated population, or, in more transactional terms, more than their social contracts. One may gainsay such priorities as window dressing for military fat cats lining their institutional nests, but in a region as violent as the Middle East it is hard to deny that national security is always at stake. This cursory treatment of military expenditures is meant merely to put educational outlays in some budgetary perspective.

The military burden is particularly high in the Middle East. Military spending as a share of GDP, for those countries in the region for which data are available, averaged 6 percent in 2016—almost triple the global average of 2.2 percent. Oman had the highest military burden in the world at 17 percent, followed by Saudi Arabia at 10 percent (data.worldbank.org). Saudi Arabia spent $63 billion in 2016 on the military, making it in absolute terms the largest spender in the MENA and the fourth largest in the world. For a number of countries, levels of spending are in fact down as a proportion of GDP from three or four decades ago—in Egypt's case perhaps misleadingly so.

Table 1.10. Military Expenditure by Country as a Percentage of GDP by Year

Country	2005	2011	2016
Algeria	2.8	4.3	6.7
Egypt	2.9	1.9	1.6
France	2.4	2.3	2.3
Iran	3.3	2.4	3
Iraq	2.2	2.4	4.8
Israel	7.6	6	5.8
Jordan	4.8	5.5	4.5
Kuwait	4.3	3.5	6.5
Lebanon	4.5	4.1	nd
Libya	1.4	nd	7.8
Morocco	3.3	3.3	3.2
Oman	12	9.8	17
Saudi Arabia	7.7	7.2	10.4
Singapore	4.3	3.2	3.4
Sudan	3.3	nd	3.1
Tunisia	1.5	1.6	2.3
Turkey	2.5	2.2	2
UAE	3.7	5.5	nd
Yemen	4.3	5.2	nd

Source: World Bank (2016), based on the IMF Government Finance Statistics Database, latest available data.

Egypt's outlays on the military sector warrant commentary. In 2009 they stood at 2.9 percent of GDP and declined thereafter, to 1.6 percent in 2016. Yet, as Robert Springborg notes, Egypt's military "is the largest in the MENA [setting aside Turkey, which is not technically in the MENA] and the eleventh largest globally" (2018: 51). Egypt's military expenditures are opaque. It is not alone in that respect. At least since the Mubarak era, Egypt's leaders have tried to hide the true weight of military expenditures on the economy, and on the social contract, by touting its myriad enterprises, which compete directly and often unfairly with the private sector, as funding expenses that would otherwise come out of the country's operating budget. Moreover, the conventional parts of the military budget, as well as the financing of its commercial operations, are not subject to parliamentary scrutiny or any public audit. The 2014 constitution vests budgetary oversight of the military in the National Defense Council, which is chaired by the president of the republic (Springborg, 2018: 53; Sayigh, 2019).

I have reviewed military expenditures merely to point out that a shift of only 2 percent in military outlays, from 6 percent of GDP on average to 4 percent, could free up funds for investment in education, job training, and R&D that would be nearly twice current levels. It is hard to believe that national security would be significantly weakened by such a reallocation.

Most Arab states impose obligatory military service on all able-bodied males. In Egypt, for example, military service kicks in at age eighteen. It is for three years, unless one is a university graduate, when it becomes one year. The age of compulsory service, roughly eighteen to twenty-two, corresponds to the cohort on which GERs are calculated. It is also a cohort that is statistically susceptible to unemployment.

There is scant documentation on what may be a huge missed opportunity to combat youth unemployment; for example, to use military service to build skills among young conscripts. The opportunities for technical and vocational training, consonant with military duties, seem vast. The needs for skilled maintenance personnel, communications technicians, accountants, coders, and so forth are clear. It is possible that in Egypt's sprawling complex of military enterprises, from farms to engineering firms, such training is going on, but I have seen no description of it.

Youth and Other Types of Unemployment

The crisis posed by youth unemployment, the alleged 'job mismatch' of the inappropriately educated (see Chapter 6) for what the market wants, and the reluctance, albeit temporary, to remain idle until the right (preferably public sector) job comes along are not unique to the MENA. As the 2011 *Economist's* special report on the future of jobs notes, "Early in the millennium 35–40% of surveyed employers indicated that they had trouble finding qualified hires. The fields that had inadequate supply are all what universities purportedly produce: technicians, sales reps, skilled trades, engineers, management, ICT staff, etc" (Bishop, 2011). The MENA simply has an acute case of a widespread disease.

Combining the disciplinary choices of undergraduates, the massification of higher education, the shrinking of public employment opportunities, and the timidity of the private sector, we arrive at the dismal outcomes for youth employment, especially among women, that characterize the

Table 1.11. Unemployment and Labor Participation Rates, 2009–2016, Select Countries

Country	Overall Unemployment Rate: Females (%)	Youth Unemployment Rate: Males (%)	Youth Unemployment Rate: Females (%)	Female Labor Force Participation Rate (%)
Algeria	10	21.6	40	15
Egypt	12	27.2	38.6	23
Greece	23.5	44	51	45
Iran	12	29	44	15
Iraq	8	nd	nd	nd
Israel	4.8	8.2	9.1	59
Jordan	12	nd	nd	12.6
Korea	3.7	11	10.5	52.1
Kuwait	1.8	nd	nd	57
Lebanon	6.4	nd	nd	nd
Libya (2012)	19	41	67	34
Morocco	9.4	19.4	18.2	25
Oman	15.4	nd	nd	32
Saudi Arabia	5.7	17	46	22
Sudan (2009)	13	16	32	23
Tunisia	15.7	36	42	26
Turkey	10.5	17	24	32
UAE	1.6	5.1	9.5	37.5
Yemen	13.5	24	35	6

Source: http://www.ilo.org/ilostat/ (ILO database)

MENA. Unfortunately, the situation is not likely to change for the better any time soon. This means, among other things, a prolonged legitimacy crisis for incumbent regimes, during which bold measures need to be taken merely to reduce building internal pressures.

The data confirms a general pattern of exceptionally high female unemployment, low female participation in the workforce, high overall unemployment, and high male youth unemployment. A few GCC members show fairly high female participation rates and fairly low overall unemployment.

Tunisia is particularly striking. It has a deserved reputation, dating back decades, for promoting gender equality, but that has not affected its low female participation rate. Nor has its large investment in education paid off in lower overall unemployment or lower male youth unemployment. In fact, Tunisia appears to have been penalized for being a star performer in producing university graduates. It has suffered from especially high rates of educated youth unemployment. Not only does this fact signal the problems of the content of university education relative to the demand for graduates but, as well, the growing frustration among the educated unemployed (Assaad et al., 2017).

Greece shows that economic crisis can devastate labor markets despite positive achievement such as high female labor force participation. Israel and South Korea show the kinds of numbers that the MENA can only dream about.

Caution is required in assessing employment data for the GCC, including Saudi Arabia. It is not clear if the data covers the national work-force only or if it includes the expatriate workforce. The latter outnumber the former sometimes five to one and by definition are employed, otherwise they would not be granted visas to enter any GCC country. They also presumably contain a large quotient of employed females (nurses, housekeepers, clerical staff). Saudi Arabia's official estimate of unemployment among nationals for 2017 is 12.8 percent, contrasted with the 5.7 percent in Table 1.11. The 5.7 percent figure presumably includes ex-pat employees. This means 12.8 percent is the correct figure for nationals. Importantly, native citizens of the GCC enjoy privileged access to public sector positions.

I posit that this situation of high youth unemployment, especially among the educated, has caught and held the attention of political leadership because, as 2011 showed, it is regime-threatening. But to deal with it requires policy measures that are destabilizing in their own right (see especially Chapter 6).

The Public–Private Balance in Higher Education

In 2008, 89 percent of all students were in public institutions and 11 percent were in private ones (UNESCO, 2009; Bhandari and El-Amine, 2011). If one compares public and private education in terms of institutions, the private sector is catching up fast. Public universities tend to be huge, however, with enrollments in the tens of, and sometimes hundreds of, thousands. Private enrollments lag far behind public enrollments, but there, too, the private sector is coming on fast. When I began researching this study, private enrollments stood at about 10 percent of the total. By 2017, according to Adnan Badran (2017), private enrollments had risen to 30 percent. In Jordan, where Badran was once minister of education, private tertiary education is a fairly recent phenomenon (since 1991), but growth in enrollment has been rapid. In 1999 private institutions accounted for 35 percent of total tertiary enrollment. We know that in Iran private enrollments are now over 50 percent of the total.

Private sector tertiary education, by and large, is of lower quality than that of the public sector and less selective. It is exploiting a robust market. Going back to GERs, if we take the unweighted average for the Arab world in 2015 of about 33 percent, it follows that 67 percent of the eligible cohort is not in tertiary education. Many did poorly on their high school exams and thus were rejected by their preferred public university. Again, using 2015 as our base year, in excess of 16 million Arabs were eligible to attend IHLs but were not doing so. It is the demand generated by this segment of the cohort that the private sector is trying to meet. For tuition and other fees, it will provide an education to the rejects of the public system—sometimes nothing more than undergraduate business and computer science diplomas. For the public sector, this investment-based private sector (many institutions are for-profit) is welcome as it lowers the pressure on the public sector to absorb ever more students. A direct participant in Egypt reported:

> I taught in six private universities in Egypt, and I can confirm that in spite of the high potential of private universities and the opportunities they offer if well managed and closely supervised, they are for the most part investment projects that aim for profit at the end of the day regardless of the quality of the service. Like other public and private institutions, corruption and cronyism rule. (Abou Setta, 2014)

In this sense private tertiary education becomes a prop for tattered social contracts. The founding and governmental licensing of private institutions becomes a facet of crony capitalism.[18]

Regionalism

The Cultural Treaty concluded over half a century ago at the end of the Second World War in 1945 between the member states of the Arab League provided for the exchange of teachers and students at various levels of studies and education.[19] It was a step toward promoting mobility in the Arab world. The signatory states expressed their intention to standardize their own stages of education, while maintaining the basic tenets of their national education systems (Zand and Karrar, 2010).

Creating an Arab space for higher education is a goal often invoked but toward which little progress has been made. In that respect the creation of an Arab educational space, emulating the European Union's Bologna process, has been a failure (UNESCO, 2009, and Chapter 6). This is hardly surprising given the track record of failed regional economic integration, the existence of four failed or semifailed states since 2011, and fierce inter-state rivalries involving Iranian and Saudi-backed coalitions and their more distant foreign sponsors.

A decade ago, the biggest number of non-national students were in the following countries, in order: Jordan (22,600), the UAE (19,800), Lebanon (19,600), and Egypt (12,000). Lamine (2010) expresses reservations about these figures, as not all universities in these countries responded to his questionnaires, and not all universities that responded provided complete information about the nationalities of students.

The mobility of faculty is similar, with a slight increase in favor of both Arab and non-Arab professors: 7.3 percent are from other Arab countries and 2.8 percent are non-Arabs. Saudi Arabia is the leader here (32.5 percent are Arab, non-Saudi professors and 6.2 percent are from outside the region), followed by the UAE, which has a high percentage of Arab professors (48 percent) and non-Arab professors (43 percent), compared to very low levels of Emirati professors (only 9 percent). Likewise, the distribution of students in this country is different from the pattern mentioned above: 33.8 percent of the total are Arab students and 14.4 percent are foreigners, compared to 51.8 percent Emirati students.

That situation may be changing as Arab public universities seek to recruit paying students from abroad or to lure back their own nationals from the diaspora. International rankings often emphasize diversity and internationalism among faculty and students, so the ranking game provides an added incentive. Working against this are Arab animosities and rivalries. Gulf students, for example, are discouraged from studying in Lebanon as they could be endangered by the presence of Hezbollah.

Conclusion

The MENA region is undergoing a demographic transition that has led to sharply lower fertility rates and is trending toward stable population numbers. This phenomenon has opened the possibility of a 'demographic dividend' whereby the cohorts of the relatively young expand in relation to dependent populations of the very young and retirees. It is only a matter of time before the growth of the older cohorts begins to raise dependency ratios once again. The MENA is already in transition and may have thirty to fifty years before the dividend evaporates.

Despite declining fertility and stabilizing populations, higher education is still a growth industry. The region's relatively low GER of about 30 percent on average means that if the target is 40–50 percent (a number of countries are already there), as seems likely, the numbers enrolled in higher education are likely to grow significantly. One may add to this adult or continuing education to underscore that tertiary education will grow robustly for some time.

There are close to 9 million tertiary-level students today (ca. 2017). That number may grow to at least 15 million students by 2050. If average costs per student are $3,000 per annum in today's dollars, that would mean annual outlays of $4.5 billion. The costing assumes BAU, which may not be a reasonable assumption. Disruptors are likely to compete on cost and come from the private sector (see Chapter 8 and the Conclusion).

We have an incomplete image of dropout rates and graduation rates. Fairly high rates of attrition are a worldwide phenomenon, and the MENA does not appear to perform significantly worse than other major regions. But that fact should not be cause for complacency. Dropouts are the sign of wasted resources and wasted talent. It is the less privileged who are most likely to drop out. A system ostensibly designed to promote social mobility is doing the opposite.

Growth in the numbers of those who do graduate has been feeble— under 3 percent per annum. This is another token of wasted resources and talent.

The Arab world and the MENA invest a lot in higher education in terms of shares in GDP, total government expenditures, and percentages of per capita income. The outlays have clearly not borne the fruit that might have been expected. Throughout the region, including in countries like Tunisia that have made the greatest effort, youth unemployment, especially among women, remains stubbornly high. Moreover, waves of structural adjustment, beginning in the 1970s, have put public budgets under severe pressure, and most MENA governments have had to curtail outlays on education at all levels.

This factor has opened the door to private investment in tertiary education, a domain that had been the preserve of the public sector for decades. Some countries, like Iran, have been transformed in a few decades. Others may well follow suit. At present, nearly two-thirds of eligible citizens in the Arab world are not receiving tertiary-level education. Not all of them aspire to it, but many do. This pool drives demand for private higher education.

Much of what follows in this book is focused on what is possible or likely by way of public policy change and initiatives. This chapter has outlined some of both the goals of and the constraints on public policy. The ultimate constraint, the mother of red lines, is regime survival. In that context, I have long ago ceased to heed Cassandra-like warnings that the status quo is not viable. To the contrary, the status quo and BAU usually are viable, albeit suboptimal. Failing to understand why they are viable and who their beneficiaries are will consign any advice proffered to incumbents to the back of a dusty drawer.

2

The Modern Flagship Universities of the Arab World

The institutions of higher learning that mushroomed throughout the Arab world in the post-independence period produced scientists but not science, medical doctors but not medical science, social scientists but not social science, and so forth. Their graduates were on the whole anti-Western, but they were culturally and psychologically profoundly Western-oriented, forming the most culturally dependent sector of society. (Sharabi, 1988: 81)

Higher education in the MENA can be seen, in the sum of its parts, as an institution. It evolved in fits and starts over centuries, but most of its institutional history has been written since 1900. I initially thought I would emphasize here the sharp breaks and discontinuities of institutional growth—the advent of Atatürk after the First World War, the revolution in Egypt in 1952, the rise of the petro-states after 1973, the founding of the Islamic Republic of Iran in 1979—but continuity is equally present, in the form of political interference, bolstering national strength, and education as a right. The founders of the region's universities were from the outset supremely conscious of the need for university autonomy and for firewalls against the political system. Their fears were justified and their defenses futile. 'Massification' was not born with the socialist republics of the 1950s and 1960s, but, at least in Egypt, much earlier. Turkey and Egypt in the interwar years built the quasi-organic links between university education and the civil service that came to mark the region as a whole. Governance issues were well understood over a century ago. Nothing significantly new has been added to the debates about shared governance and university autonomy since then (see Chapter 4).

53

There has been one major discontinuity. The few institutions of higher learning founded in the early centuries of Islam have had only a minor role to play in modern higher education in the MENA. At least for two centuries, as Europe exerted its military and scientific strength in the region (Napoleon's invasion of Egypt is the epochal marker of this dominance), traditional Islamic universities came to be seen by local rulers as obstacles to 'progress' rather than catalysts. Colonial powers that asserted themselves in Algeria, Tunisia, Egypt, and the wreckage of the Ottoman Empire at the end of the First World War were not advocates of higher education, at least not for the 'natives' of the territories under their control. What I am calling the 'flagship' universities of the region were founded by local elites to escape the model of traditional Islamic education and to counter the colonial project that prevailed throughout the MENA.[1]

Just as Europe can boast ancient seats of learning in the Sorbonne, Oxford, Cambridge, and Bologna, so the Arab world can invoke the Zitouna in Tunis, Tunisia (737 CE), the Qarawiyyin in Fez, Morocco (859 CE), and al-Azhar University in Cairo, Egypt (969 CE). All three practiced traditional modes of learning, dispensed by learned religious scholars to small groups of students. Interestingly, given the current initiatives in competency-based education (CBE), these ancient institutions did not have any standard curriculum or course formats. Students would be awarded certificates of competency in specific fields once they had convinced their instructors of their mastery. No significant scientific research was carried out in their confines. They are not, today, the leaders in tertiary education in the way of Oxford or the Sorbonne. They have either been preserved and isolated by central authorities or bureaucratized and integrated into the 'modern' public university system. That system, started in the Ottoman Empire in the 1870s, was set up as an alternative to, not a modification of, the older institutions.

Much in the way we stress the Confucian legacy in higher education in the Far East, it is tempting to invoke the Arab world's Islamic heritage to explain its educational institutions today. Arabs and Muslims do not hesitate to decry Muslim obstructionism of speculative thought, an Islamic proclivity for rote learning, a preference for blind obedience to authority, and a bias against women that cripples societies and economies (for a very contemporary critique of this kind, see Masri, 2017; Pollock, 2019).

I discount the impact of Muslim history on the contemporary functioning of Arab public universities. That legacy has received wide attention, and I believe there is not a consensus on how to interpret it. The basic question is why, after a few centuries of flourishing scientific advances after the founding of Islam, did the regions in which it prevailed enter into centuries of intellectual torpor? There is an extensive literature on this issue, and I refer here only to a few recent participants in the debate. Timur Kuran (2011; 2016), Khalil Bitar (2013), and Eric Chaney (2015) have emphasized Islamic institutions such as the *waqf* (a religious endowment whose original purposes cannot be modified with the passage of time) and the gradual control of the *ulama* (the formally trained *savants* of Islam) over education as having choked off scientific enquiry in the Arabo-Muslim world by the fourteenth and fifteenth centuries CE. They stress that there were no institutional equivalents to the Western university corporation with its trustees and independent endowments whose purposes could be periodically redefined. In the 'Muslim world,' a vibrant scientific tradition atrophied over time. In the Arabo-Muslim world, perhaps with the exception of medicine, scientific research and enquiry were the undertaking of individuals operating without institutional underpinnings and capturing students' and colleagues' attention only once the exigencies of religious education had been met.

There were graduates of the old institutions who played major roles in launching the new, such as, in Egypt, Taha Hussein or Saad Zaghloul (both students at al-Azhar), but they wanted to break with and end-run the old institutions, precisely because they doubted that they could be 'modernized,' and to embrace missions that they had eschewed or were legally restricted from adopting. So, the Muslim legacy of education is important to understand, but it has had little bearing on the evolution of higher education in the MENA since about 1870.[2]

I will focus here on four flagship universities in the Arab world in order to bring us up to the contemporary period, which is the heart of this book. They are Cairo University (founded 1908), Damascus University (founded 1923), Lebanese University (founded in Beirut in 1951), and Mohammed V University (founded in Rabat, Morocco, in 1957).[3] All four in their beginnings reflected European best practice and to some extent the strengths of their colonial masters. Damascus University arguably was the least influenced by French models, while Cairo University borrowed liberally from both French and British higher education. Mohammed V University (MVU) hewed closely to French practice, as did Lebanese University. Each of them came into being in significantly different ways. Those differing origins reflected the very different moments in colonial and postcolonial history in which they were founded. By the time they reached maturity, around the turn of the twenty-first century, they suffered from common pathologies and shared more similarities than differences.[4]

Cairo University and Egypt's Higher Education

The impetus for the founding of what would later be called Cairo University came from Egypt's social and political elite but not from the government itself. At its inception it was called the Egyptian University, and it was a private venture, led by reformers and nationalists like Mustafa Kamil, Muhammad Abduh, and Saad Zaghloul. Kamil first called for a *jam'iya ahliya* (a popular university open to rich and poor alike) in 1904. Egypt at the time was under British occupation. The British high commissioner, Lord Cromer, was at best indifferent to educating Egyptians (Tignor, 2010: 234). The Egyptian ruler, Khedive Abbas, kept a prudent distance from the university project. The founders eventually excluded Mustafa Kamil from the founding committee because of his difficulties with the khedive.

In contrast to Cromer, founding fathers, like Qasim Amin, had a vision that presaged generations of reformers and advocates. In 1908, Amin wrote, "The main reason for the rise and decline of nations is their way of training and education" (Reid, 1990: 32). Amin, who championed women's education, died the same year.

Another early advocate was Jurji Zaydan, a Lebanese emigré to Egypt. Kamal Mughaith (2018: 29) claims Zaydan published an appeal for an Egyptian "college" *(kulliya)* in 1896. Zaydan had been a medical student at the Syrian Protestant College (SPC) in Beirut (to become the American University of Beirut (AUB) after the First World War) in 1882 when Edwin Lewis, a member of the tiny faculty of the SPC, gave a commencement speech in which he obliquely praised Charles Darwin and his theory of evolution. Evangelical Presbyterians on the SPC board were outraged and forced Lewis' resignation. This split the faculty, with about half resigning from the college in protest. In turn, students in medicine, including Zaydan, also resigned and made their way to Egypt to continue their studies (Juha and Khal, 2004). Zaydan wound up in publishing and was a major figure in the Arab renaissance *(al-Nahda)*. In 1910, he was given a faculty appointment at the new Egyptian University but soon had to give it up because of pressure from conservative Muslim figures who found Zaydan's combination of freemasonry, Christianity, and secular proclivities too much to bear. Thus, twice in his life Zaydan was the victim of academic freedom issues. He died in 1914.

In the Egyptian University's "Declaration of the Founders" from October 12, 1906, it is stated, "The University we aim to establish is a school of science and arts. Its doors are open regardless of sex or religion."

It is further stated, "This University has no political tint, no links to politicians, and to no one working (in politics). There will not enter into its administration or its studies anything whatsoever that is connected (to politics)" (al-Minawi, 2007: 105). But the founders called upon Prince Ahmad Fuad, the son of Khedive Ismail, to be president of the founding committee, thereby giving the lie to the commitment to firewalls between politics and the university (Mughaith, 2018: 30). Prince Fuad became the university's first president, a post from which he resigned in 1913.

In contrast to al-Azhar, religion was to play no prominent role in the new institution. It was to be open to males and females, Muslims, Jews, and Christians. A segregated women's section was opened, apparently populated by well-to-do young ladies of Egypt's bourgeoisie. It was closed in 1912. Arabic was to be the main language of instruction, in keeping with the spirit of the Arab renaissance. The founders were adamant about granting the new university full autonomy in all matters. They inveighed against political interference as if they understood that it would be the university's Achilles' heel.

In this respect, it is interesting to note that US President Theodore Roosevelt was awarded one of the first honorary doctorates by the university in 1910. He gave a political speech, noting that in Egypt the call for a constitution and independence put the cart before the horse and that only a long period of careful preparation could ready a people for independence and democracy. The nationalist press criticized his speech vehemently (al-Minawi, 2007: 22–23).

From the outset, the issue of adequate financial resources plagued the new university. Despite the prominence of its early backers, the first subscriptions amounted to less than a 1,000 Egyptian pounds. Its first home was the Gianaclis building in central Cairo, close to what is now Tahrir Square. That building eventually became the seat of the American University in Cairo (AUC).

In 1907 Lord Cromer left Egypt, to be replaced by Sir Eldon Gorst. Gorst was much more open to promoting education, especially at the primary level. The Egyptian state, through direct subsidies and payments from the Ministry of Awqaf (religious mortmain properties) supported the Egyptian University with 7,000 Egyptian pounds per year. Total subscriptions reached 26,000 Egyptian pounds, with 1,000 coming from the Coptic Patriarchate. The most notable gift to the new institution came from Princess Fatma Ismail, daughter of Khedive Ismail. It is a tale any contemporary advancement officer would immediately recognize. Mohammed

'Alawi Basha, a member of the Egyptian University founding committee who was also personal physician to Princess Fatma, in 1913 convinced the princess to dedicate part of her charitable waqf to the university. The gift consisted of the rent from 661 feddans, the transfer of six feddans of land in Giza to the university, and 18,000 Egyptian pounds as a cash gift (al-Minawi, 2007: 25).[5]

Although Mughaith (2018: 34) provides a different figure for initial funding—13,845 Egyptian pounds in donations and subscriptions—the modesty of the level of support for what was supposed to be a national project is striking.

For all the talk of autonomy and absence of political interference, the Egyptian University was gradually absorbed by the state. The First World War made funding the private university difficult, added to which Khedive Abbas, regarded by the British as too pro-Turkish, was stripped of his position as khedive.

The Egyptian University struggled to find both students and faculty. Initially the main feeder schools were the seven high schools founded earlier by Khedive Muhammad Ali. To gain admissions to the university applicants had to have completed the high school general exam (thanawiya 'amma), first introduced in 1887. By 1920 only 607 students had passed it. This was the pool from which the university had to attract students. It offered a curriculum consisting mainly of arts, philosophy, and humanities, although science, medicine, and law were added by 1917. It charged modest fees. In contrast, al-Azhar was completely free and made no requirement of the high school general exam. At the end of the First World War, al-Azhar registered 12,000 students, compared to the Egyptian University's peak year enrollment in 1916 of 400.

There were virtually no faculty available of the required level. The university had to raid the Dar al-'Ulum (House of Sciences), founded earlier by Khedive Ismail (again, to end-run al-Azhar) and the Madrasat al-Qada' al-Shar'i (the Shari'a College), created by the mufti, Muhammad Abduh, and attached to al-Azhar, to prompt its pedagogical overhaul. Missions were sent to Europe to recruit faculty (although the language of instruction was and is Arabic). The above-mentioned seven high schools did not have faculty appropriate for the task at hand. It was in this context that Jurji Zaydan was briefly hired.

In 1914 Taha Hussein, a towering figure in Egyptian letters and academia, received his doctorate from the Egyptian University. In 1919 he became a full professor.

The disruption of the war and dwindling enrollments (they stood at 107 in 1922) pushed the founders to consider ceding control of the university to the Egyptian state. According to Mahmoud Fawzi al-Minawi (2002: 29), the projected establishment of the AUC spurred the public project along. Eventually in December 1923 'ownership' was transferred to the Ministry of al-Ma'arif (Knowledge) (al-Minawi, 2007: 30; Mughaith, 2018: 37). The first rector was another Egyptian public intellectual and staunch Egyptian (as opposed to Arab) nationalist, Ahmad Lutfi al-Sayyid. He was instrumental in propelling the Egyptian University toward excellence.

Well prior to the transfer of ownership, in 1917, a commission was appointed to prepare a feasibility study for a national university, including by-laws for the university and for faculties. It is in many ways a model exercise, showing full awareness of all the governance issues that are inherent to university management. It even presents dissenting opinions, especially with regard to insufficient autonomy from the state, as laid out in the main recommendations, and the insufficient proposed level of Arabization (Egypt, Ministère de l'Instruction Publique, 1921).

A central aspect of the recommendations was to amalgamate the seven high schools, which in 1920 enrolled 2,158 students. There were another eight hundred students enrolled outside Egypt. The amalgamated schools would be the core of the new public university.

Target enrollment was put at two thousand. The bulk would be boarders, organized in 'pavilions' of four hundred students each. In the event, the first dormitories were not built until 1949.

The issue of gender was handled less directly than in the private Egyptian University, which explicitly provided for admission of both sexes (see the "Declaration of the Founders" above). The university said it was open to all Egyptians and then without fanfare admitted women beginning in 1929. In that year, seventeen female students gained entry, eight in the Faculty of Science. Women still faced a major hurdle in that they were not allowed to enroll in the high schools (Mughaith, 2018: 39). By 1945, 32 percent of the students in the Faculty of Arts were women, 6 percent in the Faculty of Sciences, 7.5 percent in the Faculty of Medicine, and 2 percent in the Faculty of Law (al-Minawi, 2007: 68).

While once again insisting that the Egyptian University would have its own legal personality, its own budget, and full autonomy, the feasibility study recommended that the minister of education be its chancellor, that there be a university board, a president, secretary-general, and the university Senate, consisting of the chancellor, the president, a vice president, the deans, and three elected members from each faculty. The Senate and the board would share many oversight duties.

The 1921 report stresses the importance of research, noting, "If a university wishes to achieve its mission, it must concern itself not only with the preparation of its students for a career, but also to extend the limits of knowledge and to inspire in the students the spirit of research" (Egypt, Ministère de l'Instruction Publique, 1921: 22). It also emphasizes that "control of teaching will be as decentralized as possible, granting Faculties broad latitude in regulating all questions regarding the teaching of materials within their purview" (1921: 9). Each faculty was to prepare its own budget and submit it to the Senate, which would refer it to the board and then to the Ministry of Finance. Tuition was recommended to be set at 30 Egyptian pounds per year for sciences, engineering, and medicine and at 15 Egyptian pounds for letters, business, and teaching. There is no evidence in the feasibility study of any core curriculum across the seven schools or faculties. The main innovation is in governance, not in pedagogical content.

The public university opened in 1926 in temporary headquarters with faculties of arts, law, medicine, and sciences. Its cornerstone was laid in Giza on February 7, 1928. In 1930, Taha Hussein was appointed dean of the faculty of arts. This was a few years after the publication of his book, *Fi al-shi'r al-jahili* (On Pre-Islamic Poetry), in 1926. The book unleashed a hornet's nest of condemnation by Muslim scholars, and Hussein was forced from the deanship in 1931.[6] The Ministry of Education then arrogated the appointment of deans and unilaterally added five new members to the university's senate. What authority or process leads to the appointment of deans has been a 'hot' political issue in Egypt ever since.

Before the term 'academic freedom' gained currency, this violation of it was opposed by the rector *(mudir)*, Ahmad Lutfi al-Sayyid, and he in turn resigned from his position. I know of no other incident of such institutional defense of academic boundaries in the contemporary Arab world, although violations of academic freedom have been legion. So inspiring was the conduct of both men that several decades later, in 2004, a group of Cairo University faculty members established the March 9 group to commemorate the firing of Hussein and resignation of al-Sayyid ('Abbas, 2008: 76–88; Reid, 1990: 120–25; Geer, 2013). Mughaith (2018) is or was a member of the March 9 group.

Decades later, another common experience focused many contemporary faculty members' attention on academic freedom: that of Nasr Abu Zayd, a Cairo University faculty member who was persecuted by Islamists, starting in 1993, for his work on Qur'anic hermeneutics, and who went into exile in 1995 (Najjar, 2000). Abu Zayd's colleagues, such as the novelist Ahdaf Soueif and Mohammed Abul-Ghar, a professor in the Cairo University's medical school, rallied to his defense.

The first annual March 9 event was held at Cairo University in 2004. At that time, it was impossible to use a hall or room for any sort of event, whether on or off campus, without the permission of the security apparatus. Abul-Ghar led a delegation of March 9 founders to ask the university president for the use of a large hall. According to Benjamin Geer (2013), the president tried to dissuade them, claiming that academic freedom was well protected. A security officer whose office was in the university administration building, and who controlled the university president's fax machine and his international calls, instructed him to deny the request.

In the autumn of 2008, March 9 members raised a court case to remove the campus security force controlled by the Ministry of the Interior and to create a new, civilian campus security unit under the authority of the university president. The court ruled in their favor, the government appealed, and the plaintiffs won a final appeal in October 2010 (Association for Freedom of Thought and Expression, 2010). The initial implementation of the ruling, at Cairo University, was merely a façade in which police officers were given civilian uniforms. Real implementation began after the mass uprising of January 2011 and the fall of Mubarak.

By the mid-1930s, the Egyptian University's enrollments reached seven thousand. Egypt, despite nominal independence in 1936, was still very much under the control of Great Britain. It was in that context that the nearly organic links of the university to the civil service, and to the political elite more broadly, were developed. These were the years of the Great Depression that hit exporters of primary products, like Egypt's cotton, particularly hard. Jobs were scarce, and the 'great mismatch' between inappropriately educated white-collar workers and a weak job market was already apparent. (We will have much more to say about the mismatch in Chapter 6.) The de facto role of the state as employer of last resort had thus taken hold (Fakhsh, 1977). At a loftier level, university faculty and graduates became aware that university credentials could lead to high political office (Reid, 1990: 120, 126). Indeed, Taha Hussein went on to become minister of education on the eve of the revolution of 1952.

In 1936, King Fuad passed away and Farouk succeeded him. Given King Fuad's long association with the Egyptian University, it was renamed in 1940 as Fuad I University. After the 1952 revolution, the Egyptian monarchy was abolished and the institution was yet again renamed, as Cairo University. Likewise, what had at first been a branch of the Egyptian University in Alexandria became the autonomous Farouk I University. After 1952 it became Alexandria University.[7] In 1950, Ain Shams University (Abbasiya, Cairo) was founded, followed by Assiut University (Upper Egypt) in 1957, Tanta University (Nile Delta) in 1972, Zagazig University (eastern Delta) in 1974, Helwan University (south of Cairo) in 1975, Minya University (Middle Egypt) in 1976, Menoufia University (Nile Delta) in 1976, and Suez Canal University, also in 1976. Before it was done, the public system had twenty-three universities. Much of the expansion took place during the presidency of Anwar Sadat (1971–81), with seven new universities opening between 1972 and 1976. This had a massive, negative impact on the quality of Egyptian higher education. At the time of the 1952 revolution total tertiary enrollments had reached 32,600. By 1982 they had risen to 480,000 (al-Azhar not included). New universities sought temporary shelter in clapped-out high schools and recruited faculty without proper credentials (Mughaith, 2018: 46).

The seeds of what became the hallmark of the Nasserist era after 1952—education as a universal right provided at no cost to all citizens—were planted in the monarchical era. The nationalist Wafd (Delegation) Party, founded at the close of the First World War, was in power during the Second World War, and in 1943 ended primary-school fees. In 1950, again under a Wafd government, Taha Hussein served as minister of education. In that capacity he abolished high school fees. He famously remarked, "Education should be free, not bought and sold like leeks and onions" (Reid, 1990: 109). Similarly, by 1955, 71 percent of university students attended without paying fees, either because of need or for having scored 75 percent or better on the *thanawiya 'amma*. In 1962, the Egyptian government, under President Gamal Abd al-Nasser made all university education free—a commitment subsequently enshrined in Articles 38 and 39 of the 1964 constitution (Mughaith, 2018: 44). At the same time (1961, according to Khalid Ikram (2018)), successful completion of university studies would be rewarded with a guaranteed public sector job. This promise, replicated de facto or de jure in a number of other Arab states, became a central element of the populist 'social contract' and, before long, an albatross around the neck of public finances. Almost single-handedly, it created the mismatch of skills provided by tertiary education and the needs of the nongovernmental employment sector. Malcolm Kerr presciently saw what was at stake by the early 1960s: "The result of mass higher education has thus been to redistribute poverty in the name of social equality, in a manner that threatens simply to replace an illiterate class of unemployed proletarians with a literate and more sharply alienated one" (1965: 169; Fakhsh, 1977).

In July 1952, the so-called Free Officers seized power. They established the Revolutionary Command Council (RCC) nominally led by General Muhammad Naguib but with much real power vested in Colonel Gamal Abd al-Nasser. The RCC enlisted a prominent civilian Egyptian politician, held over from the prerevolutionary system, Ali Maher, to prepare an assessment of Egypt's higher education. The report was issued on August 23, 1953, stating "the imperative that the state grants to universities the greatest amount of autonomy such that scientific independence is complete; such that science advances and flourishes in the shadow of this independence; similarly that it (the state) sees to it that the university is autonomous in administering financial affairs specific to it" (al-Minawi, 2007: 198–99). This recommendation and much of the report were ignored by Egypt's new rulers (Reid, 1990: 160).

In 1954 there was a serious split in the new military regime. Muhammad Naguib and Gamal Abd al-Nasser contested leadership. Nominally, Naguib wanted to lead Egypt in a more liberal direction, including restoring political parties and open elections, while Nasser backed a more corporatist vision of a single party and popular democracy. In the struggle, Naguib found allies in the Muslim Brotherhood, some trade unions, and Cairo University. Nasser outmaneuvered Naguib and in 1954 solidified his grip on power. Any notion of real university autonomy evaporated along with Egypt's so-called liberal experiment (1922–52). Cairo University, given its behavior in 1954, was viewed as a threat, something that needed to be coopted into the new regime's corporatist structures. In subsequent years, other Arab military/populist regimes (Syria, Iraq, Algeria, Yemen, Sudan, Libya) all borrowed from Nasser's playbook.

In September 1954, after the ouster of Naguib, one of the members of the RCC and a military officer, Kamal al-Din Hussein, became minister of education. He replaced all three rectors of Egypt's existing universities, changed a number of deans, and fired sixty to seventy academics (Reid, 1990: 170). Henceforth, deans were no longer elected by faculty but recommended by the rector and appointed by the minister of education, until President Sadat reintroduced the election of deans in 1972. Under Hussein, the secret police (generically referred to as the *mukhabarat*) became a fixture on Egyptian campuses. Hussein changed the name of his ministry from *ma'arif*, knowledge, to *tarbiya wa ta'lim*, instruction and education, thereby, in Mughaith's (2018: 70) view, transforming the ministry from one devoted to spreading culture to one designed to regiment the university in the service of the military regime.

Just how quickly the regime's social contract rooted itself in the new political order was made clear in 1957 when Hussein tried to introduce some measure of selectivity in university admissions. The otherwise rubberstamp People's Assembly (Maglis al-Sha'b) defied the minister and rejected the proposal. This is one of the rare instances in which Egypt's parliament actually held a minister accountable.

Early in its life the Egyptian University became the locus of student protests against the British and against the Zionist settlers in Palestine. Students mobilized in 1919 to protest the arrest of Saad Zaghloul and other nationalists and to support the revolutionary movement of the same year. On February 9, 1946, student protests and a march across the Abbas Bridge to present their demands at Abdin Palace led to the deaths of a number of students. Events like those of 1919 and 1946 became part of the folklore of student activism in Egypt, and they had their counterparts in other Arab states.

All that was, in principle, to come to an end with the advent of the Nasserist regime. The notion of the university as an autonomous zone of creative thought was to be replaced by the university as a docile support of the 'revolution.' Nasser drew heavily on Egypt's universities to provide ministers and other high-level officials for his governments, but any manifestation of activism at Egyptian universities was repressed. Mustafa Amin, who, along with his brother Ali, founded one of Egypt's major daily newspapers, *Akhbar al-youm* (News of the Day), before the revolution, quickly bought into the new regime's outlook. In *Akhbar al-youm* on September 26, 1954, he argued that, with the evacuation of the British troops, there was no need for student agitators but rather for scientists, engineers, and investors (Reid 1990: 171).

Meanwhile, the public universities were drained of their foreign faculty. In 1951 all British faculty were repatriated. In 1956, after the Suez Canal nationalization, all French faculty left, followed in 1960 by all foreign staff of any nationality.[8] Nasser's regime created twenty-eight higher research institutes, directly under state control, with 25,000 students. This was a political control issue, but it also led to a separation of research from teaching functions in the universities.

After 1955 Egypt struck a strong strategic alliance with the Soviet Union and the Soviet Bloc. It encompassed military cooperation, direct economic support, the move into central economic planning, and sending Egyptian students to the Soviet Bloc for advanced training.

The socialist decrees of 1961 that led to the nationalization or expropriation of swathes of private assets marked Egypt's 'socialist transformation.' For the first and perhaps only time, Egypt's universities became foci of indoctrination in the state's official ideology. In 1965 the regime created the Socialist Youth Organization, arousing only tepid interest among university students. Following Egypt's crushing defeat at the hands of the Israelis in June 1967, students rioted throughout Egypt in protest of the lenient sentences handed out to the nation's military leaders. Those riots led to the disbanding of the Socialist Youth Organization (Reid, 1990: 202).

Nasser died of natural causes in 1970 and was succeeded by his vice president, Anwar Sadat. In October 1973 Egypt launched a partially successful offensive against the Israelis, who had been ensconced in the Suez Canal zone since 1967. The Arab members of the Organization of the Petroleum Exporting Countries (OPEC) raised crude oil prices in support of Egypt's campaign. This brought sudden and massive wealth to OPEC nations, including Iran. One of the direct results was a huge expansion in tertiary education in the OAPEC member states, especially Saudi Arabia, the UAE, Kuwait, Bahrain, Libya, and Qatar. There was sudden demand for tertiary-level instructors, and Egypt led Jordan and Sudan in exporting faculty to the newly rich countries. The well-paid stint abroad became a staple of Egyptian university life.

Sadat was determined to curb the 'leftist' remnants of the Nasser era, and he did so by taking the Muslim Brotherhood off a tight leash. As Carrie Wickham (2013: 34–37) recounts, the rise of Islamist student associations in the 1970s became the dominant force in student politics. Mohammed Osman Ismail of the Arab Socialist Union (ASU) was a key liaison person. He was made governor of Assiut (1973–82). At Assiut University and on other campuses, the Islamic *jama'at* (societies) swamped leftist organizations in student elections. Consultative councils *(shura)* headed by 'princes' or commanders *(amirs)* spread throughout Egyptian universities. The head *amir* in the mid-1970s was Hamdi Gazzar, a Cairo University medical student. By 1979 the *jama'at* had captured the General Egyptian Students' Union at the expense of Nasserists and Arab nationalists. Abd al-Mun'im Abul-Futuh became president of the Cairo University union, Essam al-Eryan *amir* of the Medical Students' Union at the university, and Abu 'Ala al-Madi *amir* of the Engineering Union at Minya University. Al-Madi was to found the Wasat Party in 1996.

The Sadat era also saw a massive and ill-prepared expansion in Egypt's universities, outlined above. The creation of seven new universities in four years was an improvised affair, especially in that the pool of eligible faculty was reduced by the exodus to the oil-rich OAPEC countries. Premises were more often rented than built, and underqualified instructors were brought into service. A 1983 UNESCO study, cited by Donald Reid (1990: 221), decried the deterioration in standards: an academic year of effectively twenty weeks, teacher-to-student ratios in some faculties of 1:600, and curricula sometimes twenty years out of date.[9]

But this state of affairs needs to be put in context. The chaos of the 1970s expansion was creative. Forty years later, for example, Suez Canal University was one of the best in Egypt and in the region, producing an undergraduate who went on to a tenure-track professorship in molecular biology at Princeton University. Benha, Zagazig, and Beni Suef Universities have improved dramatically since the 1970s. Bringing universities close to home also encouraged higher female enrollments. Sending one's daughter off to Cairo or Alexandria was a step too far for many Egyptian parents, but educating them within commuting distance of home was far more palatable.

An intended consequence of founding regional and provincial campuses was to avoid large concentrations of students in the major urban centers. An unintended consequence was the 'parochialization of' Egyptian higher education and the erosion of the flagship universities' role in educating all Egyptians. Other Arab nations replicated this dispersion with the same intended and unintended consequences.

Past Glory?

Whatever the role of the state in university affairs, there is a perception that the Egyptian University maintained higher levels of quality in education (albeit perhaps not in research) than have prevailed since the Nasser era. But the deteriorating standards were not the direct result of the populism of the post-1952 era and the resultant massification of higher education (from 7,000 in the mid-1930s, Cairo University's enrollments rose to over 150,000 in the mid-1980s). The seeds of massification and the suborning of the university to the political authorities was already apparent before the Free Officers seized power in the summer of 1952 (Reid, 1990: 160).

But there is no gainsaying that prior to the 1970s, numbers were manageable, the faculty was of high caliber, and commitment to teaching was higher. The list of Egypt's who's who over the past decades features an overwhelming number of Cairo University graduates and faculty members from the 1930s, 1940s, and 1950s. A notable figure was Ali Moustafa Mosharafa, an Egyptian theoretical physicist and professor of applied mathematics in the Faculty of Science at the Egyptian University, who was appointed its first dean in 1936 at the age of thirty-eight. He contributed to the development of quantum theory as well as the theory of relativity and corresponded with Albert Einstein. He died under mysterious circumstances on January 15, 1950. Press reports at the time suggested that he was assassinated in one of the Israeli Mossad's operations against prominent Arab scientists (see Chapter 4).

Another figure of international stature was Mostafa Tolba, who was a student in the Egyptian University's Faculty of Science, joining in 1939. The total enrollment then was ninety students. The links between professors and students "were very personal" (Tolba, 2006). Tolba noted the introduction of the "university family" in 1946, after he graduated, in which each professor was responsible for mentoring twenty students. Tolba went on to an illustrious career during the Nasser and Sadat eras, helping design the state-centric system of university education and national research. In 1959, another outstanding academic, Hilmi Abdurrahman, at the time secretary-general of the Council of Ministers, invited Tolba to be secretary-general of the Supreme Council of Science. By 1960 he had launched three new research institutes, for schistosomiasis, ophthalmology, and tumors. In 1971, President Sadat asked Tolba to establish an Academy of Science, like that of the Soviet Union, which he did. The resulting Academy of Scientific Research and Technology was directly under the prime minister, and its president had the rank of minister. Rather than work toward university autonomy, the tendency was to create entities reporting directly to ministers and divorced from the universities. Tolba gained international recognition as the executive director of the UN Environmental Programme from 1975 to 1992. During his tenure, the Montreal Protocol on reducing the depletion of the ozone layer was enacted in 1987.

A nuanced portrait of the Egyptian University in the late 1930s and 1940s is given by Rushdi Said (2000). Having reached the age of eighty, Said felt that he could comment without inhibition on 'red line' issues one must be silent about in Egypt, such as the *nizam* (order, regime), in which every responsible official from the president to the *'umda* (village head) is appointed. All affairs are conducted in secrecy and with lack of accountability. Said shows that much that is wrong today was wrong when he was a young man, and that pre-revolutionary figures, like Prime Minister Ismail

Sidqi, resorted to the same stratagems as their successors. In the immediate post–Second World War era, standards were already slipping, favoritism dominated promotions, and research was not respected.

Said was born to a Coptic Christian family in Cairo in 1920. He joined the Faculty of Sciences of the Egyptian University in 1937. He paid no tuition. He notes that most of the faculty were foreign. His class had about seventy students, so interaction with professors was easy and frequent. Egypt could attract top-quality scientists because lab costs were quite modest in those days. Professors at the University of London shared in reading and grading undergraduate examinations. In 1948 Said went to the US for graduate studies and did not return to Egypt until 1951. He took his PhD at Harvard in 1950.

Upon his return, Said joined the Geology Department in the Faculty of Sciences at Fuad I University (the renamed Egyptian University) in 1951. Most of the foreign professors, as noted above, had left during and after the war. Simultaneously Ain Shams and Alexandria became fully fledged universities, producing strong demand for qualified faculty members. Said notes, somewhat ruefully, that many of his peers, more recently credentialed and of lesser talent, jumped ahead of him by transferring to the two new universities (2000: 67).

Said faced constant hostility from a colleague, a member of the Muslim Brotherhood who was hostile to Copts. The 'religious right' had been given considerable leeway under Prime Minister Sidqi, who wanted to use the Muslim Brotherhood as a bulwark against the Marxists. Thirty years later, President Sadat took the same tactic out of mothballs.

Believing himself systematically sabotaged in pursuing scientific research—no funding, research assistants told to stay away, and so forth—he built his own small research unit, finding outside funds to do so. He was able to publish *Geology of Egypt* in 1961. In 1968 he moved to the governmental Mining Institute, which was home to Egypt's Geological Survey. He remembers the period in his memoirs with nostalgia. The 'revolution' had a pragmatic reason to encourage the survey: uncovering exploitable mineral deposits to support Egypt's industrialization. Great advances were made in geophysical and geochemical surveying, as well as drilling and mining techniques. Said managed to enlist UNESCO in sharing carbon-dating technology with the survey (Reynolds, 2013: 181–205). This conforms to a common pattern in the Arab world of islands of excellence, harnessed strictly to state objectives and priorities and largely divorced from universities. Said's success in this context exemplifies another theme we shall come upon repeatedly: the development of epistemic communities or communities of practice that integrate isolated national experts into international networks of expertise, often with their own sources of funding.

The Faculty of Law at Cairo University has always enjoyed a solid reputation. Nabil al-Arabi, the former secretary-general of the League of Arab States and former foreign minister of Egypt, attended the Faculty of Law in the mid-1950s. His father had been a professor and dean of the faculty. When al-Arabi was a student, the faculty's total enrollment was about 1,200. Today it is on the order of 30,000. Al-Arabi has noted, "Only the students who study in French or English are of interest to reputable firms. Presumably those trained purely in Arabic will be hired, if at all, by the public sector" (interview, 2014).

Chemistry Nobel laureate Ahmed Zewail took his undergraduate and master's degrees at Alexandria University in 1967 and 1969, respectively, commuting from his home town of Damanhur. In his memoirs, Zewail recalls his time at Alexandria University: "The classes were exemplary. Many of the professors were worth emulating; they were role models for us. They had a professionalism about their responsibilities to their students" (2002: 33). Zewail remembers especially Professor Gouda in mathematics and Dr. al-Shinawi in geology. Lectures were mostly in Arabic. A third of his classmates were women. He notes that his high scores attracted the attention of research professors.

After 1999, Zewail, with the support of President Hosni Mubarak, became the lead figure in the establishment of the Zewail City of Science. As we shall see (Chapter 7), it had a troubled history. As he remarked to me in 2005, the president and others confused infrastructure with real science and thought that if you had the former the latter would follow automatically. Zewail died in 2016 in Pasadena, California. He had been a professor at the California Institute of Technology (Caltech) for most of his professional life (Devran, 2016).

Third-party Leverage

After the June War of 1967, Egypt severed diplomatic relations with the US. They were restored only after the October War of 1973 and Egypt's recovery of full control over the Suez Canal. The post-1973 period saw Egypt distance itself from the Soviet Union and reestablish close ties with the US. There was a flurry of joint projects, many under the auspices of USAID.

One such collaboration took place between Cairo University and the Massachusetts Institute of Technology (MIT). The Technological Training Program was established in 1976.[10] It aims to build capacity in the government of Egypt in project evaluation, especially to help USAID develop a sound project list. An autonomous center called the Development Research and Technological Planning Center was inaugurated in 1977. Its major foci were:

- Technological planning, transfer of technology, and technology adaptation,
- Educational technology,
- Regional and local planning and the related topics of urban-rural development,
- Improving population programs,
- Health care delivery systems and improving health conditions,
- Management development,
- Energy planning and new energy supplies, and
- Macroeconomic planning and socioeconomic studies. (USAID, 1980).

It is significant that this project sought to bridge divides among the government, the private sector, and Egypt's leading university, a triangle that we will scrutinize in other chapters. As one of its founders remarked, "The government types we saw said, 'We don't want to deal with the universities, they're all communists,' and the university types said, 'We don't want to deal with the government, they're all crooks'" (from an interview with Nazli Choucri and Fred Moavenzadeh, 2012).

The center was nominally autonomous, with a governing board drawn mainly from Cairo University and MIT. Each project, say on water management, would have an MIT and a Cairo University principal investigator. Because at that time and today, serious research was not essential to one's academic stature at Cairo University, high-quality research did not result. The center did provide research and salary support. Those incentives, said Fred Moavenzadeh, who participated on MIT's side, mitigated the exodus of faculty to the oil-rich Gulf states (based on an interview with Nazli Choucri and Fred Moavenzadeh). Some of the researchers went on to high office. Ahmad Nazif was prime minister from 2004 to 2011, when the Mubarak era came to an end. The president of Cairo University at the time the center was founded was Sufi Abu Taleb. He was speaker of the People's Assembly in 1981 at the time of the assassination of President Sadat and briefly served as acting president of the republic. Abu Taleb was representative of those senior academics with national political careers.[11]

The project ran for about a decade. The center still exists at Cairo University but appears to be a shell of its former self (based on interviews with Fred Moavenzadeh and Nazli Choucri, 2012; and John Blackton, 2012). This experiment was a forerunner to several underway today that seek to link universities to R&D and applied research. The more recent experiments, which we will touch on elsewhere, have an explicit goal of training students for work in the private sector. In the mid-1970s, MIT and Cairo University were not concerned with that. The public sector was still the main, and frequently only, employer of university graduates. The experiment was, it seems to me, a typical instance of third-party leverage aimed at far-reaching reform. Many more followed as structural adjustment crises accumulated in the Arab world in the 1980s and 1990s. Financial crises give third parties a window of opportunity to leverage change that goes beyond the strictly economic.[12] The collaboration between Cairo University and MIT did not result in significant change. The most one can say is that it probably did no harm.

The Supreme Council of Universities

Many nations have experimented with broad oversight committees or councils of public tertiary education. Such bodies may review and approve curriculum, working conditions for faculty and non-academic staff, and levels and types of financing (see Chapter 5). Britain's University Grants Commission was something of a model.

In the Arab world Egypt pioneered with a much more invasive model: the Supreme Council of Universities (SCU). Although it developed its full range of authority after the 1952 revolution, the SCU was created by royal decree in 1950. At that time, as we have seen, there were only three universities, not counting al-Azhar. Unlike today they had full control over admissions and real autonomy in other domains. By the same token, qualified students were free to apply to the university of their choice. Today the Coordination Office (Maktab al-Tansiq) in the Ministry of Education, in coordination with the SCU, distributes students, generally to the university nearest to where they reside.

Ali al-Din Hilal Dessouki, who was secretary-general of the SCU between 1991 and 1995, sees it as part and parcel of the Nasserist move toward central planning and tight political controls. Two other supreme councils were founded at about the same time: the Supreme Council for Production and the Supreme Council for Services. Nasser probably saw them as roughly similar. Their secretaries-general had the rank of minister (Dessouki, two interviews, 2013; Hatem, interview, 2013).[13]

The SCU is presided over by the minister of higher education. The presidents of all twenty-three of Egypt's public universities are council members. The SCU has an expert staff that assists the member universities. It is empowered to:

- determine degree equivalencies,
- define professorial specializations,
- organize admissions and set the numbers to be admitted,
- set general policy on university publications and books,
- outline the general framework for technology, finances, and administration,
- establish protocols for special research and other units,
- coordinate instruction, exams, and credentialing, and
- coordinate and supervise academic promotion.

According to Youssef Rashid (interview, 2014), the SCU does not engage in financial planning. Each university is responsible for the development of its own budget.

Damascus University and Higher Education in Syria

Like Egypt, Syria was part of the Ottoman Empire until the end of the First World War. Unlike Egypt, it did not experience direct European colonial control until France was awarded a League of Nations mandate over Syria as part of the peace settlement. It was also awarded a mandate over Lebanon, which was hived off from modern-day Syria.[14] The nominal purpose of these mandates (Great Britain was awarded mandates in Palestine, Transjordan, and Iraq) was to prepare these countries for full independence.

When higher education was initiated in Syria, it was under Ottoman auspices. Sultan Abdulhamid (1876–1909) was facing separatist movements throughout the empire, including in its Arab territories. The first call for a Syrian IHL came from high-ranking Ottoman officials in 1894. They were partly motivated by the need to counter the growing influence of the SPC and the Université Saint-Joseph (USJ) in Beirut.

In 1901, the sultan encouraged the establishment of a medical school in Damascus. It opened in 1903 and was under the supervision of the Istanbul medical faculty, and the language of instruction was Turkish.

Professors were either Turks or Syrians who had trained in Istanbul. One of the sultan's objectives was to reach out to the Arab elites of Damascus and to impede the spread of Arab nationalist ideas among them (Rafiq, 2004: 9–11; al-Samar, 2018: 94–95). The SPC had begun medical education in 1870 and was thus able to supply the new school in Damascus with some of its staff.

It is important to note that Damascus University in all its incarnations has been a public institution, unlike Cairo University between 1908 and 1925. On that basis, Abd al-Karim Rafiq (2004) claims that Damascus University is the oldest "national" university in the Arab world, and in his case study 'Ammar al-Samar (2018) calls it the "first governmental university in the Arab world."

The Ottoman Medical School in Damascus began operations in July 1903 with forty students, drawn mainly from Damascus. It graduated its first students in 1909. After graduation, students were required to fulfill five years of service, mainly in the Syrian countryside, a practice that endured up to the civil war beginning in 2011. The faculty numbered fifteen, and the course of study was six years. The curriculum replicated what was being taught in Istanbul. In 1909 the Committee of Union and Progress (CUP), known popularly as the Young Turks, overthrew Sultan Abdulhamid. They had a pan-Ottoman project, equally at odds with Arab nationalism, and were therefore as interested in higher education in the Arab territories as was the sultan. They initiated some instruction in Arabic in the medical school in Damascus. It suspended instruction in 1914 because of the First World War, but the CUP moved a law school from Beirut to Damascus in the same year. Ottoman suzerainty came to an end in July 1918, and a year later the French Mandate was formally established. A short-lived Arab Kingdom of Syria (1919–20) was snuffed out by French military force. Between 1903 and 1918, when the Ottoman Empire ended, the school graduated 110 physicians and 152 pharmacists (Rafiq, 2004: 27).

The medical school closed in 1918 because of the war, and then reopened in 1919 as the Arab Medical Institute, with Rida Said as its director (al-Samar, 2018: 100). Along with the Arab Law Institute, it became the core of the new university. The *wazir al-ma'arif* (minister of education) had the right to appoint both directors and presidents. One French High Commissioner, General Georges Catroux (1941–43), saw the university as useful in France's relations with Syria and with the Muslim world more generally.

In June 1923, the Syrian University was born, composed of the Institutes of Law and Medicine, the Arab Scientific Group, and a museum. Decree No. 132 of 1923 stipulated the election of the president by the faculty, confirmed by appointment by the head of state. Rida Said was elected president. Arabic was decreed the language of instruction (al-Samar, 2018: 106). The use of Arabic at the university, even in scientific fields, has been one of its hallmarks since its founding and up to the present time.[15]

Both the Egyptian University and the Syrian University were blessed by founding presidents who can legitimately be described as towering figures who served long and well. Ahmad Lutfi al-Sayyid was president of the Egyptian University (then Fuad I) from 1925 to 1941. Rida Said (1876–1945), who built the Syrian University almost from scratch, demonstrated not only staying power but remarkable political agility. He had begun his medical studies in Istanbul in 1903, then continued in Paris in ophthalmology in 1909 as well as the study of viruses at the Institut Pasteur. He was made dean of the Medical Institute in Damascus under the Ottomans in 1919, was kept on during the short-lived Arab Kingdom of Syria, and then retained by the French with the advent of the Mandate. Like the British in Egypt, the French saw the national university as much as a threat as an opportunity.

Said wanted the Syrian University to embody the best in European and US higher education (he had the AUB in his backyard). He was the force behind the founding of the Syrian Medical Association in 1925 and the launch in 1924 of the journal of the Syrian University Medical Institute. The journal published monthly until 1946, mainly articles in translation and some original research (Rafiq, 2004: 96–98; al-Samar, 2018: 111). Almost a century ago, Said and Syria took steps to organize the medical profession, anchor it in the university, and give it a forum for scholarly production. As Tony Zahlan (2012) has lamented, throughout the Arab world, such efforts were snuffed out, at least in substance, with the advent of the populist republics of the post-Second World War years.

Governance

The Mandate authorities, led by the French high commissioner, brought the Syrian University under close financial and administrative control. The new Ministry of Education (*al-ma'arif*) took on supervision of the Institutes of Law and Medicine. The basic operating order for the *Université scientifique syrienne* was drawn up by the French in 1922 (reprinted in Rafiq, 2004). One of the tenets of the order was a total ban on politics at the university.

Students could be expelled for engaging in politics. This goal was quixotic. Although the numbers were tiny, students engaged in the 'revolt' of 1925–26, protested the proposed 1933 treaty with France, boycotted Lord Balfour's 1925 visit to Syria, and routinely demonstrated against Zionist settlement in Palestine.

The basic university law provided for two councils, one made up of professors and the other of administrators, both headed by the university president. The Syrian University president was to be appointed by the president of the Syrian Union (as the Mandate was known) for a period of one year. In 1926, in the wake of the 'revolt' against the Mandate authorities, the tenure of the president and the deans was extended to three years. Said had to survive this regime of frequent review and reappointment. The Mandate authorities did not attach the Syrian University to any French university, a practice common to other IHLs in the French Empire.

Rida Said was successful in safeguarding some modicum of autonomy for the university. The bulk of the university administration remained Syrian, and Arabic remained the language of instruction. It was the strength of his professionalism and the respect he nurtured within the Mandate administration and Syria's political class that afforded Said and the university some room for maneuver. The university, however, lost its autonomy bit by bit, especially in finances, probably leading Said to resign in 1936. His successor, Abd al-Qadir al-Azm also resigned three years later, in 1939 (al-Samar, 2018: 108).

The French had a very mixed record of promoting education in their dependencies,[16] but in the case of Syria they saw an opportunity to construct an 'Arab' institution that could win respect throughout the Arab and Muslim world and steal the thunder of Baghdad, Cairo, and Beirut. The Syrian University and AUB aspired to educate the best and the brightest of the Arab world. AUB came closer to that aspiration than the SU. In the contemporary period there is no Arab institution that reaches out to all Arab youth. In fact, the trend is the reverse: the fracturing of Arab universities into regional entities, recruiting students from their hinterlands.

In 1928–29 the Ecole Supérieure de Literature was added to the Syrian University. In 1933, however, Minister of Ma'arif Haqqi al-Azm abolished it, and all its staff was dismissed. Abd al-Karim Rafiq does not explain why this happened (Rafiq, 2004: 119–20), but it demonstrates that Rida Said was unable to protect the Syrian University from administrative fiat. The école, or faculty, was not resurrected until 1946, after Syria became fully independent. The 1930s saw the rise of meddlesome Syrian politicians and a financially strapped Mandate administration, which by the end of the decade was preparing for war with Germany. Said was helpless in the face of such a concatenation of forces. He was only sixty when he retired in 1936.

As was the case with enhanced autonomy, Said was not successful in building a first-rate course of instruction. Local education experts, some of them French, were not kind in their assessment of the Syrian University, deploring the lack of scientific research and the poor quality of the library: "It is, said one, 'not a true institution of higher education but rather a trade school to graduate judges, employees, lawyers, dentists, pharmacists'" (Rafiq, 2004: 247).

Stability eluded the country until 1958, when it entered into a union with Nasser's Egypt, known as the United Arab Republic (UAR). The UAR reflected fears in Syria that Syrian communists, with Soviet backing, might seize control of the state. It lasted only three years. During that time the grip of the intelligence arm of the Syrian state asserted its control over the university. In 1958 the name of the Syrian University was changed to Damascus University.

Leading up to 1958, the Syrian University was blessed by the leadership of another great figure, Constantine Zurayk. Zurayk was a Greek Orthodox Christian, born in Damascus, educated at AUB, Michigan, and Princeton, and a prolific writer on the Arab renaissance and the challenge of the West.

On March 30, 1949, Syria's Chief of Staff Husni al-Za'im seized power. He lasted only four months and was toppled and executed by another military officer, Sami al-Hinnawi. During his brief tenure, Za'im asked Zurayk to take over the Syrian University and to reform it top to bottom. The irony here is thick. An eminent Syrian academic and leading light of the Arab renaissance takes command of a flagship university from the hands of an army officer who seizes power in a coup. Za'im gives him "exceptional authority." Ends and means are totally confused. Within months Zurayk's patron was dead and two more succeeded him in rapid succession.

Zurayk termed his tenure at the Syrian University "the best of his life" (I rely here on al-Azmeh, 2003). He navigated his reform agenda between gradualists and big-bang advocates. He brought female enrollments up to 25 percent, sent two hundred students abroad for PhD work, and encouraged student associations, including al-'Urwa al-Wuthqa (The Trusted Bond), which was originally founded by Muhammad Abduh and Jamal al-Din al-Afghani. In April 1950 he supported the law that made secondary education free in Syria.

Zurayk resigned from the presidency on March 8, 1952, for personal reasons. He had physically opposed security forces entering the Syrian University campus because of demonstrations against Adib Shishakli, the third coup master who overthrew Sami al-Hinnawi. Zurayk was not able to raise academic salaries. He was criticized by students for trying to quash political activists at the university. He had approved the expulsion of seven students (al-Azmeh, 2003: 66–72). Zurayk quickly went on to become acting president of AUB after the death in office of President Stephen Penrose. The contextual turmoil that both presidents, Said and Zurayk, had to cope with may be extreme, but the average university president in the Arab world will have faced similar challenges.

It is understandable that with the war in Europe after 1939 and the advent of the Vichy regime after Nazi Germany's occupation of France, the SU would fall victim to a number of years of emergency rule and regime change to and from Vichy, liberation, and full independence for Syria in April 1945. But that transformation did not bring calm. In May 1948, Syria, along with other Arab states, entered into the first Arab–Israeli war on the occasion of the founding of Israel. Over two rounds of fighting, Israel overcame its Arab adversaries. This was a source of great humiliation for Arab nationalists and especially for their armed forces. It was the defeat of 1948 that ultimately led Nasser and the Free Officers to overthrow the Egyptian monarchy in 1952. Similarly, in Syria, the military in 1949 launched a coup against the elected civilian government of Shukri Quwatli. It was to be the first of three such coups.

Despite this regional turbulence, the Syrian University regained some of its autonomy in the early years of independence. Both the president and the university council had real power. The council helped the university fulfill its basic mission and it assisted in promotions and recruiting, budget preparation, and organizing the university calendar. The university's budget was its own, although, as noted, the state made a hefty contribution and modest fees were charged to students. The president of the university was appointed, not elected (al-Samar, 2018: 119). Syria today would only be acknowledging its own past if such governance structures were reinstituted.

In 1958 the Nasserist corporatist model was extended to Syria. By 1975 university autonomy had totally disappeared. Most effective power had devolved to the Council for Higher Education (see pages 82–83), modeled on Egypt's SCU. The minister had ultimate power in all matters. The president was appointed for a period of three years, renewable once. If the presidency were to become vacant, the minister would exercise the powers of the president. University councils were stripped of their nominal prerogatives (al-Samar, 2018: 129). The advent of Hafez al-Assad and the consolidation of Ba'th Party power through the 'corrective revolution' of 1970 saw the transformation of the university into a "government institution like all the rest" (al-Samar, 2018: 125).

In the period since 1958, and especially since 1967 when the Ba'th Party and its military allies seized power, universities have been reduced to instruments of the Syrian state and of the party. In the period 1975–80, Rifaat al-Assad, the brother of President al-Assad, ran the Ba'th Party's Regional Bureau of Higher Education. In 1974, the Ba'th created the National Union of Students, and each university has a party branch (Starr, 2012: 26–27). The student union actively repressed student protests in 2011.

The Ba'th Party is involved in teaching appointments and promotions. "Even more than other institutions, the universities are saturated with agents and informers of the *mukhabarat*, or secret police" (George, 2003: 145). As a former university leader recalled,

> The whole system, like the polity itself, was party-dominated. There was no formal process for selecting a new president. It depended on the most senior party leadership and personal connections. I was not a [Ba'th] party member but I was well known to the Assad family. It helped push through my appointment. There is a University Governing Council with deans, student representatives, and the party leader for the university branch, but the council had no formal role in leadership selection. (interview, 2014)[17]

The branch party leader would normally be more powerful than the president and would involve himself in all sorts of academic business, especially appointments.

The same official recalled that "there is no real budget process, but in any event the minister of higher education has little to do with it. It is worked out between each university and the Ministry of Finance based on a capitation formula." He added, "According to the results of the *baccalauréat* exam, a coordinating committee would assign successful *bacheliers* to the four main universities, with Damascus getting the cream of the crop. If there are 25,000 successful students, DU would get 10,000."

Unlike in Egypt, top scorers could go to Damascus University regardless of place of residence, but they could also opt to stay in their home region.

It is generally argued (for example, European Commission, 2017) that Syria's public higher education system is highly centralized. It is thus interesting to note that Aleppo University was in 2014 considered almost as good as Damascus University. This is because the president of Aleppo University was the brother-in-law of Mustafa Tlass, minister of defense under Hafez al-Assad. He could defy the general policy of sending faculty for advanced training to Russia or East Germany. He sent his faculty to the UK. The returning faculty transformed Aleppo University.

As Hani Murtada was minister of education, he opened nine branches of the main public universities, Damascus, Aleppo, and Latakia, and did so in Dar'a, Suweida, Deir ez-Zor, Qamishli, Hasakah, Idlib, Hama, Tartous, and Raqqa. Curiously, the Ba'th Party was opposed. Unlike in Egypt under Sadat, the Ba'th favored concentrations of students in a few cities. Through the student unions they could maintain strict control of student affairs and always produce big noisy crowds in support of Hafez or Bashar al-Assad. Decentralization looked too loose and potentially uncontrollable to the party *apparatchiki*. Eventually Murtada gave up struggling with the party and submitted his resignation. His successor as minister was also head of the party leadership group.

After the death of Hafez al-Assad in 2000 and the succession to the presidency of his son, Bashar, some very important legislation was enacted. The first was Presidential Decree No. 36 of 2001, which for the first time legalized the establishment of for-profit private IHLs. Soon thereafter Kalamoon University was founded, followed by eighteen others (in general see European Commission, 2017).

The major legal framework that regulates both private and public higher education in Syria is Law No. 6 of 2006. This law amends and replaces previous legislation and seemingly gives IHLs greater autonomy, especially with respect to faculty appointments and promotions.[18] Nonetheless, as the European Commission (2017) survey concludes, the system is highly centralized.

Civil war in Syria since 2011 has crippled higher education. It has been particularly devastating to Damascus University, which has seen its international ranking plummet, even relative to a few other Syrian universities. It is now ranked 10,902nd worldwide. It is not among the hundred best in the Arab world. Tishreen University is now ranked 188th in the Arab world and 5,073th worldwide (Abd al-Razzaq, 2018).

Enrollments

While perhaps not the beacon to the region the French had hoped for, the Syrian University was significantly diverse in its student body. Over its first quarter-century it graduated 1,066 lawyers, of whom 746 were Syrian, and 367 physicians, of whom 282 were Syrian (Rafiq, 2004: 136, 305). About 10 percent of all students were women, first admitted in 1922–23 and concentrated in medicine (the first female physician graduated in 1931).

Neither Egypt nor Palestine, while under British control, ever granted equivalency to the Syrian University degrees, relenting only in 1939. In 1946, when Syria had won independence, the Syrian University, in keeping with its mission, invited the prominent Egyptian legal expert and dean of the Faculty of Law at Fuad I University, Abd al-Razzaq Sanhuri, to advise it on what we would now call a strategic plan. Sanhuri recommended the establishment of three new faculties: a normal school, a Faculty of Arts, and a Faculty of Engineering. He won acceptance in Syria for inviting Egyptian professors to the university (Rafiq, 2004: 302).

In 1928, successfully passing the Syrian *baccalauréat* exam was made a requirement for entry to the Syrian University. As in Egypt, the numbers in secondary education were small. In 1940 there were 38,870 male secondary students and 15,483 females spread over 358 schools (Rafiq, 2004: 300). Massification would not begin for another two decades. The small numbers feeding out of the high school system reflected the elitism of Syrian education at that time.

The period after 1958 marked the beginning of the massification of Syrian higher education. In 1958, Aleppo University was founded, then Tishreen University in Latakia in 1971, al-Baath University in Homs in 1979, al-Baath University in Hama in 2014, the Syrian Virtual University in 2002, and al-Furat University in Deir ez-Zor in 2006. In 1970 it was decreed that all those obtaining the Syrian *baccalauréat* would automatically be admitted to university. This represented a kind of quick win for the Ba'th (Hafez al-Assad was just consolidating his grip on power, having pushed out Salah Jadid). Just as in Egypt at the same time, this big step toward massification overwhelmed the system and led to a marked deterioration in quality (al-Samar, 2018: 135).

Massification notwithstanding, the Syrian GER stood at about 15 percent at the turn of the millennium. In the following year legislation was passed to allow the establishment of private universities. Twenty came on stream in short order. Still, to go from one university with two faculties and some six hundred students in 1945 to thirty IHLs and 470,000 students in roughly sixty-five years, and to over 700,000 students a decade later, is an achievement, although one not unique to Syria in the Arab world. By 2009 Damascus University had 120,000 students and 1,748 faculty members for a ratio of 68:1 (al-Samar, 2018: 138–39). The European Commission (2017) advances a figure for public tertiary enrollments of all kinds for 2014, two years into the civil war, of 764,242 and for private tertiary of 30,136. I assume that a significant part of these enrollments is through open learning courses.

As the civil war has unfolded in Syria, massification looks like this: Maher Malindi, dean of the Faculty of Law at Damascus University, told *al-Ayyam* newspaper that the law school had around 25,000 students and only sixty-five professors. This "represents a huge challenge," he said. "International standards necessitate that no single professor should supervise more than fifty students, while in this faculty we have five times this rate" (Shahla, 2018). Indeed, Zina Shahla (2018) describes a kind of death spiral of migrating students and professors, plummeting public expenditure, declining quality, and a job market so disrupted that it is almost impossible to know what skills are needed. By one estimate, faced with violence and $100 per month salaries, 40 percent of Syrian faculty in public institutions have migrated. I argue elsewhere in this study that crisis is the most fecund mother of policy change, but we can expect little meaningful policy response to the current Syrian crisis.

Finances
In its origins over a century ago, what became Damascus University was partly funded through a dedicated tax on animals slaughtered in the slaughter-ter houses of Damascus, Beirut, Aleppo, Deir ez-Zor, and Jerusalem. It is not clear if these levies carried over into the protectorate era. As we shall see in the chapters on university finances (Chapters 6 and 8), dedicated revenue streams for IHLs have rarely been used in the contemporary era in the Arab world.

The Syrian University was heavily dependent on the state budget for funding. By the late 1930s, 85 percent of the budget came from the state and the rest from fees. It is hard to know in today's currency how onerous fees may have been. Rafiq (2004: 77) claims they were high, reaching a level equivalent to half a professor's annual salary. Twenty percent of Syrian students were granted full or partial tuition waivers. With time, waivers were extended to Palestinian refugees and Syrians from outside the provinces of Damascus and Aleppo and to the poor of all regions, and fees were reduced for children of civil servants, the military, retirees, and faculty members (al-Samar, 2018: 122). In 1965 university education was made free.

The Council for Higher Education

The main body governing the higher education sector in Syria is the Council for Higher Education. The council is headed by the minister of higher education and consists of the presidents of public universities and a few selected private universities, the heads of higher education public institutes, representatives from the student unions and teacher unions, the deputy ministers of finance, education, and health, and representatives from the State Planning Commission. According to the European Commission,

> All universities have to follow the organizational structure defined in the 2006 University Law with little flexibility. In terms of academic autonomy, decisions can be taken at academic departmental level. However, for decisions related to replacing curricula and other relevant academic matters, departments need to have the necessary approvals from the Council for Higher Education. The possibility of increasing financial autonomy is still a matter for debate. . . . In terms of academic appointments, the system is highly centralized. All academic staff appointments are issued by ministerial decree. (2017: 3)

A government committee called the University Admissions Committee, headed by the prime minister and in consultation with the Ministry of Higher Education and the universities, determines the number of students to be admitted to the higher education system each year and their distribution. The Council for Higher Education, according to Law No. 6, has the following authorities:

- Propose higher education policy across all disciplines within the framework of the general policy of the state,
- Develop public policies for scientific research in universities and research institutes, directing research toward addressing social, economic, and cultural problems in the Syrian Arab Republic,
- Develop general plans for higher education institutions, developing scientific, technical, and linguistic standards as well as educational qualifications for teachers and researchers to evaluate their performance,
- Develop rules for admission of students to universities and institutes,
- Coordinate among universities and institutes with regard to upholding educational standards and degrees, scientific disciplines, research, and training,

- Develop a system for the evaluation of performance, as well as rules for accreditation of universities and terms for granting accreditation and revoking it,
- Propose the draft general budgets for all universities, institutes, and organizations that are under the aegis of the ministry,
- Determine the duration of the study and exam schedules, holidays, and training workshops,
- Determine models of education with their pros and cons,
- Establish rules and conditions for selecting those who will repeat classes or years, and
- Establish rules and conditions for the appointment of members of the teaching staff and for their promotions.

The council is, if anything, more powerful and more invasive than Egypt's SCU. This kind of oversight makes sense when the unit of analysis is the entire system of higher education rather than individual universities. What was different in Syria, at least until the outbreak of civil war in 2011, is the role of the Ba'th Party at all levels. The party historically has been the glue of Syria's 'deep state.'

The Path to the Civil Service

Syrian government employees make up roughly 23 percent of the labor force, a level similar to that in Egypt. In 2001, however, the Syrian government ended its policy of ensuring employment of graduates of postsecondary intermediate institutes (two-year vocational institutes), which had previously been the main path to careers in SOEs. Up to 2000, Syria guaranteed public employment for graduates of two- and four-year tertiary programs but abandoned that policy in keeping with its larger transition to a market economy and an associated concern to slim down the public sector. The decoupling of the public university system from public sector employment meant that higher education no longer promised the security it once did. As of 2007, unemployment among those aged fifteen to twenty-nine stood at 27 percent for four-year university graduates and 41 percent for graduates of two-year vocational institutes (Buckner, 2013: 7).

Returns to education in Syria are very low, averaging less than 2 percent for preparatory schooling, around 2.5 percent for high school, and around 4.5 percent for higher education. Thus, returns to education increase with the level of educational attainment, but are far lower than the international averages of 10 to 15 percent or the regional averages of around 6 percent (Kabbani and Salloum, 2010).[19]

Lebanese University

Of the four countries under examination in this chapter, Lebanon is something of an outlier. It is a civilian republic, a vibrant if flawed democracy, and confessionally the most diverse country in the region. Its education system is also unique. The first 'modern' universities in the region, the SPC and the USJ, were founded as private institutions in 1866 and 1875, respectively. Both were initiated by religious groups, the US Evangelical Mission for the SPC and the Jesuit Compagnie de Jésus for the USJ. Unlike Syria, the French Mandate authorities did not sponsor or promote a public university in Lebanon. Over time the SPC, which became AUB at the end of the First World War, evolved away from its missionary origins to become a non-confessional, co-educational independent private institution that would be familiar to anyone acquainted with US higher education. The USJ has maintained organic links to the Jesuit order. For example, the rector must be from the Compagnie de Jésus.

Lebanon is also unique in its concentration of higher education in private institutions. By 2013 there were forty-five private and one public IHL, Lebanese University. Lebanese University's enrollments as a proportion of total tertiary enrollments peaked in 1999–2000 at 60 percent, then declined to about 38 percent in 2014–2015 (El-Amine, 2018: 200). In the Arab world, only Palestine has similar levels of private higher education. Lebanon did not have any ideological barriers similar to those of Syria or Egypt to impede the launching of private IHLs. To the contrary, in the late 1990s, but especially between 2000 and 2003, when Abdul-Rahim Mrad was minister of education and higher education, there was an explosion of private, for-profit institutions. Mrad himself founded a for-profit university in the Bekaa valley, where he is from. Conflict of interest does not resonate very loudly in Lebanon.

Despite their pioneering role and undisputed excellence, neither the SPC/AUB nor the USJ served as models for subsequent generations of IHLs in the Arab world. The two exceptions were the AUC, founded in 1919, and the American University of Sharjah, founded in 1999 with initial assistance from AUB. With the opening of the educational sphere to private actors in the 1990s, the governance structures of AUB and AUC were emulated to varying degrees in some of the new private institutions.

As a relatively open, unplanned economy, Lebanon had and has a significantly smaller public sector than most of the rest of the Arab world. The civil service, including the military, accounts for only about 15 percent of total employment. So, the state has not taken on the role of employer of last resort. And, as a relatively plural political system, with several parties, sometimes with armed wings, student movements probably have greater resonance in the political system than elsewhere. Indeed, Emile Shahine (2011) argues forcefully that students were instrumental in the founding of Lebanese University (see also Barakat, 1977).

It was not until 1951, five years after independence, that Lebanon took the first, halting steps to launching a public university (El-Amine, 1999; 2018).[20] The corner stone was the Ecole Normale (teacher training), founded in 1932. But it was not until after independence that primary education was made compulsory and another ten years before public secondary education was begun. Until that time all secondary education was in private, often confessional, hands. Georges Tohmé (Tohmé, n.d.), who went on to be president of Lebanese University, recalled training to be a high school teacher at a time when there were only three public high schools in all of Lebanon. In 1951, the Ecole Normale Supérieure (ENS) was founded. Khalil al-Jurr became its first director and effectively the first president of Lebanese University. He was born in 1913 and was the first Lebanese to obtain a French *doctorat d'état*. He served as Lebanese University president until 1953. Like Cairo University and Damascus University, in its early years Lebanese University benefitted from a long-serving 'founding' president, Fuad Afram al-Bustani (1953–70), a faculty member at the USJ since 1933.

Serving Lebanon's confessional political system, the early advocates of a national university were powerful leaders *(zu'ama)* of major sects. In the third UNESCO conference of 1948, Hamid Franjieh, Kamal Jumblatt, and Camille Chamoun all called for the founding of a national university. In contrast to the founders of the Egyptian University in 1908, there were no contributions forthcoming from these and other advocates. If this was to be a public university, it would have to secure public funding.

The finance committee of the parliament, chaired by Emile Lahoud, who became minister of education, approved a special budget (Shahine, 2011: 48). Three specializations of Lebanese University were under study: statistics, education, and social sciences. In February 1951, the Riad al-Solh government provided a budget of 300,000 Lebanese pounds. The university was officially founded by Decree No. 6267 on October 20, 1951. It started with sixty-eight students in the ENS (Shahine, 2011: 58). It did not open fully until 1953 when Bustani became the first official president.[21] By 1963 it enrolled 6,092 students and a decade later,

14,826. In 1994 it reached 35,000, and then 72,000 by 2010 and 80,000 in 2018.

For many, like Bashshur (1997; also Shahine, 2011: 16), the real launch of Lebanese University was not until 1959, when the president of the republic, Fuad Chehab, put all his weight behind it. Three faculties were added to the ENS: literature, sciences, and law. Law turned out to be the main attraction for students.

The law organizing Lebanese University was not issued until December 1967. In 1969, it was decided to build a new campus in the southern part of Beirut, at Hadath. The campus was not completed until after the end of the civil war (1975–89).[22]

Chehab entrusted Lebanese University with the mission of building a nation out of a confessional hodgepodge that had led the country to a short-lived civil war in 1958. In that era, pressure on the university came from students and faculty, not the political system. That came later, with the long civil war that started in 1976, which, in El-Amine's (2018) view, killed the university.

Law instruction in Lebanon had been the monopoly of the USJ since 1913. It was Lebanon's *'grande école.'* Its students had to be fluent in French. It provided a Christian elite that was the backbone of the protectorate administration. The Lebanese government hesitated to open a public law school but bit the bullet in 1959, when, under Prime Minister Rashid Karami and President Chehab, Lebanese University was authorized to offer the law *licence* with both a French and an Arabic track. At the same time, the Faculties of Law, Political Science, and Economics were launched. Law was to have two branches: one entirely controlled by the university and the other still under the control of the USJ (Shahine, 2011: 101). All of this is in the context of protecting confessional advantages through control of credentialing. In the end the USJ was unable to defend its monopoly.

A new actor entered the scene in 1960–61: the Beirut Arab University. Although sponsored by a local Sunni Muslim charity, al-Birr wa-l-Ihsan, it was and is officially a branch of Egypt's Alexandria University. Its president is chosen by Egypt's minister of education. Bashshur (1997: 37) unequivocally characterizes the launch of the Beirut Arab University as a "Nasserist" project, a forward bastion of Arab (Muslim) nationalism, and a counterweight to perceived American/Christian dominance of Lebanon's higher education.[23]

The Beirut Arab University wanted to offer law diplomas to students with no foreign language competency. The Lawyers Union went on strike in protest. All union members were graduates of the USJ and feared that Beirut Arab University graduates would one day take over the union

(Bashshur, 1997: 31).[24] Parliament tried to adjudicate, but one result was that Lebanese University saw a big surge in law students. It was the only bilingual law school—Arabic-French.

Universities were in Lebanon, as elsewhere in the Arab world, critical pieces in the political chess games played out in the region. They provided ample opportunity for confessional patronage and spoils, an arena in which politicians could test their strength, and a key link in Lebanon's national projects. But unlike under the populist regimes elsewhere in the region, the tight embrace of the *mukhabarat* and the subordination of IHLs to centralized political authority were not prominent features in Lebanon. Spoils rather than coercion was the dominant politics of the university.[25] Despite the legal and practical ability to mobilize and agitate politically, the system of confessional *zu'ama* (political patrons) and the lifeblood of spoils and state patronage were never threatened, even after fifteen years of civil war.

Lebanon enshrined checks and balances among confessions in its constitution. Those checks and balances were increased by practice over time and redefined at least once, in the Taif Accords of 1989, which ended the civil war (El-Amine, 1997b: 564). The Taif Agreement gave rise to a new national education strategy, emphasizing reconciliation among the heretofore warring factions. Confessional formulae may have also been treated in 2008, in Doha, after forces of Hezbollah stormed West Beirut and nearly triggered a new civil war. Qatar mediated a settlement that in effect endowed Hezbollah with veto power over any government actions.[26]

The impact of confessionalism was felt everywhere, and for Lebanese University in particular was a kind of scourge. Senior posts were dedicated to specific sects. The basic rule was to take the confessions of all of Lebanon's 'class one' employees (director general and above) and use that as the distributive model. Thus, the university president was to be Shi'i. Hassan Diab, minister of higher education (himself appointed by Sunni Prime Minister Najib Miqati), appointed Adnan al-Sayyid Hussein (Shi'i) as president of Lebanese University (Diab and Jammal, interview, 2013).

The formal and informal checks and balances in the Lebanese political system have led to paralysis in decision-making and routine government activities such as approving budgets and confirming key appointments. Lebanon's basic higher education law (Law No. 66) was first enacted in 1961. It was obvious by the new millennium that the law needed thorough revision. A draft revised law fell victim to confessional politics, but after years of delay was enacted in 2014.

In 1988 Tohmé stepped down as Lebanese University's president. It was not until 1993 that his successor, Assad Diab, was officially appointed. Diab's appointment came after the Taif Accords, and he was the university's first Shi'i president. Interestingly, he had studied law at the USJ. He served as president until 2000 and passed away in 2010. More recently, a stand-off between Prime Minister Najib Miqati (Sunni) and Speaker of the Chamber of Deputies Nabih Berri (Shi'a) prolonged the non-appointment of Lebanese University deans. The positions had not been filled since 2004 and would not be until 2014 (see Hussein, 2013; El-Amine, 2018: 193).[27]

The long civil war clearly had major negative effects on all aspects of university life in Lebanon. Over the war years there was a clear deterioration in the quality of Lebanese University: the physical infrastructure deteriorated, branch budgets varied according to the relative strengths of political patrons, the curriculum was shattered, and the credentials offered by one branch differed significantly from those offered elsewhere in the same subject matter (El-Amine, 2018: 184).

Confessionalism became the first and last refuge of citizens under constant threat. In 1977, Lebanese University branches were set up in all governorates *(muhafazat)*, formalizing the de facto grip of sectarian militias (Shahine, 2011: 18). This was by Decree No. 122, which along with others gave the university president and the minister of higher education the authority to direct the affairs of the university, including appointing professors and administrators. University autonomy was effectively gutted (Shahine, 2011: 18).

The Taif Accords enshrined sectarian quotas. That may have been acceptable for civil service positions but had no precedent for professorial appointments. It led to the intimidation of faculty and administrators by students, some of whose other day job was serving in armed militias. At the same time, given the pervasive and random violence in Lebanon, international enrollments in the country's IHLs dwindled from around 50 percent in the mid-1970s to 12 percent by 2000 (Nahas, 2009: 8). The new Lebanese University branches had considerable de facto autonomy. All that linked the units together was the university council, which was sometimes paralyzed by the inability of the 'authorities' to appoint deans, and by the faculty union *(rabitat al-asatidha)*. One of the few positive results of the 'parcelization' of Lebanese University was that the proportion of female students rose from about 20 percent at the beginning of hostilities to over 50 percent at their close (El-Amine, 1997b: 568). As elsewhere in the region, having higher education close to home allayed the fears of worried parents about sending their daughters far away for education.

During some of the most challenging years of its existence, 1980 to 1988, Lebanese University was led by Georges Tohmé. In 1963 he had joined the ENS as a faculty member and in 1972 became the first person to attain the rank of professor (biology) at the university. The faculty at Lebanese University at the time had overwhelmingly been trained in France, amounting to 60 percent, while 20 percent had been trained in Lebanon and only 4 percent in the US (Nizam, 1997). Tohmé told me that he blocked hiring faculty credentialed in the Soviet Bloc (interview, 2013). The proliferation of Lebanese University branches necessitated the hiring of part-time, contract faculty who were not properly credentialed.

Tohmé's appointment, initially for five years, was renewed in 1985. He resigned voluntarily in 1988 in order to take up a position at UNESCO. He presided over the establishment of the Faculties of Engineering, Public Health, and Medical Sciences. For the latter, he used Damascus University as his model. The USJ's president and AUB's 'deputy' dean of medicine opposed the launching of the new medical faculty (Tohmé, n.d.: 13). Many politicians opposed its founding in solidarity with the two private universities and also with support from the eight hundred students in the Soviet Union who feared their degrees might come under increased scrutiny by Lebanese authorities. The Faculty of Agriculture was also launched during Tohmé's tenure. Its first dean was Mouïn Hamzé, who later became director of the Lebanese National Council for Scientific Research (CNRS-L).

Throughout his presidency, Tohmé had no secretary-general or chief administrative officer (Tohmé, n.d.: 28). He and the 'politicians' could not agree on candidates. It is the prerogative of the university president to appoint the secretary-general but Tohmé preferred to appoint no one rather than someone resulting from political interference. He used instead two adjunct faculty members to fill the position, who, apparently, both served pro bono.[28] Only one new dean was appointed during his presidency. In the same spirit, Tohmé claims that at the beginning of his presidency he resolved to make no senior appointments without the formal approval of the Council of Ministers. This was in order to shield himself from direct approaches of politicians on behalf of their clients (n.d.: 29). So he abjured authority rightfully his and deliberately eroded university autonomy.

Early in his presidency, Tohmé engineered a major salary adjustment for professors but also required that they cease working, with or without permission, for private universities to earn extra income. Some were teaching in high schools. He never publicized individual cases, and he negotiated with private institutions to end what he called "theft." Tohmé believed and believes passionately in the full-time professor, devoted to teaching and research. After all, that is what he was (Tohmé, n.d.: 33; see also Chapter 9).

Turning to students, Tohmé is polite but critical, especially of the student–politician nexus. He confirms the crucial role of students in launching Lebanese University in 1950–51 (as argued in Shahine, 2011), but after that he does not have much kind to say. He deplores "professional" students who shift their registration from faculty to faculty to pursue their political agendas (Tohmé, n.d.: 48). With the connivance of faculty members such students obtained representation on faculty committees involved with exams. In the Faculty of Science (where Tohmé had been a professor) the success rate on exams prior to the war did not exceed 40 percent. Some years later it was 90 percent. Some professors argued that students "participating" in the war merited some compensation for their efforts (n.d.: 49).

It is important to keep in mind that Lebanese University had more than 70,000 students. As a graduate who went on to a professorship at AUB recollected (Sabra, interview, 2013), in his time (1981–83) the bulk of students were from modest or poor backgrounds. They worked very hard (much harder than students at AUB), and the faculty, with their modest means, responded in kind.

Governance

A 1959 decree put Lebanese University under the supervision (tutelage: *wasaya*) of the Ministry of Education. The university enjoys administrative and financial autonomy and a legal personality. The university council nominates three candidates for the presidency. The minister chooses one among them and recommends him/her to the Council of Ministers.

The president is considered 'class one' in civil service rankings, equivalent to minister. The president's powers are delegated to him/her by the minister. Among those powers are the right to prepare the agendas for the university council, propose the operating budget for review and approval by the council, and to appoint the secretary-general of the university. In 1967 the president's tenure was set at five years, nonrenewable except after the passage of one full term.

The university council, when it occasionally convenes, consists of the president, the deans, the directors of branches, one representative elected by the tenured faculty from each unit, four students representing the National Union of University Students, and two individuals known for their expertise (El-Amine, 1997a: 200). Students have voting rights on some matters. All members of the faculty and nonacademic staff are state employees, subject to civil service regulations.

The deans are appointed for three years and their terms can be renewed (El-Amine, 2018: 164). Their appointment needs approval of the Council of Ministers. If the council cannot agree on the appointment of deans, the university council is effectively paralyzed, as was the case in 2004–2014. There is a secretary-general for each faculty and for the university. The secretary-general (amin sirr) is the chief administrative officer.

Promotion to the rank of professor must be approved by the Council of Ministers. Branch directors typically have had more clout than deans because of their political connections. Nonetheless they have had to come from the Lebanese University faculty and their term has been three years (Lebanese University, n.d.: 19).

Importantly, and in contrast with Cairo University and Damascus University, the promotion process is internal to Lebanese University. There are two executive committees that handle promotions, one for applied and basic sciences and one for humanities and social sciences and law. There are no student or administration representatives on them.

The creation of Lebanese University branches began in 1977, one year into the civil war. The directors of branches were chosen, de facto, on the basis of 'geopolitical' considerations. Academic life in the branches followed suit. Capture of the branches by the zu'ama was probably inevitable.[29]

When Boutros Harb was minister of education (1990–92), he claimed there was corruption in the university administration. In April 1991 it was announced in the newspapers that the president of Lebanese University and the deans were to have their academic duties separated from their administrative and financial duties. The minister in effect took direct administrative control of the university (El-Amine, 2018: 182–83). In 1977 a decree established an advisory council for Lebanese University, with representatives from the business sector and professional associations. The university president was to chair this committee and set its agenda. The council had the right to make its own suggestions to the university administration. This council was in fact never set up. Under President Assad Diab, in 1993, the council was constituted exclusively of professors, and Diab used it as a substitute for the university council, causing the full-time professors' association to protest (El-Amine, 2018: 187). From 1992 the presidency became part of Shi'i political spoils. Up to 2005, the Syrians were involved in the selection of Lebanese University's leadership. After they withdrew their military from Lebanon in 2005, leadership decisions fell victim to tussles between the Shi'i factions, Amal, and Hezbollah.

Reforms

The European Union (EU) initiated the so-called Bologna process in June 1996 and with it the *licence, master, doctorat* (LMD) (see Chapter 6) system to encourage student mobility among its campuses. On June 28, 2005, Lebanese University formally adopted that system. Zuhair Shaker, who became president in 2006, concludes that the experiment has not lived up to expectations because implementing legislation lagged, people did not understand the objectives, the university council could not be formed, and the university's infrastructure was not up to the task (Republic of Lebanon, 2011?: 8).

Third-party leverage came into play. With support from Tempus, in 2007 doctoral institutes were founded in sciences and technology; law, political, economic, and administrative sciences; and literature, humanities, and social sciences. The goal was to become a first-rate teaching and research university, accredited and ranked, capable of competing with the most respected universities. It is hard to square this aspiration with the university's research budget, which is only 1 percent of total operating outlays (see page 93).

In recent years, fifteen 'applied' institutes have been founded with selective admissions. Otherwise admission to the Lebanese University is open to those who successfully pass the Lebanese *baccalauréat* exam. Students were "sorted out" at the end of the first year. Attrition was apparently high (Republic of Lebanon, 2011?: 15). In recent years, first-year students constituted about 40 percent of all students. In 2010–2011 that meant 29,108 entering students and 15,000 graduating students (2011?: 17). The number of doctoral candidates went up from 2,500 in 2005–2006 to 6,300 in 2010–2011.

Finances

The dispersion of branches raised the costs of education per student. Nonetheless, in 2009–2010 average outlays per student at Lebanese University were 4 million Lebanese lira or $2,656 (Republic of Lebanon, 2011?: 19). By way of comparison, outlays per student at AUB at about the same time were ten times higher, even when netting out the operating budget of AUB's hospital (Nahas, 2009). Lebanese University's administrative staff was about three thousand—a surprisingly small number given a student body of more than 70,000 and dozens of 'campuses.' The budget in 2009–2010 broke down as follows:

Salaries and wages: $110,323,820
Research: $1,381,429
Operations: $18,632,814
Financial aid: $478,758
Capital: $8,854,699
Total: $139,671,520

In 2013 the total budget increased to $238 million, of which the state contributed $197 million (Diab, 2013: 1082).[30] In the same year the gross numbers of faculty members were as follows: 1,396 tenured and full-time faculty, 725 hourly contract faculty, and 1,997 de facto hourly contract faculty.

In 2012, after years of stagnant or declining salaries, Minister of Higher Education Hassan Diab (no relation to Assad Diab) managed to push substantial salary increases through the Council of Ministers. Different official sources list different base salaries before and after. The discrepancies may be the result of special allowances and research premiums. My best estimate is that salaries for the equivalent of an assistant professor rose from $23,000 to $30,000 per year and for full professors from $58,000 to $67,000. Professors of all ranks are supposed to be full time, allowed one day a week for approved outside activities (see Lebanese University, n.d.; Diab, 2013).

Ahmad Jammal, the director-general for higher education in the Ministry of Higher Education, pointed out that relative to Egypt and many other Arab countries Lebanese University and private university salaries are good, starting at 4 million Lebanese lira and rising to 8 million Lebanese lira for someone like himself, which is more than what he earns as director-general (interview, 2014). Therefore, faculty out-migration is not much of a problem. Nor do faculty spend significant time in tutoring and private lessons, in contrast with Egypt. That said, in the spring of 2019, faculty went on strike to protest proposed cuts in salaries to help Lebanon meet requirements for international credits and loans totalling $11 billion.

The Council for Higher Education

Like nearly all its neighbors, Lebanon has a Council for Higher Education that oversees all tertiary education, whether public or private. It is described in the draft Law for the Organization of Higher Education (full text in Republic of Lebanon, 2010?: 10–46):

Article 14: The formation of the Council for Higher Education

- The formation of a Council, called Council for Higher Education, chaired by the Minister of Education and Higher Education, and consists of Lebanese members as follows: Director General of Higher Education; Judge from the State Council; two representatives of Lebanese University; five representatives of private higher education institutions; three experts in higher education; president of the professional syndicates.

The Board shall hold the following powers and functions according to what is outlined in the provisions of this law:

- Contribute to the development of a national policy for higher education in general, particularly those [institutions] belonging to private higher education sector;
- Make suggestions for the organization of higher education within the national policy framework for higher education;
- Propose guidelines and criteria for the establishment of private institutions of higher education or their branches;
- Make recommendations with regard to requests for permission to set up or found institutions;
- Recommend the introduction of new programs at colleges and institutes;
- Approve programs, regulations and amendments submitted by higher education institutions;
- Recommend cancellation of permission to create institutions, branches or programs that do not meet the required academic standards;
- Authorize higher education institutions and programs after undergoing an independent evaluation by the national body or through external assessment and quality assurance;
- Establish committees made up of appropriate experts in order to support tasks outside the framework of the functions of the Technical Committee;
- Advise the minister on all aspects of higher education.

Compared to Egypt and Syria, this is a very limited set of authorities and functions. In particular the council has no role in budgets, admissions, and promotions, and only limited oversight of curriculum and programs. This is not surprising in that its attention is focused on more than forty-five private institutions with considerable autonomy and only one public institution.

While Lebanese faculty may not emigrate abroad for better career opportunities, its university graduates do. Lebanon has a long tradition of out-migration, but now its university system operates in direct support of it. The big investment that Lebanese citizens make in private education makes sense only if the higher private rates of return to education afforded in external job markets are taken into account.[31]

Other Arab countries may tacitly encourage out-migration of the university educated. Lebanon tolerates this, one suspects, to generate the billions of dollars in remittances that allow the political spoils system to function. If the country could avoid periodic civil war, it might be a second-best solution to several problems. Unfortunately, civil, confessional strife seems always to be lurking on the horizon.

Mohammed V University

The last of the flagship universities chronologically is Morocco's MVU, founded in 1957 in the capital, Rabat. The French established a protectorate in Morocco in 1912. Over the next three decades France slowly 'pacified' all of Morocco. It encouraged much more limited direct colonization of Morocco than it had in Algeria, which was legally part of French territory. The Moroccan Protectorate authorities, led by Resident General Hubert Lyautey (1912–25), founded no Moroccan university and kept primary and secondary education to a level sufficient to the needs of the Protectorate for literate civil servants.

It is also important to note that Morocco had an old and powerful merchant bourgeoisie, mainly from the city of Fez. Branches of these families had long been established abroad in cities such as Manchester and Cairo. It seems that this bourgeoisie never had the opportunity or imagination to sponsor a 'modern' university.

Like Egypt and Tunisia, Morocco had one ancient seat of Muslim learning, Qarawiyyin University in Fez, founded in 859 CE. Like its two equivalents, it did not become the cornerstone of the modern Moroccan university system. It was and has remained a center for the propagation of the Maliki rite of Islam (one of the four dominant schools of Sunni Islam). At the turn of the last century, Eugène Aubin termed the university "the only seat of learning in the Maghreb" (1906: 223). Tunisians would likely protest that the Zeitounia should be equally ranked.

Students selected their professors from the fifteen to twenty normally available. The students (tolba) came from Fez for the most part and lived with their families. Those from outside Fez would live in one of five 'schools' (*madrasas*) supported by *habous* (elsewhere in the Arab world known as *waqf*, or religious endowments). The boarders had to find private support for daily subsistence. Once graduated, they would have the rank of *fqih* (jurisprudent) and work their way up to professor. Qarawiyyin University was thus devoted to the production of legal scholars and practitioners. That is its vocation today.

An interesting custom was introduced in 1665 under Sultan Moulay Rachid. In his contest for the throne, he had the support of some forty students from Qarawiyyin. In recognition of their support he allowed the *tolba* to elect a sultan for one week. The *tolba* sultan was proclaimed in early April every year thereafter. The sultanate was auctioned off among the *madrasas*. In 1906, 406 students participated and the sultanate was won by a student from the Sous, a southern, Berber region. He would have the right to have some special request granted by the Moroccan government, or *Makhzen*. The sultan appointed trustees (*umana'*) to raise funds from the families of Fez for a multiday feast. They also raised money from local officials and ministers (Aubin, 1906: 228). Buying oranges and other fruit from the *tolba* reputedly brought blessings (*baraka*). The *tolba* sultan reigned for about a week, and the real sultan would send him a gift. The true and the faux sultans would meet via a jesting contest between their respective courtiers. At the end, the faux sultan kissed the stirrup of the real sultan. At dawn the next day the faux sultan fled to his *madrassah*. This theater could be enacted only so long as the spiritual majesty of the sultan was unquestioned. For most of Morocco's recent history that has been the case, although the ceremony was long ago abandoned.

The Protectorate did take two early initiatives. In 1912 it founded the Ecole Supérieure de Langue Arabe et de Dialectes Berbères. In 1921 this became the Institut des Hautes Etudes Marocaines and published the journal *Hesperis-Tamuda*. The Institut Scientifique Chérifien was founded in 1920. Both institutes were small training and research facilities designed to strengthen the Protectorate, not educate the natives (*indigènes*). Morocco won its independence in 1956, and a year later Crown Prince Hassan opened the Institut des Hautes Etudes as the Faculté des Lettres et Sciences Humaines, the nucleus of what was to become MVU, named after King Mohammed V, who led Morocco to independence. The crown prince also affiliated the Institut Scientifique to the new university.

Because of his anticolonial stance and academic eminence, the Sorbonne professor Charles-André Julien was appointed founding president of MVU for the period 1959–62, supported by André Adam, director of the Moroccan Ecole Nationale d'Administration for 1955–60. Julien had been doyen of the Faculté des Lettres beginning in 1957. He had flirted with communism but returned to the French Socialist Party during the era of Léon Blum in the mid-1930s. As both a politician and a scholar, he was strongly critical of France's colonial legacy, especially in North Africa. He died in 1991, just shy of his hundredth birthday.

Mohammed al-Fassi succeeded Julien as president and ran the university for nearly a decade. In 1959 total enrollments were 2,730 students, half of whom were not Moroccan. The great majority of faculty members were French. Within a decade the student body grew to 10,000, mostly Moroccan. Only 164 out of 399 professors were Moroccan.

Student politics were lively throughout Morocco's recent history. Less than a decade after independence, student demonstrations in March 1965 led the government to proclaim a state of emergency, suspending the parliament. This lasted for five years. The riots were set off by a ministerial circular limiting movement from primary to secondary cycles of the school system. They were violently repressed by Minister of the Interior Mohammed Oufkir.

President al-Fassi's departure coincided with extensive student agitation in the spring of 1968, itself a reflection of student movements that erupted around the world. Until that moment MVU had enjoyed considerable autonomy, but in 1968 the Ministry of Education and Minister Mohammed Benhima took it under government control (Vermeren, 2002: 327).

In 1975 the regime launched the great march into the Sahara to claim a vast territory controlled until that time by Spain. Algeria and the indigenous population of the Spanish Sahara opposed Morocco's unilateral action. Low-intensity warfare ensued. By 1978 all internal political voices had to be lowered in the name of Morocco's claims. In addition, King Hassan II, like Sadat in Egypt, used Islamists as a counterweight to the student left. Indeed, several came as political refugees from Egypt and Syria. A small number wound up in the Faculty of Law at MVU (Bildu, 2013: 12)

The Path to the Civil Service

As elsewhere, there was a direct link between university education and civil service employment. It was especially pronounced in Morocco because the middle and upper echelons of the civil service were still staffed by the French. Said Yaqtin (2017: 100–101) references a report prepared in 1957 by Mehdi Ben Barka,[32] which explicitly states the mission of the university as the training of civil servants *(formation des cadres)*.

Indeed, demand was high for university graduates. But once sated, the civil service in Morocco remained relatively small. By 2014 it employed 580,000 out of a total workforce of about 17.2 million, or around 3.5 percent. That is vastly below Egypt's, Syria's, Jordan's, or even Lebanon's rates. If we take Jordan as a comparator—like Morocco a monarchy without oil—we find rates of civil service employment at least triple Morocco's (Mrabi, 2013; World Bank, 2016). By contrast, civil service salaries in Morocco were higher than in other Arab states, so that public outlays on the civil service were similar despite the lower number of employees.

Enrollments

Morocco saw rapid expansion in total university enrollments, beginning in the 1970s with the founding of new campuses. Like Cairo, Damascus, and Lebanese Universities, MVU spawned branches in Casablanca, Fez, and elsewhere that eventually became independent universities. The university describes itself as "the mother university of the Moroccan university system" (Kingdom of Morocco, 2007: 67). Given the violent events of 1965 and 1968, there was clearly a security aspect to this regionalization of the university system. New campuses were often located in the suburbs of their localities so that student demonstrations would be less disruptive, less visible, and more easily repressed (Vermeren, 2002: 437).

The supply of students from the *lycée* system surged in the 1980s (Mellouk, 1997: 77–83). In 1983–84 secondary education was Arabized. This was followed by a new *baccalauréat* system. Under this system the proportion of high scores increased dramatically. The universities were swamped. University enrollments went from 105,600 in 1983–84 to 233,400 in 1993–94 and 260,000 in 1995–96. This period corresponded to measures of structural adjustment that impacted public outlays negatively.

In 1999 the National Charter for Education and Training stipulated that all students who pass the *baccalauréat* examination are eligible for tuition-free studies at one of the public universities. The result in 2010–2011 was that the total number of students reached 360,668, growing at over 15 percent per year. The Mohammed V University, Agdal (MVUA) campus reached 24,001 and the Mohammed V University, Souissi (MVUS) campus 17,977, the first growing at 6 percent per year and the latter at 14 percent.

While Arabization of high school instruction opened the gates to university education for thousands, it was a poisoned gift because significant portions of university studies were in French. The new entrants struggled with French, and first-year dropout rates soared. As Vermeren (2002) has argued, the seeming democratization of high school Arabization in fact thinly veiled a major element of socioeconomic bias. The more well-to-do students who had French instruction throughout their *lycée* years were far better equipped to handle university-level studies, particularly in STEM disciplines. It is, therefore, not surprising that many graduates could not find regular employment. The average youth unemployment rate in Morocco has been 19 percent, and in 2018 it reached 28 percent.

Governance

Moroccan universities do not have separate mission statements. Instead, there are 'common tasks' for all public universities specified in Law No. 01-00 of 2000, which are considered the universities' mission. Broadly speaking, the higher education system, and not the university, is the unit of analysis (El-Amine, 2014). Among the tasks are: contributing to the strengthening of Islamic and national identity; providing basic and continuing education; development and dissemination of science, knowledge, and culture; preparing youth for integration into the labor market, especially through the development of skills; performing scientific and technological research; undertaking tasks of expertise; and contributing to the overall development of the nation and of human civilization. With regard to any particular university, the specification of tasks to be undertaken is based on a plan called the University Development Project, a document submitted by the candidate for the presidency of the university that s/he is expected to implement if s/he is appointed to the job (see Chapter 5 on governance).

In 1993 Mohammed V University (MVU) was divided into two independent universities: Mohammed V University at Agdal and Mohammed V University at Souissi. The two reunited in 2015, but remain separate campuses. Leadership at both universities could not provide an explanation for the division. It was surely not pedagogic and may likely have been related to patronage opportunities. The former president of Mohammed V University at Agdal, Wail Benjelloun (email, August 13, 2018) reflected:

> The split of Mohammed V was for little pedagogic reason, and I did manage the initial phase of the reunification. I believe it was necessary to bring the two units together because each was a big university, yet incomplete. Some examples: Mohammed V Agdal had a Faculty of Science but the Medical School was in

Mohammed V Souissi; Mohammed V Souissi had no Faculty of Letters and Humanities; Mohammed V Agdal had the country's biggest Engineering School but Souissi had the Institute of Computer Science. Between them the two universities had three Faculties of Law. So not only was each incomplete but the distribution of schools really made no sense. The reunification recreated a university that is a repository for the intellectual history of modern Morocco since it in fact trained all of the post-independence cadres which replaced the agents of the French protectorate. The split also weakened the position of the university nationally. I oversaw the administrative reunification of services (academic, secretary-general, finance, communication, etc), and although there was much initial apprehension, it all worked out very rapidly and I think efficiently. Since then I have closely followed the development of the situation and, other than a Faculty Council which I think has too many members, things have worked out nicely. (Email, 2018)

While the combined campuses did moderately well in international rankings (QS and THE, various years), MVU became merely one among several universities. It was no longer 'national' but rather regional, serving the Rabat-Salé region. It helped that King Mohammed VI was a graduate, but that could not mask the decline in status. Despite that, the research output of MVUA alone was about a quarter of the national total (Kingdom of Morocco, 2007).

Access to the faculties of MVU is of two types: open or free access to *lettres et sciences humaines*, *sciences*, and *sciences juridiques, économiques, et sociales*; selective access to the Ecole Mohammedia d'Ingénieurs (EMI) and the Institut Supérieur de Technologie; and research institutes. The EMI was and is one of Morocco's *grandes écoles*, modeled on those of France. The students wear uniforms and receive military instruction. Admission is highly selective and dropout rates are low. Although quasi-independent since its founding in 1959, it has been affiliated to MVUA. It has between eight hundred and nine hundred students, a quarter of whom are female.

Faculty recruiting, as of 1999, is carried out by scientific commissions that are elected by their home 'establishment' (Kingdom of Morocco, 2007: 35). The president of the university has the authority to appoint professors and administrators and to assign them. However, s/he cannot determine their compensation.

In 2017 total faculty for the combined MVU campuses was 2,034, not including part-time faculty *(vacataires)*. The student body in the *licence* cycle was 64,920. There were 591 in the master's cycle and 151 in the doctoral cycle. Again in 2017, 10,614 students graduated. If we assume that 20,000 to 22,000 would be the expected number of graduates if there were no attrition, then we can estimate the dropout rate at about 10,000 over three years. One source, citing official reports, estimates dropouts at 58 percent of all enrolees *(Moroccan World News,* 2017).

As a result of the National Charter for Education and Training of 1999 and Law No. 01-00 of 2000, all universities are linked to one of Morocco's regions. The charter emphasizes practical links to regional and national development. Article 7 of the law stipulates that representatives of economic and social sectors, including presidents of professional chambers, will be represented on university councils. For MVU, the mayor of Rabat, the president of the Rabat-Salé Regional Council, the director of the Education and Training Council, the president of the Ulema Council, deans and directors of university institutions, elected representatives of the faculty, the administration, and students constitute the university council. Total membership has been on the order of forty-six, which is unwieldy (see Benjelloun's comment above). Most councils have in fact been plagued by the absenteeism of their nonacademic members.

Finances

Government expenditure on all levels of education in recent years reached 18 percent of total expenditures and 6.2 percent of GDP in Morocco, according to the World Bank Collection of Development Indicators. Nearly three-quarters of public education expenditures go to personnel, while only 1.3 percent goes to scientific research.

MVUA received in 2005 a state operating budget of 41,423,100 Moroccan dirhams ($3.7 million) and a capital budget of 19,032,400 dirhams ($1.7 million). Sponsored research in the same year totaled 7,757,329 dirhams ($700,000) or about 16 percent of total revenues (Kingdom of Morocco, 2007: 87).

Faculty salaries in 2012 ranged from the lowest of about 13,000 dirhams per month ($1,170) and the highest of about 26,000 dirhams ($2,342). There is no distinction by discipline and no differences among universities. Physicians earn more through clinical practice. Faculty members were allowed twenty hours per month to teach elsewhere (Mrabet and Benjelloun, interviews, 2013).

The Supreme Council for Education, Training, and Scientific Research

The Supreme Council for Education, Training, and Scientific Research is provided for in Morocco's constitution. It is one of a number of like councils in different socioeconomic domains. It is an advisory body to the king, the government, and the parliament. It is authorized to review and comment on all public policies in the three components of its title. The council is both proactive, taking initiative to review or evaluate policies and make recommendations based on its findings, and reactive, taking instruction to carry out such analyses by the king, the government, or other concerned parties. It is meant to act as a partner to all national and international entities engaged in its areas of oversight. It issues an annual report of its main activities.

This body differs substantially from the councils in Egypt, Syria, and Lebanon. It does not directly or indirectly control any university or ministerial functions. It is not empowered to issue any binding instructions or rules. It is a valued partner only insofar as it is found useful. It can be ignored.

Private Education

Private education was first introduced in Morocco in 1984–85, with two private institutes for business administration enrolling under a hundred students. The private sector now comprises over two hundred institutes, 39,000 students, and over four thousand professors, of whom some five hundred are full-time. Two-thirds of enrolled students are in business administration and management (Jaramillo and Melonio, 2011: 66).

A hybrid institution is Al Akhawayn University, founded in 1995 in the ski-resort town of Ifrane. Its name means "the two brothers" and refers to King Hassan of Morocco and King Fahd of Saudi Arabia, the university's major benefactor. Al Akhawayn has 2,200 students, largely undergraduate, and a board of trustees composed mainly of public officials. In most respects it is a stand-alone institution rather than a model for the future.

The Rabat School of Governance and Economics (EGE) is a smaller private IHL, established in 2008 and owned by a nonprofit foundation. EGE currently trains about a hundred students and aims for elite/semielite status. It has fifty-five professors (ten are permanent) and fifty administrative staff. It also hosts research centers, including one on Africa and the Mediterranean. EGE's goal is to contribute to the diversification of Morocco's leaders, who are currently mostly engineers trained in the French *grandes écoles* (Jaramillo and Melonio, 2011: 70). Given Morocco's ongoing fiscal difficulties and the outlook of significant parts of the political elite, further expansion of private tertiary education is in the cards.

Conclusion

A half-century separates the founding of Cairo and Damascus Universities from those of Lebanese University and Mohammed V University. Those were tumultuous decades both regionally and globally. Two world wars and the Great Depression marked them and had profound effects on the pioneer universities. Lebanese University and MVU came with the advent of national independence and became integral parts, at least conceptually, of the construction of a new society. That of course also became the mission of Cairo and Damascus Universities, but after a half-century of experience as elitist institutions under the thumb of colonial authorities.

Despite these differing origins and experiences, by the 1970s the main characteristics, as well as pathologies, of all four exhibited more similarities than dissimilarities. All became factories for civil servants. None developed organic links to private sector employment. All were regarded by the central authorities as potential political threats rather than vital sources of ideas and innovation. Egypt and Syria in those years were governed by highly centralized autocracies, while Morocco and Lebanon maintained a modicum of political liberalism. Lebanese University fell victim more to Lebanon's confessional spoils system than to the *mukhabarat*, but in all four cases the universities were the captives of the political system. The official chatter was about university autonomy while the reality was political subordination. In this respect it is tempting to pin the blame on the radical, populist regimes that emerged in the 1950s and 1960s, but colonial practices had fundamentally eroded the 'best practice' aspirations in governance and academic freedom that the pioneers' founders had sought. Worst practice has deep roots and many sources.

Both the universities and the civil service became integral parts of social contracts upon which the four regimes saw their political survival riding. All but Lebanon experienced more or less severe fiscal crises that made funding the social contract problematic. For its part, Lebanon threw in fifteen years of civil war that made fiscal crises look like picnics. For the periods of their rapid expansion, the four universities were seriously underfunded, leading to a deterioration in their standards and the quality of their graduates. Just when these countries needed to be creating millions of new jobs, the reverse occurred, with soaring rates of youth unemployment coupled with severe restrictions (often ignored) on civil service hiring. Lebanon may have coped the best because its tertiary system is at least half private and its citizens are used to investing directly in their children's education. The other three, by the 1990s, threw in the towel and took legal steps to open tertiary education to private actors and investors. We are unlikely to see many new public universities, and the balance in enrollments will shift gradually in favor of private institutions.

Despite this shift, one suspects that the four flagship universities will maintain their claims on significant public resources and that they may, like several of their counterparts in Latin America, constitute real centers of excellence, joined in depth and quality by only a few private institutions. That evolution will take place on the battlefield of the quest for rapid economic growth and the creation of millions of new jobs.

3

Politics and the University

Middle Eastern universities suffer from all known forms of political interference and manipulation. No particular instance of interference will sound unfamiliar to those following higher education in other parts of the world. To understand what is different in the MENA, we need to disassemble interference into component parts. The initial cut is to distinguish between political interference with a small 'p' and that with a big 'P.' It is the latter kind that is so pervasive and so pernicious in the MENA. The basic distinction is between that of the university as a pawn in mundane political games of influence and patronage (small-p) and the university as a critical element in regime survival (big-P). Everywhere in the MENA the university is perceived in the mindset of political leadership as critical to survival.

Small-P Politics and the University

Like all parts of the state apparatus, the public university is a field of and for patronage: finding jobs for clients, getting clients' offspring into the university, fixing failing grades, maybe even locating a branch of a university in a favored constituency.

In 1993, Mohammed V University in Rabat, Morocco, founded one year after independence in 1957, was divided into branches in Souissi and Agdal. Morocco's flagship university thus became a couple of corvettes. When I enquired into the reasons for this initiative, I received embarrassed smiles. The suggestion was that the Ministry of Education and the minister saw a whole range of new staffing opportunities by

105

which clientele could be rewarded. There was no obvious institutional or pedagogic rationale for the split.

Rahma Bourqia, herself once a Moroccan university president, sees small-p politics systemically, noting that "what characterizes these policies is discontinuity. The political orientation and the governance style change with each minister. . . . In other words, each change of minister returns the system to a period of transition, even of hesitation, that prolongs the temporality of system change" (2011: 7).

In Lebanon from 2004 until 2015, there were no appointments of academic deans at Lebanese University, Lebanon's largest, as required by law. The statutory tenure of a dean is three years so over three cycles had been skipped. In 2015 a new minister found a formula to satisfy all political and sectarian claimants, and new appointments were made. This de facto process is not at all reflected in the Law on Higher Education. One of Lebanon's leading students of education has compared Lebanese University to a pasture on which politicians graze their sheep (El-Amine, interview, 2012).

Lebanon's confessions are the framework for patronage and spoils. Insiders differ on when such considerations became crippling for Lebanese University. Clearly the civil war (1975–89) led to the 'confessionalization' of specific campuses (for example, the Shi'a came to dominate at the main Hadath campus). Some see the Taif Accords that brought the civil war to an end as enshrining confessional patronage at the university. The Doha Agreement of 2008, which headed off a renewed civil war, solidified the arrangements. The basic rule was to take the confessional distribution of all 'class one' employees (director general and above) across the government and use those proportions as the university model. It became accepted that the president of Lebanese University would be a Shi'a. Two prominent confessional leaders, Najib Miqati, a Sunni prime minister, and Nabih Berri, the Shi'i speaker of the house, deadlocked over appointing deans. The issue was not resolved until 2015.

Over a thousand faculty positions in 2015 were filled by part-time, contractual instructors. Despite the efforts of some senior academic leaders to elaborate clear academic criteria for contractees, the political leadership could not resist the temptation to use contract instructors as patronage fodder. The same minister who appointed new deans also added six hundred new contract positions to the original thousand, again along political-sectarian lines and without proper academic credentialing.

Universities in the Palestinian territories have fallen victim to the patronage needs of the Palestinian Authority. Al-Quds University in East Jerusalem may be exceptionally burdened with Palestinian Authority clients, to the extent that it has not been able to meet its payroll for some time and has essentially been borrowing from its faculty through salary IOUs (Anonymous, interview, 2016).

The dean of the Faculty of Medicine at Jordan's Hashemite University has accused members of the kingdom's Higher Education Council of conflicts of interest by deliberately evaluating sitting university presidents negatively and then positioning themselves to become president (Younes, 2015).

The Arab Spring of early 2011 forced the resignation of Egypt's president, Hosni Mubarak. There was a brief moment of open debate and investigative reporting on the now-defunct regime. It transpired that Mubarak and his dominant party, the National Democratic Party (NDP), had stuffed university administrative positions with retired military officers who performed no university functions. This interlude corresponded to one in which presidents in Egyptian universities were elected by their colleagues.

This moment did not last long. General Abdel Fattah al-Sisi, who came to power in 2013, reintroduced the fetters of the Mubarak regime and then some. For example, the University of Alexandria made what appears to be a preemptive move against any tendency that Egyptian researchers might have to inquire into sensitive areas or express nonapproved views. An article on the *al-Ahram* newspaper website (in Arabic) reports that the university decided recently that all postgraduate dissertations would have to conform with Egypt's Vision 2030. In other words, they would be censored (Shepland, 2018).

In fact, that policy applies nationwide. The University of Liverpool was approached to open a campus in Egypt in 2017 but ultimately declined out of fear for its "institutional reputation." Severely curtailed academic freedoms in Egypt were deemed incompatible with Liverpool's values (Holmes and Aziz, 2019).

There is a bridging function among universities, leading from small-p to big-P politics. It is the role of universities as theatrical stages and political testing grounds. Despite an often mediocre product and being manipulated for political ends, universities still enjoy a measure of prestige and respect for service to truth that makes them an ideal stage for political theater. When Egyptian President Anwar Sadat's wife, Jihan, defended her master's thesis at Cairo University, it was televised nationally. It probably did Sadat's political image more harm than good, but he could not pass up the opportunity.[1] US President Barack Obama chose Cairo University to deliver his 2009 address to the Arab and Muslim worlds. On June 20, 2011, as Syria moved to the brink of civil war, Bashar al-Assad went to Damascus University to deliver his unyielding denunciation of his opponents as agents of terrorism and to launch the horrendous armed conflict that has ground on for years.

In the overwhelmingly authoritarian systems that characterize the Arab world, the university can serve as a testing ground for political strength. Elections to student unions, which are legal and ubiquitous, are watched closely, as they may reflect shifting balances of power off campus. Professional association elections (engineers, lawyers, physicians) serve the same purpose. Such elections can be manipulated from outside, but they are often allowed to reflect the real balance of forces at play. Sudan's National Islamic Front, founded by Hassan Turabi, was born at Khartoum University (inter alia, on Sudan see Shibeika, 2014; on Tunisia see Camau and Geisser, 2003).

In North Africa, plunging into student activism has been a way to attract the attention of the political authorities. Student leaders may be chastised in various ways, then 'recuperated' by the regime. Mohamed Charfi was a vocal critic of the Bourguiba regime in Tunisia, then minister of education under the man who deposed Bourguiba, Zine al-Abidine Ben Ali. Similarly, in Morocco, Abdellah Saaf was part of the radical March 23 movement of 1970 but became minister of national education (2000–2002) (Saaf, in Ait Mous and Ksikes, 2014: 321–43).

Student and professional elections and 'militating' one's way to high office can easily morph from small-p politics to big-P politics. When Bashar al-Assad uses the cover of Damascus University to launch a ferocious war on his adversaries, he is not merely engaging in theatrics but stating unequivocally that the university will do his bidding, that it will act as the pillar of his power structure that it is. There will be no student demonstrations against his presence, no public dissent by the professoriate. The cameras are rolling, and the message is there for all to hear and see.

Big-P Politics

"A national consensus is required among public, private, and civil society decision-makers on the overriding importance of building the knowledge society. This consensus would amount to a new social contract reflected in all Arab spending and investment decisions" (UNDP and AFESD, 2003: 138).

This plea for a new social contract more than hints at the political stakes involved in the sphere of higher education. Along with a new social contract, there would need to be a new 'authoritarian bargain,' or, perhaps, the erosion of authoritarianism itself.[2] The extent of improvement in Arab higher education in recent decades has been so modest because its implications are potentially so far-reaching. All the players understand this.

There have been significant moments in the history of Western democracies when universities and students shook the foundations of governing elites. The year 1968 just about everywhere was such a moment. Charles de Gaulle had to helicopter to French garrisons in Germany, commanded by General Jacques Massu, to ensure their support if the rioting in France got further out of control. Student-led antiwar protests in the US led Lyndon Johnson to abandon his quest for the Democratic nomination for president in 1968. But such moments in the West, where political structures tremble due to the university and its citizens, are relatively rare. Ironically, I would argue, they are also rare in the Arab world, but that is because of the formidable repressive grip that is constantly maintained on the academy. When that grip is defied, autocrats feel the ground move under their feet.

One of the most spectacular challenges came from Sudan's Khartoum University in October 1964, when students demonstrated against an incursion of security forces into the campus. The protests spread throughout civil society, and Sudan's president, General Ibrahim Abboud, was forced to resign. University students were again prominent in the demonstrations that drove Jaafar al-Nimeiry from power in 1985. Sudan was quiet during the Arab Spring, despite the loss of the south to the newly independent South Sudan, plunging oil revenues, and Omar al-Bashir's indictment by the International Criminal Court as a war criminal. But then in 2019, as the economy continued to nosedive, university students, civil servants, and professionals mobilized to drive al-Bashir from power altogether. At the same time, a similar movement gathered momentum in Algeria.

The obsessive need of authoritarians to control all the component parts of civil society is well recognized in the region. That was a major focus of the 2005 *Arab Human Development Report*, but its roots in several countries go back to the 1950s and 1960s. In September 1961, for example, the UAR of Egypt and Syria came apart when Syria, after an internal coup, withdrew from the union. Students at Cairo University demonstrated in support of Egypt's president, Gamal Abd al-Nasser, the father of the union, and denounced the Syrian reactionaries and separatists (*infisaliyyun*). The Egyptian authorities closed Cairo University for some weeks because the law forbade student demonstrations of any kind on campus. The late Mohamed Sayed Said summed up the basic principle (as cited in Ghobashy, 2016: 16): "Authoritariansim does not spare any social institutions but works to control them all through monitoring and stringent subordination to security."

University autonomy, so often enshrined in law in the Arab world, serves as a model for other parts of civil society—professional associations, the press, trade and labor unions, NGOs—that worry political leaders, none more so than the university itself. Autonomy combined with the inherent range of issues explored in a university setting is potentially a potent mix. So real concessions on autonomy may appear to political leaders to be the camel's nose poking into the authoritarian tent.[3] Because they share or pretend to share in a supranational, universalist culture, universities are seen as particularly vulnerable to foreign penetration by the regime's enemies. Velvet revolutions fomented by intellectuals are deeply feared by authoritarians. From the outset the Islamic Republic of Iran has had a tortured relationship with universities that predated its advent. Ayatollah Khomeini in 1980 set the tone: "We fear neither economic boycott nor military intervention. What we fear is cultural dependence and imperialist universities that propel our young people into the service of communism" (quoted in Maloney, 2015: 127).

A 'cultural revolution' was launched in Iran in April 1980. Universities were shuttered for four years. The Council for Cultural Revolution was charged with drawing up new curricula. Universities were suborned to the task of fighting Iraq from 1980 to 1988, but by 1997, with the election of the reformist cleric Mohammed Khatemi to the republic's presidency, hardliners once again saw the shape of a velvet revolution. The election in 2005 of Mahmoud Ahmedinejad to the presidency stopped reform in its tracks. But then came the massive demonstrations in 2009, protesting what were regarded as rigged elections that saw Ahmedinejad reelected. The demonstrations were brutally crushed and the organizers, many based at universities, denounced as foreign agents.

Similar accusations of foreign agents and treasonous behavior were made at the beginning of the Arab uprisings of the winter of 2011. The more demonstrators chanted "peaceful," the more autocrats smelled velvet revolutions. Concessions to any part of civil society could spread to other parts. Even huge and distant China tried to suppress news of Tunisia's 'Jasmine Revolution' (Wikipedia, 2011, "Chinese pro-democracy protests").

The Iranian parliament's hardliners in August 2014 forced out of office Science Minister Reza Faraji-Dana, an electrical engineer who had tried to unshackle the universities. One of his initiatives was to depoliticize the appointment of chancellors and rely principally on merit.

Regional autocrats probably do not regard universities as more important to their legitimacy and survival than other institutions of civil society, such as professional associations and labor unions. All three enjoy symbolic legitimacy and all can harm the regime and its economy. There is an important distinction, however. Universities are home to hundreds of thousands of young students, some of whom seek political adventure and have relatively little to lose. The faculty, for their part, identify with a culture of speaking truth to power.

A particularly graphic example of big-P politics emerged in Sudan when al-Bashir seized power in 1989. He put paid to whatever fiction remained of university autonomy. His main concern was the venerable flagship, Khartoum University, but for the entire higher education system he abolished a recently approved academic freedom act, ended elections of deans and other university officials, and proclaimed himself chancellor of all universities. He created five new universities and doubled admissions to existing ones (Bishai, 2008).

Schizophrenia: Choking and Stroking

In Chapter 4, we will explore the trade-offs between degrees of systemic democracy and academic freedom versus intellectual creativity and innovation. Here, the goal is to analyze the ambivalence autocratic regimes feel toward their universities. The challenge they face is to keep universities politically quiet and supportive, all the while producing the 'cadres' to staff the state and contribute to progress in technological fields. This is a dilemma, rather than a trilemma—that is, the balance between control and academic excellence.

Autocrats are both fascinated and terrified by universities. They have always seen them as essential tools in building new societies and new citizens. Here, the avatar is perhaps Mustafa Kamal Atatürk, the founder of the Turkish republic, built out of the rubble of the Ottoman Empire. He wanted to instill pride in being a Turk and a citizen of the republic. He introduced the Latin alphabet to transcribe Turkish, replacing the Arabic alphabet that linked Turks to Islam and the Qur'an. There are famous photographs of him, in civilian dress, visiting a rural school and writing the letters of the new alphabet on a blackboard. As Jenny White observes, from the beginning of the republic, academic disciplines had been manipulated to corroborate the definition of the Turkish nation: "That identity today clearly still has the force of truth, validated—as it was then—by its professional academic setting" (2012: 570).

The experiment of the Turkish republic was observed by a generation of Arab leaders, still under colonial domination. Many shared with Atatürk, once their countries became independent, a desire for secular republics built on ethnic nationalism. They understood how the education system could play a crucial role in that venture. Indeed, the Ba'th Party that eventually came to power in both Syria and Iraq was founded by high school teachers, Michel Aflaq and Salah Bitar. Although he clearly eschewed secularism, it is worth noting that Hassan al-Banna, who founded the Muslim Brotherhood in 1928, was also a schoolteacher.

In several Arab states, the single or dominant party became instrumental in controlling the university and in the attempt to wed academic competence with political loyalty. In Egypt, Nasser's showdown with General Naguib in 1954 saw a part of Egypt's universities and intelligentsia align with Naguib. The relations between Nasser and academe got off on a particularly poor footing. Just as Nasser looked on universities with suspicion, so too did Hafez al-Assad of Syria, whose seizure of power in 1970 provoked student demonstrations. In 1979, students from Aleppo University marched on *mukhabarat* headquarters. Some were killed by security forces and a hundred faculty members were fired (George, 2003).

As was said in the construction of communism, the goal was to be 'red and expert.' The party was to provide a framework for ideological correctness and for setting societal, economic, and strategic priorities to which the university was called upon to contribute.

By 1961, Nasser had tamed Egypt's universities and sought to mobilize them in support of Egypt's 'socialist revolution.' Ideological courses were introduced. In 1965 the Socialist Youth Organization was created. In the wake of the 1968 riots,[4] following Egypt's defeat in the 1967 war with Israel, the organization was closed down (Reid, 1990: 197, 202). In 1977 political activity on Egyptian campuses was criminalized (Mughaith, 2018: 56).

Nasser favored academic technocrats in his cabinets, alongside military figures in the security sector. He moved out the lawyer politicians and moved in the academic technocrat (Reid, 1990: 188). Algeria, in the heady days of burgeoning petroleum rents following the OAPEC-engineered price hikes of 1973, witnessed the same resort to highly educated technocrats (Minister of Industry Abdessalam Belaid foremost among them).

By the 1990s, after economic crises, neoliberal reforms, and some ideo-logical exhaustion, older 'socialist' parties like Egypt's ASU, Tunisia's Neo Destour Party, and Algeria's Front for National Liberation (*Front de libéra-tion nationale,* FLN) morphed into patronage machines without any ideo-logical agenda. Only in Syria and Iraq, where the Ba'th Party prevailed, was there any pretense of the old socialist model. In both instances the model had eroded significantly. Eight years of war with Iran had led Saddam Hussein to embrace some Islamic symbols, while neoliberal reforms and crony capi-talism transformed Ba'thi Syria. The collapse of the Soviet Union in 1989 removed an effective patron from the scene. Everywhere political Islam chal-lenged the old order, especially after the Iranian revolution of 1979, followed by the triumph of the Taliban in Afghanistan a decade later.

In both Syria and Iraq, the Ba'th was an integral part of the security 'deep' state. In Syria, the National Union of Students was a creation of and beholden to the Ba'th Party (Starr, 2012). One Syrian insider described the situation at Damascus University on the eve of the 2011 uprising in these terms:

> The whole system, like the polity itself, was party-dominated. There was no formal process for selecting a new university president. It depended on the most senior party leadership and personal connec-tions. . . . There is a Governing Council of the university with deans, student representatives, and the party leader for the university branch, but the council had no formal role in leadership selection. The branch party leader would normally be more powerful than the president and would involve himself in all sorts of academic business, especially [faculty and staff] appointments.[5] (Anonymous, interview, 2014)

In his study of Ba'thi Iraq, Joseph Sassoon (2012) does not pay much attention to Ba'thi control of the universities. He suggests that all faculty members were also members of the Ba'th. Under the party secretariat, there was a Central Bureau of Students and Youth, with branches in all universities and members who sat on university councils.

Mukhabarat

More important than the party in nearly all regional states has been the police and intelligence apparatus commonly referred to as the *mukhabarat*. An observer of Syria wrote simply, "Even more than other institutions, the universities are saturated with agents and informers of the *mukhabarat* or secret police" (George, 2003: 145).[6]

Even Lebanon, listed as 'partly free' by the polity index of Freedom House, has its *mukhabarat*. I recall vividly attending a dinner hosted by Prime Minister Rafic Hariri in honor of Pakistan's President Pervez Musharraf, where I was seated with a half-dozen university presidents and Director of Internal Security Jamil as-Sayyid. I knew this was the prime minister's way of having a little joke but also of sending us a not-so-subtle message.

A former student at Baghdad University remembered the *mukhabarat* as indeed present but mostly among the nonacademic staff, and they were mostly Shi'i (Saddam Hussein being Sunni). That was a long-standing fact. For the Shi'a, work in intelligence was a good form of social mobility, as was the army. Presumably Saddam did not feel threatened by them, although they did not rise to the most senior positions. People did not talk much about police and party presence, as the faculty were increasingly concerned with finding ways to make some money—private lessons, and contracting services to the government (as the state retreated somewhat).

The former student cautioned me against overpersonifying Saddam's regime, noting, "It takes many people to build a system like Iraq's Ba'th. Getting rid of Saddam in 1991 [after Operation Desert Storm] would not have fixed anything any more than getting rid of him in 2003 did."[7]

Iraq, like Iran, used universities to identify and recruit talent for the intelligence services and for the party. Ba'th students received a five-point bonus on university entry exams. Political indoctrination took place in the party, not in the university (Blaydes, 2018: 172, 184).

Iran has developed its own unique control instrument known as the Basij (Volunteers), a paramilitary group notable for its size, resources, and ability to reward its members. Its mission is defense of the revolution and it offers unquestioning loyalty to the supreme leader. It works alongside and is subordinate to the Revolutionary Guard. Mahmoud Ahmedinejad, a university professor, was drawn from its ranks. It brutally put down 'reformist' demonstrations in universities in 1999, supported Ahmedinejad's election to the presidency in 2004, and once again suppressed demonstrations against Ahmedinejad's reelection in 2009. When Ahmedinejad broke with Ayatollah Khamenei after 2010, the Basij remained loyal to the supreme leader. Its mission is to 'educate,' inform on, enforce, and intimidate.

There are probably over five million Basij members. They all go through fairly intensive religious training. Their numbers are greater than the four million university students. The Basij has about 900,000 student members and some 20,000 faculty members. It is important, if not crucial, for faculty promotions to be a Basij member. Likewise, 40 percent of admission places at Iranian universities are reserved for Basij members.

Sharif University of Technology, seen by some as Iran's MIT, was not immune to Basij penetration. Mehrdad Bazarpash was head of the Students' Basij there and went on to important positions under Ahmedinejad. Hamid Behbahani from the Professors' Basij became minister of roads and transportation, and Kamran Danesjhoo became minister of sciencific research and technology (Golkar, 2015: 137–54).

After Egyptian President Sadat's assassination at the hands of Islamic extremists in 1981, the *mukhabarat* under Hosni Mubarak watched campuses especially for Islamist activists. This did not mean that they were repressed at all times. Indeed, members of the Muslim Brotherhood were occasionally allowed to run for university offices in student and faculty associations. Arrests, often accompanied by torture, would give all but the most reckless reason to act prudently.

Violence and Repression

Being a student or a faculty member in the Middle East exposes one to violence and repression on a scale and with a frequency that would be hard to replicate in the West. At the time I wrote this section, the city of Mosul in Iraq was being freed from the grip of Daesh. The videos coming out showed the rubble that was once the University of Mosul, reputedly Iraq's second best after the University of Baghdad. The university's students and faculty had scattered or were being held hostage by the jihadis. Its president was living in Erbil in Iraqi Kurdistan. Perhaps only the presidents of Tulane or Louisiana State, New Orleans, at the time of Hurricane Katrina could begin to imagine what the University of Mosul was facing in 2017.[8] Given their weight in the population, students may pay a disproportionate price in life and limb in situations of generalized violence (Egypt, 1967–68; Lebanon, 1975–89; Sudan, 1954– ; Algeria, 1990s; the Iraq–Iran War, 1980–89; the Syrian civil war, 2011–). A forensic photographer for the Assad regime smuggled out of Syria his photo archive of prisoners and victims of torture. Based on them it is estimated that 60,000 Syrians have died in Assad's jails since 2011. Students must surely have been a significant proportion of them.[9]

Purges, jailings, and extrajudicial killings are commonplace throughout the region. The cruel irony for Iraqis is that the Ba'thi grip on universities led to a purge of nominal Ba'this after the US invasion of 2003. Some three thousand university professors were expelled because of their political leanings. Thereafter and up to 2009, 413 faculty members in Iraq were killed by various parties (Majeed, 2010; Barakat and Milton: 2015).

Morocco had its 'years of lead' under King Hassan II, during which students and faculty disappeared on a wide scale. Lucky ones, like Abraham Serfaty, survived.

Libya's Muammar Qadhafi employed death squads to hunt down and kill dissident Libyan students abroad, whom he referred to as 'stray dogs.'[10] In 1976 students at Tripoli and Benghazi Universities organized their own unions in defiance of government-sponsored unions. There were widespread arrests, then most were released. A year later many of the same students were rearrested and given long prison sentences. Some were publicly executed. The executions were televised live (Rajabany and Shitrit, 2014: 79).

Throughout the MENA, prison terms and the scars of torture can be worn as badges of honor, and many, especially students, can show them.

I have emphasized autocracies in defining the role of universities in the MENA, but there is one quasi-democracy in the region that has emulated and outdone its Arab neighbors in repressing its system of higher education. Turkey began its democratic transition in 1950, when it held its first relatively free and fair elections. The dominant Republican Peoples' Party lost the elections that year to the Democratic Party. Thereafter, the democratic transition was periodically interrupted by military interventions, especially in 1960 and 1980. Important segments of the intelligentsia supported the putsches in the name of defending secularism or progressivism (Dinçşahin, 2015).

The 1980 military coup was particularly far-reaching.[11] It followed upon years of bitter, often violent clashes between leftists and right-wing nationalists. The military leaders who took over mainly targeted the left. In a massive purge, 650,000 people were taken into custody and 1.6 million people ended up being barred from public sector employment (De Bellaigue, 2016).

The coup led to the creation of the Council of Higher Education (YÖK), the military's arm for purging the university system of opponents. Its first chairman was İhsan Doğramacı (1981–91). He founded Bilkent University in 1984. Bilkent today is probably Turkey's most successful private university. The YÖK in all the succeeding years has never relinquished its role of overseeing the university system. It has become a powerful instrument in the hands of Recep Tayyip Erdoğan and his AKP, which was voted into power in 2002.[12]

For a time Erdoğan was allied to Fethullah Gülen, a charismatic Islamic mystic with a widespread movement in Turkey. In 2013 the two men fell out, and Erdoğan moved to close the Gulenist network of tutoring schools, the *dershane*s, which were both a source of funds and recruits to the Gulenist movement (Çağaptay, 2017: 136).

On July 15, 2016, there was an attempted military coup in Turkey. It was successfully thwarted by Erdoğan with considerable and courageous civilian support. The coup attempt was both cause and pretext for a purge of the Turkish polity to rival that of 1980. The target was all suspected clients, allies, and sympathizers of Fethullah Gülen, but also Kurds, liberals, and just about anyone opposed to Erdoğan.

The 2016 purge resulted in the firing of 40,000 teachers, the closure of fifteen universities and schools with 200,000 students, and the forced resignation or firing of 1,577 deans and some 5,000 academics. Those purged by government decree were removed from their academic positions and barred from other academic employment. Their passports (and those of their spouses) were canceled, effectively foreclosing their ability to seek positions outside the country (MESA, 2017; Ashdown, 2016; De Bellaigue, 2016; Pettit, 2016; Kaya, 2018).

The Turkish example is a cautionary tale. Illiberal democracy does not preclude the same repression and brutality exhibited in more autocratic settings. Erdoğan is said to have remarked that democracy is like a bus. You ride it until you reach your destination. Then you get off.

University Activism

Can we assess the real threat level of universities to autocrats? Students and faculty are always part of broader movements of protest, but it is not obvious that they lead them or have a decisive weight within them. They were players in the protests against colonial rule (as in Egypt in 1919 and 1946) and they have joined in socioeconomic protests (Morocco, 1965; Egypt, 1977; Algeria, 1989). Unable to confront their political masters head-on, they could use the Arab–Israeli conflict to embarrass their leaders into greater risk-taking, failing which the leaders would look like cowards. Lebanese students always had a greater degree of freedom than their counterparts elsewhere. In 1968 Israel bombed Beirut airport, prompting widespread student demonstrations against the impotent Lebanese government. Fifty Lebanese University professors signed a protest of government inaction (Barakat, 1977: 64–65; Shahine, 2011).

Students were the leading elements in the early period of the Arab uprisings of 2011, but were swamped early on by Islamist organizations that mobilized constituencies far broader than those centered in universities. In 2019, both Algeria and Sudan seemed to be living through the 'springs' they missed in 2011.

Students are both political players with considerable agency (such as Muslim Brotherhood student members in Egypt) and pawns of political actors external to the university (for example, all Lebanese political patrons have loyal student factions in universities). During the years of socialist populism (mainly the 1960s and 1970s) campuses were dominated by nominally leftist groups. That was the case in Egypt, Algeria, Tunisia, Syria, and Iraq, but also in more liberal, pro-private-sector, and pro-West Morocco, where the left-leaning Union Nationale des Etudiants Marocains prevailed.

Postsocialist/populist regimes such as Mubarak's in Egypt, Ben Ali's in Tunisia, or Bashar al-Assad's in Syria encouraged the mobilization of Muslim student groups in universities to check and ultimately drive out leftist organizations. Both the autocrats and the *mukhabarat* believed they could manage this game without running serious risks. Anwar Sadat initiated this strategy in the mid-1970s, especially at the Assiut University (Wickham, 2013: 34–37), and then paid with his life in October 1981 when Muslim extremists assassinated him at a public ceremony in Cairo.

King Hassan II of Morocco was a descendant of the Prophet and head of a dynasty that enjoyed immense religious legitimacy, but he too resorted to Islamist proxies at Moroccan universities to counter the left. The perceived threat emerged first in March 1965, when widespread rioting broke out in Casablanca protesting a ministerial circular limiting the movement from primary school to the high school cycles. The protests soon morphed into cost-of-living protests. Minister of the Interior Mohammed Oufkir violently repressed the demonstrations, and the king declared a state of emergency that was to last five years. The Moroccan parliament was suspended.

The contagion of the student demonstrations of 1968 in France spread to North Africa. The *Makhzen* (royal government) resorted to the same methods as Sadat in Egypt. In the 1970s, after the Muslim Brotherhood was hounded from Egypt and Syria, a small number wound up in Morocco. At the same time Abdulkarim Khatib, one of Morocco's leading politicians, broke from the Mouvement Populaire, a party defending Berber interests and close to the *Makhzen*, and founded his own Islamist party, also close to the palace. A small number of Muslim Brothers were at MVU in the Faculties of Letters and Law. Hassan II wanted to use them to thwart the left at the universities. They wanted to break the grip of 'the communists' on the curriculum (Bildu Ali, 2013: 12).

Then, in 1975, the regime launched the great march into the Western Sahara to lay claim to the former Spanish possession. In so doing the king tapped into strong nationalist sentiments, and by 1978 all opposition voices were lowered in the name of national unity (Vermeren, 2002).[13]

Hassan II was still concerned by both the dominance of the left among students and, more generally, in university affairs, and also, in 1979, by the repercussions of the founding of the Islamic Republic in Iran. In 1981 he did by decree to Qarawiyyin University, the oldest Islamic university in the Muslim world (founded in 859 CE), essentially what Nasser had done to al-Azhar University (founded in 970 CE) a couple of decades earlier—turned the religious professoriate (ulama) into civil servants. The minister of education at the time, Azzeddine Laraki, not only ordered the opening of a department of Islamic Studies at MVU but also ordered the closing of its philosophy department. He enlisted Syrian Muslim Brothers on the faculty to organize the new department ('Ida, 2013).[14]

There is some evidence that the university in the MENA is more a perceived than an actual threat (see Chapter 5 on governance). Rare are the examples of university leadership defending university autonomy against the predations of central authorities. The resignation in 1932 of Ahmad Lutfi al-Sayyid as president of the Egyptian University in protest over the firing of Dean of Arts Taha Hussein is a notable exception.[15]

That firing and resignation inspired the launch of the March 9 movement at Cairo University in 2004, seventy-two years later. Its founder was Professor of Medicine Mohammed Abul-Ghar. The movement sought to enhance the independence of universities, especially with respect to the presence of security forces on campuses. The academic appointment system was identified as corrupt and as leading to the deterioration of university quality. Its members were prevented from running for university office in 2010. Many joined the 2011 Tahrir Square protests as individuals (Geer, 2013; El-Mikawy et al., 2017: 181). Once General Abdel Fattah al-Sisi came to power in 2013—after unseating Mohammed Morsi, Egypt's first freely elected president in decades—he reasserted the state's grip on universities, bringing security forces back onto campuses and ending the election of university presidents and deans. The March 9 movement offered little meaningful resistance.

Against the periodic bursts of university activism there are long periods of torpor. For students, the costs of activism are high and only a few ever explore its risks. Protesting students are a minority among their peers. Even more so are those who join student unions or campus party organizations. Gertel and Hexel (2018: 287) found that only 7–10 percent of their sample had participated in campus union or political party activities. Alaa Shibeika, writing about Khartoum University in 2014, captures the dichotomy between the few activists and the many 'nibblers' plotting their escape from Sudan altogether:

> As the students marched silently to the chancellor's office on April 4 in remembrance of Ali [a classmate who had been killed], they threw away the gown of politics and put on that of humanity. Others strongly criticized the idea of a strike and saw it as hindering education. They felt more comfortable nibbling at their books. They believe their education will one day give them a much better life beyond the borders of this troubled country. (Shibeika, 2014)

The opposite of exit is represented in the Union of the Credentialed Unemployed founded in Tunis by Hassan Ben Abdullah in 2006, partially in reaction to the perceived cooptation of the Tunisian General Labor Union by the Democratic Constitutional Rally party in quashing the Gafsa phosphate strikes. Abdullah was jailed for three years, two in solitary confinement (Chomiak, 2014: 28).

For the professoriate, the incentive structure that has been built into university life may have been a more important factor in assuring political quiescence than the *mukhabarat* and political surveillance. The professoriate multitasks, holding more than one job in a rat race to provide a decent standard of living for their families, one reflective of their professional attainment. Students are often absentees, for the most part showing up only for exams. Despite the huge concentration of human talent and energy, the overall context is not conducive to action. When it occurs, the *mukhabarat*, the campus police, and regime-sponsored associations among faculty and students can disrupt the aspirant disrupters.

University administrations, even down to the level of deans and department chairs, are extensions of dominant parties and do the bidding of the central authorities. Executing the regime's broader political agenda is more important for these leaders than promoting the university itself. We are not likely to see the likes of Ahmad Lutfi al-Sayyid again.

In the authoritarian cage, the professoriate has had Albert Hirschman's (1970) famous three options: exit (migration and exile), loyalty (sycophancy), and voice (protest). Variants of loyalty for those toiling in the system have prevailed. According to Sari Hanafi and Rigas Arvanitis,

Over the last ten years, in every Arab country, scientists and policymakers involved in education and research (very often former scientists themselves) have been trying very hard to transform their research systems. They have tried to do this by creating a space for science inside the political arena and inside their administrations and institutions. They have worked diligently at a very slow pace and have secured, finally, a few small and fragile commitments. Governments usually discovered for themselves that when scientists began working, all sorts of unpredicted benefits appeared. However, many of these Arab governments have not yet taken the political risks entailed by the scientific activity: they discouraged, if not prevented, any intermediary scientific association that might have significant inputs. (2016: 306)

As much as the political fetters on the university, it may well be the constraints on scientific associational life that have stunted it. Travel to conferences requires a lengthy approval process. Scientific papers must be vetted by government authorities. Academic associations do not effectively set standards for and govern and monitor their members' professional lives. International professional associations have weak linkages to the MENA. As autocrats fear their own universities, they also fear linkages among universities, especially those across borders.

Exit from the system has been significant. In the 1980s an estimated half of all Arab scientists with PhDs left the region (Massialas and Jarrar, 1991: 193). Hanafi and Arvanitis (2016: 149) show that the situation has not improved since then. After the repression of 2016, Turkey's professional class began an exodus. A quarter of a million Turks emigrated in 2017, up 42 percent over 2016, when about 180,000 left. They are mainly professionals, journalists, professors, and members of the old secular business class (Gall, 2019).[16]

This brain drain does not reflect the movement within the Arab world of faculty from poorer countries (Egypt, Jordan, Palestine, Morocco, Sudan) seeking multiyear employment in GCC countries to increase their salaries exponentially. Because this movement is between politically controlled entities in both the sending and the receiving country, the political risks may seem minimal.[17]

Most of the drain is in the STEM disciplines, probably because some mastery of English is required to win degrees in those disciplines, which in turn opens doors to teaching and research outside the MENA. Tony Zahlan notes that autocratic regimes are not unhappy with this situation, which they see as exporting trouble (interview, 2013). They will fete and praise their exiled brain power but not try to lure it back. This is in sharp contrast to China, as authoritarian as any Arab state, where the Communist Party is the coordinator of the Thousand Talents program, launched in 2008, to lure back to China the cream of its students abroad. It has succeeded in recruiting on average about 80 percent of the half-million Chinese studying in other countries. The calculus must be that this talent will contribute to strengthening China's economy, to the creation of careers for the educated, and ultimately to enhancing the regime's claims to legitimacy.

Arab leaders seem to see only the dangers and not the pay-off. In one respect, fears of 'scientists' may not be misplaced. Diego Gambetta and Steffen Hertog (2016) found that engineers were disproportionately represented in the ranks of extremist Islamic groups in the MENA. A survey in Tunisia, conducted by the Tunisian students' union, similarly found that around 20 percent of students in STEM disciplines gravitated to extremist organizations.

> "Engineering students are considered strategic targets for terrorist groups, because of these students' knowledge of army weapons and mastery of media, photography and communication," said Ahmed Al-Zawady, leader of the General Union for Tunisian Students. (Abdul Nabi, 2015)

Our concern throughout this study is the crisis fueled by the educated unemployed. They are the victims of a system that was supposed to give them the skills to prosper but has left them adrift (see Chapter 6). Once outside the educational system, they may become politically dangerous. The combination of some education and shattered expectations has driven many to Islamist extremism. Georges Fahmi and Hamza Medded (2015) examine this phenomenon in Tunisia, both before and after the overthrow of Ben Ali in 2011. Tunisia has supplied an astonishingly high number of recruits to jihadi causes, including the Islamic State.

The Social Contract and the Supply of Technocrats, or How to Have It Both Ways

After the relatively brief period of socialist populism, autocratic leaders were content to use the universities to produce bureaucrats and school teachers. They were a critical cog in the production and protection of a professional and entrepreneurial middle class on which the autocrats founded their legitimacy. In this sense education in general was a critical part of the social contract that bound autocratic leaders to their polities. If nothing else, the autocrats would provide the children of their citizens the means to escape. Failing that, there were formal or de facto guarantees that university graduates would be absorbed into the civil service.

The autocrats did not, however, abandon the hope that their systems of higher education could produce quality science and innovations to sustain their countries' development and military strength. Reflecting these aspirations, Nasser's Egypt propagated the phrase "from the needle to the rocket"—that is, all those things an independent, modernizing Egypt could produce on its own (or with a little help from the Soviet Union).

Perhaps borrowing from the experience of France with its *grandes écoles* and Soviet experience with its academies of science (Fox, 2005), Middle Eastern leaders tried to address the quality issue through enclaves of relative excellence, for the most part divorced from universities and completely under the control of the central authorities (on hubs and enclaves, see Chapter 7 on innovation).

As usual Nasser's Egypt set the tone. Early on, the Nasserist regime began to create independent research units, separate from universities and without even the fiction of university autonomy: the Atomic Energy Commission, the Desert Research Institute, the National Research Center, and the National Center for Criminal and Sociological Research, among others (Reid, 1990: 192). To the extent there was cutting-edge research, universities found themselves cut off from it.[18]

Thus, in the sea of mediocre mass production of diplomas, select faculty could find intellectual challenges and advantageous compensation in elite institutes and academies that bore little of the political unpredictability for incumbent elites of the sprawling university system.

It is not likely that the autocrats of the region are familiar with what Robert Barro has called the Lipset/Aristotle thesis, to wit that education leads to or generates democracy. Edward Glaeser and colleagues (2007) adduce some statistical support for this hypothesis based on the average number of years of schooling correlated with polity scores. In their abstract, the authors state:

> In our model, schooling teaches people to interact with others and raises the benefits of civic participation, including voting and organizing. In the battle between democracy and dictatorship, democracy has a wide potential base of support but offers weak incentives to its defenders. Dictatorship provides stronger incentives to a narrower base. As education raises the benefits of civic participation, it raises the support for more democratic regimes relative to dictatorships. This increases the likelihood of democratic revolution against dictatorships and reduces that of successful anti-democratic coups.

It is important to note that they are considering education as a whole, not simply higher education, but the logic of their summary should apply to all levels. It is also important to note that other analysts do not find this linkage in the Arab world (inter alia Daqu, 2017).[19]

Thus, much *is* at stake for the autocrats, but they do not have the option of neglecting education (see Rougier, 2016). At a minimum they need the technocrats that will contribute to economic growth and hence to the expansion of rent-seeking opportunities. They need the cadres to staff the deep state and keep tabs on internal and external enemies. They need the scientists who at least understand the latest developments in ICT and military technology.

The shredding of social contracts as a result of economic crisis has played out over decades (Mossalem, 2015). It has provoked mass protest movements, often led by students, who have the least to lose and a historical reputation to maintain. Every decade has witnessed protests against the erosion of the social contract, including: Morocco in the spring of 1965; Egypt in 1968 and 1977; Iran in 1977–78; Jordan in 1989;[20] Algeria in 1989 and 1990; and Sudan in 1985 and 2019.

The global crisis of 2008, followed by the Arab uprisings of 2011, created new structural crises and a new round of contract-eroding reforms. In 2018 alone, demonstrations racked Jordan, Iran, Morocco, and Tunisia. Egypt has remained quiet despite hyperinflation and the elimination of fuel and other consumer subsidies. Rising prices and unemployment led to major demonstrations in Sudan and Algeria, where the overthrow of Omar al-Bashir and the denial of a fifth term to Abdelaziz Bouteflika were the primary goals of the demonstrations. Predictably, students were at their forefront. Also predictably, getting rid of the head autocrat is not the same as hobbling the 'deep state.'

4

Excellence in Higher Education: Enabler and Enabled

> The essentiality of freedom in the community of American universities is almost self-evident. . . . To impose any strait jacket upon the intellectual leaders in our colleges and universities would imperil the future of our Nation. . . . *Scholarship cannot flourish in an atmosphere of suspicion and distrust.* (US Chief Justice Earl Warren, quoted in Cole, 2009: 345, emphasis added)

Chief Justice Warren's judgment would strike a chord with any academic and probably with the public at large in almost any country. It is intuitively appealing. For those of us fortunate enough to live in or with relatively free and open academic systems in which academic freedom and institutional autonomy are respected, it seemingly affords us the ability to warn those who restrict those freedoms that they can never achieve excellence in education, the creation of knowledge, and the promotion of innovation without loosening their stranglehold on their universities. Unfortunately, such a judgment and admonition would be in error. All depends, of course, on how we define the various terms of the proposition: excellence, autonomy, academic freedom.

How do we define and rank factors of institutional autonomy or degrees of political oversight? How do we assess sources of funding, for example as universities rely less and less on the public purse and more and more on corporate support? Is there a direct linear relationship between degrees of authoritarian control, say from totalitarian (North Korea) to illiberal democratic (Russia or Turkey), and degrees of creativity? Is creativity the right output measure, even if we could operationalize that term? (Patents filed and granted might be the appropriate metric but it says nothing about basic research, which might be measured through Nobel laureates.)

This conundrum needs to be broached before proceeding further because I focus on political systems that are mostly highly autocratic, which view institutional autonomy as a threatening model for all parts of civil society (professional associations, unions, religious organizations, NGOs) and academic freedom often as a fig leaf for treason and subversion.

I enter this discussion with trepidation. It is at the heart of centuries, if not millennia, of debate and analysis of the purposes of education. I am a rank novice in this domain despite having spent most of my adult life in academe. I hope the real experts will cut me some slack. I come at it from a particular vantage point, that of the ability of authoritarian regimes to foster academic excellence of some sort. Are such efforts doomed to failure? Are there certain kinds of excellence that politically closed systems can hope to achieve? Or must we conclude that such systems must change profoundly, in a more liberal or open direction, before high-quality academic performance can be realized? And, as we have asked earlier, is the 'reformer' merely helping the autocrat to perpetuate his or her control, or is the 'reformer' engaged in a cat-and-mouse game where reform may ripple out across the entire political system?

Perhaps unsurprisingly, there is not consensus on the answers to these questions. Jonathan Cole is in one camp, although his focus is on a specific universe, that of the leading US research universities. Although this 'model' is under heavy and persistent attack, it nonetheless vaulted dozens of US universities to the top fifty or hundred in world rankings and became the envy of the rest of the world. I suspect that Cole would find the presence of the NUS—the product of an authoritarian nanny state—in the top twenty as an anomaly.

In fairness to Cole, he does suggest that 'creativity' in academia may be relative, that although other, more repressive systems may not be able to match the creativity of US higher education, they can be creative in some ways. He goes on to say that there have been no empirical studies of the relationship between academic freedom and creativity (2009: 347, confirmed by Salmi, email, 2012). I think that is true. One of the principal data-based empirical studies in fact measured the inverse relationship: the 'causal' link of education levels to the practice of democracy (Glaeser et al., 2007). There is a rich empirical literature on the relationship of education to political participation (Bourguignon and Verdier, 2000; Campante and Chor, 2012).

With the research university as the unit of analysis, we find little mystery in what it takes to be good or great. Cole, in a chapter entitled "Building Steeples of Excellence," summarizes the ingredients as a "relentless talent search, visionary leadership, innovation, great research, excellent students" (2009: 345). For Jamil Salmi (2009), the three critical factors are the best talent (both for faculty and students), adequate funding, and university governance (principally effective decision-making authority regarding selection of faculty and students, design of curriculum, and securing and dispensing funds).

In various ways and with varying emphases there are many who share Warren's and Cole's views. Philip Altbach (2007) focuses on academic freedom. I would argue that academic freedom may be seen as a proxy for a broad range of institutional rights and responsibilities. Altbach posits that universities cannot achieve their potential nor fully contribute to the emerging knowledge-based society without academic freedom.

Charles McPhedran (2013) notes that most of the world's 'elite' educational institutions are located in democratic nations. He cites an interview with Phil Baty of the Times Higher Education ranking organization, who opined, "I do believe on a personal level that . . . you won't see yourself challenging Harvard or Oxford or Cambridge without a very open and free approach to higher education." China, Saudi Arabia, and Singapore would demur.

Various editions of the *Arab Human Development Report* (especially 2005) have pounded away on the same theme. Still, in the near euphoria following the Arab uprisings of 2011, Mohammed Faour and Marwan Muasher summarized the systemic challenge:

> A self-evident but often ignored fact is that democracy will thrive only in a culture that accepts diversity, respects different points of view, regards truths as relative rather than absolute, and tolerates—even encourages—dissent. Without this kind of culture, no sustainable system of checks and balances can evolve over time to redistribute power away from the executive. Nor can a mechanism be developed to check abuses by any state institution. (Faour and Muasher 2011: 1)

Experts in the public policy of higher education, like Salmi, point out that we do not understand the political chemistry of academic output and quality. Indeed, in a study of successful and new research universities that he and Altbach edited (Altbach and Salmi, 2011), relatively little was said about the political context in which these universities operated.

Education: The Enabler

Probably the bulk of the literature on education and democracy focuses on the hypothesized causal relationship between education and democratic practice. That is not my primary concern. Mine is the relationship between democratic practice and educational excellence. But the dominant concern in the literature, running from Aristotle, through John Dewey and up to Seymour Martin Lipset, Amy Gutmann, Derek Bok, and many other contemporary luminaries, is immensely important and so closely related to my concern that I need to review its premises.

There are two major ways in which education leads to or strengthens democracy. The first might be called institutional impact and the second, the weight of an informed citizenry.

Institutional Impact

Amy Gutmann makes the case for institutional impact on the polity as a whole. A "primary purpose" of higher education, she writes, is to provide the environment for "sanctuaries of non-repression." However, she states that the pursuit and creation of knowledge is what members of the academy must undertake, and the institution must nurture this pursuit however distant its impact on citizenship may be (1999: 184).

Gutmann does not deal with the purposes of education in authoritarian systems. Referring to Alexis de Tocqueville, she says that autonomy is necessary as protection against 'democratic tyranny.' Given the weakness of democratic practice in the MENA, we may posit that only Turkey runs the risk of democratic tyranny, especially since the attempted coup d'état of July 2016. Indeed, in Turkey the risk to date is that of the tyranny of the plurality.

Universities, Gutmann continues, should be "communities of critics" who "make it more difficult for public officials, professionals, and ordinary citizens to disregard their own standards when it happens to be convenient" (1999: 188). This applies to autocracies as well as to democracies, but the risks critics run in the former are much greater than in the latter. Universities are not the only such communities: so, too, are (or should be) the media, professional associations, and legislatures. The institutional autonomy of universities is not derived from property rights but from the scholarly right to autonomy. Therefore, it is equally important to public and private institutions (1999: 179).

Academic Freedom[1]

Academic freedom—the right of university faculty and students to adopt and espouse views and opinions without fear of (unreasonable) restriction by university or extra-university authorities—is an integral part of the architecture of university autonomy. It both enables democratic practice, considered here, and may be essential to strengthening the excellence of higher education. We will consider this latter aspect in the second section of this chapter (see pages 141–51).

Academic freedom is relevant mainly to the tertiary education level. Students and faculty in the compulsory years of pre-university education cannot normally expect to enjoy the rights and obligations of academic freedom. For Gutmann, academic freedom is needed not primarily to create knowledge but rather to act as a bulwark against political repression (1999: 174–77). One can infer that the creation of knowledge is not necessarily good (or bad) for democracy, although it is likely to be a public good. The knowledge is most often not appropriated by its inventors nor its institutional home but is brought into the public domain, where its benefits are available to all. Academic freedom is conceived of as both individual and institutional. As such it radiates well beyond the institution's walls to the rest of society.

Altbach (2007), while placing greater emphasis on the role of academic freedom in producing knowledge and innovation, cautions that historically, academic freedom has never been absolute. It is frequently violated even in the most liberal of systems. Continental universities in the nineteenth and early twentieth centuries made socialists ineligible for academic appointments. Although obviously illiberal and autocratic, the Third Reich in Germany directly restricted the teaching content of German universities and fired Jewish, non-conformist, and politically dissident tenured professors. Despite Germany's glorious Humboldtian past, few German voices were raised against these developments. German professors' organizations and student unions supported the Nazi suppression of academic freedom, and the universities themselves often implemented the changes. So, too, during the McCarthy period, and the Cold War era more generally, the US witnessed moves to restrict academic freedom if the views espoused were Marxist or leftist.

Just as lip service is paid to university autonomy in official documents in the Arab world (see Chapter 5), academic freedom is similarly enshrined. Nowhere is it respected. It is mostly international, off-shore professional bodies that protest violations of academic freedom in the region. It is too dangerous for local associations to do so. This situation is generally recognized. As a result of the various pressures faced by teaching personnel, most adopt a policy of self-censorship and refrain from engaging in discussion of issues that may be considered sensitive or controversial by those in power. According to Ramzi Salamé,

"This has led to the reduction of the role of teaching personnel in leading scientific research, in producing knowledge and debating issues that can contribute to the advancement of society and its institutions. Furthermore, it hinders the education of intellectual elites who would possess the critical thinking needed to lead societal progress" (2010: 339).[2]

In its bid to join the EU, Turkey has implemented political reforms to bring it in conformity with European nations in terms of human rights, freedom of expression, abolition of the death penalty, and, of course, free and fair elections. By all these measures Turkey is far ahead of its Arab neighbors, save Lebanon. It is thus disturbing to see the growing violation of these norms in recent years under the AKP government of Recep Tayyip Erdoğan.

In the summer of 2015, after terrorist attacks in southeast Turkey attributed to the outlawed Kurdish Workers' Party (PKK), the Turkish armed forces resumed attacks on alleged PKK strongholds. Over one thousand Turkish intellectuals signed a petition that called on Turkey to end the violence and to resume talks with the PKK. President Erdoğan responded by vilifying the academics and warning that they would pay for their "treachery." Three were subsequently jailed for "making terrorist propaganda" (Bollag, 2016).[3]

Matters deteriorated further after the attempted coup of July 2016, led, it is alleged by the Turkish authorities, by Fethullah Gülen, a Turkish religious leader who was formerly allied to Erdoğan, living in exile in the US. The coup failed, and there followed a massive sweep of all the AKP's adversaries, involving arrests and suspensions from work of tens of thousands of suspects (see Chapter 3). A state of emergency was declared under which academics could be dismissed on grounds of "supporting terrorism." Dismissal on these grounds remains on an individual's official employment record, endangering future employment prospects. They also risk losing university-owned housing and the special passport issued to government employees (Scholars at Risk Network, 2017).[4]

In Egypt, the Muslim Brotherhood had tens of thousands of members and probably millions of sympathizers. It won the presidency and a relative majority in parliament in Egypt's first open elections after the ouster of President Hosni Mubarak in February 2011. President Mohammed Morsi, a senior leader of the Brotherhood, was then driven from power by the Egyptian military in the summer of 2013 in a move that resulted in the deaths of nearly a thousand Egyptians, mostly affiliated to the Brotherhood. The Muslim Brotherhood was outlawed and declared a terrorist organization.[5] As in Turkey, the security services rounded up and jailed thousands of alleged supporters. To be a sympathizer, let alone a member, is to support terrorism, a crime under Egyptian law. How can one prove that one is not a sympathizer? As in Turkey, one risks being guilty until proven innocent, but what proof would be sufficient?

Recall that academic freedom protects the faculty member or the student against *unreasonable* actions by university or extra-university authorities. Are Turkish and Egyptian authorities acting unreasonably in sacking, suspending, or jailing academics who appear to sympathize with terrorists and subversives? Islamic State does operate in Egypt's Sinai Peninsula. There is a Kurdish insurrection of sorts in southeastern Turkey. Tenure and other safeguards will do the academy little good when the political winds are blowing so strongly.

A Democratic Citizenry

According to John Dewey, "Democracy has to be born anew every generation, and education is its midwife" (quoted in Bok, 2017). In addition to providing institutional buttresses to democratic practice, education provides the practitioners themselves. Gutmann (1999) posits that the major purpose of education in democratic polities is to form good citizens who can help maintain the system and improve it. Education is not for the sake of education and the enrichment of the individual, although that may be a by-product. It is to serve democracy, which in turn serves society and its individual members. This proposition is endorsed and analyzed for the Arab world by Cammack et al. (2017), El-Amine (2014), Masri (2017), and Faour and Muasher (2011).

Lending empirical support to the basic proposition, François Bourguignon and Thierry Verdier (2000) show evidence for a statistically significant relationship between years of education and approval, if not practice of democracy. Similarly, Glaeser and colleagues state, "The political success of a democracy hinges on having a large number of supporters whose benefits of political participation are sufficiently high that they fight for it even in the absence of direct rewards. *Education supplies such supporters and stabilizes democracy*" (2007: 79, emphasis added).

Glaeser et al. correlate average years of schooling in the population (running from one to ten years) against the polity democracy score and find a strong correlation suggesting causality (2007: 81).[6] Alberto Chong and Mark Gradstein (2015) likewise find robust correlations between years of schooling and preferences for democracy (as measured by the World

Values Survey). These correlations hold whether or not the respondent is from a democratic or nondemocratic system.

The 2016 *Arab Human Development Report* finds, in ten Arab countries, a correlation between years of schooling and civic engagement (civic engagement is obviously different from democratic practices and preferences, but at least kindred). The World Values Survey of 2015 revealed that those with tertiary education, worldwide, are more likely to stress the importance of living in a democracy than those with only primary education. For the Arab world a majority of respondents at all levels agreed with the proposition, but the levels agreeing in specific countries varied widely. The overall levels of positive response were not significantly different from those of the US.

Why would education contribute to a preference for democracy or to democratic practice itself? Education teaches interactive skills and heightens the influence of participants on non-participants. Education thus reduces the costs of political participation for its beneficiaries. The authors have to net out from their sample of countries strong authoritarian regimes that compel participation of certain kinds (party or syndicate membership), giving a false image of participation rates.

In a similar economistic vein, Filipe Campante and David Chor (2012) seek an explanation for the Arab uprisings of 2011 by correlating rising levels of education, declining job prospects for the educated, and the resort to political protest (protest is their dependent variable, whereas for Glaeser et al. it is levels of political participation). Campante and Chor find that the rate of return to education (RORE) in the Arab world is relatively low and declining (see Chapter 6). As a result, the opportunity cost of engaging in political protest is low; that is, educated Arabs have little to lose in engaging in protest. So, Campante and Chor add the dependent variable of (inadequate) employment opportunities to that of the reduced costs of participation to propose a dynamic producing political protest.

The Arab Barometer and other surveys of Arab youth present ambiguous evidence for the basic propositions above. UNDP and AFESD (2016), in its Table 1.1, shows that Arab youth are most concerned by employment and the economy (more than 80 percent), and then corruption (more than 15 percent). Democracy was way behind at 2–3 percent of respondents. The frustrations of the job market coupled with the corruption and unresponsiveness of the autocratic regime would seem to support the proposition that the educated unemployed are willing to challenge their masters but not the proposition that education sharpens their appetite for democracy.[7]

Table 4.1. People with Higher Education in the MENA Hold Stronger Beliefs about the Importance of Democracy. Percentages measure proportions by level of education of those who find democracy important.

Country	Primary Education (%)	Tertiary Education (%)
Algeria	54	64
Egypt	63	81
Iraq	47	52
Jordan	52	64
Lebanon	49	54
Libya	66	65
Morocco	61	74
Tunisia	64	72
Turkey	58	61
West Bank	45	58
Yemen	60	79
Singapore	17	33
USA	58	71

Source: Derived from World Bank (2017), Figure 1.3.

'Amir Mahdi Daqu (2017) bases his analysis on Arab Barometer data for ten Arab countries. He finds no significant correlation between university education and the demand for democratic institutions and practices. Only Jordan and Palestine in his sample support the relationship. Daqu suggests that Arab higher education in its content is authoritarian and hostile to democracy, hence the result. He notes that, overall, the Arab Spring produced regression and deepened authoritarianism and "fascism" (2017: 354). Kathrin Thomas (2018), also using Arab Barometer data (Wave IV), finds tepid and declining voting, civic association membership, and political party membership. She, too, sees the declining quality of Arab political life as the cause.

It appears that inculcating civic values is most effective at the pre-university levels when it is made part of the compulsory K–12 curricula, but that assumption is questioned by Gutmann (1999) and rejected by El-Amine (2014), who argue for a major university role in educating citizens. Derek Bok (2017) points out that there is always a risk of indoctrination in civics education and that the leadership of many US universities find it inappropriate at the tertiary level.

Perhaps what we could agree on is that outside the formal university curriculum, there are important learning experiences at the university level that can shape future citizens. The university's procedures for student evaluation and faculty recruitment and promotion should be reasonably transparent and based on measurable performance. Rewarding merit can be seen as essential to citizenship. University and student government should be 'democratic' within the constraints imposed by funding sources (often the government) and the board of trustees. Student government should be an opportunity to engage in democratic practice and in the shared governance of the university. Increasingly, Western universities are encouraging or obliging students to engage in community service projects and programs to enhance awareness of major challenges facing society as a whole. Perhaps most important is the general context of learning, which should encourage a consistent questioning of received wisdom and an analytic approach to understanding, both of which contribute to critical thinking. These kinds of experience, more than formal civics instruction, may shape future citizens and are less laden with indoctrination than civics classes (in general see Zakaria, 2015).[8]

The autocracies of the MENA at some point in their past have invoked a kind of meta mission to fulfill God's will, overthrow imperial hegemony, or establish revolutionary social justice. Some regimes, such as the Islamic Republic of Iran, invoke all three. With time the meta mission erodes. What is surprising in the MENA is the limited extent to which the educational system was ever mobilized to indoctrinate young citizens in the regimes' professed ideals. The *mukhabarat* was more present on university campuses than party *apparatchiki*. Even when Egypt's socialist ideology was most vaunted and its ASU set itself up as a vanguard organization, universities were spared formal indoctrination. This was also the case in Algeria in the three years after independence in 1962 and up to the military coup of 1965, when most productive assets in the country, including agricultural land, were brought under state control. Algeria's Front for National Liberation spearheaded the country's socialist transformation in those years, drawing heavily on Yugoslav experience and expertise. The military after 1965, led by Houari Boumedienne, throttled the socialist fervor. The Ba'th Party in both Syria and Iraq adhered to the Egyptian model of heavy-handed security control of campuses with only token efforts to create revolutionary citizens.

It is said that after Libya's leader Muammar Qadhafi issued his *Green Book* in 1975, Libyan schoolchildren were obliged to study it two hours a week. The book covered Libya's socialism, direct rule by the masses (*jamahiriya*), the failings of Western democracy, and Libya's revolutionary role in international politics. How seriously it was ever taken inside Libya is a matter of pure conjecture.

The defeat suffered by Egypt, Jordan, and Syria in June 1967 during their brief war with Israel brought an end to the militant phase of Arab socialism and secularism. The trappings were kept, especially in Syria, Iraq, and Algeria, but the spirit flagged. Moreover, the defeat, and the need to rebuild Arab military forces, opened the door to the religious and financial weight and influence of Saudi Arabia and the propagation of Wahhabi religious doctrine on a broad scale. Egyptian President Sadat, who succeeded Nasser in 1970, touted his religiosity, while Saddam Hussein, in his eight-year war with Iran employed religious symbolism to rally his troops.[9] In general, regimes with religious agendas have engaged in indoctrination through education more than the socialist secularists (on Egypt, see Cook, 2000). It is also the case that faculties of religious studies have more relaxed admission standards than, say, engineering, economics, or medicine, and they are more accessible to students who are comfortable only in Arabic. The same may be said for the faculty who teach in them. In short, many monolingual young Middle Easterners are exposed to Islamic indoctrination.

The universities of Saudi Arabia include compulsory religious instruction. The revolution in Iran in 1979, establishing a republic in the debris of the shah's 'empire,' drove the House of Saud to grant even more control over all phases of education to the Wahhabi *ulama*. This in order to deflect scrutiny from the drift of parts of the sprawling Saudi royal family from the tenets of their religion and its special relationship with the US.

In an empirical analysis of civics education in the Arab world, Mohammed Faour (2012) compares the civics content of schoolbooks in Egypt and Tunisia shortly after the Arab uprisings. At the time, the Islamist Ennahda Party was in control of Tunisia while the Freedom and Justice Party, which is close to the Muslim Brotherhood, was in power in Egypt. Despite this, Faour found that Tunisia's civics education was much more 'universalist,' emphasizing, for example, religious tolerance, than was Egypt's, where fashioning the Muslim citizen was more the goal.

The Islamic Republic of Iran was founded in revolution and war. In April 1980 Iran launched a cultural revolution and simultaneously shuttered its universities for four years.

During that time, the Council for Cultural Revolution was charged with drawing up new curricula. A prime instrument of control and the object of the new 'civics' were the Basij (Volunteers), the foot soldiers of the revolution (see Golkar, 2015: 137–54). The mission of the Basij was and is defense of the revolution. One of its most famous members is Mahmoud Ahmedinejad, formerly a university professor, who went on to be elected Iran's president twice, in 2004 and 2009. As noted in the previous chapter, there are probably five million Basij members. They all go through fairly intensive religious training. Their numbers are greater than the four million university students. Around 900,000 are themselves university students, and some 20,000 professors are also from the Basij. Being a Basij member helps with academic promotions.

In the early years of the Turkish republic, when Atatürk was president, the K–12 education system was a prime instrument in building the new Turkish citizen to support the republic and its secular values. A half-century later, as Erdoğan and the AKP consolidated their power, an Islamist set of values was imparted in sectors of the K–12 system. There has been a huge expansion in Imam Hatip schools, first encouraged after the 1980 coup and designed to train mosque preachers, such that enrollments have risen from 60,000 in 2002 to 1.1 million today (*The Economist*, 2017). Subjects perceived as antithetical to Islamic values, such as the theory of evolution (see pages 150–51), are no longer taught in public schools at the pre-university level.[10]

Despite the relative absence of indoctrination in Arab higher education, there is a more subtle and widespread process of shaping attitudes and fundamental political understandings that is embedded in the style and content of the pedagogy and the methods of university authorities. It is this conditioning that Daqu (2017) believes is the cause of the apparent divorce of education from a desire for more democratic institutions.

Citizenship or Education as a Public Good

Human capital, embodied in one's people, is the most fundamental part of the wealth of nations. Other inputs, such as natural resources and financial capital, can be acquired at world prices in global markets, but the efficiency of one's labor force rarely can be. Not only does more education make the labor force more efficient, it makes people better able to embrace all kinds of change including the introduction of new technologies. And for some extraordinary individuals, more education enables them to create new technologies. (Goldin and Katz, 2009: 41)

There is no universal right to education at the tertiary level. We look in more detail at GERs in Chapter 1, but it is common for half or more of those in eligible age cohorts (usually eighteen to twenty-two) *not* to be enrolled. This would seem to pose a huge equity issue for the polity that funds public tertiary education. How can the general taxpayer be asked to pay for the education of a fraction of the eligible citizenry? What benefit does the taxpayer whose children do not go to university derive from those who do? Tertiary education must be regarded as a public good, the benefits of which are available to all citizens and all taxpayers. In this sense, too, education must be seen as an enabler. Thomas Melonio and Mihoub Mezouaghi (2015: 114–15) review the economic literature on the impact of education on productivity and growth (as does Anomaly, 2018), while Claudia Goldin and Lawrence Katz (2009) advance a powerful argument for the near-universal spread of secondary education in the US after 1910 as the major causal variable in the economic dominance of the US in the following century. Taher Abdessalam (2010), writing on the financing of higher education in Tunisia, sees public funding as an implicit loan from the parents' generation to their children's generation, who will pay back the debt through their own taxes. However, he notes that with 19 percent unemployment (in Tunisia) among the children's generation, the theoretic payment of debt does not hold up.

Tertiary education may produce citizens with two characteristics. First, building on values and skills learned in compulsory education, the university educates young adults who can contribute to the smooth functioning of the political system. Ideally that system would be democratic, but, as I suggest above, a functioning autocratic system is better for citizens' welfare than one that is dysfunctional. Think of Singapore as opposed to Venezuela (as I write in 2019).

Second, the university produces economic actors who possess the skills to make the economy function more or less smoothly, thereby ensuring a level of economic activity that can generate the taxes to pay for public services, including education itself. The most gifted actors will be innovators who can transform economic life. The challenge is to keep them within the system. Everyone benefits, at least in theory, so the equity issue is resolved.

The Autocrat's Dilemma

Our discussion of the impact of education on democratic practice through institutional autonomy, academic freedom, and the inculcation of civic responsibility raises a difficult question. If one may assume that incumbent autocrats would welcome neither product of education—for example, neither the transition to greater democracy (Glaeser et al., 2007; Gutmann, 1999) nor the greater incidence of political protest (Campante and Chor, 2012)—why then do autocrats invest in education if they know it will undermine them?

Suspending for the moment the hypothesis that higher levels of education correlate with increasing political apathy, Bourguignon and Verdier devote much of their essay to precisely this question. Assuming that political participation depends on the educational level of economic agents, which is itself under the strict control of an oligarchy, they imagine three pathways for the oligarchs: first, choke off democracy by denying mass education; second, educate a middle class that can help the oligarchs make money and control rents, and third, educate broadly and concede a transition to democracy (2000: 387).

"The driving mechanism of the whole model" is that the oligarchy will promote some education among the nonoligarchs to spur growth (2000: 291). It seems that, for Bourguignon and Verdier, the assumption is that the oligarchy is solely concerned with maximizing wealth, which can be done through the private returns accruing to educating the offspring of oligarchs and through the public good of an expanding middle class.

The more skewed the initial wealth distribution, the more reluctant the oligarchs will be to expand education. In so claiming, Bourguignon and Verdier raise a chicken-and-egg problem: how or why would some polities be more egalitarian than others?

Their model is complex, involving two time periods and varying sizes of the poor, the middle class, and the oligarchs. If I read the analysis correctly, the oligarchs seek growing wealth for themselves and an unchallenged grip on political power. They understand that using education to broaden the middle class can stimulate growth and hence their incomes but also strengthen currents seeking greater democracy. Misjudging equilibria between their two goals could lead to their overthrow (Diwan et al., 2019, explore this in their treatment of Middle Eastern cronyism). They may attempt to solve the puzzle by conceding more education but also rigging democratic processes. That in fact seems to be the most common solution.

Glaeser and colleagues (2007) attempt an answer but it is not fully convincing. Autocrats, they suggest, may prefer democracy to being overthrown by another autocrat. They need educated cadres to promote growth and hence the field for rent-seeking. They need the rents to maintain their cronies. When autocrats have to choose between growth and survival, they opt for growth, which in turn enables democratic transitions.

I, too, do not have a good solution to this puzzle, but here goes. First, autocrats think of themselves as somehow unique, impervious to the forces that bring down their peers. The others simply are not as smart as they are. Bashar al-Assad of Syria said as much after the 2011 uprisings in Egypt, Tunisia, Libya, and Yemen. His regime, he insisted, was close to the people, unbeholden to the US empire, and therefore not at risk. Second, autocrats have no choice. In the twentieth and twenty-first centuries, it is inconceivable that a leader would deny his people education (see Goldin and Katz, 2009: 17). It is at the heart of the social contract (or authoritarian bargain) that they have struck with their people. Moreover, countries that lag in educational indicators suffer international opprobrium. Finally, they think they can get away with high levels of education.

Figure 4.1 shows that autocracies such as Libya, Tunisia, and Saudi Arabia extend education to citizens at the same rate as more liberal systems such as Lebanon and Kuwait. Egypt, Syria, Iraq, Algeria, Sudan, and Morocco may show autocracies reluctant to extend education to their citizens, but for some time Algeria, Morocco, and Sudan have expanded tertiary education significantly, while Syria and for a time Iraq sank into civil war. There is little evidence here that the region's most determined autocrats fear education.

Reading backward from the evidence, I surmise that autocrats know they need strategic, educated technocrats for the 'deep state,' propagandists, military leaders, and enough simple civil servants, nurses, and schoolteachers to keep the system turning over. They are only beginning to see the private sector as something that needs a robust source of human talent. The rest of the newly educated can leave altogether and seek their fortune elsewhere. It is difficult to study the impact on the system of people who are no longer in it, but surely in the Arab world (and Iran) it is immense.

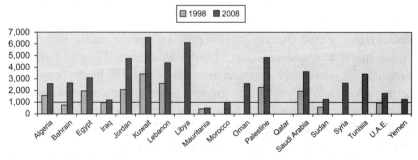

Figure 4.1. Number of Tertiary Students per 100,000 Citizens, Arab World
Source: UNESCO (2009: 9)

The basic hypothesis that the more education there is, the more likely is a rise in civil activism and a demand for democracy has itself been questioned by some. An inconvenient fact, noted by Ishac Diwan (2012b), is that over the decade prior to the uprisings, as university enrollments grew exponentially, the Arab world became less democratic and more repressive—its exceptionalism was intensified. GERs are not the same as average years of schooling, the base measure used by Glaeser et al. (2007), but there is no obvious reason that rising GERs would be associated with *declining* levels of democratic practice. In a 2017 article, he identifies an "emancipation gap":

> The average Arab has a lower preference for democracy (with a gap of 11%), is less active civically (a gap of 8%), respects authority more (by 11%), values the patriarchal system more (by a whopping 30%) and is more religiously conservative (by 18%). . . . Instead of university education allowing Arab youth to catch up with their global counterparts, it actually increases the distance in their values. (2017)

The culprit, according to Diwan, is not culture, nor a selection bias toward educating the already conservative, but rather using education as a tool of indoctrination. The measured views demonstrated in the World Values Survey are the result of deliberate policy.

Education is thus not only the midwife of democracy but also of autocracy. It can foster engrained respect for authority, uncritical acceptance of orthodoxy, and a compliant citizenry. In another essay, Ishac Diwan and Irina Vartanova (2018) provide empirical evidence based on a worldwide sample of countries in the World Values Survey that education effectively and lastingly indoctrinates students. They are able to identify respondents who were educated under autocracies but came to live in democracies, whose attitudes were significantly more authoritarian than counterparts who had experienced only democracy. They add another variable: the contested claim that democracies tend to be more equal in terms of wealth than autocracies, giving well-off citizens of autocracies an *interest* (rather than just an attitude) to support the autocratic order. The authors see these two facts as an answer to Bourguignon and Verdier's question, why do autocrats educate their citizens?

All these are plausible explanations for why autocrats play with educational fire, but I submit that the evidence for indoctrination over the last decades in the MENA is weak, even in highly ideological systems like Iran's (see pages 135–36). Rather, the widespread repression of anything resembling civic mobilization among students or faculty may in itself weaken the links between education and political action.

Education: The Enabled

> Other factors such as the rule of law, the level of democracy, the existence of a national vision for the future of tertiary education, articulation mechanisms, and location are certainly significant. *Yet the jury is still out regarding the ability to determine, in a conclusive way, whether research institutions can excel without these supporting dimensions or whether these factors represent significant elements of vulnerability over the long term.* (Salmi, 2011: 338, emphasis added)

What can we expect of policymakers in autocracies in terms of creating an enabling environment for educational and research excellence? Are maximum freedom of thought, expression, and debate prerequisites for high-quality intellectual life, innovation, and high-quality education? If Earl Warren's encomium at the beginning of this chapter regarding unfettered enquiry and thought is correct, then we shouldn't bother to interact with the autocrats. There will be no pay-off in enhanced excellence in higher education.

The evidence, however, would suggest that Warren's ideals are neither sufficient nor necessary. High-quality research, innovation, development, and advanced education can be combined with autocracy, repression, research redlines, violation of academic freedom, and in general the subordination of higher education to systemic political objectives.[11]

What is the mission assigned to higher education by its political masters? Is success in higher education not also measured through the training of a skilled workforce? Is it not measured through the education of responsible citizens? Are authoritarians less successful in these latter tasks than more democratic systems?

We have to conceive of the trade-offs as lying along a continuum. Even the most authoritarian and interfering regimes can nurture pockets of creativity—a theme we explore below. By the same token, democracies can foster widespread educational mediocrity (India is a notable case in point). What can be said is that maximizing intellectual and institutional freedom enhances educational excellence and perhaps accelerates the process of creativity and innovation.

This fact is well understood by the academy in the MENA and is summarized by a group of Lebanese scholars regarding their country's enabling environment:

> *The kind of open and liberal mindset that defines us as individuals and as a cohesive group we owe to years of osmotic interaction in Lebanon's fine educational venues as well as through a thousand other occasions for shared experiences and the exchange of uplifting influences within the country's rich civil society.* (*Daily Star*, 2014, emphasis added)

The history of the Soviet Union, Nazi Germany, and the People's Republic of China should tell us a lot about what it takes to produce educational excellence and good science. There is no doubt that all three systems have been able to nurture excellence in strategic areas, determined by the state and party. They have educated and indoctrinated students who became the citizens and economic actors needed by the system. In areas related to strategic strength, from heavy industry to advanced military technology, all three systems, generally qualified as totalitarian, were able to achieve world-class results. These achievements came despite political purges of Jews or anyone suspected of hostility toward the 'revolution' and the incorporation into political orthodoxy of theories of racial superiority.

Autocratic or totalitarian regimes maximize unpredictability at both the individual and the institutional level. That can hardly be good for intellectual life. We have already noted that the Islamic Republic of Iran closed universities after it came to power and launched a 'cultural revolution' thoroughly at odds with all the traditions and habits developed at Iranian universities under the shah. China acted similarly shortly after the communists seized power in 1949. In 1951–52, according to Douglas Stiffler (2005), forty-nine old institutions were closed and faculties were redistributed and amalgamated regionally. New, comprehensive universities and specialized institutes were created. In 1956, the infamous "let a hundred flowers bloom" campaign began, followed by purges and repression. Even before this, an exodus of academic talent to Taiwan had begun. It is a wonder in both China and Iran that any academic life survived the initial years of revolution, purges, and war, but survive it did.

Academic freedom is a relative concept. In Nazi Germany it was reserved, to the extent it existed at all, for true Germans: "We will continue to stand firmly for the freedom of conviction provided it arises from German nature" (Grüttner, 2005a: 83). One could imagine similar constraints being put forward in Iran or Turkey. Perhaps prior reputation and renown could protect an individual academic. Russia's Ivan Pavlov, who built the theory of conditioned response, was an open critic of the Soviet system until his death in 1936. His eccentricities were tolerated perhaps because he had won a Nobel (physiology) in 1904. Conceivably, Egypt's Ahmed Zewail, who received a Nobel for chemistry in 1999, would have been similarly tolerated had he criticized the regime of Hosni Mubarak, but he chose not to. The difference between Pavlov and Zewail that we should note is that Pavlov registered his achievements within the authoritarian constraints of tsarist Russia and the totalitarian constraints of the Soviet Union.[12] Zewail developed and matured largely at Caltech.

These nondemocratic systems are capable of corrective actions when evidence mounts that they are not meeting strategic goals. John Grüttner (2005a: 75–111), writing on Nazi Germany, reminds us that by 1943 the senior Nazi leadership, including Joseph Goebbels, realized German science was lagging and that good German character was no substitute for good science. That realization may have come too late to save the Nazi experiment, but the evidence was at least assessed.

Enclaves

Perhaps the most widespread form of adaptation was and is the creation of academic and research enclaves. Under Middle Eastern autocracies most tertiary education is devoted to producing the skills needed to run the economy, the civil service, and the military-intelligence apparatus. It is mainly undergraduate education. Research is not an essential element in this undertaking. The Humboldtian ideal of wedding research to instruction is not observed.

In the totalitarian systems mentioned above, high-quality research was carried out in state-sponsored academies of science and specialized research centers. That model was partially adopted in the MENA above all when the Soviet Union played a significant role in supporting the institutional development of the socialist experiments in the Arab world. This meant that advanced research was carried out in state-sponsored and state-supervised institutes, academies, and centers that did not have organic relations with universities despite recruiting their experts from them. Nor did they have organic links to the private sector, which, until the structural crises of the 1970s and 1980s, did not enjoy much standing in several Arab countries. This double isolation of the enclaves was ideal from a political control point of view, as it precluded the development of civil society webs across and between universities, the private sector, and innovative research.[13]

In the past few decades, however, the isolation of the enclaves has been breaking down. The pressures of neoliberal reforms and energizing economies to raise demand for job-seekers and thereby reduce unemployment has become part of the survival strategy of several MENA regimes (see Chapter 6). It is important to note that some universities have themselves become enclaves of excellence.[14]

I describe below a few examples of such enclaves in the MENA. Some are of long date; others recent initiatives. A lot is happening. The question is whether or not the regimes can control the experiments.

In 1966 Ayramehr University of Technology was founded in Tehran under the auspices of the shah of Iran, Mohammed Reza Pahlavi. It was inspired by and linked to MIT. It is now over fifty years old, all of them passed in an authoritarian context. When the Islamic Republic of Iran was founded in 1979, it was renamed Sharif University of Technology (SUT) to honor a student 'martyred' in 1975. Its student mix is atypical for most Middle Eastern universities: about 6,000 undergraduates and 4,000 graduate students. That heavy weighting of graduate students is rare. As for the undergraduates, they are very rigorously selected. Undergraduate admission to SUT is limited to the top 800 of the 500,000 students who pass the national entrance examination *(konkur)*.

Despite the turbulence and hardship that has characterized the Islamic Republic, SUT has maintained high standards and international ranking, as high as number five among MENA universities and in the top hundred worldwide of universities founded in the last fifty years. Recently it was ranked thirty-eighth in the world for citations per faculty.

Ali Akbar Salehi, MIT PhD in nuclear physics, was chancellor in 1982–85 and 1989–93, ran Iran's Atomic Energy Organization, and was also Iran's minister of foreign affairs. SUT has had many famous graduates, none more so than Maryam Mirzakhani, winner of the Fields Medal in mathematics.[15] She received her BSc at SUT in 1999, went on to teach at Princeton and Stanford, and sadly died of cancer in 2017 at the age of forty.

After 2002, when international sanctions were applied against Iran, the pursuit of advanced scientific research in support of Iran's strategic goals did not end. For example, the country invested $300 million in the Iranian Light Source Facility (synchrotron) as a source for "brilliant x-ray light" (Stone, 2015).

It is no surprise that many of the high-quality enclaves in the MENA are located in the resource-rich countries of the GCC. One member of the GCC, Kuwait, is a quasi-democracy, while the rest are run by monarchs, a sultan, or emirs. Their political survival is based on two strategies. The first is a very generous social contract that encompasses the native population but not the huge expatriate workforce that dwarfs the native workforce. The second is to make themselves useful to the most powerful members of the OECD, who can, in turn, protect them from local powers, such as Iran or Iraq.

The UAE and Qatar have entered into collaborative arrangements with Western institutions of higher learning to establish high-quality universities and institutes. A few, like the United Arab Emirates University in al-Ain, Abu Dhabi, cater mainly to native Emirati students. That is also the case with all Saudi Arabian universities. Others, however, have mainly non-Emirati student bodies, such as the American University of Sharjah or NYU Abu Dhabi.

One of the best of these institutions is the Masdar Institute in Abu Dhabi. It was launched in 2007 in collaboration with MIT as a graduate school (MSc and PhD) in engineering, more specifically energy and alternative energy. Over a third of its students are Emirati. It interacts with the international private sector in R&D, has an incubator function, and raises funding for research. Its faculty have filed for several patents. It merged in 2016 with the Khalifa University of Science, Technology, and Research (KUSTAR) and the Abu Dhabi Petroleum Institute. By 2019, the Times Higher Education organization ranked it third in the Arab world.

In 2009 Saudi Arabia opened the KAUST, literally in a desert enclave (or gated city) some distance from Jeddah. Nearly all of Saudi Arabia's normal rules of gender segregation are suspended at KAUST. Like Masdar it is a graduate studies institution with a broad range of specializations and foci. Its faculty are given generous start-up research funding, and KAUST itself has a multi-billion (some allege $20 billion) dollar endowment.[16] Its presidents have included Choon Fong Shih, former president of the NUS, and Jean-Lou Chameau, former president of Caltech. The giant Saudi parastatal, Saudi Aramco, has managed the project since its inception and sometimes supplies its senior leadership.

While it helps to be rich, it is not a prerequisite, as Egypt demonstrates. Enclaves, we have argued, are often established to promote a country's strategic goals. This was the case of the Geological Survey of Egypt, which saw a period of growth and dynamism over the period 1954–76, under Rushdi Said's leadership. He remembered the period in his memoirs with nostalgia (Said, 2000; Reynolds, 2013; Chapter 2). The 'revolution' had a pragmatic reason to encourage the survey: uncovering exploitable mineral deposits to support Egypt's industrialization. The survey led to great advances in geophysical and geochemical surveying as well drilling and mining techniques. Said managed to enlist UNESCO in sharing carbon-dating technology with the survey. Throughout this period Said remained a professor of geology at Cairo University.

The late chemistry Nobel laureate Ahmed Zewail spent most of his career at Caltech. Egypt naturally celebrated his Nobel, and he and the entourage of President Hosni Mubarak began to discuss launching a cutting-edge research facility and technopol that came to be called the Zewail City of Science and Technology. It has had a tangled history, marked by the ouster of Mubarak in 2011 and the death of Zewail himself in 2016. Its set-up costs have been estimated at $2 billion.[17]

According to Robert Service (2016),

> A key element of Zewail's vision was difficult for Egypt's autocratic leader to swallow, however. At most of the country's research institutions the federal government holds sway over university faculty hiring decisions and research funds. But Zewail wanted to promote an independent, merit-based scientific culture in Egypt. He insisted that the university be run by an independent board of trustees with complete authority over hiring and admission decisions. (Service 2016: 632)

Mubarak balked at these conditions, but apparently his eventual successor, al-Sisi, was more accommodating. In the meantime Zewail City became embroiled in a land dispute with a new academic institution called Nile University, which was launched in 2006 by Egyptian Prime Minister Ahmad Nazif (see Lawler, 2011; Iskandar, 2014). The dispute was settled by dividing up property and facilities between Zewail City and Nile University.

A unique enclave has been established in Jordan. It is a joint research facility called Sesame (the Synchrotron-light for Experimental Science and Applications in the Middle East), supported by Middle East countries including Egypt, Jordan, Turkey, Iran, Israel, and Palestine. It is not only meant to promote scientific excellence but also peace and understanding. Sesame is modeled on the European Organization for Nuclear Research (CERN), which was developed after the Second World War to enable science that individual members could not afford and improve the relations of former adversaries that had been at war.

To date the value of investments and contributions to Sesame have exceeded $90 million. Iran, Israel, Jordan, Turkey, and the EU has each contributed $5 million. Sesame opened in 2017 (Abe, 2012; Overbye, 2017; Fox, 2019).

Virtually all countries in the MENA are experimenting with academic and research enclaves. They are attractive to political leaders because they help advance strategic objectives without sacrificing control, and they are attractive to academics because they provide research support, a partial suspension of the political rules and red lines, and legitimate contacts with valued scientific communities abroad.

The Nuclear Option

It is hard to imagine a field of inquiry anywhere more fraught than that of the civilian and military uses of nuclear energy. The line between civilian and military use is blurry, and to maintain it requires invasive reporting and inspection regimes. If specific states are determined to cross the line they must be prepared to play the most high-stakes international politics imaginable. My question here is, can autocracies foster the scientific and managerial capacities to sustain significant nuclear programs? I rely on the important studies of Jacques Hymans (2012a; 2012b) to explore this question.

First, we may speculate that top scientists are drawn to this field precisely because it is of supreme national importance. The nuclear scientist can serve his or her nation in a critically important way. Understanding this helps put in perspective issues of academic freedom and unfettered thought. They pale in significance against the risks involved in the field.

Being a nuclear scientist in the MENA can be a matter of life and death. Israel is widely suspected of having assassinated its rivals' nuclear experts and has jailed at least one of its own on charges of espionage (Mordechai Vanunu). One of Egypt's most brilliant nuclear scientists, Ali Moustafa Mosharafa, died mysteriously in 1950 at age fifty-two, and was followed by Jameera Moussa, dean of Cairo University's Faculty of Science, at age thirty-five. Between 2010 and 2012 four of Iran's leading nuclear scientists were killed (two had connections to the Sesame project, mentioned above) and a fifth severely injured, allegedly by Israeli operatives.

Hymans (2012b) is quite clear in his overall assessment of autocratic science: it has a high risk of failure and is characterized by long development cycles. Even with outside assistance, as has been provided by Pakistan and North Korea, it is hard to internalize the science and manage its applications. Libya, which benefited from A.Q. Khan's (Pakistan) toolkit, is a case in point.

Autocrats often have love/hate relations with their leading scientists. Grüttner (2005a) asserts that Hitler held his scientists in contempt. Despite Sassoon's claim (2012: 78) that Saddam Hussein was in awe of scientists, Hussein jailed one of Iraq's leading nuclear scientists, Dhulfiqar Dhia, only to release him after Israel bombed the Iraqi nuclear facility, Osirak 1, in 1981. That attack, according to Hymans (2012a: 118), led Saddam Hussein to grant the Iraqi Atomic Energy Commission the autonomy that is crucial to nurturing professionalism and innovation. But, typical of autocrats, Saddam soon took away what he had grudgingly granted, placing his cousin, Hussein Kamil Hassan al-Majid, in charge of the commission. By the time of the Kuwait invasion in 1990 the weapons program was moribund.

Hymans looks at every significant effort to develop nuclear weapons capacity worldwide. Contrary to what proliferation experts had predicted, the time to weaponization has been increasing. It took France six years and North Korea twenty-nine to weaponize (2012a: 4). More recent aspirants have consistently underestimated the managerial challenges, rather than the scientific hurdles. The Manhattan Project in the US employed 130,000 people. The Iraqi Atomic Energy Commission built up to seven thousand employees (2012a: 23).[18] More than underperforming scientific communities, it is underestimating managerial challenges that has thwarted progress in nuclear development. As in other scientific sectors, autocracy may slow but does not preclude significant progress.

Disciplinary Bias?

Do autocrats fear some disciplines more than others? Specifically, is a scholar safer in the confines of the STEM disciplines than in the social sciences (including economics) and the humanities? The STEM disciplines are seen as directly relevant to national strategies and security. They are also not as obviously threatening to the autocrat as are academics in the social sciences, economics, history, and philosophy. The heart of these 'soft' disciplines goes directly to the study of power, equity, and citizens' well-being. As a result, STEM scientists may be able to cut deals with autocrats that social scientists cannot. It is hard to imagine a philosopher or sociologist having the prominence in Pakistan of A.Q. Khan, who for many years ran the country's nuclear program.

According to Hazim Kandil (2014: 34–42), Egypt's Muslim Brotherhood appears to distinguish between the natural sciences (dealing in facts not argumentation) and the social sciences (dangerously speculative and argumentative), tolerating the former and condemning the latter. Similarly, in Iran, Mahmoud Ahmedinejad and most of the conservative clergy in the legislative assembly have assaulted social science departments in Iranian universities. Kandil asserts that 'critical thinking,' questioning received wisdom (read party orthodoxy), earned one a ticket out of the Brotherhood. By contrast, STEM disciplines seem to offer irrefutable truths not open to question and debate. It is no coincidence, he notes, that Mohammed Morsi and Mahmoud Ahmedinejad, both elected president of their countries, were engineers with university backgrounds.

Cole (2009: 337) notes the distinction between disciplinary types but argues that healthy academic life is organic. One cannot attack one part without damaging the whole, precisely because the STEM disciplines lead to practical applications with enormous impact on life and well-being. It may be the scientists in those disciplines who engage most directly with the moral issues they pose. The Pugwash Conferences on Science and World Affairs and the Union of Concerned Scientists have engaged nuclear scientists in the quest for nuclear disarmament and arms control. It is scientists who shape the debate on the environment, genetically modified organisms, cloning, hacking and cyber crime, and so forth. In the final analysis, STEM scientists may be more dangerous than academics in the humanities.

The People's Republic of China has laid down no-go areas for academic enquiry. In November 2017 China's Communist Party issued communiqué no. 9, which contained seven points that it termed problematic as subjects for investigation by academics or to be covered in teaching:

1. Promoting Western Constitutional Democracy: An attempt to undermine the current leadership and the socialism with Chinese characteristics system of governance. (Including *the separation of powers, the multi-party system, general elections, and independent judiciaries.*)
2. Promoting 'universal values' in an attempt to weaken the theoretical foundations of the Party's leadership. (That *"the West's values are the prevailing norm for all human civilization,"* that *"only when China accepts Western values will it have a future."*)

3. Promoting civil society in an attempt to dismantle the ruling party's social foundation. (That is, that *individual rights are paramount and ought to be immune to obstruction by the state.*)
4. Promoting Neoliberalism, attempting to change China's Basic Economic System. (That is, *unrestrained economic liberalization, complete privatization, and total marketization.*)
5. Promoting the West's idea of journalism, challenging China's principle that the media and publishing system should be subject to Party discipline.
6. Promoting historical nihilism, trying to undermine the history of the CCP and of New China. (For example, *to deny the scientific and guiding value of Mao Zedong thought.*)
7. Questioning Reform and Opening and the socialist nature of socialism with Chinese characteristics. (For example, saying *"we have deviated from our Socialist orientation."*)

The seven points cover subject matter that falls under the general rubric of social science and economics with a bit of philosophy thrown in. However, as they are matters of personal belief, any academic, regardless of discipline, might have views on them that run counter to the party line. One does not have to be a historian to have thoughts on number six or an economist to have thoughts on number seven. It is the case, however, that an economist or a historian is much more likely to teach about them than a physicist or a chemical engineer. I would add that few countries in the MENA, no matter how much they might share the spirit of the seven points, have the party apparatus to enforce them.

Throughout the MENA (including Iran and Turkey) the most politically and culturally sensitive area of academic inquiry is Darwinism and the theory of evolution. The theory is at the core of life sciences much more than of the social sciences. As in fundamentalist Christianity, Darwin's theories directly contradict Islamic beliefs in divine creation. While evolutionary theory is taught below the radar, it is increasingly a no-go area for teaching and scholarship.

The pressure has been building for some time. In 2008 Ismail Serageldin wrote:

Throughout the Muslim world, we are witnessing an increasingly intolerant social milieu that is driven by self-appointed guardians of religious correctness, who inject their narrow interpretation of religion into all public debates. Rejecting rationality or evidentiary approaches, they increasingly force dissenting voices into silence and conformity with what they consider acceptable behavior. (Serageldin 2008)

The teaching of evolution is outright banned in Saudi Arabia (but not in KAUST). It is taught at MVU in Morocco, the only public university to do so. Elsewhere, it is widely if surreptitiously taught in majors that require some reference to it. Mustafa El Tayeb (2015: 96) bemoans the fact that it is taught "in a fragmented way at the undergraduate level" and that "the teachings always conform to tradition, not to science as taught in the West." He adds that the damage is often done in the "closing remarks from the instructor" (see also Khatri, 2014; Plackett, 2016).

Have Your Cake and Eat It Too?

Tunisia under Zine al-Abidine Ben Ali shows the ability of autocracies to produce superior performance in certain areas. Ben Ali's regime after 1990 became notorious for its police repression and strict controls on political life while developing a network of cronies (built around his wife's family, the Traboulsis) who engaged happily in high-level corruption. At the same time Tunisia suffered from all the ills of high youth unemployment and sluggish growth.

Yet in some ways Tunisia under Ben Ali was a high achiever. Its civil service functioned relatively well, and its educational system was among the best in the Arab world. Using data from around 2007, Ashraf El-Araby (2010) shows Tunisia's educational system to be the best performing of six Arab countries. It had introduced a meaningful quality assessment program, performance-linked incentives, and rules granting universities greater autonomy. It implemented institutional reforms that made it the leading investor in R&D outside the oil-rich countries and a relatively productive country in terms of research papers, citations, and research scientists per million people (see Hanafi and Arvanitis, 2016b: 145; Blackton, interview, 2012). We noted above that Faour (2012) found the civics content of Tunisian school materials to reflect universalistic values significantly more than do Egypt's.

Conclusion

There is a long tradition in Western political thought linking education to citizenship and democracy. In the Arab world there is little democracy so a crucial element in the equation is missing. That notwithstanding, there is still a need for educated citizens, even in autocracies. Morocco's

1999 National Charter of Education and Training puts citizenship front and center: "The educational system of the Kingdom of Morocco is based on the principles and values of the Islamic faith. It aims to train a virtuous citizen, a model of rectitude, moderation and tolerance, open to science and knowledge and endowed with a spirit of initiative, creativity and enterprise."

As in democracies, the production of such citizens at the tertiary level poses a major equity issue. Few countries approach South Korea's GER of ca. 90 percent, which is near universal. The OECD average is around 60 percent. In the MENA it is more like 30 percent on average. While a large minority, or in the MENA, a majority of citizens do not send their children to university, they pay the taxes to defray the costs of the students who do attend such institutions. The only way to resolve the equity issue is to assume that the graduates of colleges and universities provide some combination of professional skills, knowledge of how to make the political system function, and innovative talent in support of the economy that is of benefit to all citizens, making their contribution to the public good justifiable. It then becomes a question of empirical investigation to determine if this assumption is correct. The answer will be, I am confident, in shades of gray.

There is a second paradox. Some analysis seems to prove that education may be a catalyst to democratic transitions. The MENA has made great progress in promoting education at all levels. The efforts have had the strong backing of local autocrats. Why would they engage in efforts that might cut the grass beneath their feet? First, they may be unaware of the hypothesis, or they may doubt its validity. After all, as Bok (2017) points out, political participation in the West, or at least in the US, seems to be declining as average educational levels increase, and in the MENA we have witnessed a strengthening of autocracy as the tertiary education population grows.

I frankly doubt that Hosni Mubarak, Muammar Qadhafi, Bashar al-Assad, or Saddam Hussein paid much attention to any part of the hypothesis. Rather, education was an indispensable part of the social contract with their peoples, on a par with consumer subsidies and some level of guaranteed employment. Their blind eye to the massive out-migration of the educated from their countries suggests that they recognized the trade-off between education and political participation and, borrowing from Albert Hirschman's (1970) *Exit, Voice, and Loyalty*, preferred exit to voice, and loyalty to both.

Grüttner argues in his concluding chapter that the proposition that "true science can flourish only in democracies . . . cannot be reconciled with the facts" (2005b: 285). Grüttner is right. Autocracy can enable academic excellence and high-quality science. All that can be said is that democracies may (but not always will) produce excellence more broadly and more consistently than autocracies.[19]

Tony Zahlan (interview, 2013) pointed out that in autocracies the scientist cannot be an independent, self-motivated innovator. S/he needs political cover before acting. No matter how compelling the science, the scientist needs a green light from the authorities. That means that many good ideas remain locked in the scientist's brain, and that many bad ideas that somehow excite the interest of the leadership are given precious resources.

But if we look at the world through the eyes of the autocrat, there is the distinct possibility of having some of the best of both worlds: political control and educational excellence.[20] It is probably no coincidence that Lee Kuan Yew, the author of Singapore's remarkable success in all fields, was himself a schoolteacher. Singapore is a soft autocracy, a nanny state with a very limited field for political life. Yet it has been enormously successful economically. It prides itself on foreseeing global economic change and putting the educational system to work to produce the talent needed to meet the next challenges. It has built one of the world's best universities, the NUS, which is at the apex of a high-quality feeder system from preschool through high school. Significantly, NUS and other institutions of higher learning enjoy the kind of autonomy that Jamil Salmi, Jacques Hymans, and others see as critical to education quality. But, as Zahlan would surely predict, this autonomy is highly conditional, shaped by the signals and the cover coming from the topmost leadership.

The MENA has not had the equivalent of Lee Kuan Yew, although I would argue that Atatürk came close as leader of the Turkish Republic. My reference to Ben Ali above is only to show how faint is the resemblance.

The question I ask repeatedly in these pages is, if the trends are moving in the right direction, and if the international benchmarks are slowly being matched, what is the cost of letting this process take its course? One answer is that desultory change will claim many victims and constitute a significant opportunity cost for the economies and polities of the region (see Chauffour, 2017). A second answer is that, as we have seen with the collapse and malfunctioning of at least four states in the region, desultory reform can be reversed. Finally, the relative neglect of the reform process may open the possibility of hostile takeovers. I submit that this happened in Saudi Arabia after 1979, and other regimes have shown a tendency to treat the educational sector as part of a spoils system rather than as a national asset.

On the larger question of enablement, the jury is out. The MENA has vastly expanded K–12 education and reached respectable levels of coverage at the tertiary level. The quality of what is being offered is questionable, but the quantity is laudable. Does it translate into higher levels of political participation or a demand for democracy? The answer would appear to be 'not yet.' The uprisings of 2011 could, as Campante and Chor (2012) argue, reflect the catalyzing effect of education on political protest. But the uprisings have been quashed, either by civil war or by determined autocrats. Only Tunisia offers an exception. Some believe that 2011 was only the first wave of some sort of democratic transition (Elbadawi and Makdisi, 2017), but opinion polls show that Arab youth are more interested in social justice and an end to high-level corruption than in democratic practices per se (see Gertel and Hexel, 2018). Perhaps the theater we should be watching is China, where high levels of education and a burgeoning middle class seem to be contained within Chinese autocracy.

The obverse of the previous question is: what are the institutional requisites for high-quality education and research? Here the answer is mixed. Liberal, open systems that are willing to tolerate, even privilege the autonomy of the educational sector and its institutions may do better by most measures than systems that regard autonomy as a potential existential threat. But liberal politics are no guarantee of educational excellence. All we can say is that liberal systems do less harm than autocracies. The latter can and do create enclaves of excellence that achieve the limited aims of the autocrats. But again, looking at China, how many of us would be surprised if over the next fifty years China places five of its universities in the top twenty and remains an autocracy led by the Communist Party?

5

Governance: Why Does It Matter?

> We have yet to arrive at academic, organizational and financial indepen-
> dence for institutions of higher education. (Cairo Declaration on Higher
> Education in the Arab States, 2009, quoted in Bechir, 2010: 62)

The most common theme in the extensive commentary and analysis
of the 'crisis' in Arab higher education (UNDP and AFESD, 2003;
World Bank, 2008) is that Arab IHLs do not have the independence
to manage their own affairs properly. I will argue that the single most
important variable in governance is, therefore, the institution's relative
degree of autonomy. That conclusion makes intuitive sense, but it needs to
be questioned closely.

As with many other sacred cows in higher education, several respected
experts and colleagues have questioned the benefits of autonomy. I will
reference their reservations below. At the end of the day, I posit that while
institutional autonomy has drawbacks, if you are an institutional leader, it
is better to have it than not to have it.

Autonomy

According to the UN Committee on Economic, Social and Cultural Rights
(CESCR), university autonomy is a prerequisite for the exercise of professors' and students' individual rights. The committee defines autonomy
as "that degree of self-governance necessary for effective decision-making
by institutions of higher education in relation to their academic work,

standards, management and related activities" (Human Rights Watch, 2005: 14).

Analysis of autonomy must be coupled with analysis of accountability. They are two sides of one coin.[1] All forms of autonomy are accompanied and constrained by forms of accountability. All other components of governance are of significantly less importance than these two. Finding the right equilibrium between autonomy and accountability is the most crucial part of good governance (in general, see Salmi, 2002: 89; El-Amine, 2014).

The British have long experience in this issue and a century ago settled on a solution that was both liberal and minimalist. Robert Berdahl (1983: 83) cites a 1918 meeting of British university heads with the chancellor of the exchequer. They told the minister, after asking for an increased grant, "No one but ourselves can have any idea of how that money can best be spent from time to time. The doors are open and if we make fools of ourselves, you can take it away. Inspect freely, but there must be absolutely no control." That balance of accountability and autonomy has not survived in the UK and probably exists nowhere, but, from the point of view of university leadership, it is something to be longed for.

The fundamental question that we must ask with respect to autonomy is, autonomy to do what? This question is the core of this chapter. There is nothing intrinsically good or bad about autonomy. It all depends on what one is trying to achieve. Morocco's great historian, Abdallah Laroui, captured autonomy's downside:

> The people in power . . . wanted to reform while giving the impression of conserving. . . . I wanted, for example, university autonomy, hoping that responsibility, liberty of action, variety in recruitment (even outside Morocco) would make it a *foyer* of modernization. But *le pouvoir* (the regime), by deciding to give the university maximum autonomy, re-enforced the camp of tradition. (Ait Mous and Ksikes, 2014: 83)

Full autonomy in the real world does not exist. No institution can do as it pleases. There is always some instrument of the owners that holds management responsible and accountable. Autonomy, and good governance more generally, are means to an end. But what is that end?

I posit that in its most commonly accepted usage of universities having effective authority over the major policy issues facing them, autonomy is most relevant in competitive environments in which universities seek to build their strength and quality vis-à-vis other universities (in general, see Salmi, 2009). I will develop this idea in what follows.

In laws governing higher education and universities in the Arab world, the ideal of autonomy is often enshrined. Law No. 285 of the Republic of Lebanon, which came into effect in April 2014, is representative: "Institutions of higher education, established by law, enjoy a moral personality and academic, financial and administrative independence [*istiqlaliya*] including the rights conferred upon them by the constitution and laws." Those who live and work in the system in Lebanon and elsewhere, however, know a different reality. Taher Kanaan (2010) sums up the situation in Jordan as follows:

> All post-secondary education is the responsibility of the Ministry of Higher Education and Scientific Research (MoHESR) which was established by the Higher Education Law in 1985. The Ministry includes the Higher Education Council (HEC) and the Accreditation Council (HEAC). In principle, Jordanian universities enjoy a degree of autonomy. In reality, however, they are subject to fairly severe constraints imposed by the HEC and the HEAC.

The leader of the March 9 movement (see Chapter 2) at Cairo University, Mohammed Abul-Ghar put the matter briefly: "The deans are the eyes of the government inside the university" (Abul-Ghar, 2005). In his history of Damascus University, 'Ammar al-Samar cites the venerable Nicola Ziyadeh, who dismisses the notion of university autonomy anywhere in the Arab world: "Every university belongs to the Ministry of Instruction and Higher Education; the university, with respect to the state, is a department among departments, like the post office, transportation, or . . . ." (al-Samar 2018: 145).

Ministries of Finance seldom relax their grip on funding and often smother the university in red tape for approval of budgeted positions, importation of lab equipment, or disposition of assets nominally owned by the university. Reaching out to the private sector to promote sponsored research can prove more onerous than it is worth. The Ministry of Higher Education and Scientific Research may closely control curricular content and the selection of deans and presidents, while national coordinating committees may decide how many students will go to which public institutions. In some countries, Supreme Councils control the academic promotion process (such as Egypt).

Academic freedom that, ideally, protects individual faculty members from harassment on the part of political authorities or even elements of civil society is a fundamental component of institutional autonomy. Who but universities can, ultimately, protect the academic freedom of the teaching staff? Precisely because university autonomy in the MENA is so circumscribed, academic freedom has little practical relevance.

Supporting the senior university leadership, all of whom are beholden to the nation's political authorities, are the Ministry of the Interior and the *mukhabarat*. They interfere in academic and student elections and place personnel in key sectors of the university's administration. The Lebanese law, for example, guarantees the sanctity of the campus. Police can enter the campus only upon the request of the president, but is it really up to the president to decide when to issue the invitation?

Like any component of civil society, universities seem to strike inordinate fear in the hearts of political leaders. They do not like to see *any* part of civil society—unions, the press, civic associations, religious groups—asserting their autonomy. So, they cannot help themselves from meddling in university affairs, using the university as a facet of regime power (see Chapter 3 on politics and the university).

It is curious to me that universities arouse these fears. It is true that they always seem to harbor unruly students and individual faculty members who raise awkward questions, but by and large as institutions universities in the Arab world have been fairly tame. Ahmad Lutfi al-Sayyid's defiance, as rector of the Egyptian University, of his dean, Taha Hussein, in 1932 was exceptional if not unique.

In 2011 the February 20 movement in Morocco was largely driven by students and intellectuals. Arguably that movement forced King Mohammed VI to issue a new constitution, giving the prime minister expanded powers. But despite these important events, in general, universities have not been hotbeds of opposition, let alone subversion.

In addition to the university's multiple missions, there is the unannounced agenda, which is to reinforce the legitimacy of the regime and to shore up the authority of the nation's leadership. This mission will not appear anywhere in fundamental laws governing higher education and the structuring of universities. Nonetheless the primary task of the minister of higher education and of university presidents may well be to support and protect the regime. All other announced missions in education, research, and the creation of knowledge will count for relatively little in light of the unannounced political mission.

While not necessarily contradictory, these missions are difficult to achieve simultaneously. They overlap with the trilemma defined in the Introduction whereby universities, or their masters, must choose which two of the three mission goals they most want: quantity, quality, or 'reasonable' cost.

There are always solutions to the trilemma but they are never ideal. The decision-making that goes into choosing what will be sought and what will be sacrificed is dynamic and ongoing. Broadly speaking we can imagine those choices residing within the purview of university leadership and boards or at some higher, systemic level (for a general survey of the Arab world, see El-Amine, 2014). The quantity-quality-cost trilemma can be broken down into policy areas.

Accountability

Public institutions are mostly paid for by the taxpayers (see also Chapter 8). I do not distinguish here between direct and indirect taxes. I also assume that taxpayers pay for the bureaucracies that collect customs or absorb natural resource rents. The taxpayers are the ultimate owners (the principals), and the university officers and administrators are their 'agents.' Ministries and other public bodies operate on behalf of the owners to whom they are nominally responsible. The taxpayers have a right, at a minimum, to financial oversight—how their tax money is spent. Ideally the public oversight bodies would in turn be monitored and guided by the elected representatives of the taxpayers grouped in national legislatures. In the Arab world legislatures are weak, so this type of taxpayer oversight is not effective. In fact, depending on the institution, there are only two kinds of effective monitoring and oversight: formal governmental authorities and/or institutional boards of trustees or university councils.

There are many ways to structure oversight. One I call trust-based, in that the owners trust their managerial agents to do what they say they want to do. The most trust-based would be the British model after the Second World War: the British University Grants Commission, headed by a senior respected academic and a senior representative of the Treasury, recommended five-year block grants, based very loosely on a plan of action, but allowing university authorities considerable latitude in the expenditure of the funds (see pages 162 and 164). There is far less trust manifest in the British system today.

Some countries have a model of quasi-autonomy based on their own parastatals or SOEs. The parastatal governance structure could be transferred to universities, adding to the latter external boards with the authority to supervise mission, finances, and broad strategy (World Bank and OECD, 2010: 28).

Boards could have broader membership, with representatives of the community (again, in Morocco, universities are to serve regions, and regional stakeholders are represented in their councils), elected legislators, and representatives from other ministries. Boards or councils could insist on annual budgets and perhaps calibrate them with strategic plans and key performance indicators (KPIs) in a multiyear framework.

Governments could allow for different funding formulas across institutions or insist on uniformity, perhaps using some sort of student capitation formula. Variation, I argue, would signal the willingness of political authorities to accept competition among public institutions. That has not yet happened in the Arab world, outside the GCC, although there is a growing fascination with international rankings in which Arab public universities, with the exception of Saudi Arabia and the UAE, tend to do poorly. Arab governments and societies seem most comfortable with public systems of uniform quality even if that quality is mediocre.

At the heart of accountability are university finances. Current funding formulas rely overwhelmingly on the public purse. One approach to finances might be to dedicate specific revenue streams, especially from taxes, to support higher education. Brazil, notably the State of Sao Paolo, dedicates certain percentages of tax revenue to university operating budgets and research. Dedicated revenues would reduce some of the uncertainty in annual funding levels.

Diversification of funding sources would enhance university autonomy. Better that the piper has several payers rather than just one. In this respect, the most unusual instrument I have found is that of the Monterrey Institute of Technology in Mexico. It is a private institution, first established through local business persons. It did not have access to public funding. Beginning in 1947, however, it took advantage of a law that permits nonprofit organizations to conduct lotteries to support social causes. The Monterrey Institute conducts lotteries three times a year, grossing on the order of $100 million per annum (Marmolejo, 2011).

Such revenue sources (dedicated taxes, lotteries) introduce a much higher level of predictability into university finances than annual trips to the minister of finance and the minister of higher education. Tax revenues fluctuate, of course, but within a tolerable range. Dedicated tax revenues allow university administrators to engage in multiyear planning. It gives universities a stake in the overall health of the economy inasmuch as a growing economy will mean increased tax revenues and thus greater amounts of funding for universities.

An early example of dedicated funding sources in the Arab world comes from the forerunner to Damascus University. In the early 1900s the Ottoman authorities in Damascus imposed a levy on each animal slaughtered in the city's slaughter houses to help fund a medical college in Damascus (Rafiq, 2004).

In its most recent constitution, Egypt has committed to certain targets of expenditure on education, scientific research, and higher education as percentages of GDP. The levels are not very ambitious, but even at these modest levels one wonders how they will be achieved when there are so many claimants on public expenditures.

Both public and private IHLs could benefit from endowments. I know of no Arab public university that has a significant endowment except for a few in the GCC, such as the KAUST or the Cornell Weil Medical College in Qatar. Endowments are typically in support of a single institution, but they could be in support of a research consortium or a cluster of like-minded IHLs. The endowment 'owner' is the board of trustees. The board thus becomes the keystone of university autonomy, and university leadership (the agents) are accountable to the trustees, who act as the representatives of the principals (the taxpayers).

Whether in public or private institutions, the trustees may have interests that run counter to those of parents, students, and faculty. I use interest here in the 'disinterested' sense of persons whose official responsibilities for the financial health of the university may lead them to positions the faculty and/or the students may find debatable or even reprehensible. The endowment is a portfolio. It is invested in certain ways. Implicitly it may lead trustees to pressure the university to take positions that will not offend any of the major enterprises in which the endowment is invested. In the crony capitalism that is common in the Arab world, institutional conflicts of interest are to be expected.

An endowment could appear to some like a kind of silver bullet—a great pile of funds from which the university can draw revenue and by which it can defend its 'autonomy.'[2] But as indicated above, that is seldom the case. Endowments and their managers are not neutral. Protecting the investment portfolio may lead to actions that conflict with university values and mission.

In public systems budget autonomy is the last concession made by governments to IHLs. It does not come about because the owners think it is a good idea, but out of economic necessity (as in Jordan or Egypt in the past few decades). A recent Moroccan government report on higher education openly advocates greater university autonomy precisely to endow university leadership with the levers to engage directly with the private sector and to create new revenue streams for the institution (Kingdom of Morocco, 2018: 98). There simply are not sufficient public funds to meet the core needs of universities. At the same time, public control over other areas (admissions, senior appointments, curriculum, promotions) continues to be exerted by the owners. This mismatch of contributions by the owners and the degree of accountability of the managers is probably not sustainable. Since the 1970s in the US, state and federal funding of public university operating budgets has fallen from over 60 percent to about 34 percent today, yet few public authority controls have been relinquished. As universities shift their sights to fundraising and wooing out-of-state students, they will be faced with a new set of owners with their own agendas.

Universities will always have owners, and they will call the tune. At different times and in different political climates, one kind of owner may seem preferable to another. Is it better to answer to the government or to a large corporate sponsor? Both raise issues of academic integrity and values. It would probably be best to diversify one's funding sources as much as possible.

Admissions

Should public institutions independently set their own admissions criteria, admissions targets, and levels of fees or tuition? The latter issue falls as well under financial or budgetary policy. Control over admissions criteria and targets will only be devolved if it is accepted that there is a hierarchy of public institutions and that they have reputations to protect and standards to meet. That is not the case in most Arab states.

More common is a nationwide coordination board that administers the high school exams that determine the levels of high school students and the 'majors' in the university for which they are eligible. Universities can only await the decisions of the national board. The numbers, aptitudes, and disciplinary interests of incoming students are unknown to university authorities quite literally until the last minute. The ostensible logic behind such boards is to guarantee impartiality and fairness in the national admissions process. This logic is not without merit, but the subtext is that admission to university is left directly under the authority of the nation's executive.

Tuition and other fees, however, will always go straight to the core of taxpayer concerns, as the education, no matter how good or bad, must be accessible to the taxpayers and their children. On average, the Arab GER of those aged eighteen to twenty-two is about 26 percent (as of 2011) (see Jaramillo et al., 2012), meaning that 75 percent of eligible youth do not receive a tertiary education. Yet those young people and their parents pay taxes just like the direct beneficiaries. This may be seen as equitable only if it is accepted that higher education is a public good from which everyone benefits. Those who are educated come away with the skills needed to serve the economy and the values needed to assure an effective political system. Everyone, in theory, benefits from these outcomes, but it is easy to anticipate that those who do not benefit directly will not see it this way.

Certain taxpayers may expect that they or their children will be direct beneficiaries of the education dispensed by public institutions. Like the general taxpayer, these principals in theory have their representatives to defend their ownership rights. Some, with independent means, may withdraw their children from public institutions and send them to private institutions at home or abroad. It is obvious that when unemployment is highest among those with high school or university diplomas, both general taxpayers and those who directly benefit from public education are being shortchanged, to put it mildly. How does the Moroccan taxpayer react when King Mohammed VI says that higher education in the kingdom "is becoming a factory for unemployment"?

Finally, there is the phenomenon of corporate financing of programs, scholarships, and research facilities at both public and private institutions. Indeed, this is one of the mechanisms that allow private institutions to maintain some autonomy from public authorities and keep their costs within reason. But such funds have strings. During the Vietnam War, US public and private universities were the scenes of fierce opposition to research grants from the US Department of Defense and related private industries. Today the issue might be research on genetically modified organisms funded by Monsanto or climate research funded by Exxon or British Petroleum. State enterprises, like Saudi Aramco or Morocco's Office Chérifien des Phosphates (OCP), are heavily involved in higher education (see page 172). By comparison, the taxpayer provides the most funds but is a dwarf in terms of influence.

Possible Governance Models

We can imagine ideal types of governance distributed along a continuum from most to least centralized. In the most centralized, the entire public education system is totally subordinate to the president and prime minister acting through their preferred agencies of higher education, finance, planning, internal intelligence, and sometimes, the regime party (see Connelly and Grüttner, 2005). Before 2003 in Iraq and 2011 in Syria and Tunisia, this kind of model prevailed. Universities had no effective autonomy in any significant policy realm, and university missions were subordinated to regime consolidation and survival.

A second centralized model is one in which the educational *system* is itself autonomous. That is, all the IHLs constitute an organic whole with a collective mission and some mechanism for collective oversight. The broad mission is set by the central political authorities, but the line ministries responsible for various pieces of the system may act autonomously. Supreme Councils may be created to coordinate among the owners. The education sector's mission is to achieve excellence in select facets of the educational enterprise. This may serve to buttress the political regime, but it is not the primary goal of the sector. I believe that this kind of systemic autonomy does not exist anywhere in the Arab world, but all the moving parts are there, and it could be coming.

Then we have a model in which universities are treated like public enterprises. Egypt's Law No. 49 of 1972 recodified university governance. Each university was to have a special budget on the model of the public general organizations (Mughaith, 2018: 54–55; World Bank and OECD, 2010: 28). Morocco went further. In theory, the Moroccan state draws up a broad educational strategy to which all IHLs adhere, but the leadership of each IHL can and must develop its own institutional strategy. Once the state authorities agree to the IHL plan and the metrics to measure progress, they will commit the resources necessary to carry it out.

Morocco has gone far to implement this model, and for that reason it is worth spending some time on it. The Education Law of 2000 (Law No. 00-01) seeks to transform universities from public institutions to a kind of state enterprise: "That means, above all, to consolidate their status and their administrative, financial and academic autonomy in a contractual relationship with the supervisory authorities. It is the best arrangement to make them true locomotives for regional and national development and to allow them to contribute towards the insertion of our country into the knowledge society and into the economies of emerging countries" (Kingdom of Morocco, 2015a).

The basic notion is that university leadership is selected on the basis of a plan submitted by candidates for the presidency that in turn becomes the foundation of a contract between the state and the university to provide the resources to carry out the plan. The plan has a four-year horizon so that the state is committing to multiyear funding. Abdallatif Miraoui, president of Cadi Ayyad University (CAU), told me that for his second term as president he totally rewrote his strategy in the open competition for the office (interview, 2018).

Different public universities will have different plans. The one-size-fits-all approach is thus discarded. Plans will inevitably focus on building or maintaining the institution's strengths (see Benjelloun, 2010?). The seeds of competition are thereby planted—maybe.

A hard-hitting analysis published by Morocco's Supreme Council for Education, Training, and Scientific Research concluded:

> Article 7 of Law 01-00 authorizes the university to invest its capital and diversify its resources, notably by the creation of affiliated businesses or financial stakes, but these dispositions have not been implemented. Moreover, the absence of 'contractualization' between the government and the university on the basis of their strategies of development seriously limits accountability and the responsibility of the actors. (Kingdom of Morocco, 2018: 63)

Similar models (known in France as *contrats plans*) have been tested in managing public sector enterprises, and they are beset with difficulties. It is not obvious what happens if the owners, the state, or the agents—the university administration—fail to live up to their side of the contract. If the state fails to provide the agreed-upon resources, what recourse does the university have? It can't very well take the owners to court. The state, however, does have options if university leadership does not implement its plan. It can redirect public resources to institutions that are performing better. This is the primary manifestation of competition among universities: those that are better able to fulfill their plans will capture more of limited public funding.

This is a very different approach than that initiated by the Obama administration in the US. There, the effort involved ranking universities according to a set of metrics (a scorecard), such as graduation rates and job placement, and distributing federal funds, largely in the form of loans and scholarships, to the highest-ranked institutions. This is perilously close to the one-size-fits-all of centralized systems and ignores the specific strengths, weaknesses, and unique missions of individual institutions (Stripling, 2016).

Supreme Councils

Several MENA countries (led by Egypt and Turkey) give sweeping oversight authority of the entire tertiary system, including private institutions, to Supreme Councils for Higher Education and Scientific Research. The nomenclature and the scope of authority varies, but such councils are critical to the governance of entire systems as opposed to individual IHLs (see Chapter 2). At first blush, such councils would seem to be the antithesis of university autonomy, as they have great weight in financial, curricular, admissions, and hiring decisions. Their defenders counter that they assure common, equitable standards throughout the system, thwart favoritism and parochialism in the management of university affairs, and assure a basic level of social equity in higher education. This argument cannot be easily dismissed.

Egypt's SCU is especially powerful. I interviewed two of its insiders, Ali al-Din Hilal Dessouki, the SCU's former secretary-general, and Amr Salama, former president of Helwan University and minister of education. Dessouki cast the SCU in a positive light, in that it overcomes the tendencies of university leaders to give in to internal pressures, while Salama saw the SCU as entirely the creature of the minister of higher education, who appoints the secretary-general as well as the university presidents, who are members of the SCU. It is a closed loop, ultimately an instrument of the president of the republic. It has, according to Salama, gone far beyond its original intent, which was coordination, not management.

A softer variant of the Egyptian model is to be found in Morocco, where the Supreme Council for Education, Training, and Scientific Research is one of ten 'autonomous' councils provided for in the constitution, appointed by the king but enjoying only advisory powers. Other such councils are the Economic and Social Council, the Human Rights Council, and the Diaspora Council. They constitute a kind of parallel structure to the government and parliament, and, as creatures of the throne, can and do offer solid critiques of policies and practices. In 2014 the minister of higher education proposed revisions to the Higher Education Law of 2000. The Supreme Council for Education, Training, and Scientific Research published a critical analysis of the minister's draft reforms (Kingdom of Morocco, 2015b).

The last macro-model is one in which fully autonomous institutions compete for students, faculty, and resources. The institutions could be public as well as private, for-profit or not-for-profit. This is basically how the US model looks. It is worth noting that it is to some extent the model of higher education in the Palestinian homeland, where all but two universities are private.

It is the case that elements from all five models can be combined, as China has demonstrated. Strong Communist Party controls, restricted academic freedom, some university autonomy, and a quest for excellence as measured by international rankings are all elements of the Chinese system. The model in many ways has been quite successful (Kapur and Perry, 2015).

Universities and Regional Development Councils
Public universities in Morocco are linked to regional development. University councils have representation from regional interests and economic actors. Aspirationally, Moroccan universities are to become the poles of regional development and innovation. This is a worthy mission. It addresses directly the critical issues of local development and employment. It tries to bring all relevant stakeholders onto the same sheet of music with the university. Implementation, however, has been less than satisfactory, apparently because all or most of the stakeholders are derelict in their participation.

Morocco might well look across the Strait of Gibraltar to Spain, where universities are run by regional governments: "With the tacit consent of the politicians, they have used their legal autonomy to turn themselves into closed shops" (*The Economist*, 2018d: 11). They do not collect data that would facilitate their evaluation, such as how their graduates fare in the job market. Democracy plus autonomy lead to the shackling of animal spirits.

No model is inherently superior to any other. It depends on the overall mission. Academics may instinctively place great value on academic freedom, shared governance, research excellence, and institutional identity, while politicians may value stability, adherence to regime norms and values, and education to serve national priorities. Whom should we respect more: authority-questioning academics or stability-obsessed politicians?

Internal Governance
This is the second level of the autonomy and accountability puzzle. To whom is university leadership ultimately accountable? To external political authorities? To a university board of trustees? To internal faculty, staff, and student constituents? To the parents of students? The simplistic answer is to all of them, but political authorities and boards will almost always trump internal constituencies.

Georges Tohmé, who was president of Lebanese University from 1980 to 1988 (see Chapter 2), by law had the right to appoint some of the university's most senior leaders, including its secretary-general. At the beginning of his presidency he resolved to make no senior appointments without the formal approval of the Council of Ministers. In this manner he hoped to shield himself from direct approaches of politicians on behalf of their clients (Tohmé, n.d.: 29). So, he delegated authority rightfully his and eroded university autonomy deliberately.

Another Lebanese expert on higher education compared Lebanese University to a 'commons.' All the politicians want to graze their sheep on it (El-Amine, interview, 2012). Autonomy consists of the fences and barbed wire needed to keep the sheep out. Most Arab academic leaders do not fence off the commons.

Recognizing that reality, we may still ask to what extent faculty, students, and staff are involved in the institutional decision-making process. Are certain leadership positions elected by faculty? If internal participation in such matters is extensive, essentially through faculty senates or councils and internal elections, this will reflect considerable institutional autonomy. In the Arab world, faculty- and university-wide councils may have some elected members and may influence the selection of deans and sometimes university presidents. In most instances, however, it is recognized that political authorities will have their way in selecting senior university leadership, and the locus of decisions affecting all university policies will reside in the supervisory ministries (primarily higher education and finance) and occasionally in Supreme Councils (inter alia, Egypt and Turkey).

We may posit that shared governance is only meaningful if the university has considerable autonomy in designing its academic strategy and deploying its financial and infrastructural resources. Absent that, there will not be much at stake in shared governance. Elections will be important mainly as a barometer of the strengths and weaknesses of political forces external to the university. For example, in 1992, because of the growing influence of the Muslim Brotherhood among students and faculty, Egypt's legislature passed legislation ending faculty elections of deans and empowering university presidents to appoint deans. Elections were briefly restored in 2011, after the ouster of Mubarak, then done away with again after 2013. Indeed, in 2014, legislation was enacted that placed all public and vital facilities, including universities, under military jurisdiction until 2021 (Sayigh, 2019: 31).

Rhetorically, Latin American institutions have attached considerable importance to shared governance as the core of university autonomy. The Universidad Nacional Autónoma de México (UNAM), Mexico's flagship public university, built the term into its official name. The same concept of autonomy prevails in Turkey (Barbalan et al., 2008). In reality, in both instances, oversight and financial controls are highly centralized. In Turkey since the 1980s the effective tool of the owners has been the YÖK, which adheres to the political agenda of incumbent authorities.

Like university autonomy, shared governance has, in academia, an almost sacred ring to it. But a number of experts see its downside. As the American Academy of Arts and Science warned, "In practice, shared governance has often meant 'divided authority,' with faculty controlling curriculum, administrators controlling the budget and regents, and trustees attending to the institution's long-run financial viability" (AAAS, 2017: 67).

Students and parents in private institutions are likely to be quite powerful. They pay the fees common in private education. They have a contract with the university and are upset when the contract is seemingly violated. Students may withdraw, parents may litigate, the 'market' may direct demand to other institutions—like any enterprise the private university may have to adjust or atrophy.

The faculty are the guts of the enterprise, public or private. They build the institution's reputation and they can destroy it. Faculty in the MENA's public universities cannot easily vote with their feet. They cannot always choose to move from one public university to another. But they can migrate: from public to private, from home country to another country, from education to some other career. Short of all that, they can make life miserable for all the other constituents.

Promotion and Compensation

Faculty members are often, de jure, civil servants and thus compensation is regulated according to civil service rules. Universities do not have the right to adjust compensation on an individual basis. Performance reviews may have little practical impact on compensation for either faculty or staff, or, more likely, there are no performance reviews. University leaders do have some discretion in granting bonuses, allocating special allowances, and making research awards.

Academic promotions are effectively controlled by most Arab universities. However, in Egypt, it is the SCU that reviews and acts on all promotion cases. A former secretary-general of that council argued to me that promotion and personnel decisions, if left to the discretion of university officials, would descend rapidly into favoritism and nepotism (Dessouki, interview, March 2013). He believes that the SCU's management of the promotion process is necessary to avoid this kind of introversion (see also Hammoud, 2010).

Curricular Policy

Once again, the issue is whether or not one size fits all, and that public IHLs offer a standard curriculum with only minor variations to reflect institutional strengths. Control over the curriculum becomes relevant only when the institution seeks to distinguish itself from others and to advertise its strengths to prospective students. That in turn means the institution is allowed to practice selective admissions.

Whatever the degree of autonomy regarding curriculum, the educational oversight ministry and the ministry of finance will almost always have a final say in the creation of new programs with budgetary implications. Parliamentary committees of jurisdiction, as in Lebanon, may have to approve the creation of new programs and academic units. Elsewhere, boards of education and accreditation bodies would have a voice in the approval process, but they are weak in the Arab public sector.

When Institutional Autonomy Matters

Autonomy is only worth having if the university has a specific mission and strategy and wants to compete for resources to achieve that end. It will want students that respect the mission and faculty that can help pursue the strategy. If innovation, cutting-edge research, and interactive teaching are highly valued, then autonomy will contribute to achieving them more than centralized, command-and-control systems.

By contrast, if, like Egyptian universities, each institution has the same mission and strategy and there is no competition among them for resources, then autonomy is meaningless or irrelevant. We can extend the question: if shared governance and the election of academic leaders is what defines autonomy, what is the purpose of elections if most aspects of university life, including salaries and perquisites, are centrally controlled? Elections should matter only if the university controls its own mission and internal affairs.

A university would seek autonomy to design curriculum, recruit faculty and students, and conduct research that gives it a character and reputation that in turn becomes its 'brand.' Autonomy becomes a core element of its mission and is crucial to helping the mission evolve in response to new challenges and to adjust financially and substantively to these challenges.

In this competitive environment, it is also accepted that there will be a pecking order of universities that, ideally, changes over time. Universities will compete for the best faculty and the best students and will call attention to their success in specific research fields. When Cairo and Damascus Universities were founded at the turn of the last century, that kind of autonomy and competitive environment was probably what their founders had in mind. It was not, however, central to the vision of the populist Arab regimes of the 1960s and 1970s.

In Arab countries outside the GCC, there are major constraints on public financing (and in recent years, even inside the GCC). This is a worldwide phenomenon as countries try to raise their GERs, enhance their research output, and contain costs that routinely increase at rates exceeding that of inflation or growth in GDP.

Competition among IHLs may act as a mechanism for the distribution of scarce resources. For example, Germany's Excellence Initiative, worth 4.6 billion euros, was launched in 2006. Annual grants now total 533 million euros. It rewards groups of researchers that form 'excellence clusters.' About fifty a year will receive up to 10 million euros. Universities that host two such clusters can apply to be 'excellence universities,' which may bring them 15 million euros a year (*Science*, 2016: 499). We noted above that Morocco's model of contractual support for universities could lead to periodic reallocation of resources based on the monitored performance of individual universities.

The growing concern with international rankings signals a growing openness to competition among universities. Some of the highest-ranked Arab universities are public, such as King Abdulaziz University in Saudi Arabia or CAU in Morocco. Playing the ranking game is not always transparent or honest. The data that feed into the rankings can be cooked and manipulated. But playing the game is a sign of institutional pride, the determination to hold one's place or to advance in the league tables. Institutional behavior may well change.

We must recognize that autonomy, like academic tenure, can lock in mediocrity. It all depends on how institutional incentives are structured and applied. But better to have autonomy than not to have it. Once lost, autonomy is very hard to regain, so it makes sense to fight for it and protect whatever one gets. In the end, competition may render mediocrity unaffordable.

The Private Sector and the Corporate Sector

There are now over eight hundred universities in the Arab world. Their number has quadrupled in a decade. The total student body in tertiary education is now about nine million. Yet, it represents only about a third of the eligible population aged eighteen to twenty-two. There will be continued rapid growth in the coming decades and much of it will be in the private education sector. It may, however, take a generation before the majority of students are enrolled in private IHLs (see Bhandari and El-Amine, 2011).

The public sector will try to regulate this growth, but it will be hard to exert effective controls because, first, the private sector will help meet the strong demand for tertiary education, and, second, money talks. The investors in private education often have deep pockets and friends in power. We may assume that private institutions will enjoy considerable autonomy, but it may be only the marketplace that can hold them accountable.

We are already seeing some new actors in higher education, and there will surely be more. The Arab Open University has been in existence for some time, and online education will doubtless grow in the future (see Chapter 6 on reform). The first massive open online course (MOOC) in the Arab world was launched in 2014 by the Queen Rania Foundation for Education and Development (Sawahel, 2014). Online education could play a big role in 'solving' the trilemma of quantity, quality, and cost.

Corporations may enter directly into higher education by founding or managing universities.[3] Saudi Aramco plays a central management role in the KAUST. Morocco's OCP, a state enterprise, in 2012 launched the Mohammed VI Polytechnic University. So far there have not been Arab emulators of Turkey's private corporations that gave rise to the not-for-profit Koç, Sabanci, and Bilkent (Doğramici family) Universities. The Bilkent example is particularly interesting in that the university is the owner of a conglomerate of companies that finances the university's operations (see Chapter 8). The managers of companies in the conglomerate are accountable to the university, not the other way around.

The corporate university is spreading quickly and for the STEM fields may prove particularly attractive. In 1986 the South Korean parastal Pohang Iron and Steel Company established the Pohang University of Science and Technology. The company was privatized after 1998. The university was ranked number one among the top hundred universities under fifty years old by the Times Higher Education ranking system (Mezue et al., 2015).

The Political Dimension

We recognize that autonomy in any of the institutions of civil society is politically charged. If we think of politics with a small 'p,' then autonomy may involve protecting institutions from politicians who want to use those institutions to pay off their friends by placing students, faculty members, or staff on their payroll.

If the challenge was merely small-p politics, it might be manageable. But autonomy has major big-P implications. Conceding legal autonomy to civil society organizations may appear too risky to entrenched autocrats. It may be that because Lebanon, for all its political problems, has not suffered from entrenched autocrats, it has fostered a great deal of de facto and de jure autonomy in its civil society institutions, including, of course, universities.

So, we can pretend, in the manner of many external funding agencies, that university autonomy can be discussed in isolation from its broader political implications. But that is an illusion. The *Arab Human Development Report* for 2003 states flatly that Arab universities are run according to political logic, not educational logic. The unannounced red lines and agendas I outlined lie in the political realm. They involve the overriding task of university leadership to keep the institution politically quiet, if not supportive of the regime. All official goals are ultimately subordinated to this critical but unannounced mission.

There is widespread consensus that Arab universities are underperforming, delivering educational and research outcomes that do not reflect the size of the investment. There is no similar consensus on how to remedy this situation. There is a prior question, almost a meta question, and that is, do political leaders really want excellence in higher education in some form? Judging from the results to date, one would have to answer "no," or, more charitably, "yes, but . . . ." There have been no Lee Kuan Yews in the Arab world, that is, authoritarians who accept the risk of university autonomy for the sake of excellence in training the leaders of the economy. Until there are leaders ready to take similar risks, improved university governance may prove to be an illusion.

At the same time cautious reforms, as in Morocco, are underway. Powerful external actors, like the World Bank, UNESCO, private foundations, and bilateral aid agencies have been building communities of practice and leveraging some modest changes through project financing.

The private educational sector is expanding rapidly. This is so mainly because public authorities have tacitly admitted their inability to mobilize the resources necessary to meet their original aspirations for free education for most, if not all, of their citizens. One would think that unleashing the private sector would be as threatening to autocrats as empowering public institutions. The fact that the leadership of private universities is the beneficiary of political favors rather than of professionalism may explain the puzzle.

In Latin America today, over 50 percent of all students in tertiary education attend private institutions. Because of its giant Islamic Azad University (with 1.5–2 million students), Iran has a similar level of private education. In both Latin America and Iran the most prestigious universities (Sao Paolo and Buenos Aires, like UNAM in Mexico and SUT in Iran) are public. That might provide a model for the Arab world. The private institutions would enjoy considerable autonomy. Public centers of excellence would have to be granted considerable autonomy, de facto or de jure, in order to compete.

We may see, as in Morocco, experiments in qualified autonomy built on a strategic plan and multiyear budgetary support. The university leadership would be granted significant authority to recruit faculty and staff to carry out the plan and to mobilize university resources in support of it. Accountability is built into the drafting of the plan, the metrics of evaluation, and the monitoring of its implementation.

What we might call the Eastern European/Soviet model may not be obsolete. This combined a command-and-control system for providing general university education with quasi-autonomous centers of excellence built around research groups and academies of science. The centers of excellence were determined by central authorities, had relatively lavish funding, and enjoyed considerable internal autonomy. While faculty may have been shared with universities, the research and funding were not. China appears to want to have it all: some world-class universities, dozens of well-funded, prestigious research centers, some of which are affiliated with universities, and a lower-quality stratum of universities designed to reach most of the eligible population. The entire system is closely aligned with and monitored by the Communist Party.

A final speculative note. There are four failed or quasi-failed states in the Arab world: Libya, Syria, Iraq, and Yemen (Somalia is a failed state as well, although we often forget it is a member of the Arab League). Their higher education systems are in shambles. Like the countries themselves, they will have to be rebuilt. This is an opportunity for radical thinking and solutions outside the box. Does one rebuild the University of Aleppo or of

Mosul, physically and organizationally, as it was? Could tertiary education in all four or five countries be totally rethought? Could new, disruptive models developed in failed states have repercussions in other Arab states? I am not at all optimistic, but the possibility needs to be seriously considered. It would be a pity to let the opportunity slip by out of timidity or fatigue.

6

Reform in Tight Places

I n this and the following chapter, I survey major efforts in the MENA to reform higher education and to stimulate innovation. For purposes of exposition, I separate the two, and the section headings in both chapters purvey a somewhat false sense of clear divisions. We are in fact dealing with phenomena that overlap and blend into each other.

The Oxford English Dictionary defines innovation as a "new method, idea or product, etc." Reform is defined as making "changes in something, especially an institution or practice, to improve it." Reform, I argue, may not involve innovation, but innovation always involves reform. In that sense, reform is the master narrative. Reforms may entail applying old rules and practices that have been neglected over time or fallen from use. While president of AUB, my administration concluded that our liberal arts core curriculum had fallen into desuetude during and after the long period of Lebanon's civil war, so we launched a major interfaculty effort to redefine and redesign it. In hindsight what we did constitutes reform, as defined above, but not innovation. By contrast, any innovation is likely to require organizational and institutional reform. If it does not, it is probably super- ficial or at least nonsystemic.

Reform and innovation are both emblematic of an existing situation that needs positive change. That change can be organizational, technologi- cal, cultural, or some combination of all three. Remote monitoring devices allow hospitals to monitor patients in their homes, thus freeing up hospital beds for more acute or complicated cases. That impact is organizational. The increased use of nurses and paramedics in medical diagnosis and remote monitoring is organizational and cultural, and, in terms of liability, legal as well. Both reform and innovation are at play in this example.

Innovation often involves new technology that allows old problems to be solved in new ways. The digital revolution has affected every aspect of academic life, from impact analysis of scholarship to applying for financial aid and checking students' work for evidence of plagiarism. Needless to say, new technologies often create new opportunities to wreck or abuse existing systems as much as they contribute to solving existing problems. We are all familiar with malware, hackers, personal data theft, bots, and the like that either seek to compromise data and programs or put them to criminal, commercial, or political use.

Reform

> [This] Memorandum speculates that, even in the absence of changes to "the rules of the game" strictly speaking, informing the actors (enterprises, households, and citizens) of the causes and consequences of the public policies adopted, sharing new concepts and ideas, and discussing the existing rules of the game may shift the equilibrium among the various components of the society and thus engender the desired change in the actors' positions (such as education reform). Increasing the level of knowledge, scaling up accountability and transparency, and encouraging policy evaluation are three mechanisms that enable players to constantly revise their positions. (Chauffour, 2017: 6)

The passage above is from a World Bank memorandum on Morocco, a country in which the World Bank has been particularly active. As I will develop below, the World Bank and other IFIs have not-so-subtly slipped in a range of political reforms under the guise of economic reform and restructuring. The Moroccan government, from King Mohammed VI on down, may be forgiven for sniffing out some velvet revolution in the memorandum.

Given the perceived and real political stakes involved in higher education, reform may strike political leaders as particularly dangerous. There is likely to be a strong preference for the status quo and BAU, even if both are significantly dysfunctional.[1] That explains why so little real reform takes place even though a 'crisis' in higher education is frequently acknowledged at the highest levels. The progress that has taken place has been uneven, often superficial, and more quantitative than qualitative.[2] Does it matter that progress is slow if the overall direction is toward best practice? The answer is no, but only if one is willing to write off all the students and faculty who are shortchanged by the slow pace of reform and receive an inferior education or suffer through stunted careers.

Reform will come about through public policies. Even in systems where private education prevails (such as Lebanon), both the public and private sectors are governed and regulated by public policies.

Where might one expect reforms? In this and the next chapter we will give consideration to the following seven areas. They are by no means exhaustive, but they are either intrinsically important or areas in which reforms have been attempted.

- Governance and finance (dealt with in Chapters 5 and 8),
- Education for the job market,
- Quality assurance,
- Regional cooperation,
- ICT (dealt with in Chapter 7), and
- Research/R&D (dealt with in Chapter 7).

Of these, two are of paramount importance in terms of reform. Governance is of great significance because the main issue under it is enhanced autonomy. Institutional autonomy is the link between reform at the level of the system and reform at the level of the institution (see Chapter 5). Without autonomy an institution cannot undertake the internal reforms that would affect everything from curriculum to salaries, unless the reforms are centrally mandated and apply to all.

Any moves toward institutional autonomy, it is feared, will set precedents for the rest of civil society. Moreover, autonomous universities may be seen as offering one's foreign and domestic enemies privileged access to the nation's educated elites.

The second reform issue of exceptional importance is education for the job market. Inappropriate training is widely identified as one of the major failings of Arab higher education. It contributes directly to exceptionally high rates of educated youth unemployment. That in turn links the issue to an implicit political threat to incumbent elites, made manifest in the uprisings of 2011. It links the issue, as well, to the broad and highly disruptive economic reform efforts underway in the region since the 1970s. The linkage of structural economic crises and educational reform have afforded points of leverage to the advocates of reform in the donor community and their allies in the domestic policymaking community.

What Do We Know about Policymaking?

If educational reform and innovation are integral parts of the public policy process, what do we know of that process? Policymaking in the MENA is opaque. That is part and parcel of autocratic regimes with very weak instruments of accountability. There are many academics, expert members of NGOs or IFIs, technical advisors, and public officials who do understand at least parts of the policymaking process but feel unable to comment on it in any detail. They are bound by political prudence or rules of confidentiality.[3] It is thus surprising to find Morocco's Supreme Council for Education, Training, and Scientific Research take a highly critical look at the course of educational reform in the kingdom (Kingdom of Morocco, 2018). In my experience, this report is one of a kind.

With respect to external, third parties, Khalid Ikram, a senior economist at the World Bank who worked on Egypt for some forty years, chose to ignore any World Bank or Egyptian restrictions on his fine analyses of the economic reform process in Egypt (email, 2018). His books of 2006 and 2018 on Egypt's decades-long reform process are able to link outcomes to policymakers. Two World Bank colleagues, Syed Akhtar Mahmood and Meriam Ait Ali Slimane (2018), invaded the politics of policymaking in their prescriptive analysis of thwarting privilege and capture in all aspects of public policy. These, too, are rare analytic forays.

For the rest of us outside the policy black box there is the risk (noted in the Introduction) of two major analytic traps. First, we observe the outcomes of policies and then may read backward to assume that the policy's beneficiaries were responsible for its adoption. Our understanding of cause and effect may be off target. I fall into this trap where I deal with R&D policy and brain drain. Similarly, it is common to invoke crisis as the key variable in policy adoption. As a result, whatever context produces the policy is thus by definition one of crisis.[4] The weakness of legislatures means that interest groups do not engage in lobbying of a kind common in Western democracies but rather intervene directly with the executive to secure desired policies or ignore or bribe their way around laws and regulations after they are issued. In other words, stakeholders may influence policies *after* they are made, rather than before, by subverting or ignoring them. In this context there is no higher education lobby in Arab states, let alone regionwide associations that act as advocates for specific policies.

Weak accountability also means that the scope of public debate of existing and new policies is limited. The media do not provide robust fora for the discussion and analysis of policy alternatives.

In contrast to weak legislatures, the donor/financial community and nonregional state actors play a major role in the policy process. Their leverage comes through the support they can offer in times of stress or crisis. That support may take the form of investment, financial lines of credit, military/security backing, or a combination of all three. The support is contingent on policies (sometimes maintaining the status quo, sometimes representing sharp departures) that the third-party actors deem desirable. These actors focus on policies *before* they are made, seeking to shape their form and substance.[5] They are generally alert to the distortions that may be introduced in the implementation phase.

Top-down Reform

Top-down reform is, probably, the only way reform will be initiated, let alone sustained. For example, Saudi Arabia's Crown Prince Mohammed bin Salman in 2016 announced with great fanfare the kingdom's Vision 2030 for a post-oil economy. This was a classic top-down initiative, involving little or no public vetting or consultation. A major component is training Saudis for employment in the private sector, in which they have been relatively absent (Elgayar and Fox, 2018). What can be seen as the groundwork for Vision 2030 was laid as early as 2010 (Lindsey, 2010b).

The kings and royal families of Jordan and Morocco have spearheaded educational reform. In Egypt, it has been the minister of education who has driven reform. Yousry al-Gamal, minister of education from 2005 to 2010, laid the foundations for reform of the K–12 system (Bond et al., 2014?: 46), while Tarek Shawki, former professor at the AUC and minister of education after 2017, has pursued reforms in the role of the high school general exam (*al-thanawiya al-'amma*) and in bringing ICT to the pre-tertiary system. Baseera, an Egyptian polling outfit, found him to be Egypt's most popular minister in 2018.

As a counterfactual we can try to imagine what bottom-up reform would look like. It would involve much greater activism on the part of elected officials, parents' groups, and coalitions of universities. Such activism is relatively absent in the Arab world. Far more significant are student, teacher, and staff unions, but they usually become ferocious defenders of the status quo, not reform.

It is easy to assume that weak accountability affords authoritarian leaders the ability to make unpopular decisions and to take bold action.

Shawki, part of President al-Sisi's team, would seem to confirm that. But weak accountability is a two-edged sword. Along with bold action, leaders may prefer to remain relatively passive, even in the face of discontent or immanent crisis. In the education sphere, as in others, weak accountability in the Arab world is as likely to lead to inertia as it is to bold action.

That said, few leaders are indifferent to unemployment rates running at 10 percent of the eligible workforce and reaching 25 percent among the educated (secondary or higher). It is a long-term crisis that leads to periodic bursts of violence but is manageable in the short term through brain drain, the quiet tolerance of huge informal sectors that provide precarious, low-skill employment, and the creation of fictive jobs in the public sector. But these 'solutions' do not obviate the long-term erosion of political legitimacy that unemployment causes.[6]

So, leaders do act, and reformers try to get their ear and persuade them of a given course of action.[7] So do third parties in the donor community. There was a long era, not yet over, in which Arab autocrats, at least in the oil-poor, labor-rich countries of the region, broke sharply and repeatedly with BAU. It involved the 'fiscal crisis' of the Arab state first manifest in the 1970s, which has recurred periodically in the decades since then. Leaders dismantled long-standing social pacts, narrowed their coalitional support, and surrendered some of the levers of state control over their economies. There was plenty of popular protest during these decades, but the leaders adopted policies of change more in response to the pressure of the donor community than in response to their own people.

Fiscal crisis drove the policy-change process. Leaders were faced with untenable situations in the short term. Their nations' credit ratings were being periodically downgraded, creditors and investors were reducing their exposure, public expenditures were covered by printing money, inflation surged, and debt-servicing along with it. Stop-gap measures, such as lifting select consumer subsidies, succeeded only in arousing popular anger without solving the structural problems. The fiscal crises forced open the door to the entry of the private sector into university education. It led to or accelerated the decoupling of university education from public sector employment.

It can be reasonably argued that the Arab uprisings of 2011 grew out of the slowly evolving fiscal crisis and the abandonment of social contracts, but the cause and effect are not clear. Whatever the causes, the uprisings represented a full-blown crisis that led to regime change and civil war. The status quo and BAU were shattered in some countries (Egypt briefly, and

Tunisia) but not in others (such as Algeria, Jordan, Lebanon, Saudi Arabia, Sudan, and, to a lesser extent, Morocco).

The Arab uprisings of 2011 were not about education per se, but they destabilized systems to the extent that a certain range of reforms, such as electing presidents and deans, became possible. The window shut pretty quickly.

In Iraq, Syria, Libya, and Yemen the physical infrastructure of the educational systems has been badly damaged or destroyed. To rebuild will entail both institutional and physical reforms. If we begin to hear the slogan "build back better," beware. The example of Haiti after the January 2010 earthquake should show us how hollow that phrase can be. Nowhere have the uprisings triggered structural reforms in higher education. The old maxim "never let a good crisis go to waste" in this instance is likely to be ignored.

Third-party Leverage

The reform process has been driven significantly by outside actors armed with money and expertise. They are the usual suspects: the World Bank Group, regional development banks, bilateral aid agencies, and occasionally, foundations and NGOs (the latter often have expertise but not equivalent financial leverage).

These institutions have exploited the economic crises of the 1970s and 1980s to involve themselves in human resource formation in the broad sense and in education at all levels. The focus was and is on unemployment, the overstaffing of the public sector, and the stimulation of the private sector. The economic reforms, inspired by the so-called Washington Consensus, earned the epithet 'neoliberal,' and so did the educational reforms (Bou Hassan, 1997; World Bank, 2008; Buckner, 2011).[8] For many, if not most, intellectuals neoliberal reforms were seen as a perversion of the mission of higher education; its 'commodification' and its 'corporatization' (inter alia, Chaaban, 2015).

In parallel, European universities were entering the Bologna process (1999) to develop common standards and procedures, including accreditation, to encourage student and faculty mobility among them. The Bologna process led to the establishment of the European Higher Education Area. Turkey joined it in 2001 (Barbalan et al., 2008). The EU sought links with universities in the MENA through exchanges, joint degree programs, and research. Tentative but so far ineffective steps have been taken to create an Arab Education Area. This would involve establishing degree/diploma equivalencies, setting benchmarks against which to measure performance, and perhaps moving toward regional accreditation mechanisms (Lamine, 2010).

There are two European third parties that warrant special mention: Tempus and the Center for Mediterranean Integration (CMI). Tempus describes itself as the EU's program to support the modernization and reform of higher education in the EU's surrounding area, especially in the partner countries of Eastern Europe, Central Asia, the western Balkans, and the Mediterranean region. It aims to promote voluntary convergence of the higher education systems in the partner countries with EU developments in higher education. The Tempus program is implemented in close coordination with the Erasmus Mundus program, which provides scholarships to third-country students, allowing them to participate in top-level master's courses and doctorate programs.

The CMI was founded in 2009 and has several public policy foci. One is centered on education and reform: advancing university governance reforms, quality of technical and vocational skills, youth entrepreneurship, and innovation. The CMI enjoys support from the World Bank Group and the European Investment Bank. Several bilateral aid agencies are partners, such as the Agence Française de Développement.[9]

Reform by Stealth

In the Introduction, I discussed the reformer's dilemma: how does one move an autocrat to tolerate or even advocate reform *when part of the success of such an effort may be to prolong the life of the autocracy*? In contrast to reform through crisis, the driver here is reform through stealth, or what autocrats often call 'velvet revolutions.' Jean-Pierre Chauffour (2017) makes it clear that his goal is systemic change. But Mahmood and Slimane offer a more subtle approach. They see the challenge as one of institutional reform, a long-term affair that requires some opportunism to succeed: "What is possible in these cases, however, is a more granular understanding and awareness of barriers to change, even if at the end, little can be done in the present configuration, while waiting—literally—for the 'right time'" (Mahmood and Slimane 2018: 6).

Mahmood and Slimane's concern is not higher education but rather, insulating policy and public institutions from 'capture,' cronyism, and rent seeking. These 'bads' are likely to be part of the autocrat's political survival strategy. Their unlikely heroes in reform are mid-level bureaucrats who to some extent fly beneath the radar. These bureaucrats make choices along an indifference curve between 'living quietly' and 'doing the right thing.'

Living quietly is the expedient, safe course, while doing the right thing could entail political, career, and even physical risk.

The authors suggest, but do not require, a *deus ex machina*, a minister with a limited reform agenda upon whose coattails the mid-level bureaucrats may ride. Although their efforts must be "surreptitious," the bureaucrats may be able to take modest steps toward reform that, in turn, may have ripple effects: "Although it is challenging to address the problem of policy capture and privilege seeking, many technical solutions exist that may be politically feasible. A well-sequenced set of a critical mass of such reforms may have a cumulative effect over time and create a dent in a privilege-ridden system" (2018: 124).

This may be the logic behind quality assurance reforms that are widespread in the MENA (see page 199), but it is safe to say the autocrats know the game that is being played: "We will pocket your money and good will and make some gestures at reform."[10]

Morocco

Morocco illustrates well the role of external actors in the reform process, as well as the considerations lying outside the educational sector that may move reform along. Relative to other Arab states Morocco has been a vigorous reformer at all levels of education. At the same time it has been something of a laggard in terms of basic socioeconomic indicators such as literacy levels, female participation rates, and (in)equality of income distribution.

Morocco's king appoints the government. He is directly responsible for security, defense, the judiciary, and religious life. He supervises but is not directly responsible for the ministries involved in social and economic policy, including education. Therefore, he can criticize those whom he has appointed without implicating himself. King Mohammed VI has often been unsparing in his criticism of educational and other reform efforts, noting their failure to reach their self-assigned goals. For example, in his speech from the throne in July 2004, he set 2010 as the deadline for "reaching quality education." The Plan d'Urgence of 2009 signaled that that goal was receding. Even the mass demonstrations of February 2011 did not galvanize the reform effort, and in 2013, again in his speech from the throne, Mohammed VI talked of certain (university) specializations being factories of unemployment.[11]

The experience of Morocco since 1983 provides a representative example of the role of third parties in promoting educational reform. In that year Morocco entered into a structural adjustment program to correct macroeconomic imbalances. One of the main economic reforms was to contain public spending and to lower the deficit. The World Bank and the IMF identified the public sector wage bill as one of the problems (Clément, 1995; Bou Hassan, 1997). Early retirement programs were implemented across the civil service (Kleich Drey, 2008; Mrabi, 2013; Kingdom of Morocco, 2018).

The structural adjustment process led to a reduction in outlays on education of 11 percent between 1983 and 1989. It was accompanied by a program to deregulate and privatize parts of the education system. A series of reform programs was launched, beginning in 1999 with the National Education and Training Charter, followed by the Education Emergency Program of 2009–2012 (Plan d'Urgence) and the Education Action Plan of 2013–2016. By this time Morocco was led by the moderate Islamist party, the Party of Justice and Development (PJD), under Head of Government Abdelilah Benkirane. He was clearly comfortable with the spirit of neoliberal reform. Speaking in November at the fiftieth anniversary of the African Development Bank, he declared that "it is time that the state withdraws from certain sectors, such as healthcare and education and that the role of the state should be limited to assisting private operators who want to engage in these sectors" (Moroccan Coalition for Education for All et al. 2014).

In Chapter 5, we noted some of the governance reforms of these years in Morocco. There was the move to strengthen the universities' corporate identity, including their right to invest in or create private enterprises. They were linked to Morocco's seventeen regions in order to promote regional development and employment. University councils consisted of the presidents of regional councils, including the president of the regional council of *ulama*, and seven representatives of regional economic and social sectors. From the university there was the university president, three faculty members, and three student representatives.[12]

In the spirit of greater corporate identity, incoming presidents were to be selected on the basis of four-year plans for the university. The successful candidate could expect his/her plan to be the basis of a contract between the government and the university for the requisite level of funding.

The World Bank Group and allied third-party institutions mobilized substantial resources both for structural adjustment and for education reform. Figure 6.1 illustrates the leverage these entities can exert on the reform process.

More specifically, the World Bank has mobilized two education sector loans worth a total of $200 million. It is important to note that they

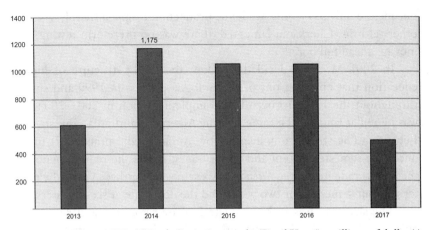

Figure 6.1 Morocco: World Bank Commitments by Fiscal Year (in millions of dollars)*
*Amounts include IBRD and IDA commitments
Source: http://www.worldbank.org/en/country/morocco/overview

focus mainly on pre-university education. The first loan, Educational Development Policy Loan 1, boosted coordination between key ministerial departments and contributed to better use of government resources through improved coordination among donors, aimed at maximizing the benefits of technical assistance-enhancing strategic planning. The loan was in support of the Plan d'Urgence. The World Bank helped mobilize other supporters: the African Development Bank, the European Investment Bank, the EU, the Agence Française de Développement, and the Spanish International Cooperation Agency for Development.[13]

The same institutions came forth with follow-up support for the period 2014–2017. The World Bank Group committed $100 million to the loan and another $50 million to support small and medium enterprises (SMEs), the hoped-for source of job creation for all levels of education.

One component of the structural adjustment support involved an early retirement scheme for the entire civil service, which went into effect in 2002. Some 39,000 civil servants took advantage of it. It was extended to university faculty as well. Full-time university faculty declined from 12,689 in 2002 to 12,194 in 2006 (Kleich Dray and Belcadi, 2008; Mrabi, 2013). Substantial bonuses were paid to those taking retirement. The impact on university faculty, according to Cherkaoui (2011: 164; Kingdom of Morocco, 2018), was negative. The best-trained, bilingual professors, frequently in law, architecture, and economics, with good job prospects outside the university, left. Academic production dropped sharply. As with other reforms, Cherkaoui lamented, there was no prereform testing, just moving ahead full bore.[14]

In 2001 Morocco decided to adopt the LMD structure of higher education that emerged out of the Bologna process in 1999 and spread throughout the EU. Morocco began implementation in 2003–2004 and was joined at roughly the same time by Algeria, Mauritania, Tunisia, and Lebanon. The structure is inspired by 'Anglo-Saxon' practice. It introduces the semester system and credit hours. It sets the requirements for the undergraduate degree *(licence)* at six semesters or three years, the master's at four semesters or two years, and the doctorate at six semesters.

The structure was to be characterized by rigorous standards of frequent student evaluation. Institutions would have a certain leeway in designing the structure of degree programs and curricular content, subject to central evaluation to measure equivalency.

A major objective was to harmonize higher education with European practice, thereby enhancing student and faculty exchanges and, to some extent, shared research. I am not sure why the LMD reforms have been limited to institutions in the region with a strong francophone background when the inspiration came from North America.

It is safe to say that implementation of the LMD reforms met, unsurprisingly, with considerable resistance just about everywhere. It involved a brutal shake-up of BAU, placed major demands on faculty to rewrite and restructure their offerings, and probably raised the quotient of supervisory work substantially. In Morocco, Cherkaoui characterized it as a disaster (2011: 43; interview, 2013; also Kingdom of Morocco, 2018: 35–47). Like the early retirement program, it was introduced without trials and testing. While we cannot claim cause and effect, the proportion of part-time faculty in Moroccan universities shot up. Significant reforms seldom go smoothly (one reason why leadership prefers inaction), and the LMD system may one day prove its worth, but we are still very much in the 'sea trial' phase.

Political agendas only tangentially related to education can and do produce reforms of considerable significance. It has long been a well-known feature of the Moroccan monarchy's effective political control to encourage a certain amount of division between those Moroccans identifying themselves as Berber and those who emphasize their Arab and Islamic origins. Rather than suppress these identities, the monarchy celebrates them and plausibly claims to incarnate both. King Mohammed VI, soon after inheriting the throne, issued a decree *(dahir)* on October 17, 2001, creating the Royal Institute of Amazigh Culture. By 2004, Morocco's three Berber dialects were being taught in the schools of the Berber regions. The *tifnagh* script was officially adopted as the alphabet for Berber. The institute signed agreements of cooperation and collaboration with the Ministry of Education to further develop the teaching of the Amazigh language and culture. The Universities of Agadir, Fez, and Oujda have each created a Department of Amazigh Studies to improve the teaching and the learning of the Amazigh language and culture (Silverstein, 2004; Saoud, 2014).[15]

Similarly, the creation of Morocco's seventeen regions, and the place of regional universities in them, was in part driven by Morocco's claims to the former Spanish Sahara, going back to 1975. Morocco's annexation of that region has not been fully accepted in the international community. It is bitterly contested by next-door Algeria. Regionalization in Morocco is partly designed to make the Western Sahara look like just another Moroccan region. Like the official blessing of the Berber languages and cultures, regionalization has had potentially profound effects on higher education.

There are solid indications that Morocco sees its way forward as being a kind of Singapore West. It aspires to become a trade and educational corridor between Europe and Sub-Saharan Africa. Morocco invests about $500 million a year in the latter, focusing on renewable energy, ICT, agriculture, and manufacturing. This engagement is about a decade old (Sharqi, 2016: 10; Oubenal, 2019: 323). At the same time Morocco is trying to lure European capital into manufacturing platforms that can export to Sub-Saharan Africa, the Middle East, and Europe. The automotive, aeronautic, and solar sectors are already substantial in Morocco (Chauffour, 2017).

In terms of education, the hope is that Morocco will become a pole of attraction for West African students (French would be a kind of lingua franca and Islam a spiritual and cultural bond). Special training institutes and research ventures, funded by Europeans, would assure a supply of relatively low-cost, highly skilled Moroccan employees to the manufacturing joint ventures. As Lahcen Daoudi, former minister of education and member of the ruling party, saw it, this kind of education could have a strong appeal for the 52,000 Moroccans studying abroad (as of 2013), bringing them and what they spend on fees back to Morocco. Morocco had and has a chance to get a leg up on its competition (interview, 2013). Like the head of government at the time, Abdelilah Benkirane, Daoudi saw education reform as a business proposition. "Le Maroc se vend bien" (Morocco sells well), he said to me.

Morocco's strategy would offer political dividends, as well. It could be sold as helping to stem the flow of refugees across the Mediterranean to Europe and to shrinking the field for extremism. Morocco could also curry favor with its African neighbors for its claims to the Western Sahara. Reform is often helped by pay-offs in other areas.

I quoted Chauffour at the beginning of this chapter to indicate the far-reaching political implications of education reform. As he was writing about Morocco, I will end this section with excerpts from Chauffour that I suspect set eyes rolling in Rabat. First, he sketches out a kind of crisis. At current rates of change, he warns, it will take fifty years for Morocco to "converge" with the economies of southern Europe. Morocco, he argues, must accelerate and boost its productivity growth substantially:

> Place education at the heart of development. For the education reform to be effective, it will have to be realistic and selective. It should tackle major constraints in a "shock therapy" approach designed to trigger an "educational miracle," that is, a huge improvement in the Moroccan students' level of education. This would require a complete overhaul of the education system, improved teacher recruitment and training, the adoption of a new brand of public-school governance, the development of alternative educational options (charter schools, school vouchers and home schooling), and the promotion of 21st century skills. (2017: 4)

Chauffour then takes on the "system" as a whole: "For example, the behavior that hampers free competition and the country's economic openness by protecting special interests and maintaining nepotism and rent-seeking *is often rooted in the players' history, culture and way of thinking*. Those within the system who benefit from its protection find it normal that so many others should be deprived of it" (2017: 59, emphasis added).

Third-party experts prefer to couch reform in bland and neutral terms that imply that reform can be reached through existing institutions and practices without any abrupt challenge to BAU. Talking of "shock therapy" to the host government is certainly bold and probably foolhardy.

Governance

We reviewed the basic trends in governance and governance reform in Chapter 5. The political dangers contained in governance reform were reviewed in Chapter 3. Here, a few summary remarks will suffice. The linkage of economic reforms to education reforms means that progress toward greater institutional autonomy, albeit slow, is underway. If its progress does not shake the rest of the system, then political leaders may not impede it. As a result, there is some cautious optimism among various experts in the education field. As Andris Barbalan, Üstün Ergüder, and Kemal Gürüz note, "The emergence of national quality assessment agencies and the switch from 'line-item' to lump sum budgets accompanied by the strengthened role of the university head and the increased discretionary powers given to the central administration of the institution represent basic features of what characterizes the transformation from the regulatory to the evaluative state" (2008).

"It is likely that the Arab Spring will certainly affect the governance system of higher education, probably in the direction of more independence, participation and partnerships," said Rajika Bhandari, deputy vice president of research and evaluation at the Institute of International Education (quoted in Hamdan, 2011).

The sad fact is that, with a few partial exceptions (Tunisia, Morocco, Jordan), the Arab uprisings have resulted mainly in the reassertion of authoritarian controls, physical destruction of much educational infrastructure, and, in the case of Turkey after the 2016 attempted coup, sweeping purges of university faculty and administrators.

Education and the Job Market: The Great Mismatch[16]

There is now an extensive literature on the 'youth bulge,' the 'demographic dividend,' 'waithood,' and the educated unemployed (in the Maghreb, *les chômeurs diplomés*) in the Middle East (see, inter alia, Handoussa and Tzannatos, 2002; Dhillon and Youssef, 2009; Dyer, 2009; Amin et al., 2012; Assaad and Barsoum, 2009; Salisbury, 2011; Kolster and Matondo-Fundai, 2012; UNDP and AFESD, 2016; EBRD, EIB, and IBRD, 2016; Van Diesel and Abu-Ismail, 2019). Lower fertility is creating a youth bulge and corresponding relative growth in the working population. This has reduced the 'dependency ratio,' the number of people outside the workforce (mainly the young, the old, and those doing unremunerated housework), to low levels. That fact should produce the demographic dividend—an abundant, educated workforce with relatively few dependents to support. The economies of the Middle East have the opportunity to ride this favorable dependency ratio to higher and sustainable growth and prosperity.

It is not happening. Outside the oil exporters, economic growth has stuttered. Regional turmoil since 2011 has been a factor, but the basic statistics before and after 2011 do not differ much. Overall unemployment seems stuck at 10 percent in most countries, while youth unemployment averages 24–25 percent of the relevant cohorts. Most analysts emphasize that in the Arab world unemployment is structural, not cyclical (inter alia, Assaad, Krafft, and Yassin, 2018; Kabbani, 2019). In Morocco it surged to 28 percent in 2018 after decades of reform efforts. Women's participation rate as a proportion of all eligible women seldom exceeds a third. Even Turkey, in relative terms a star performer, with the world's eighteenth largest economy, and not benefitting from petroleum rents, has an overall unemployment rate of 10 percent and a youth unemployment rate of 19 percent. Its female employment rate is about 33 percent. The International Labour Organization estimated that youth unemployment will keep rising, reaching 29.1 percent in the Middle East and 30.7 percent in North Africa by 2019, whereas the peak rate in other world regions would not exceed 18 percent (UNDP and AFESD, 2016: 80).

The Kingdom of Jordan is not alone in underlining the severity of the problem:

> Over many years the progress of education in Jordan exceeded other countries in the region, in both quality and quantity. Over recent years, however, that progress has stalled, and our education system is no longer producing the results the Kingdom needs. There is an oversupply of university graduates and chronic undersupply of skilled craftsmen and technicians. As a result, youth unemployment is running at 31.8% and total workforce participation is only 41%, one of the lowest rates in the world. (Kingdom of Jordan, 2015?: 4)

It then suggests KPIs on youth unemployment that are striking in their modesty: the unemployment rate among university graduates in five years is to go down to 24 percent and in ten years to 20 percent (2015?: 4; see also Abu Farha, 2015).[17]

The great majority of unemployed youth have had at least a primary-school education. Everywhere youth unemployment is inversely correlated with level of education. The basic trope is that once the public sector had sated itself on high school and university graduates, it fell to the private sector to take up the slack. But, so the story goes, the private sector found the products of the education system unsuited to their needs, hence the mismatch. Once again, the MENA is not alone,[18] and after the crash of 2008 a number of southern European economies spawned unemployment that looked much like that of the Middle East. But the region's problem appears more deep-seated, persistent, and resistant to reform.

The job–skills mismatch is twofold. Formal-sector employers allegedly cannot find the type of employees they need. The informal sector, that vast gray economy beyond the tax collector and state regulation, soaks up educated and uneducated youth in low-skill, low-tech jobs (El-Haddad and Gadallah, 2018). The educated are overqualified for the work they find in the informal sector. On average, the informal sector absorbs about 40 percent of all new entrants to the job market, the public sector 25 percent, and the formal private sector around 10 percent. The remainder are unemployed. The informal sector is where many young Middle Easterners spend their 'waithood,' that is, the time between graduation and finding a suitable formal-sector job. At the time of the uprisings, waithood averaged 1.7–2 years in a number of Arab countries (Amin et al., 2012: 56–57; Dhillon and Yousef, 2009; Assaad and Krafft, 2016a).[19]

There is significant variation among Arab economies in the employment role of the informal sector. Assaad, Krafft, and Salemi (2019) compare Egypt, Jordan, and Tunisia, and despite some differences, those who make the most rapid transition to informal-sector employment among the educated tend to come from lower socioeconomic strata and do not pursue the highest-quality degree programs in tertiary education (engineering, medicine, economics). The bias toward the better-off in access and completion of tertiary degrees is thus reinforced by access to the workforce, with the poorer strata with inferior credentials forced into the informal sector, while the better-off with more prestigious diplomas move into the formal private sector or the civil service.

In contrast to the 1970s and 1980s, when the demand for higher education graduates was strong, above all in the civil service and the rapidly expanding education sector itself, it is now the case just about everywhere that the returns to higher education are diminishing (Salehi-Isfahani, 2009; Kolster and Matondo-Fundai, 2012; Tzannatos, 2016; Tzannatos et al., 2016; Boughazala et al., 2016; Rizk, 2016). According to Zafiris Tzannatos and colleagues (2016), "the general picture that has emerged so far is that RORE (rates of return to education) in the MENA are:[20]

- Lowest compared to other regions, with an additional year of schooling adding around 5.4 percent to labor earnings compared to a world average of 7 percent
- Particularly low for secondary education (3.5 percent) followed by tertiary education (8.9 percent); both are almost half the respective world averages (6.9 percent and 16.9 percent)

- High for primary education (9.4 percent), which is almost equal to the world average (10.3 percent)
- Higher for women than for men (nearly 8 percent versus 5 percent)
- Higher in North Africa/ Maghreb than in the Middle East" (Tzannatos et al., 2016: 3; see also Kabbani and Salloum, 2010, on Syria).

The causal argument they advance goes to the heart of the political regime:

> Under the traditional "social contract" the population (or, at least, part of it) exchanged political freedom in return for public sector jobs (as well as free public services, low taxes, subsidies and other state handouts). This is the cause that, apart from resulting in low quality services that required few real qualifications on behalf of public sector workers, it [sic] created low incentives for families and individuals to invest in education beyond the point of credentials. Getting employment became a matter of entitlement rather than a privilege to be earned through merit, effort and productive service. Under these conditions, the quality of the education output is low resulting in workers having low productivity. This pushes the demand for labor down giving rise to low returns to the acquisition of additional education. (Tzannatos et al., 2016: 18)

The low returns to education have, it is suggested (Campante and Chor, 2012), a direct political effect: an unemployed or poorly employed youth faces a low opportunity cost in engaging in political protest. They do not have much to lose.

The Arab world has unusually high rates of brain drain (Hanafi and Arvanitis, 2016: 149). The continued investment by students and parents in tertiary education may reflect the inclination of the region's educated youth to go abroad for employment, where the RORE will be much higher (Nahas, 2010). The phenomenon is old. In the early 1980s it is estimated that half of all Arab PhDs had left the region and that only two of every five Arab researchers were working in the region (Massalias and Jarrar, 1991: 193). Three decades later it was estimated that Algeria had 22,000 'researchers' working in-house while 40,000 were abroad (Sawahel, 2011).

The 2016 *Arab Human Development Report* attributed brain drain to the exclusion of youth in Arab society and to the "barriers of patronage, wasta, nepotism, and autocratic controls" (UNDP and AFESD 2016: 155–56). It indicates that over time the willingness of tertiary graduates to emigrate has grown enormously, from about 20 percent twenty years ago to over 60 percent in 2015. In 2010, 62 percent of Jordanian migrants abroad were university graduates. All Arab countries, it claims, promote such migration to varying degrees for political and economic reasons (2016: 161).[21]

We have seen how Morocco intends to address this problem through business partnerships with Europe aimed at supplying African markets. The goal is to bring innovative education to Moroccans and Africans in Morocco. Jordan adopted a much more radical approach, albeit one that can only address a small part of the problem. It is considering establishing an advanced polytechnic school aimed at graduating skilled students from all over the Arab world whose ultimate destination would be the skilled labor market in Europe. The logic is that the demographics of Europe's aging population favor this sort of export. If the local markets for educated talent are evolving slowly, then brain drain by design may relieve some of the pressure (Al Adwan, 2013).

The destabilizing effect of the mismatch has been evident for some time. To provide something like sixteen years of education to young Arabs (male or female) and then leave them without meaningful or appropriate employment leaves them with every incentive to attack the 'system' (see Elbadawi and Makdisi, 2017: 52–57; on Tunisia, see Fahmi and Medded, 2015). In one of the more thorough empirical studies of the causes of the Arab uprisings, Campante and Chor conclude: "Taken together, these different pieces of information build a narrative that suggests that the combination of rising levels of education and poor job prospects—particularly for the relatively skilled—was present in the Arab world, and particularly so in those countries that have witnessed the Arab Spring in its fullest bloom" (2012: 174).

The uprisings of 2011, even in countries that were relatively spared (Morocco, Algeria, Jordan), elicited measures to address employment, productivity, and innovation. Morocco created over four thousand new civil service jobs to satisfy a few of the *chomeurs diplomés*. It earmarked over $60 million to support "innovation centers, R&D, and business-university partnerships." The General Confederation of Moroccan Businesses pledged to support the effort through "special training contracts, developing apprenticeships, building better bridges between enterprises and universities, involving businesses in career guidance for students, and special conversion training for graduates in subject areas with no economically viable openings" (Sawahel, 2011).

Jordan started earlier. In 2003 it launched its Faculty for Factory program at Jordan University to "engage academia and industry in structural assistance programs for their mutual benefit." The focus is primarily on SMEs, and expert faculty are to provide diagnostics and project designs to strengthen private enterprise. It currently fields over eighty academics, mainly in engineering, from nine Jordanian universities. The great majority still come from Jordan University and the Jordan University of Science and Technology (summary provided to me by Yousef Al-Abdallat, the program's director). The program, according to some close observers, has not worked well. Professors do not actually help solve problems. They are chiefly interested in the salary and the ability to generate publications from their work (Elkarmi and Al-Mulki, interviews, 2015).

At the time of the uprisings, Jordan, under the auspices of the King Abdullah II Foundation for Development, started a student-centered program called the University Summer Training Program (DARB) to acclimate students to work in the private sector and to afford them practical training. The first cohort of 388 students was placed in the summer of 2011, and by 2015 some 2,800 students had benefited from DARB. Subsequently 324 were offered jobs.[22]

The job mismatch is usually measured in terms of private sector employers' dissatisfaction with the skill set university, vocational, and high school graduates bring to work: too many graduate in the humanities or social sciences and too few in the STEM disciplines.[23] Masses of graduates come out of diploma mills like Egypt's 'commerce' *(tijara)* faculties. While the graduates nominally have business degrees, they are quintessential products of the culture "you pretend to teach us, and we pretend to learn." University graduates reach the job market without critical thinking skills, experience in problem solving, or training in 'citizenship skills' (Faour and Muasher, 2011).

The private sector, however, has a lot to answer for (for useful surveys, see UNDP and AFESD 2016: 81–88; EBRD, EIB, and IBRD, 2016: 73–87; Assaad, Krafft, and Salehi-Isfahani, 2018: 970).[24] For decades, in the 1960s through to the 1980s, it was repressed and discouraged in many Arab states. Its natural refuge was the informal sector, rent-seeking behavior, and quick profits. That era was succeeded by the structural adjustment phase when, all too often, regime 'cronies' in the private sector got inside deals on undervalued privatizations, state contracts, monopolistic licenses, and the like. The Alawi-minority regime in Syria captured a significant part of the Sunni capitalist class in Damascus and Aleppo in this manner. Cronyism became the glue of what we now know was a dysfunctional political system (in general, see Diwan et al., 2019).

Even in the more market-friendly era, the private sector has been most comfortable in sectors with quick returns, such as real estate, tourism, and the financial sector, or in sectors that do business with the state. Morocco, which has an old and experienced capitalist class and which has always been market-friendly, nonetheless looks, in terms of unemployment, much like the more populist regimes of the region. Education reform without an overhaul of the private sector will be like one hand clapping.

So once the civil service is saturated, university graduates turn to a private sector that in many instances does not need them. As we shall see, the Middle Eastern private sector is not heavily invested in STEM areas (in contrast, say, to Israel), and it invests relatively little in R&D (see Chapter 7). The financial sector, of course, needs graduates with business training. All institutions, public or private, need ICT support. But the tourism sector, outside the ranks of management, does not really need university graduates.[25] Universities may have failed the job market, but the job market has also failed the universities.

There is imperfect congruence in the views of political elites and private sector employers on the nature of the challenges, but there are also significant differences. The eight-country survey of private sector firms by the European Bank for Reconstruction and Development (EBRD) and other institutions (EBRD, EIB, and IBRD, 2016) reveals that political instability was the most commonly cited private sector concern. That reflects the major concern of the MENA political leadership, especially after the 2011 uprisings.

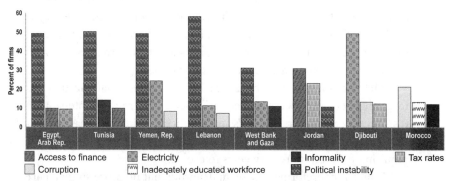

Figure 6.2. Political Instability is Most Commonly Chosen as Top Obstacle by MENA Surveyed Firms (2013–14)

Source: EBRD 2016: Fig. 2.5. *Note:* For each economy the three obstacles most frequently chosen as the top obstacle by firms are shown.

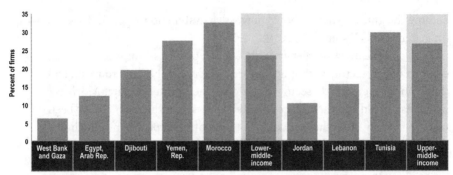

Figure 6.3 The Proportion of Firms Reporting an Inadequately Educated Workforce as a Severe Constraint
Source: EBRD, 2016: Fig. 4.11

By contrast, whereas political leaders see the problems of higher education and the job mismatch as regime threatening, the private sector is focused on access to finance, corruption, power supply, political instability, and the informal sector as its major firm-level challenges. An inappropriately educated workforce is not among their major concerns.

The report by EBRD and other institutions (EBRD, EIB, and IBRD, 2016) stresses that firms experiencing rapid growth are much more concerned by the skills mismatch because they rely more heavily on university-educated employees than other firms of comparable size. But size is also a predictor.

Large firms will be the most likely to employ university graduates. By contrast, formal SMEs tend not to grow very much. So large, young, export-oriented firms may be those that suffer the most from the mismatch and hold the key to employing the educated unemployed. We may conclude that there are sufficient shared concerns between governments and their private sectors concerning political stability and the need to address the mismatch to sustain a policy reform process.

Melonio and Mezouaghi (2015: 74) are correct that the time frame for such a reform process is necessarily very long, as the professional status of teachers, university admission practices, and the increase of faculty in expanding programs are all components of a higher education system requiring from ten to twenty years to evolve.

Educational reforms may seem daunting, but no more so than curtailing public employment, reducing consumer subsidies, extending lines of credit to young entrepreneurs, easing labor regulations, and enhancing the ease of doing business. Addressing the causes of informality might have the greatest reform impact, but leaving it alone to work its magic is the most tempting course.

The fact that reform is 'organic,' that is, that change in one area will impact on several other areas, has an upside: a change in one area may have a ripple effect, triggering change in other related areas (Mahmood and Slimane, 2018: 165). Thus, we need to keep the broad reform process clearly in mind. My analysis, for example, sees the private sector as a critical player, one that is increasingly recognized by policymakers. But the fact that at present it may provide only 10–15 percent of new jobs to educated youth seeking work raises the question of just how much attention it should receive.

Quality Assurance

'Quality assurance' has a soothing, almost bland ring to it. It is the gentle face of reform. It has been a major World Bank and CMI project in the Arab world since the turn of the millennium. The CMI and the World Bank sponsor the University Governance and Quality Assurance Program, which addresses issues of inadequate access to higher education, institutional quality, and discrepancies between the needs of the labor market and what the educational system produces. Quality assurance encompasses a potentially sweeping set of targets. The main thrust has been establishing standards, benchmarks and KPIs, strategic planning, and accreditation (see Hajji, 2008; Faek, 2017). These headings allow university leaders, outside agencies, and would-be reformers to raise all the structural and systemic issues of autonomy and excellence that might otherwise alarm political leaders. But even if there is an element of reform by stealth embedded in quality assurance, there is also the risk that all involved will treat it more as theater than as grasping the nettle of structural reform (for background, see World Bank and CMI, 2013).

In its human resource development strategy, Jordan's reformers, led by Queen Rania, tick all the appropriate boxes: "Our system strives to provide world-class experiences and outcomes for all involved. It aligns with the needs of the local and global economy. It is globally respected and meets, if not exceeds, international standards through accreditation, certification, and quality assurance. We continually monitor ourselves to identify and implement improvements" (Kingdom of Jordan, 2015?: 5).

In 2007 a regional organization, the Arab Organization for Quality Assurance in Education (AROQA), was founded.[26] Only a small minority of Arab universities are full members of AROQA, and only Jordan University and Jordan University of Science and Technology are top tier.

AROQA holds an annual conference that may help bolster a 'community of practice' in institutional assessment. It aspires to become a regional accreditation organization.[27]

By 2012, fourteen Arab countries had engaged in some level of quality assurance (Hassan, 2012; El-Amine, 2014). Egypt pioneered it in 2002, on the strength of a $50 million grant from the World Bank. The National Quality Assurance Agency was established in 2006, independent of the Ministry of Higher Education and the Council of Ministers. It developed a quality assurance handbook for universities, using nineteen standards for assessment. The assumption was that the university actually has the ability to deal with the standards. As noted in Chapter 5 on governance, this is not at all self-evident. Under the governance standards, there is no direct questioning of centralized budget and finance procedures. Assessment teams could find rubrics under which to comment on the relations of universities to the Supreme Council and to the ministry, but they are not obvious.

Syria got on board with quality assurance, establishing the Higher Committee on Quality and Accreditation in January 2005. It was tasked with adopting ongoing self-evaluation at universities, setting criteria for quality and academic distinction, establishing a quality assurance system for public and private higher education institutions with external auditing of quality, and setting criteria for the government's accreditation of degrees.

Tunisia joined up in 2008 (Boughazala et al., 2016), with a law to meet quality and employability challenges. It constitutes the basic higher education law, defining the main principles and objectives underlying the design of Tunisia's higher education system. It introduced formally the LMD scheme. Mongi Boughazala cautions that the test of the law will be its implementation.

Lebanon, with World Bank funding, took up quality assurance in 2002, but at the time of writing (2017), Lebanon's largest and only public university, Lebanese University, had not joined the process. It had allowed visiting teams to assess specific departments but not the university as a whole. Ironically the initiative is led by Ahmad Jammal, the director-general of the Ministry of Education and a tenured member of the Lebanese University faculty, but his clients, as it were, are all private universities. LU, he judges, sees threats and few opportunities in quality assurance (interview, 2013). It is not alone. Many Arab universities shy away from quality assurance out of fear of "unfair comparisons" or of any kind of structured evaluation (Bhandari and El-Amine, 2011; Lindsey, 2011a). Inasmuch as most universities do not have control over the variables that define their quality, their fears are not misplaced.

There is, then, a risk that IHLs will merely go through the motions of quality assurance. A self-evaluation at the Faculty of Economic, Social, and Juridical Sciences of MVU in 2007 concluded, "Because of the great number of students, the culture of quality is not a major preoccupation of the faculty. No system of quality assurance has been put in place. There is no system of evaluation" (Kingdom of Morocco, 2007: 185).

In a World Bank survey of a hundred Arab universities, there is an astonishing avowal for which the authors offer no analysis or explanation: "Although institutions report that they have mechanisms in place to monitor achievement of their goals, in reality little evidence was found of systematic use of key performance indicators" (World Bank and CMI, 2013: 35; see also Faek, 2017).

Strategic planning and the rigorous measurement of progress toward goals (KPIs) are almost always unpopular, both among university administrators and among faculty. Accrediting agencies insist on these exercises, but they may result in formulaic behavior without producing change.

Regional Cooperation and Exchange

The Arab world, despite its aspirations, has never achieved the levels of economic and political union of the EU. Its relative disarray has only been accentuated since 2011. There is nothing in the region like the European education space set up by the Bologna process. On the eve of the 2011 uprisings the situation was already bleak. Of 3.76 million students enrolled in Arab universities, 3.6 million were citizens, or 96.3 percent. There were 109,000 students from other Arab countries (2.9 percent) attending Arab universities outside their home countries, while non-Arabs totaled 28,816, or 0.8 percent. These data show clearly that student mobility among Arab countries is feeble, while student mobility from other regions to Arab countries amounts to a rounding error (Lamine, 2010: 57). There were no regional systems of accreditation or degree equivalency. Inter-Arab research was minimal. Faculty movement was driven almost entirely by wage differentials, with the oil-rich importing faculty from the oil-poor. External linkages were overwhelmingly with the leading universities of the OECD.[28]

Since 2011 the situation has deteriorated further. The four partially or wholly failed states of Libya, Yemen, Iraq, and Syria can play no meaningful role in regional education except to export students and faculty cut adrift by their failed systems. The civil conflict in these states has polarized regional politics roughly into pro-Saudi and pro-Iranian camps, with a few (Morocco, Jordan, Kuwait, Oman) trying to straddle the divide.

The one positive element is the universities' quest for new sources of revenue. Offering courses and degrees to Arab students with the means to pay is a means to this end. It appears, however, that private universities are more adept at attracting such students, who are often the rejects of their own public systems, than are public universities.

The international education market involves something like five million students. A number of countries have invested in attracting them (the US, Australia, the EU, Canada, inter alia). A primary motive is to capture tuition revenues, but a few countries, primary among them Singapore, see such recruitment as a direct infusion of talent into their skilled workforce. Philip Yeo, director of Economic Development Innovation Singapore, told me in an interview (2015) that he was basically a kidnapper, scouring Southeast Asia for high school and university students who would eventually help Singapore remain at the cutting edge of Asian innovation. Tony Tan (2007: 7) has written, "Singapore's openness to global talent is its key competitive advantage. There are many foreign, private institutions such that 72,000 international students study in Singapore, with 9,000 in the three public universities. At the same time, half of all students are engaged in study abroad." Even though the quality of Arab higher education lags behind that of Singapore, it can still, with its current assets, make significant progress in inter-Arab education and also in international higher education.

Conclusion

"We cannot talk of the future of the university [Damascus University] in isolation," writes 'Ammar al-Samar. "*It is part of a sinking ship*. There is no use in its reform without fundamental change in Syria" (al-Samar, 2018: 146, emphasis added). Al-Samar reminds us, if we need reminding, that educational reform is organically linked to other sectors of society and the economy. Educational reform is futile in the absence of reform in these other areas. Jean-Pierre Chauffour, perhaps with the weight of the World Bank behind him, said as much.

Because the reform process depends heavily on public authorities, we should not be surprised that little disruptive innovation, in the sense used by Christensen (1997; 2008), has occurred. The current set of government and private sector providers have left demand for specific kinds of education unmet. There are opportunities for disruptors to enter the market, but they will surely come from the private sector (see Chapter 7 and the Conclusion).

- The economic dynamic that has led to growing private provision of education at all levels will not diminish in the foreseeable future. Creative ways to meet unmet demand will be found. Policymakers will be challenged to find ways to regulate the new providers. There is the distinct possibility, however, that private providers will be part of crony networks that sustain incumbent regimes and hence will be protected from regulation.

- I have made some bold and worrying assumptions about the views of autocratic regimes toward higher education. I have followed the dangerous *démarche* of reading backward from observed results to hypothesized causes. I think political leaders are worried about survival and are willing to take some risks to avoid catastrophic losses. The private sector is passively supportive of reform initiatives, but its history over the past decades is not one to encourage private actors to lead the reform process. We have more empirical evidence of private sector views than we do of autocratic leadership views. The private sector model of relative autonomy, financial independence, and governance by boards (with oversight from Supreme Councils of Universities) is, with time and proliferation, likely to seep into the public sector.

- To date, the educational reform agenda has been modest and has relied for progress on third-party leverage. Yet it appears to be the case that political leaders can easily discern the links among education, the job market, and economic growth, all of which help define their own political legitimacy. All political leaders recognize that something must be done, but they hope that whatever that is, the basis of their rule will not be challenged in the process. They are right to be worried.

7
Innovation and Critical Linkages

We may tend to see innovation as mainly technological: self-driving vehicles, the internet of things, artificial intelligence (AI), robotics, and the like. But innovation can also involve the introduction of new programs, business models, organizational concepts, and so forth. Several Arab universities in the last decade or more have introduced the use of the credit hour as the building block of credentialing, and along with it the LMD model specifying three years of study for the bachelor's, two years for the master's, and three years for the PhD. No new technology is necessarily involved in this, but it has profound implications for teaching, curriculum, and the use of professorial and other teaching staff time. It is partially aimed at enhancing the mobility of students and faculty among institutions that adopt it. It is definitely innovative.

We should think of innovations along a spectrum from supporting BAU to shaking the foundations of regimes. If one believes that existing arrangements are basically good, then making the status quo viable is a worthy objective. If one thinks BAU is unsustainable, then more radical reform is called for. Third-party agents are in a bind. They are legally bound to work with existing authorities and would lose their leverage if they were perceived as undermining political arrangements. But they may doubt that current arrangements can foster necessary change (see, for example, Chauffour, 2017, on Morocco).

Innovation and reform may be classified under three labels (see also Chapter 6). The first is what I would call inward-looking innovation, which seeks to alter how universities carry on their basic business. The second is outward-looking innovation, by which IHLs structure their interactions with the government and the private sector. The third is disruptive innovation. In its classic manifestation, explained below, disruptive innovation is seldom generated from within the system but is more like a meteorite from outer space that one sees only when it is too late.

The three kinds of innovation blend into one another. It is less difficult to engineer changes that are contained within the walls. When they aim at external constituencies, coordination and implementation become much more difficult. All have the capacity to disrupt the IHL if fully implemented. In combination, they have the potential to reinvent the university as we know it in the Arab world. Inward-looking innovation will focus on new financial models and the use of technology to lower average costs of education and of research. It may involve redefining what it is to be a professor and consequently how professors are evaluated and remunerated. It may involve distance-learning blended with face-to-face instruction, again in an effort to reduce overall costs of instruction. It may involve new forms of credentialing, moving from the LMD model described above (itself an innovation) to competency-based credentials that consist in mastering a set of skills or knowledge. Successful innovations in inward-looking change will spread rapidly because they directly address the day-to-day concerns of university administrators who operate under severe resource constraints.

Of equal, if not greater, long-term significance are outward-oriented innovations. I see these as mainly focused on the links between the employment sectors (government and the private sector) and the university. There has never been a period in my lifetime when these external linkages have loomed larger. What the workforce of the future will look like, and thus what higher education must do to prepare for it, is not at all clear. When we do not know where we are going, it is hard to know what institutions are best able to provide both leaders and the cadres.[1]

It is important to keep in mind that of the three stakeholders in innovation—IHLs, the government, and the private sector—it is government and IHLs that have the most at stake. If governments are unable to help solve the employment riddle, they can expect new episodes of the 2011 uprisings and regime demise for some. If universities cannot contribute to the solution, they will become liabilities to the government, useless to their main beneficiaries, students, and, as they are now, irrelevant to technological innovation. For its part, the private sector must be wooed with credit and tax incentives and transformed from the transactional short-term profit-making entity that it mostly is today to one that is creating jobs and helping design the educational programs to meet its demand.

Outward-oriented innovations have to address both challenges: how to meet the demands and requirements of the existing private and parastatal sectors that define today's labor market *and* try to anticipate what the regional labor market will look like in twenty to thirty years. *It may be that Arab universities will, of necessity, deal with inward-looking innovations, but it is moot whether or not they have the will or capacity to deal with outward-looking innovation.* For instance, at the present time there is a gap and no little suspicion between IHLs and the private sector. Universities are not yet heavily involved in advanced research or R&D. Public universities have not been given the resources or the incentives to lead on issues of the 'knowledge economy.' Many reforms and innovations, especially regarding curriculum, teaching methods, and the technology of delivering instruction will involve both inward-looking and outward-looking measures. This is where universities should begin to innovate.

There has been an explosion in the private provision of higher education, more so in the number of institutions than in the number of students. How do we treat private providers? Given the quasi-monopoly enjoyed for decades by public institutions, this is a disruptive innovation, but one brought about by players within the existing system—heads of state, ministers of finance, private investors, and external sources of funding and expertise. The old model was financially and conceptually exhausted. Legal frameworks were changed to allow the private sector to provide education and to collect fees for it. This, it was hoped, would take pressure off the public sector and allow it to shore up its dwindling centers of excellence.

Private education, born in economic crisis, is a powerful example. It is gradually transforming the face of higher education, but it was initially designed to ease claims on public finances. By definition, disruptive innovations are more or less unanticipated by those who will be most affected (disrupted) by them. In this sense, public policy comes into play only as damage control.

The bricks-and-mortar university, with its large population of students and employees, and its large sunk costs, seems ripe for disruptive innovation. It has a very costly business model, whether costs are charged to students or to governments. Everywhere in the world those costs have been rising well above domestic rates of inflation. Those who pay—parents, governments, and their taxpayers—are not happy with what they receive. The 'business proposition' does not appear to be viable. There is a large, identifiable market for higher education and there are 'venerable' institutions to supply it. The question is, are there new actors who can meet the demand at a fraction of the cost and with the same or better quality?

Inward-looking Innovation

Inward versus outward is always a question of more or less, not of either/ or (see Table 7.4). An ESCWA study (2014) seeks to identify the ways in which universities can be linked to society, including government and the private sector. It comes up with six recommendations that have the virtue of being in the realm of the possible:

1. Incentivize research teams rather than individuals,
2. Establish credible refereed journals,
3. Incentivize international and regional collaboration,
4. Compensate faculty research time,
5. Structure faculty time to encourage research early rather than late in the career, and
6. Mitigate brain drain by international networking and recruiting.

Only the fourth and fifth recommendations are unambiguously inward-looking. The first might best be carried out by government-managed research funds (the CNRS-L is a good example). The second might involve establishing pan-Arab journals. The other four combine inward- and outward-looking foci. They all combine reform and innovation.

Public IHLs are appendages of the state, their finances coming from central budgets, their leadership is politically vetted, and, whatever the law may say, they are dependent on the good will of the head of state. IHL faculty are, basically, civil servants. Given this situation it is surprising to me how open to innovation the leadership of public IHLs actually is. Abdallatif Miraoui, the president of CAU in Marrakesh, told me, "We [Morocco] are a country of the south, not of the north, not like France or the US. *We have no choice but to change the paradigm.* Complaining about our situation will get us nothing. We have to innovate. . . . We need to be a smart university. We need to go digital" (interview, 2018, emphasis added). One could say that talk is cheap, but Miraoui and many others in the Arab world actually walk the walk.[2] Why this is astonishing is that the system provides few incentives for them to do so (see Chapter 8).

What has gone on at CAU involves both inward- and outward-looking innovation. "Going digital" has been the key to curricular and pedagogic innovation. In turn it has also entailed alliances with business groups and technology suppliers such as Microsoft. Most recently, CAU has built and launched an incubator, thereby carving out an entrepreneurial role for itself.

CAU's inward-looking innovation was thrust upon it by state policies. We talk casually about the massification of higher education in the Arab world, but looking at CAU's statistics is startling. In 2011, when President Miraoui took office, CAU enrolled 29,000 students. By 2016–2017 that number had risen to 76,500. In 2018 it was 102,000. Further expansion is anticipated. This is extraordinary growth, and it is the result of decisions made in the Ministry of Education, not at CAU. Morocco's Supreme Council for Education, Training, and Scientific Research (Kingdom of Morocco, 2018: 22) reported on three public universities whose enrollments had grown 170 percent over a seven-year period.

CAU has a certain buzz to it such that many Moroccan students try to go there, but the financial resources to support this massification have not followed. The corps of instructors of something over 1,500 has not grown appreciably since 2011. As a result, the student-to-teacher ratio is about 68:1. To deal with that ratio and still provide quality education has required big innovations in how one teaches and in the curriculum itself.

Pedagogy

IHLs should be enabled to test different teaching methods and to design curriculum to achieve better teaching outcomes. Not many public Arab universities are so enabled. It is argued that students have different ways of learning that fall into identifiable types. 'Big data'-driven analytics can identify those types and help maximize the effectiveness of teaching. It may be, as Pallas et al. (2017) argue, that this is best carried out in the K–12 years. Student outcomes are much more important in measuring teaching performance at the pre-university level than at the university level, where research output is significantly weighted. Indeed, the same authors urge the reform of the promotion system as an essential first step in tertiary education.

Often the training needed for employment is pitted against instruction in the humanities and social sciences (the liberal arts core), but, in reality, this is not the case. The humanities and social sciences are ideal vehicles to nurture 'soft skills' in students, emphasizing critical thinking, problem solving, group efforts, and leadership. Making the acquisition of soft skills a goal of pedagogical innovation should be a priority.

Western universities have not long addressed issues of teaching methodologies, revised curricula, and systemic sensitivity to students' learning abilities.[3] I have the sense that little has been done in this respect in Arab universities. A major driver of this process is dropout or noncompletion rates. The statistical evidence of noncompletion of degree programs in the Arab world is spotty, but in the US we know that about 40 percent of registered students in four-year degree programs do not finish their course of study, and the rate is more like 60 percent for part-time students and those in community colleges. This is a colossal waste in three respects. First, there is a wide gap between the return to education of those who complete degrees and those who do not. The personal and societal investment in the education of dropouts is thereby largely wasted. Second, those who drop out often default on student debt and tend to come from less privileged backgrounds, so there is a major equity issue at stake (see Koropeckyi et al., 2017). Third, IHLs have to cope with fluctuating enrollments and attendant staffing challenges.

The innovation challenge is, then, what can be done pedagogically to reduce dropout rates. First, at the level of IHLs, teaching must be taken much more seriously and have a well-defined weight in promotion. Probably beginning with graduate education (the source of much part-time instruction) and certainly with newly recruited faculty, training in teaching techniques and methodologies must become the norm. One component of this will involve how to identify a student's specific aptitudes for learning, and a second would be discipline-specific protocols in teaching.

Remote or distance learning is already becoming common in the Arab world, although there has been reluctance to recognize credentials achieved through it. Blended teaching is likely to prevail, but that will work only if the teaching faculty is specifically trained in it. An important innovation is the so-called 'flipped classroom,'[4] where the faculty lead from behind and the students, having absorbed through the internet what would have been a lecture in the traditional model, help lead the class and define issues for discussion.

Such innovations are underway at CAU. They have been introduced at the master's level with the hope that they will spread down and up the educational sequence. Miraoui believes that faculty cannot be ordered to adopt new methodologies. CAU encourages volunteers with incentive payments. A basic objective is to impart to students soft skills of verbal presentation, clear analytic writing, teamwork, and leadership.[5] Anyone familiar with the paradigm of Arab education at any level will recognize how absent such soft skills are.

Bridging reform and disruptive innovation is CBE. Ironically, at a time when Arab IHLs are moving to the credit hour as the unit of account in time-defined credentialing, the institutions in the US and elsewhere that originated this system are calling it into question (DeMillo, 2015). The old model assumes that all students can learn the same things in the same period of time. In contrast, information economies focus on outcomes; process and time are variables. In education, this, it is claimed, shifts the focus from teaching to learning (Levine, 2015).

Michelle Weise and Clayton Christensen (2014) see CBE as potentially more disruptive than other ballyhooed innovations, such as MOOCs. It targets a growing set of students who are looking for a different value proposition from higher education—one that centers on targeted and specific learning outcomes, tailored support, as well as identifiable skill sets that are portable and meaningful to employers. CBE is about gaining mastery of a subject regardless of the time it takes to get there.

Learning pathways can differ, as all students come to a subject with varying levels of understanding and different sets of knowledge and experiences, which, in part, lead to their learning at different rates. Through direct assessments, a student can be tested on her mastery of any competency to ensure that time is truly the variable factor and learning is fixed: assessments are built into the system to ensure students' proficiency; students can take assessments as many times as necessary until they have mastered the competency; and instructors can rely on an analytics dashboard and cater to students' needs, such as a personalized tutor, when necessary. Moreover, Weise and Christensen underscore the valuable role that employers can play in post-secondary education by creating a whole new value network that connects students directly with employers (2014: 20).

Undoubtedly, CBE contains the potential for disruption. All facets of teaching and the professorial career will be recast as it spreads. The parameters of IHL financing will be overhauled. Employers will have to learn how to evaluate radically different credentials. Despite all that, the extent of disruption may be far less than what Weise and Christensen suggest.

It is already the case that the new model is spreading in secondary education, and it is not disruptors external to the high school system that are pushing it but, rather, established schools themselves. The traditional model is, basically, one of pass/fail. A student may get an A or a C but still pass. S/he may not truly master much of the content of courses taken. Competency-based learning requires demonstrated mastery of subject matter.

The Glossary of Education Reform (2014) focuses mainly on secondary education and warns of the disruption that the new system may cause:

> When schools transition to a competency-based system, it can entail significant changes in how a school operates and how it teaches students, affecting everything from the school's educational philosophy and culture to its methods of instruction, testing, grading, reporting, promotion, and graduation. For example, report cards may be entirely redesigned, and schools may use different grading scales and systems, such as replacing letter grades with brief descriptive statements—e.g., phrases such as *does not meet, partially meets, meets the standard,* and *exceeds the standard* are commonly used in competency-based schools (although systems vary widely in design, purpose, and terminology). Schools may also use different methods of instruction and assessment to determine whether students have achieved competency, including strategies such as demonstrations of learning, learning pathways, personal learning plans, portfolios, rubrics, and capstone projects, to name just a few (emphasis in original).

Bishop (2011) refers to some examples—"'Micro-credentials' and 'nano-degrees,' for example, short vocational courses for specific skills: Udacity offers several, sometimes constructed with industry help (digital marketing with input from Google and Facebook). EdX offers such courses free. An exam to confirm competency may cost $200."

There is strong demand for this kind of credentialing for adults throughout their working lives. Some programs will grant credits toward degrees based on previous work experience. I would anticipate that there will be direct competition in the Arab world for this market between public IHLs and private suppliers.

For example, Laureate International Universities, founded in 1998, is a for-profit chain operating in twenty-nine countries with two hundred campuses and a million students. It has nine campuses in Saudi Arabia and also manages Bilgi University in Istanbul. It seeks to disrupt an existing middle-class market by providing acceptable quality at a very competitive price (Basken, 2016).

However, competing with public institutions offering the same products basically for free will be hard, unless private suppliers offer quality the public sector cannot match. Assaad, Krafft, and Salehi-Isfahani (2018) are skeptical that this is the case.

Part of pedagogical innovations are distance and blended learning, which have become widespread. The Arab Open University is the major regional player, but individual institutions, from CAU to Cairo University, have introduced distance learning. In Iran, the public Payame Noor University, founded in 1988, has dozens of sites and 800,000 registered students. Distance learning is at the heart of Syrian higher education. Distance learning helps these IHLs achieve economies of scale, thereby partially resolving the challenges of massification at a reasonable cost.

It appears that MOOCs have lost some of their luster, but they are present at CAU (in partnership with Microsoft) and through Edraak (Arabic for 'to realize' or 'to be aware'), which was launched in 2014 by the Queen Rania Foundation in Jordan (Sawahel, 2014; Bali, 2014). Up to a third of CAU's students may be 'virtual' and it offers over two hundred MOOCs. Arizona State University has partnered with the Abdulla Al Ghurair Foundation for Education to market master's level courses in the Arab world.

These inward-looking initiatives are likely to involve some very powerful corporate partners. They are partnering because they have identified significant potential markets for their services and products. While these are innovations that can be designed and to some extent implemented within the walls, they contain technical challenges that open the door to external funding and technical assistance.[6]

Incentive Systems

The hard truth is that Arab IHLs have to strengthen both teaching and research. Both have been neglected. We know from the experiences of US IHLs that the spread of adjunct faculty has been the key to freeing up time for research and, to a certain extent, reducing the teaching load of full-time faculty. Making the part-time faculty a recognized and appropriately compensated part of the IHL is a reform Arab IHLs must undertake. It may well entail heavier reliance on part-time faculty, going forward, in order to tap into a broad range of professional skills and to contain the costs associated with full-time faculty. In the conclusion to this chapter, I offer a radically different business model for IHLs that seeks to provide good-quality education at an affordable cost both to parents and to taxpayers.

Different formulae for research funding should be considered. Significant national resources should be committed to competitive research funds. Ideally, awards would favor applications by research teams, collaborative research across IHLs or with foreign partners, and have set-asides for younger researchers.

Tunisia has taken steps in this direction. In 1996 Tunisia instituted a national evaluation system to identify worthy research units to be funded directly by the Ministry of Research (see pages 217–18). In contrast to annual awards to small research teams, this approach emphasizes building research capacity over time.

According to the World Bank and OECD, in Egypt, "The establishment of the Higher Council for Science and Technology provides the basis for high-level co-ordination and prioritization of R&D aligned with national development goals and strategies. The new Science and Technology Competitive Fund and the EU–Egypt Innovation Fund provide incentives for raising research quality and linking research activity with industry development needs" (World Bank and OECD, 2010: 37). Their report goes on to warn against a phenomenon common throughout the Arab world:

> One major structural barrier to the development of future capability is the separation of research from university education and knowledge exchange. This fragmentation, which derives from centralist periods and influences, does not suit the contemporary character of knowledge formation and diffusion, gives rise to loss of synergies, impedes cross-disciplinary work, and yet does not enable the development of critical scale. (2010: 37)

This was written before the 2011 uprising, so that it is difficult to know what progress, if any, has been made since then.

New Financial Models

Bricks-and-mortar universities involve extensive physical infrastructure that is expensive to build and operate. With the increasing emphasis on STEM disciplines, there is the need to build and equip sophisticated labs that are quickly dated. There is an assumption that lower student-to-faculty ratios enhance educational quality, so the salary budget associated with the physical IHL absorbs scarce resources.

The physical IHL is likely to enjoy tax-exempt status. While it is often the case that IHLs drive up the value of the real estate in their neighborhoods, they also deprive public authorities of the tax revenues high-value property might otherwise yield. What if a 'virtual' university could convey high-quality educational content with a much smaller teaching staff and without the capital and operating costs of a bricks-and-mortar institution?

Coupled with new models of credentialing, this kind of model of reform and innovation might make education affordable for the majority of the adult population.[7]

Any financing scheme must incorporate social choices. Funding could be allocated according to institutional performance. The principle is that the best deserve to receive more, the mediocre less. But if we regard higher education as a right and a public good, then penalizing the mediocre will only add to the mediocrity and shortchange aspiring students. The two understandings may be combined: one size fits all for basic funding; performance and excellence criteria for awarding supplemental funding for research and other targeted goals.

The same protagonists define the terms of debate on charging fees. Those that believe in education as a right regard education as a pure public good that should be paid for by the taxpayer, with the rich paying higher rates than the less well-off. Those comfortable with the market argue that education produces substantial private returns that the state should tax by charging fees up front or making loans that graduates are responsible for paying off. Formulae for needs-based financial aid can address equity issues. But, as Jaramillo (Jaramillo and Melonio 2011: 59) points out, cost-sharing will work only if the quality of education offered is acceptable. In Chapter 5, we saw that the average rate of return to education, including higher education (RORE) in the Arab world is declining, a sign of declining quality.

Despite the venerable institution of the *waqf*, which could serve as a precedent and a model, most Arab universities have not tried to build endowments of liquid assets and properties, nor have they much engaged in philanthropy of any sort. This is no silver financial bullet, but public universities from Oxford to Berkeley have plunged into philanthropy in a major way and quite successfully. There is no reason that Arab universities could not follow suit. The potential to tap into MENA diasporas to build such initiatives is significant and could be used for philanthropic contributions to MENA universities.

In the future some variant on the CAU financial model may be viable, if not optimal, although the student-to-teacher ratio of 68:1 should not be emulated. Hold faculty full-time equivalents (FTEs) relatively constant, expand the conventional student body in line with or ahead of demographic change, and keep student-to-teacher ratios at acceptable levels through adjuncts, new part-time professors of practice, and MOOCs. The only element I have added is the resort to part-time professors (as distinct from adjuncts).

A variant on this course of action would be to expand the teaching corps significantly using adjuncts in parallel with expanding the student body across all age cohorts in 'life-long learning' and charging the nonconventional cohorts fees. Older students will, for the most part, not be in class for fun; they will have a career goal in mind. They can take out loans for their studies. Those who seek distraction and enrichment can pay for the privilege. In this way the IHL can introduce its own progressive taxation.

Outward-looking Innovations

Mohamed Elkhosht, president of Cairo University, stated, "My vision of Cairo University is that it becomes a third-generation university focused on grooming graduate entrepreneurs . . . . We need to train students to use their own ability to solve problems and take initiative. It's the only way to cultivate the kind of leaders needed to create the small and micro enterprises that will drive economic growth" (Wirtschafter, 2017).

Universities may have once been ivory towers but no longer. They will thrive or wither by their ability to place graduates in gainful employment. University leaders and teaching faculty must understand what that challenge means. There are two principal bridges to the job market. We have already explored pedagogic content and technique in which employers may have direct input. The second is contributing to basic research and to R&D, which can link employers and IHLs in joint undertakings and contribute to economic growth. This in turn stimulates employment.

The challenge for IHLs is not only to find appropriate employment for their graduates, but, as well, to understand the broad contours of organizational and technological change and where they are leading. IHLs must collaborate with, and, in many ways, lead the region's parastatal and private sectors toward a future that is far less clear than only two decades ago, and even that, of course, was false clarity.

Innovation and R&D

A public-policy expert in Abu Dhabi once remarked to me, "People here are transactional. They are not really interested in innovation. Their attitude is, why invest in development of things if you can buy them off the shelf? Let someone else pay for the R&D."

The stereotype, like most, has some truth to it but not much. Arabs in different institutional settings make superb scientists and innovators. In their own countries, however, there is fear of the institutions that might unlock innovation and scientific research.

The three vital partners to vigorous R&D cultures are not, in the Arab world, up to the task. Universities tend to produce bureaucrats, not scientists; the state is more concerned with rent-seeking than productivity; and the private sector lacks legitimacy and acts in a manner to sustain that image. The political system, despite the official rhetoric, acts to reinforce those roles (Hanafi and Arvanitis, 2016a). In 2008, by way of example, Cairo University's total research budget came to $4 million—this for a university with global aspirations (Kamil, 2008).

The fact is that, with rare exceptions, the private sector is not structured or motivated to respond to the call. Its overall contribution to R&D investment is no more than 10 percent (the government and public universities account for the rest). Some multinational firms with operations based in Arab countries—Renault in Morocco (where 40 percent of its total vehicle construction is located) or Boeing in Abu Dhabi—may be ready to participate, at least in form, but the heart of their R&D efforts will remain in their home countries. A few parastatals like Morocco's OCP or Saudi Arabia's Aramco, take research seriously and invest in it (1 percent of the former's annual sales goes into R&D).

There is a paradox here. In several spheres the Middle East is, de facto, at the frontier of innovation. Its future will depend on mastering the water-energy-food nexus, involving water management, desalinization, petrochemicals, alternative energy, and genetically modified crops for drought and heat resistance. There is vast potential for applied research in the treatment of medical problems with high prevalence in the region, such as diabetes, obesity, hypertension, and hepatitis C. Pharmaceuticals and ICT are both vibrant sectors in the MENA. Yet, outside of Israel, it would be hard to discern a major regional research push in these areas.[8]

That said, we do find some promising policy innovators. As noted above, Tunisia has set up a funding system that provides core financing for research as opposed to competitive applications for specific projects (the model adopted by the CNRS-L). In 1996 Tunisia instituted a national evaluation system to identify worthy research units to be funded directly by the Ministry of Research. By 2008 the evaluation council had identified 330 research units and 250 laboratories that qualified for funding. The ministry, through its core funding grants, would cover 65 percent of operating costs and contribute 35 percent toward the research itself. The funding cycle is four years with a midterm review. In parallel, the same research entities may compete for project funding. The competition process favors consortia of research units. There has been an exponential increase in

Tunisia's research output since the beginning of the millennium (Hanafi and Arvanitis, 2016: 145).

Jordan is also something of a pioneer in innovation and R&D. The country does not enjoy petroleum or other natural resource rents. It has a fairly dynamic and forward-looking private sector. King Abdullah and Queen Rania have been visible sponsors of both private sector and higher education reform. Despite all that, Jordan has not had notably more success in fostering a symbiosis between universities and the private sector. The Jordanian private sector is most active in pharmaceuticals, ICT, renewable energy, and health services. Obvious areas of university–private sector collaboration are in energy efficiency, quality improvement, and product development.

In an interview (2015), Fouad Mrad recounted the history of the ESCWA-sponsored Technology Center in Amman. In 1979, the eminent physicist and analyst of Arab scientific progress Tony Zahlan was invited by ESCWA to prepare a feasibility study for a technology transfer center for the Arab world. He did, and nothing happened. He was asked to re-do it in 2005, and once again nothing happened. Mrad finally launched the center under the auspices of ESCWA in 2010.

The center is tiny, built on soft Gulf money or contributions in kind. Its board of directors come from big, relatively well-financed national centers like the Kuwait Institute for Scientific Research (KISR) or the Qatar Foundation, with thousands of employees. Mrad has had some success in programs to inspire youth to get into innovation and science.

He confirms the conundrum of the 'broken cycle,' that is, the failure to develop synergies among governments, universities, and the private sector. He echoes Hanafi (2014), confirming that the basic innovative talent is locked up in universities where all the incentives drive it from relevance and useful creativity. Academics are discouraged from engaging in relevant, patentable research by the quest to publish in refereed international journals. The issue of how to evaluate consultancies, public-policy contributions, and the like is not engaged. Instead, academics are content to write mediocre articles for international journals that have little local impact or relevance.

In more advanced economies, something like 2–3 percent of GDP is devoted to R&D. Of that about two-thirds comes from the private sector, but, unsurprisingly, the private sector is interested in applied research and specifically in the D of R&D, the 'development' of marketable products from applied research. Governments typically foot the bill for most basic research, that is, research that may not (yet) have obvious implications for applied research (for a useful overview focusing mainly on the US, see Press, 2013). The leaders worldwide today in R&D expenditure are Finland, South Korea, Israel, Sweden, and Singapore, all vigorous and prosperous trading nations. In 2014 South Korea led the world in R&D investment at 4.29 percent of GDP (Lee, 2016). The US trails a bit at 3 percent and China at around 2 percent. The average outlay for the Arab world is 0.3 percent. Qatar, at 2.8 percent in about 2014, and Tunisia, at over 1 percent for a number of years, lead the region. The oil-rich countries can afford to invest, but Saudi Arabia lags far behind Qatar in its R&D efforts. The leading OECD countries are putting four to ten times the proportion of national wealth into R&D that Arab states are investing. Their ratios of research scientists to total population are also vastly higher.

Arab countries average 371 researchers per million, far below the world average of 1,081. Laurence Veale (2015a) summarizes the situation: "This striking underperformance is caused by several factors, including political instability, a lack of public funding for science and technology, the absence of scientific societies and the almost absent participation of the private sector."[9]

It is instructive that the regime-shaking uprisings of 2011 elicited, at least for a few years, a growth spurt in Arab R&D outlays (Lawler, 2011; Sawahel, 2011; Bond et al., 2014?; Veale, 2015c), especially in Algeria, Jordan, Morocco, Tunisia, and Egypt. Egypt's new constitution of 2014 made research funding a constitutional issue (Article 23): "The state grants the freedom of scientific research and encourages its institutions as a means to achieving national sovereignty and building a knowledge economy. The state sponsors researchers and inventors and allocates a percentage of government expenditures that is no less than 1% of Gross National Product to scientific research. It will gradually increase until it reaches global rates." In drafting that clause, Egypt's leaders must have understood the linkage among jobs, economic growth, and R&D.[10]

With the qualified exception of some of the oil-rich states, the Arab world has underperformed in R&D outlays, referred to as General Expenditures on Research and Development (GERD), covering both public and private outlays. Nonetheless, the region can take some solace from placing eight countries in the top half of the global rankings.

The Global Innovation Index, developed by the business school INSEAD, compares countries for which data is available by their levels of innovation. The variables the index uses are high and medium technology manufactures, high-tech exports, internet protocol receipts, global

Table 7.1. GERD and Full-time Researchers per Million Population: MENA plus Israel*

Country	GERD as a % of GDP			Researchers per million pop.		
	Rank	%	Year	Rank	No. per million	Year
Israel	1	4.3	2015	1	8,225	2012
Turkey	37	1.0	2015	46	1,156	2014
UAE	41	0.87	2015	38	2,003	2015
Saudi Arabia	44	0.82	2013	nd	nd	nd
Morocco	50	0.71	2010	47	1,032	2014
Tunisia	51	0.65	2014	42	1,787	2015
Qatar	66	0.47	2012	60	597	2012
Jordan	70	0.43	2008	70	308	2015
Iran	78	0.33	2012	56	691	2015
Kuwait	80	0.3	2013	83	128	2015
Oman	85	0.24	2015	74	202	2015

Source: INSEAD (2017)
* GERD refers to Gross Expenditure on Research and Development. The rank is the place among 179 countries. In the dimensions measured above, Israel is number one on both among all these countries.

R&D companies, quality of scientific publications, research talent in business enterprise, state of innovation cluster development, graduates in science and engineering, and gross capital formation. Table 7.2 shows how the countries of the MENA plus Israel and Turkey were ranked in 2017, based on combined scores.

For the record, Switzerland was ranked number one. In the MENA small petroleum exporting countries do fairly well, but Israel is both a regional and a global star. An ESCWA study from 2014 uses factor analysis to identify four innovation subtypes in the MENA: large research systems with slow growth (Algeria, Egypt, Morocco, and Saudi Arabia); small, dynamic, and integrated systems (Jordan, Lebanon, and Tunisia); very small countries with rapidly expanding research systems (Bahrain, Qatar, and UAE); and the rest, including failed or quasi-failed states (Syria, Libya, Yemen, and Iraq).

The Global Innovation Index also ranks MENA countries, plus Israel and Turkey, in terms of the quality of their business–university collaboration. In the scale, seven equals maximum collaboration and zero equals none. Again, Switzerland is number one, at 5.8.

Table 7.2. Global Innovation Ranks

Country	Global Rank
Israel	17
UAE	35
Turkey	43
Qatar	49
Saudi Arabia	55
Kuwait	56
Bahrain	66
Morocco	72
Tunisia	74
Iran	75
Oman	77
Lebanon	81
Jordan	83
Egypt	105
Algeria	108
Yemen	127

Source: INSEAD (2017)

Table 7.3. Quality of Business–University Relations

Country	Index Score
Israel	5.6
Qatar	5.2
Jordan	3.8
Lebanon	3.6
Oman	3.6
Saudi Arabia	3.5
Morocco	3.1
Iran	3.0
Tunisia	3.0
Kuwait	2.6
Egypt	2.4
Yemen	1.9

Source: INSEAD (2017)

Zahlan (2012) decries the failure of Arab governments to insist on technology-sharing in their turn-key projects. They simply buy technology off the shelf and as a result fail to internalize any of the embedded technology. This means, he notes, that they do not need their universities and research centers for a supply of R&D. They do not need, and indeed thwart, the establishment of national and regional professional scientific associations that act to build professionalism, identify research agendas, and engage with global networks of scientists. Out of exasperation, one suspects, Zahlan makes the startling recommendation that governments cut back outlays on training physicians and engineers and use the resources to train social scientists and people in the humanities who will not migrate abroad and who can educate a new generation of secondary students fit for a university education: "What the Arab world needs today is not five-star universities, hospitals or research centers, as much as a five-star enabling environment. It has the scientists, markets and resources with which to undertake the transition, but not the political culture to do so" (2012: 196).

Or, as ESCWA puts it: "To understand the riddle of under-investment in research and innovation in the Arab region, it is important to keep in mind that the agenda for science and innovation is always political" (2014: 4).

R&D, like basic research, is not a direct conduit to employment. Its effects are indirect, leading, it is hoped, to economic transformation and growth and hence to greater demand for the educated. Although the experience will not repeat itself, this was the path followed by the Asian Tigers in the last century. The Arab world must invent a new variant.

Governments can stimulate R&D by direct funding of research or by tax incentives. The latter come into play because firms generally account for R&D as a business expense that directly lowers their profit margin. To compensate, governments can offer tax credits. In 2013 OECD countries spent about $40 billion in direct R&D funding and another $30 billion in tax breaks (Haskel and Westlake, 2018: 223).

Venture capital can also act as a stimulus. The model, best represented in Silicon Valley, took many years to evolve. The basic elements are entrepreneurs (with ideas about intangible capital) seeking out venture capitalists, large companies buying out the start-up, and generations of venture capitalists and entrepreneurs mentoring one another.

The Arab world could well use the equivalent of the recommendations of UK's 2015 Dowling report on business–university research collaboration. That report stresses the complexity of reconciling different cultures (profit versus the public good). With so much internet protocol involved, there is a need to establish 'trust' between the partners, and time is needed for trial and error. This is uncharted territory in the Middle East and will require careful analysis before useful synergies can be achieved. Indeed, Jonathan Haskel and Stian Westlake, who have analyzed what intangible capital is and how it is formed, are not convinced that universities are an essential part of R&D:

> If public subsidies to private sector institutions cannot generate enough public spillovers then maybe there will be growth in the importance of publicly subsidized knowledge generators: universities. But for support to be forthcoming, they would have to be truly public knowledge–generating institutions, and experiments in organization form are probably necessary. Perhaps that is best done by research institutes rather than conventional universities. (2018: 181)

Innovation Hubs

The Arab world has several science cities, techno-parks, and other physical spaces that seek to be catalysts to innovation in both the public and private sectors. Haskel and Westlake (2018) emphasize the importance of hubs, Silicon Valley being the patriarch of them all. But they are more likely to see cities as the cradles of innovation (perhaps inspired by the work of Richard Florida (2005)) than techno-parks. They and the Global Innovation Index stress the importance of 'clusters'. The index identifies the top hundred innovation clusters in the world. The only country in the region to make the list is Israel, with Tel Aviv at number twenty-two and Haifa at number seventy-eight. No other cluster in the MENA makes the top hundred. Although Haskel and Westlake do not see universities as crucial players, a cursory glance at the world's leading clusters shows that at their heart is a university or universities, leading examples being Stanford in Silicon Valley and the NUS in Singapore.

While the Arab world is lagging, high-tech and research clusters are developing. The King Abdulaziz City of Science and Technology is one of the most ambitious cluster initiatives. It manages three broad programs in industrial property, innovation, and incubation. It contains a patent office and is home to fifteen research teams. It offers competitive grants to researchers and research teams nationwide. The bulk of its funding goes to applied rather than basic research (ESCWA, 2014: 47).

Ahmed Zewail was awarded the Nobel Prize for chemistry in 1999. He was born and educated in Egypt before doing his PhD work in the US and joining the faculty of Caltech. He and the regime of Hosni Mubarak wanted to use his fame to rekindle the scientific spirit in Egypt and the Arab world. In his own words, "A part of the world that pioneered science and mathematics during Europe's dark ages is now lost in a dark age of illiteracy and knowledge deficiency" (Devran, 2016).

In January 2000 the Zewail City of Science and Technology was launched, but politics soon reared its head. Ahmed Nazif served as prime minister from 2004 until the fall of Mubarak in 2011. He was a graduate of Cairo University and had a PhD in computer engineering from McGill University. In 2006 his government sponsored Nile University, whose mission is to prepare graduates for a tech-driven world. It is a not-for-profit (ahliya) university. It turned out later that the land allotted to Nile University had also been allocated to Zewail City. The two entities, sharing a common mission, were locked in a legal battle quite literally over turf. Some of Nile University's facilities were ultimately awarded to Zewail City. Zewail City and a university within it were relaunched in 2011. President al-Sisi has embraced the project (Iskandar, 2014). The fact that the idea was first broached in 1999 and that twenty years later it was still a start-up is some indication of the complexities involved.[11]

In parallel to the establishment of clusters or techno-parks are the first steps toward incubation. A few universities have set up technology transfer offices (inter alia, the AUC and Nile University). CAU is launching its own incubator, as is AUB. As regional IHLs take international rankings more seriously, patenting intellectual property will grow in importance. AUC's Hassan Azzazy has developed treatments for hepatitis C, a scourge in Egypt, and he has launched his own company, D-Kimia, after two years of legal work (Lindsey, 2014).

The doyen of incubators among Arab universities is the USJ's Berytech in Lebanon. It was founded in 2002 and has helped launch over a hundred companies since then. It has been active in the ICT, cement, agro-food, and wine sectors (Veale, 2015c; Hanafi and Arvanitis, 2016).

Few university incubators will ever match those of MIT or Stanford. The incubated firm that hits the jackpot, generating a significant revenue stream for the university that launched it, is as rare as a unicorn. Incubation cannot be a major facet of financing the innovative university, except in the broad sense of promoting socioeconomic transformation.

Information and Communcations Technology

The reform agenda in the MENA is conventional. The region is slowly moving to catch up with a Western educational model that many in the West believe to be obsolete. ICT is the tool to engineer new, unconventional modes of education, modes that call into question the bricks-and-mortar university. ICT is also at the heart of innovative research and stimulating the region's private sector.[12] In this latter respect, the Kingdom of Jordan has for some time been a pioneer. The Jordan Education Initiative was launched in 2003 under the auspices of the World Economic Forum (WEF), USAID, and the British Council and was designed to improve education through a public–private partnership (Bannayan et al., 2012). It is focused mainly on a hundred pre-university Discovery Schools. Jordanian public agencies, in partnership with private sector technology companies, seek to transform secondary education.[13]

Another initiative, under the auspices of the Queen Rania Foundation, is the MOOC Edraak, launched in 2013 in collaboration with EdX of Harvard and MIT ("Higher Education," 2013). It has translated or developed a couple of dozen courses in Arabic that range from child mental health and statistics and epidemiology to entrepreneurship 101. Over two million individuals have subscribed to its courses, and it boasts 1.2 million registered learners (Mustafa Habib, email, 2017).

Egypt spends about $100 million a year on printing textbooks, more than the operating budget of Cairo University. Tarek Shawki, who was appointed Minister of Education and Technical Education in February 2017 (see Sayed Ahmad, 2017), advocated a major thrust toward online texts. A few years earlier I interviewed Ali Ibrahim, president of the Central Management Services Authority in the Ministry of Finance (2014). When I suggested that digital materials and online education could offer economies of scale across Egypt's twenty-three public universities, Ibrahim seemed almost shocked. First, he noted, universities are legally autonomous, so "we cannot merge any parts of their budgets." When I suggested MOOCs or any form of online instruction, he replied, "The professors won't like it. Professors have their own style and methods. Moreover some might lose books sales revenues." Ibrahim concluded that what I was suggesting is utopian.

Similarly, Amira Sayed Ahmad (2017) found considerable skepticism among Egyptian experts regarding online education or even electronic textbooks. Power outages, highly skewed access to the internet, and even the reluctance of conservative parents to allow their daughters to go to computer labs were all cited as reasons why Minister Shawki's plans would not work.

In 2000 Prince Talal bin Abdulaziz of Saudi Arabia founded the Arab Open University in partnership with Open University UK. It offers blended learning, with online courses developed by Open University UK combined with face-to-face tutorials with local scholars. The latter must provide around 25 percent of total study time in order to satisfy the equivalency requirements of the eight countries in which it operates.[14] In 2017 it enrolled about 28,000 students.

CAU in Marrakesh, Morocco, has enthusiastically embraced MOOCs (240 courses are offered) and distance learning. In the span of five years it has doubled its total enrollment to about 70,000 students. About two-thirds are 'physical' students while the remainder are 'virtual,' connected through online open courses. CAU is in partnership with Microsoft to make it a 'smart university.'

Disruptive Innovation

The entire higher education enterprise in the MENA is vulnerable to disruption. The established models are costly to operate, they are at best doing a mediocre job of educating, and they fail to meet the high demand for education of the 'knowledge economy.' Unmet demand and poor quality are a clarion call for disruptors to enter the market.

The question is, can existing institutions anticipate it and survive? Christensen's (1997) original formulation suggests that the disrupted are always taken by surprise and that they do not survive the encounter with the disruptor. Disruptive innovation addresses markets in waiting, neglected markets, and latent demand. Existing suppliers continue to meet existing, visible demand, and they will improve their performance in these existing markets by adopting what Christensen calls 'sustaining innovations.' These will often have the effect of increasing costs. Disruption occurs not only in the product market itself (higher education) but in the entire supply chain as well (presumably in K–12 and adult education). Think of the 60 percent or so on average of Arab youths between eighteen and twenty-two who do not attend tertiary institutions. This is a huge market, only partially addressed by new private suppliers.

But public education is not like a firm offering a product or a service for which it extracts a payment. Depending on the level, public education is a public good, available to all, for certain age cohorts, consumed by law, and a quasi-monopoly. The taxpayer foots the bill.

By contrast, the providers of disruptive innovation will want to sell their product. Many customers of the existing paradigm cannot afford to switch. The only way for the disruptive innovation to become generalized is for the dominant system to buy it so that the taxpayer continues to foot the bill. Curiously, Christensen wants to see just that—the established players electing disruption—although his original theory assumes that established players will simply rearrange the deck chairs on the Titanic. As the example of CAU indicates, disruptive innovations are adopted by IHLs not to compete with newcomers but rather to survive in their current environment.[15]

As this book was in the final stages of editing in 2020, the mother of all disruptors, the coronavirus causing COVID-19 burst upon the world, shaking every aspect of our social and economic lives. It was classically unforeseen and left us all improvising and innovating in near desperation. Much of humanity was locked down and told to avoid most human contact. For higher education and education in general, the magic of place became the curse of place. The staff and students at all levels were sent home and in a matter of days, or at most weeks, distance-learning filled the breach, not with volunteers but with conscripts. All active faculty had to learn new techniques and new technologies. It is far too early to foretell the ultimate impact of COVID-19 on education, but that it will be far-reaching, potentially devastating, and long-lasting seems a safe bet.

Returning to our main argument, the logic of disruptive innovation as proposed by Christensen is to leave both principals and agents in a cul de sac. They have no capacity to meet it, deflect it, or indeed survive it. The logic is that you will not know what hit you until it hits you. So in their more general theory Christensen and colleagues (2008) in fact show that some firms, hit by disruptive innovation, do take successful action to adjust, such as Kodak and IBM. Or, in the case of education, the institutions do see what is coming (that is what the 2008 book is about) and adopt it to shift their paradigm.

The existing players can employ the lessons learned. In the online spinoffs they may launch, the weight of research in the promotion portfolio may be reduced. Tenure may be redefined or done away with altogether. Instructional roles may be compartmentalized, with different people designing courses, delivering them, and evaluating competency (AAAS, 2017: 16). By separating the varying and complicated roles that one traditional professor typically plays, organizations will be able to hire educators who do not necessarily have PhDs or expect tenure contracts. With more people available who can meet the specifications of these highly circumscribed roles, there will likely be different pathways of potentially different durations within doctoral programs that enable students to immerse themselves in either specialized research or online teaching roles. There is no minimizing the disruption such innovations would cause. We know the introduction of the LMD system in Morocco and elsewhere provoked a great deal of dissatisfaction among faculty members. The kinds of innovations we contemplate here will be even more jarring.

Table 7.4 encapsulates the permeability of the three types of innovation.

Table 7.4. Nature and Impact of Innovations in Higher Education

Kind of Innovation	Inward-looking	Outward-looking	Disruptive
R&D	Yes	Yes	Marginally
Curriculum	Yes	Potentially	Potentially
MOOCs	Yes	Potentially	Potentially
Incentive systems	Yes	Marginally	Yes
University fees	Yes	No	Yes!
Competency-based education	Yes	Yes	Yes
Teacher training	Yes	Marginally	Yes

New Corporate Actors

It is likely that big public and private corporations will continue to assert themselves in higher education (Salmi, 2002: 32). Publicly owned parastatals have led the way. In the Middle East, Gulf countries have been pioneers. In the UAE the Abu Dhabi National Oil Company founded the Petroleum Institute to train petroleum and mineral engineers. Etisalat, the telecommunications parastatal, helped found the Khalifa University of Science, Technology, and Research.[16]

These two institutions and the Masdar Institute of Technology (affiliated with MIT) have recently merged. Mubadala, Abu Dhabi's giant public holding company, has managed a number of foreign education projects, including NYU Abu Dhabi. In neighboring Saudi Arabia, Saudi Aramco has managed the KAUST, and in Morocco, the OCP (whose annual turnover is equal to 6 percent of Morocco's GDP) manages Mohammed VI Polytechnic University in Ben Guerir, founded in 2013.

The Magic of Place

Do we need the physical university or will a virtual one do just as well? Put another way, is there some magic embodied in the campus and its surroundings that is both irreplaceable and vital to the learning and research experience?

Distance has not been abolished, at least not yet (see Massy, 2016). Physical locations are needed to produce the synergies and spillovers that generate further innovation and research. Haskel and Westlake (2018: 142, 149) see cities as embodying the magic, which suggests that innovation hinges on diversity and proximity.

Physical universities perform vital socioeconomic functions. They uplift blighted neighborhoods by generating employment, sales, purchasing, demand for housing and decent schools, as well as law and order (Rodin, 2007). In some instances, through the dynamism of 'meds and eds,' they rescue entire cities (Pittsburgh, Cleveland). People like to live near universities, and they provide intellectual stimulus for retirees. But all these positive effects are not part of the core missions of universities. They are important by-products, or externalities. Communities benefit without directly contributing to the universities' bottom line, with the major exception of foregone tax revenues.

Finally, there is the experience of being a student. It involves learning the codes and mores of a living community, making friends and enemies, participating in extracurricular life, including campus politics, and observing and experiencing how the IHL evaluates its students and staff. These are important experiences, but are they vital to the educational process?

The Cold War All Over Again?

We are in a revolutionary period in terms of technological change, with huge ethical implications. Robotics, big data, genetic engineering, AI, the internet of things all have enormous and not always benign implications for humankind. We are developing them faster than we can assess their implications and potential for harm.

All of them have real or potential roles in warfare, intelligence gathering, citizen control, and disinformation. It is already the case that the US defense sector, especially the Defense Advanced Research Projects Agency,[17] is seeking close working relations and the sharing of knowledge with private firms in Silicon Valley and elsewhere that have no part of their mission devoted to such pursuits. As the specter of Russian, Chinese, North Korean, or Israeli advances in these domains is invoked, the pressure on private firms, in the name of national security and averting calamity, will become intense and probably irresistible. Universities that are linked to these private firms in their research projects will be subjected to the same pressures. It will be hard, especially for public universities, to say no. It is not at all clear that they should say no.

Ironically, the Arab world may be partially spared these ethical and security dilemmas. The Arab world is relatively far behind in this kind of research. Its universities do not have strong links to private sector firms leading in R&D of any kind, let alone AI, genetic engineering, and big-data analysis. But several Arab nuclear scientists have paid with their lives for supporting their countries' nuclear research. The three countries in the neighborhood where we may see this scenario play out are Iran, Turkey, and Israel. In the latter the close alignment of R&D in enhancing national security is of long standing and seemingly poses no insurmountable ethical issues for Israeli academe.

Conclusion

One of the most disruptive innovations in higher education in the MENA would be to simplify its core mission or missions and in so doing redefine the roles and specializations of the instructional staff, redesign curriculum, experiment extensively with distance and blended learning, separate instruction from evaluation, and link institutional performance and evaluation to a few simple metrics related to successful access to employment. I will explore these innovations further in the conclusion to this book. Suffice it here to note that they are both "sustaining" and "disruptive." They must reduce costs, but it is not certain that they will. They are not only designed to improve the suitability of current students for the workplace, but, as well, to provide serious opportunities for the 60–70 percent of eligible students who are currently unenrolled.

There may be disruptors out there who will not have institutional history or baggage to hold them back, and who will pioneer in developing new models, but existing institutions are fully capable of experimenting with new models of content, delivery, and evaluation. The Detroit automotive sector borrowed heavily from Japanese management innovations, and General Motors and Ford are still viable businesses. Higher education experiments can be fairly gradual, indeed, as suggested by Weise and Christensen, carried out though spinoffs or satellites. Disruption need not be fatal.

New models would not be driven primarily by technological change, although online learning would surely play a big part in them. They would be driven by a very different value proposition than the bricks-and-mortar model of today. It would deal with mass education (quantity) at a reasonable cost, and offer limited quality. It would sacrifice the quality of life associated with *some* campuses, the training of citizens, the networking among classmates, and the extracurricular experiences that characterize 'good' universities.

Finally, I believe the kind of innovations I have in mind are politically acceptable. They do not bear the implications for public life that reforms in university governance bear. Issues of financial and administrative autonomy, governance shared between faculty and independent administrations, and real authority over university life vested in elected councils do threaten the controls political authorities are loath to give up. Concessions in governance made to universities may become models for the rest of civil society.

The new model of higher education I have outlined does not necessarily raise issues of governance. It involves technological, curricular, and personnel innovations that in the eyes of political leaders may seem relatively harmless. The fact that they can deal with 'massification' at an acceptable cost may make them positively attractive. I do not know whether the private or corporate sectors will be more adept at designing and implementing new models than the traditional higher education sector. Both will be players.

All innovations have downsides. That is in the nature of disruption. But existing institutions will not necessarily be swept away. They have tremendous inertial power derived from their vast personnel, huge sunk costs, and powerful political patrons. The current system reinforces social privilege. Those who benefit will resist any changes that erode their advantage. The current model can plausibly be defended. Cairo University produced Naguib Mahfouz and Alexandria University Ahmed Zewail, two Nobel laureates, so they must be doing something right. But resting on their laurels will not suffice. I have seen encouraging evidence that current Arab university leadership wants a green light to innovate. Without that green light, the Arab world will never realize its demographic dividend.

8

Feeding the Beast:
Financing Tertiary Education

This chapter drills into the various funding mechanisms available to university leadership and to ministries of education and scientific research. It builds on the figures laid out in Chapter 1 on orders of magnitude. We address the trilemma of quantity, quality, and cost at two levels: that of the educational system as a whole and that of individual IHLs within it.

Who pays for education is much like the debate over who pays for water: both are treated as universal rights, although one can live without education. Indeed, in the Arab world lower levels of education correlate with higher levels of employment. Again, like water, if the demand for education *of a certain quality* outstrips supply, costs will be introduced into a nominally free system. There will be queuing for certain institutions, stiff fees for private lessons, or perhaps bribing for advance exam questions. The poor, like those in slums without piped water, will pay more, relative to income, than the rich. Private lessons can help the well-off achieve scores that gain entrance to faculties where the costs of instruction are high—engineering and medicine—while the less well-off wind up in commerce, humanities, Islamic studies, or law. One can prattle on about education as a public good (and I will), but supply and demand will trump ideals every time.

The issue of financing comes down to 'rights' versus 'markets.' The supporters of education as a right insist it should be provided as a public good, paid for by taxes, with the better-off paying at higher rates. The creation and imparting of knowledge should not be sullied by considerations of RORE, cost-containment, outcomes-based allocation of financial support, and so forth. It is an engine of social mobility and thus of benefit to all of society. Whatever the balance between public and private funding, the quality of education must improve or there will be a revolt of taxpayers, fee-paying families, or indebted students. Having said that, I acknowledge the often extraordinary tolerance on the part of those who pay for educational mediocrity.

On the other hand, those comfortable with markets argue that higher education results in better jobs with better salaries (the 'education wage premium') and prospects; people would not study further otherwise. Therefore, the existence of high private returns justifies recovery of costs from the direct beneficiaries through tuition, servicing loans, and taxing future income streams. Making the direct beneficiaries pay the bulk of the costs, it is argued, is a step toward greater social equity.

My basic premise is that there is always someone or some interest that pays the university piper and therefore calls the tune. It is perhaps fortunate that most universities have more than one payer. The possibilities of payer are basically four: the government (representing the taxpayers); private (sometimes corporate) donors; parents, or those responsible for paying fees; and the endowment itself. All four may be combined. At the present time the lament among many academics is that the university has succumbed to neoliberal reforms, introduced a range of market-friendly practices, and has in a sense sold out to big business. When I was a graduate student back in the 1960s, the lament was that universities in the US had sold out to the government and to the Department of Defense in their quest for research and other programmatic support. It is not obvious that public paymasters are to be preferred to private ones. Bok (2013) is surely right that diverse funding sources offer the greatest protection to the university's mission.

Despite the massive expansion in higher education of recent decades, and despite near universal complaints of insufficient resources, the fact is that the MENA region, relative to other major regions, spends a significant portion of GDP on education. In the period 2000–2013, the average public spending on education as a percentage of GDP was 5.1 percent in the MENA, 3 percent in Asia, 4.4 percent in Central Europe, 4.6 percent in Central Asia, and 4.5 percent in the OECD (Rizk and Abou-Ali, 2016: 2).

Given that nearly all analysts and education professionals regard the results of this spending in the MENA to be mediocre, if not catastrophic, one can only conclude that the MENA is not getting a good return on its investment. That investment has been cyclical, and in the 1980s and 1990s a perverse phenomenon emerged whereby student numbers in higher education soared while operating budgets were cut in conformity with structural adjustment conditionality. So-called 'massification' came at the expense of quality, accompanied by unreasonably low cost.

Public Expenditures: Systemic Level

William Massy, Jonathan Cole, and many others assume that the university is the relevant unit of analysis in understanding university finance and the allocation of resources. That is to some extent true in the Arab world and the MENA, but equally if not more important is the higher education system itself, with the state at its core. At this level, decisions are made with respect to funding levels, strategic objectives, and distribution of students. All IHLs within the system are bound by these decisions. In addition, several countries have constituted Supreme Councils for Education that are the locus of decision-making across a broad range of policies. The most powerful of these are to be found in Egypt (SCU) and in Turkey (YÖK) (see Chapters 2 and 5). It is not clear, however, the extent to which such councils are involved in financial planning.[1]

At the level of both the system and the university, there is wide variance among MENA practices. We could imagine a financing continuum from block grants made to all public institutions over a multiyear period (perhaps on a competitive basis) to partially autonomous IHLs with multiple sources of revenue. There is an interesting chicken-and-egg question here. Bok (2013) suggests that university autonomy can be enhanced by multiple sources of funding—corporations, philanthropy, the government—but does it not take considerable autonomy to pursue these various funding sources?

The practice of block grants was followed by the British government for many years. Morocco and Tunisia have recently experimented with variants. In Morocco, beginning in 2000 and above all with the Plan d'Urgence (2009–2012), the government initiated performance contracts with public universities. Universities committed themselves to achieve specific negotiated targets in six domains while the government worked on various reforms to reinforce accountability (such as the creation of an evaluation agency and the strengthening of ICT governance tools). One objective has already been met: the evaluative focus has shifted away from inputs toward outputs and outcomes (Jaramillo and Melonio, 2011: box 3.2).

Likewise, the higher education system in Tunisia resorted to a multiyear expenditure program through quadrennial program agreements between universities and the state that facilitate strategic planning through a medium-term expenditure framework. This reform was suspended in 2010 (World Bank and CMI, 2012).

Multiyear funding and block grants, however, are exceptional. Most central funding is on an annual basis and not tied to performance targets of any kind. Rather, levels of funding are determined by the size of the teaching and nonacademic staff, and the number of students admitted and already enrolled. Individual IHLs may make annual requests for additional staff, but, as we shall see, they are always playing catch-up with unpredictable admissions and continuing enrollment levels. They may also submit capital budget requests for necessary maintenance and infrastructure projects. By definition, the relevant ministries—finance and higher education—have limited resources. They process the requests and render Solomonic judgments.[2] Lethargic or impuissant legislatures may involve themselves in this process but usually as part of broader discussions of civil service pay.

Nonetheless, education in general remains a political priority and a relatively protected public expenditure in most countries in the region (World Bank, 2008: 105). This reflects the social contract. Several countries expanded higher education enrollment significantly in the 1980s and 1990s at the same time that they cut spending. In the 1990s many Arab countries formally legalized private education at all levels but especially at the tertiary level. This further reduced the relative size of public outlays.

For example, in Morocco university enrollments went from 105,600 in 1983–84 to 260,000 in 1995–96. For close to thirty years enrollments grew by at least 10 percent per annum, but from 1983 to 1993 the higher education budget increased by only 2 percent per annum (Merrouni, 1997: 89). A more dramatic picture is provided by Sudan. Outlays on education as a percentage of GDP rose over the period 1970–80 from 3.9 percent to 4.8 percent, then declined over the period 1980–95 to 0.8 percent. At the same time, in the period 1990–94 eighteen new universities were founded, all public, plus twelve in the private sector. University students totaled 60,000 in 1989, rising to 130,000 in 1995.

Outlays on higher education rose gently from 0.42 percent of GDP in 1989–90 to 0.51 percent in 1994–95. Per capita outlays sank from 9,184 Sudanese pounds to 4,284 over the same period (Elnur, 1998: 306–308).

Public spending on education in Egypt as a share of total public spending and of GDP is quite high, reaching 16 percent and 4.8 percent, respectively, in 2005 (UNESCO website). These figures are slightly higher than the MENA average (although lagging behind regional neighbors such as Morocco, Oman, and the UAE) and comparable to many OECD countries. This large allocation, however, comes after several decades of drastic underinvestment in education (El Baradei, 2010). During the late 1970s and 1980s, budgetary allocation to education decreased steadily in real terms, causing long-lasting damage to the quality and efficiency of the education system. By 1990 education was only 9.5 percent of total public spending (World Bank, 2008).

In Jordan, public universities are much more self-reliant than elsewhere, and the private provision of education is expanding rapidly. In 2016, outlays on private education reached 248 million dinars, well in excess of the government's 171 million dinars in outlays on public education (Kingdom of Jordan, Economic and Social Council, 2017?: 52). Over the decade 2005–2015, enrollments in public universities doubled, from 135,000 to 262,000. Total income in public universities, including fees and government support, reached 300 million dinars, while total outlays reached 400 million dinars, yielding a deficit of 100 million dinars (in 2016 one Jordanian dinar = $1.41). Jordan University accounted for 27 million dinars of the total deficit (in general, see Kingdom of Jordan, Economic and Social Council, 2017?; National Campaign for the Rights of Students, 2015).

Egypt, after the uprising of 2011, built commitments to educational funding and to R&D into its constitution, establishing a target of 4 percent of GDP. This level has already been attained, so this commitment appears to be more a public relations gambit than an aspirational goal. Moreover, there is no enforcing mechanism and no indication as to how the target will be locked in. Past experience indicates that the target will be missed if the economy faces fiscal constraints. By 2018 education spending had dropped marginally, to 3.7 percent of GDP.

Specifying revenue sources may be more effective. For example, a certain percentage of all income and corporate tax revenues could be dedicated to specific educational targets. Targets in systems where tax collection is problematic may not achieve very much, but the problem is magnified when GDP may be only superficially taxed or portions not taxed at all. For example, as much as 50 percent of Egypt's GDP may lie in the informal sector (Duchatelle et al., 2015: 187).

In contrast to Egypt, Saudi Arabia has thrown petro-dollars at education. The total Saudi Arabia education budget in 2018–2019 was $51 billion, or roughly 7.5 percent of GDP for a population of 33 million. In the same year, Egypt's education outlays reached $8.8 billion for 97 million. On a per capita basis that works out to $1,545 for Saudi Arabia and $91 for Egypt. We find similar disparities throughout the region on outlays per student in higher education (Fahim and Sami, 2010; El Baradei, 2010; Abdessalam, 2010).

Table 8.1. Higher Education Outlays per Student, ca. 2005

Country	Outlays per Student ($)
Egypt	990
Jordan	4,400
Saudi Arabia	9,946
Lebanon	3,087
OECD	11,500
Tunisia	4,300
Turkey	1,333 (2001)
USA	20,000
Yemen	515

Source: Fahim and Sami, 2010.

These figures must be treated with caution. Enrollment figures may be inflated due to double registrations or failure to account for dropouts (inter alia, see 'Issa, 1997).

The UAE live in another universe. So too Qatar, which has the highest per capita income in the world. Texas A&M has established a campus in Doha's Education City. In 2014 it enrolled 581 students with an operating budget of $76 million, or $130,000 per student. It is not alone in such outlays.

There is considerable variation in per student outlays according to the discipline involved. Average per student outlays at Lebanese University are $3,000 per year, but for engineering that figure is $10,000 and for medicine it is $25,000 (Jammal, interview, 2014; see also Lebanese University, 2003: 40).

Higher education is personnel intensive, so it is no surprise that the bulk of annual budgets consists of salaries. On average, salaries make up 70 percent of annual appropriations, and these are simply one part of the civil service budget. In Egypt salaries account for nearly 85 percent of the total operating budget of universities. Nonacademic staff receive a considerable share of these allocations. In Lebanon, this share is almost 53 percent, and in

Egypt it is 50 percent, compared to 29 percent in Jordan and 36 percent in Tunisia (El-Araby, 2010: 3).

Turkey may indicate where the Arab world is headed. The state provides 55 percent of total university funding, while the universities generate 40 percent of income and students contribute 5 percent through fees. Income generated by the universities themselves includes revenues from contract research, patient care in university hospitals, and gifts and donations (Barbalan et al. 2008). Jordan is today close to these proportions. For many years, and despite the founding of several new public universities, the government of Jordan has held core public funding of universities at 35 million Jordanian dinars, or roughly $50 million. University leaders have had to scramble to find other sources of revenue (see page 251), but they have also been given a green light to do so.

Government outlays give us only half the picture of educational funding. Household (private) outlays represent the other half. The proportions vary but in many instances payments for tuition, other fees, private lessons, books and supplies, transportation, and lodging roughly equal formal public outlays. Lebanon is an outlier in this respect. Charbel Nahas (2009: 19–20; 2010) shows that the Lebanese government spends about 3 percent of GDP on all levels of education and about 0.5 percent on higher education. But household expenditures on education are off the world charts: 9 percent of GDP for all levels and 3 percent for higher education. In total, Lebanon spent about 13 percent of GDP on all levels, and 4.1 percent on higher education, in 2004.

Egypt shows a more representative balance, with the government spending 4 percent of GDP on education, and households spending 3.6 percent. In Jordan and Palestine, household outlays are higher than in Egypt (Rizk, 2016).

Completion Rates

The issue of dropout or graduation rates is one that system planners and university leaders share. Because it is shared, it tends to fall through the cracks. Over the course of an undergraduate education a significant proportion of enrolled students do not complete their course of study. Noncompletion is a significant loss for the IHL and for the system as a whole, but the incentives to identify and cope with it are poorly aligned. Because faculty salaries are part of the overall civil service budget, university leaders have weak incentives to control faculty hiring. In addition, there are no penalties for low completion rates or rewards for improving them. At the system level, dropouts are like white noise, just one more sign of poorly aligned incentives. White noise is tolerated and ignored.

As we have seen, the statistics on completion rates in the MENA are spotty and inconsistent, but it seems safe to assume that a quarter or more of enrolled students fail to complete their degrees.[3] Attrition is highest in the first year. Because public tertiary education is mostly free, enrolling appears to be relatively costless. But then the student encounters the costs of books, supplies, transportation, meals, and housing. S/he discovers the inadequacy of her/his preparation in foreign languages. In the STEM disciplines mastery of English may be essential, or, in North Africa, mastery of French. High school preparation may prove to be deficient in terms of work habits, analytic skills, and problem solving. All these realities manifest themselves in the early months. The student drops out, and, more than likely, heads for the informal sector or to unemployment. Over time the motivation to pursue tertiary education evaporates. The study by the Supreme Council for Education, Training, and Scientific Research analyzed the open admissions faculties of three Moroccan universities and found that only a third of entering students actually completed their degrees (Kingdom of Morocco, 2018: 22).

As in most domains, completion rates in the MENA appear to be in the middle of the pack by international standards. Argentina is often cited as the world leader in university noncompletion, with over 70 percent attrition (Kelly, 2013). The United States, across all types of tertiary education (including community colleges), sees about 40 percent of enrolled students fail to complete their course of study within a reasonable period of time. An incomplete degree, in terms of future earnings, is not worth the amount of time put into it. Three years of a four-year degree do not earn three-fourths of the return on a completed four-year degree (Koropeckyi, Lafakis, and Ozimek, 2017). Others contest this (Schnepf, 2014), arguing that dropouts often go on to finish degrees later in life. Still, it is hard to put a positive spin on failure to complete a course of study, added to which is the fact that those most likely to drop out come from lower-income brackets and minorities. Increasing completion rates would strike a blow for greater equality of outcomes. There is good reason to believe that the same dynamics hold in the MENA.

Most MENA universities have a two-tiered system. Some faculties—typically medicine and engineering—have selective admissions, take only the best students, and, as a result, have relatively low dropout rates. Alongside such faculties are open (that is, nonselective admissions) programs in the arts, humanities, business, Islamic studies, law, and so forth. They have large classes and no attendance requirements, and for many students are simply holding pens until they can transfer to a more desirable program or to another IHL. If they fail exams or courses, they are allowed to repeat. Fees outside tuition are low (at Lebanese University, for instance, about $130 per year) so that the cost of repeating for many students is acceptable.

Dropouts are a dead loss to the university and to society. They diminish the public good of education. Staff is hired in light of expected enrollments that may not net out dropouts. In Morocco the costs of dropouts to the operating budgets of IHLs in nonselective faculties is about 18 percent (see Chedati, 2009: 28–30; Kingdom of Morocco, 2018: 27). The students may incur debt on which they default. Their tribulations reinforce social inequity. They reduce the social returns to education significantly.[4] The erosion of the public good of education is the main systemic cost.

Reducing attrition rates, or increasing completion rates, should be an unthreatening reform from the point of view of incumbent political leaders. The students involved have already been admitted to university, they have signaled their desire for higher education, and they could become productive citizens, but they risk falling into the ranks of the frustrated and the angry. By finding ways to help them finish their course of study, teaching would be aligned with staff and infrastructure aligned more closely with real student needs.

Some of what needs to be done will require an overhaul of secondary education so that its products need less remedial work when they arrive at university. Even though most Arab countries think of tertiary education as a system—the policy unit of analysis—the boundaries of that system exclude secondary education. In terms of pedagogic goals and methods, IHLs and high schools need to be integrated, and communication across the 'divide' should be routine and constant.

But even if high school students arrive at university better prepared, they may be financially incapable of meeting ancillary expenses. Because the state covers the direct costs (salaries) of the professoriate, university leadership have little incentive to contain staff costs. Specifically, they may not take into consideration likely attrition in estimating the staff they need to hire. The costs of attrition and of excess teaching staff are not internalized (endogenized) in the university's budget calculus. Adnan El-Amine told me, "The graduation rate [at Lebanese University] indicates massive dropout rates at the same time faculty numbers probably reflect fictitious enrollments." The problem may be compounded by the fact that many students are registered in more than one faculty at the university, adding to the problem of double-counting (email, 2018).

Attrition is but one of the causes of uncertainty in enrollments. How central authorities—the supreme councils or coordinating committees—allocate new students is another. Sometimes, with the new academic year about to start, university leadership may not have any real sense of how many students they will be dealing with. According to Wail Benjelloun, "We do not know how many students we will have until a month before classes" (interview, 2013). The hourly contractee or adjunct becomes the linchpin to dealing with this unpredictability.

The responses to attrition may be: staff as if there is no attrition after the first semester or year; in highly selective institutions (which by that token are likely to have low dropout rates), 'backfill' from transfers and waiting lists to match student numbers with available faculty; or maintain a critical minimum of regular faculty while meeting the demand of any excess students with contract or adjunct faculty. The critical minimum would be the number of full-time faculty needed for the lowest number of anticipated enrollees over a multiyear period. The driver is the planned student-to-teacher (whether full-time or adjunct) ratio.

A fourth solution is the best. Find ways through improved teaching and remedial work to reduce attrition to negligible levels (the focus of Koropeckyi, Lafakis, and Ozimek, 2017; AAAS, 2017; Massy, 2016). The response may range from conventional remedial classes and tutoring to distance and blended learning. A major part of the challenge is to train IHL faculty in teaching methodologies, identifying students' learning modes or dispositions, and helping students surmount specific obstacles and challenges. It will be an empirical question whether the savings in resources through the reduction in attrition outweigh the additional costs of remedial teaching.

Student Loans

Student loans represent a shift in the burden of education financing from the taxpayer to the student or the student's family. Of course, many loan programs are publicly funded so that the risk is shared between taxpayers and borrowers. The risk of default is highest among those borrowers with the least income. Public schemes can hedge against the disproportionate risk borne by the poor by, as in the UK, servicing a loan only after reaching a threshold income and then for a maximum of thirty years.

The issue of using student loans to finance education becomes relevant only if significant tuition is charged. In the MENA, that is the case only with respect to private IHLs, or in Jordan, where the loan market for public education appears embryonic at best. The standard framework in the theory of human capital and education returns assumes that needy students can always borrow money to further their studies and therefore will be able to continue to study as long as the returns to education are superior to its cost (Jaramillo and Melonio, 2011: 47).

Whether to justify the investment of taxes paid by the broad public or the loans incurred by private individuals, the income-earning prospects of graduates must be bright. That is not the case in the MENA, at least for those who remain in domestic labor markets. The move toward private education and toward the introduction of tuition charges is far in advance of the development of loan-based financing.

Special Allowances

Like completion rates, special allowances link the higher education system as a whole to the leadership of universities. All civil servants, including the professoriate, benefit from special allowances. They are a ubiquitous way to raise incomes, but, unlike base salaries, the state is not legally bound to maintain them. They are often discretionary and can be revoked. Not everyone receives the same allowances, so they can be used as rewards, sometimes for real merit but also for patronage. Perhaps most important from the point of view of both the state and the university, they are not considered part of the base on which retirement and other benefits are calculated. Because special allowances have become a kind of acquired right, it might not cost the state very much to include them with base salary in calculating retirement benefits.

In Egypt there are two basic allowances, the university allowances (*badl al-jami'a*) and the quality incentive (*hafiz al-jawda*). These allowances are disbursed on a monthly basis to all faculty members and their assistants (professor, associate professor, lecturer, assistant lecturer, and teaching assistant) without exception.[5] The university allowance ranges from 1,000 Egyptian pounds ($164) for a teaching assistant to 3,500 Egyptian pounds ($574) for a professor. The quality incentive ranges from 500 Egyptian pounds ($82) for a teaching assistant to 1,700 Egyptian pounds ($279) for a professor (exchange rate from 2012).

Competitive Funding

As we have seen elsewhere, funding for basic research and R&D is woefully inadequate in the Arab world. Steps are now being taken to strengthen national research centers and to stimulate competition for the award of funds. For decades, the CNRS-L has used its limited resources to support university research. Perhaps the oldest such institution is Turkey's Scientific and Technological Research Council (TÜBITAK), founded in 1963, and which manages ten research centers and acts as a bridge among universities, the government, and industry. It partners with European funding sources and universities. Its annual operating budget is on the order of $170 million (subject to rapid fluctuation in the US dollar exchange rate).[6]

Foundations like the Maktoum Foundation in Dubai, the Qatar Foundation in Doha, and the Arab Fund for Economic and Social Development (AFESD) in Kuwait are only a few of many funding agencies that can set the course for certain types of research. Competitive funding could be a very powerful tool to stimulate collaborative research (see De Moura Castro and Levy, 2000: 104, on Latin American experiences).

Tunisia since 2009 has successfully used competitive mechanisms to encourage the formation of research groups and teams (*collectifs de recherche*). After a first round of methodological explanations, public universities were invited to submit 'institutional projects,' which were discussed with the government and led to the establishment of performance contracts. This was followed by a second step: the signing of similar contracts between the universities and their faculties, institutes, schools, and other entities. In Egypt, the Science and Technology Development Fund, in 2008, took up the task of funding Science, Technology, and Informatics (STI), disbursing 500 million Egyptian pounds ($94 million at the time) in two years (Bond et al., 2014?: 23).

Private Lessons

Private tutoring and commercial cram-schools are a common feature throughout the MENA and, indeed, throughout the world. South Korea, with its GER of ca. 90 percent, is nonetheless probably the world leader in resources devoted to private lessons—some $15 billion a year, a tenth of household spending, or nearly 0.8 percent of GDP. By contrast, in Finland such outlays are virtually nil (*The Economist*, 2015b).

Private lessons should be seen as a means of topping up salaries in the public and private sectors; it is relief of general funds. In many countries, private lessons are in a legal gray zone. Instructors in public institutions may be forbidden from working for private providers or directly offering tutorials. It should be expected that as higher education becomes accessible, those who can afford private lessons both at the high school level and at university will pay for it to get a leg up in admission to highly desired faculties and thence to the job market. From the point of view of public policy, it is like the informal sector: it is tolerated but there is no coherent set of policies to reform or replace it.

Tutors and cram-school instructors are most often, but not always, the same people who teach in the public and private school systems. It would be preferable for the tutors to come from a different supply source than the school and IHL stock of teachers (Bray, 2009). For the latter, tutoring may be illegal, and it provides incentives for the tutor to neglect his/her official teaching duties. In this way the public, taxpayer-funded educational system subsidizes private lessons and cram schools. It is truly a vicious circle.[7]

If the supply of tutors comes from a separate stock, at least the issue of legality is resolved, and the sector may be more easily regulated because it is not in the informal economy. Some MENA countries, especially Egypt, are much more addicted to the private-lesson phenomenon than others. However, the structural elements that bring it about are ubiquitous: poorly paid instructors at all levels; make-or-break high school exams that govern admission to universities (*tawjihi, thanawiya 'amma, konkur*); fearful parents; and, ultimately, unwelcoming job markets.

Private lessons are just that, private. Gross outlays that may run as high as $4–5 billion per annum in Egypt (Uthman, 2015; Khairy, 2016; Elbadawy et al., 2007; Elbadawy, 2014) and Turkey (Education Reform Initiative, 2013; Tansel, 2013) are not included in the most commonly cited figures on *public* outlays on education. Yet they are an integral part of the overall demand for education.

It is estimated that 75 percent of Egyptian secondary students take private lessons (Elbadawy, 2014). Amina Khairy (2016) depicts official schools with student absentee rates of 95 percent and teacher absentee rates that are quite high as well. Port Said tried to close 'lesson centers,' prompting an outcry from local students and families who felt they were being put at a disadvantage in the *thanawiya 'amma* in comparison to other Egyptian governorates where lessons are tolerated. Private lessons have gone from competing with the official school system to become the system. Even after gaining admission to university, some 22 percent of students continue to take private lessons, as do a third in vocational schools.

In 2005, the Turkish Education Association conducted a broad survey on private tutoring centers. It found that households spent $5,322 on average in 2005 prices per year. For those able to pay, this may be the equivalent of 15 percent of their annual income.[8]

Elbadawy and colleagues (2007) find no gender bias in those who take private lessons, which puzzles them, as males have an advantage in the job market. They speculate that parents may want their daughter to complete her education so that she finds a richer and/or more educated husband and, hence, can achieve a higher social status through marriage.

In Jordan in recent years, the phenomenon has led to high levels of absenteeism in high school, as students stay away in order to meet with tutors (Alayan, 2014). In Algeria private tutoring has become near-universal since the civil war years of the 1990s. An unchanging, rigid curriculum coupled with low teachers' salaries fuels the phenomenon (Hayat, 2015).

Is there an Uber moment coming? Educated youth unemployment is very high. There is no reason why these relatively well-educated unemployed youths could not offer tutoring as good or better than what 'certified' teachers are able to offer (see Farahat, 2015). If there were an Uber moment, one could expect push-back from licensed teachers similar to the push-back of licensed cab drivers.[9]

Public Expenditures: The Unit of Analysis is the IHL

We come back to the university as the unit of analysis, the locus of decision-making for the determination and use of its revenue streams. The university must enjoy sufficient autonomy to make the relevant resource decisions. It must be held accountable to various public and private 'principals' for the decisions it makes. As we saw in Chapter 5 on governance, neither autonomy nor accountability are granted to or imposed on public IHLs in the MENA.

How do presidents, vice chancellors, and chief financial officers see their challenges and opportunities? What is their wiggle room? In this section I attempt to answer that question by looking at the contents of the leader's bag of tricks. I use the term advisedly because the leader is trying to beat a very resistant system. Third parties play an important role in promoting certain solutions, and through their financial resources can induce reluctant political masters to make certain concessions.

There is a puzzle here that I have not solved. The average tenure of university presidents in the Arab world (see Chapter 9) is not long—around five years. Bureaucratic hurdles are ubiquitous. Political leaders merely want presidents to keep things quiet. What, then, motivates university leaders to initiate and innovate, take on the bureaucracy, in short try to beat a system that is not asking much of them in the first place? Moreover, they will not last long enough to take credit for what they began. Is it professional pride, frustration at seeing so much wasted potential? I do not know, but a few interlocutors tried to help me find answers (Chapter 9).

In its study of Makerere University in Kampala, Uganda, the World Bank (1999) takes credit for university reforms in the context of an overhaul of the economy to make it more market friendly. The verbiage is very much of the Washington Consensus. The specific reforms for Makerere were to expand university consulting, commercialize services, and launch what in the Arab world are called 'parallel courses' (see pages 254–56) for 'sponsored' students, offered for fees, in off-peak hours (evenings, weekends). By doubling overall admissions and hugely expanding sponsored students, Makerere went from no registered students paying tuition to 80 percent doing so. This is reflective of reforms leveraged by the World Bank in subsequent years in the Arab world.[10]

Unsurprisingly, the Moroccan government, or at least its Supreme Council for Education, has seen the connection between these revenue-generating devices and university autonomy: "In pursuit of this development of resources, the University would be called upon to explore new modes: creation of university foundations, the setting-up of endowment funds, contributions of alumni associations, . . . fee-paying continuing education. Professional BAs/BSs (*licenses*) and masters degrees aimed at employees still suffer from a legal void that offers no incentive to universities or teacher-researchers to explore [this avenue]" (Kingdom of Morocco, 2018: 94).

Budgets

It is hard to get consistent figures for university budgets. The main problem seems to be that state allocations in the form of salaries are sometimes included in university budgets and sometimes not. The figures below on Ain Shams University in Egypt would seem to include them. One source (Abd El-Galil, 2017b) put the university's operating budget at $72 million in 2016, while another cited $400 million. Given that Ain Shams enrolls 170,000 students, either figure on a per-student basis is paltry compared to international norms.[11]

Non-tuition fees are ubiquitous and relatively light, but for low-income families nonetheless onerous. We have noted that they contribute to high dropout rates in the first year of university. In Egypt, in the theoretical disciplines—that is, subjects that are taught in a classroom rather than an equipped laboratory—fees rose from 1,200 Egyptian pounds (about $70) to 1,520 Egyptian pounds ($86) for master's degree courses, and from 1,500 Egyptian pounds ($79) to 1,895 Egyptian pounds ($107) for doctoral programs. In the practical disciplines, fees rose from 1,800 Egyptian pounds ($94) to 2,270 Egyptian pounds ($129) for master's degree programs and from 2,250 Egyptian pounds ($117) to 3,257 Egyptian pounds ($184) for doctoral programs. "I pay 3,000 Egyptian pounds ($176) each year in registration fees for the Ph.D., in addition to the expense of buying books and study materials and transportation expenses, which reach about 10,000 Egyptian pounds ($588) per year," a doctoral candidate in social sciences at Cairo University reported (Abd El-Galil, 2018). Non-tuition fees may constitute 5–10 percent of total university revenues.

Under Morocco's Education Law of 2000, the university president becomes responsible for preparing and implementing budgets. This responsibility includes managing and accounting for revenues from contract work and consulting. Article 18 of the law gives the universities and presidents the right to diversify their income sources (Kleich Dray and Belcadi, 2008). University authorities are able to retain and reuse excess funds from one year to another (World Bank and CMI, 2012: 92). The Plan d'Urgence of 2009 continues in the same spirit: "Similarly, the universities will be encouraged to diversify their sources of financing by the creation of companies (sociétés) and investments in private enterprises."

CAU in Marrakesh grew its student body over threefold between 2011 and 2018. At the same time the teaching corps has hardly grown at all, holding steady at just over 1,500. Nonacademic staff totaled 900 over the same period (see Chapter 7). The student-to-teacher ratio is about 68:1. The annual cost of educating a CAU student is around $1,000. University leaders could not control enrollments nor faculty hiring, two of the university's major cost parameters.

Charbel Nahas provides figures for Lebanese University, as listed in Table 8.2. If we take the government contributions as external to the university's budget, then the latter would be 66 billion Lebanese lira of total revenues of 186 billion. According to Ahmad Jammal, director general of the Ministry of Education (interview, 2013), once approved by the government, Lebanese University has full discretion in spending its allocations. As director general, Jammal merely transfers the annual budget request to the Council of Ministers (cabinet). Once approved, audit functions are minimal.

Table 8.2. Revenues and Expenditures, Lebanese University, 2007 (in Lebanese lira)

Revenues	Amount
Government Transfers	120,000,000,000
Entrance Exam Fees	703,000,000
Exam Fees	8,100,000,000
Training fees	108,000,000
Reserves	55,800,000,000
Total Revenues	186,000,000,000
Expenditures	
Salaries and Wages	98,000,000,000
(academic	46,000,000,000)
(administrative	9,100,000,000)
(part time instructors	14,500,000,000)
(rewards and allowances	2,300,000,000)
Total Expenditures	150,600,000,000

Source: Adapted from Nahas (2009)

The university operates forty-seven separate branches, adding substantially to operating costs through maintenance of separate facilities and duplication in staffing ('Issa, 1997).

Hossam Kamel, Cairo University's president in 2013, told me that he had to find ways to generate a third of the university's operating budget each year (interview, 2013). His successor, Gaber Gad Nasser, reported, "When I took this job, 90 percent of the budget was allocated to salaries and wages. But, when we came to work on the development of Cairo University, we reformed the finances and took on administrative corruption. Now salaries account for 60 percent" (interview, 2014). Estimates of Cairo University's operating budget, like that of Ain Shams, vary significantly, but cluster around $250 million (Wirtschafter and Nader, 2017; Nasser, interview, 2014). Despite Egypt's centralized educational and budget system, Nasser was able to take important initiatives.

The funds Nasser saved from spending cuts in salaries and other areas were redirected to improve upkeep of the university's facilities, update ICT, and improve campus life, including more arts activities and student counseling. Nasser also said he invested more in faculty research and university–business partnerships that might generate revenues. "For four years,

I have said we can self-finance, and no one in authority has accepted that" (interview, 2014). He noted that Cairo University generates about $17 million in research contracts annually: $12 million from the government and $5 million from industry. Nasser intimated to me that contract work and institutional consulting *of all kinds* might generate revenues nearly equivalent to government support.[12] As we saw in Chapter 2 with respect to MIT's involvement with Cairo University, external third parties may be the source of contract funding. By contrast, while onerous for many students, fees represent less than 5 percent of the university's total budget.

Menoufia University is one of Egypt's oldest and most reputable provincial IHLs. In 2014, its president, Moawad al-Kholi, reflected on his experience:

> Some things shocked me. I have enough staff in the university administration for 10 universities. While the university has the capacity to provide much higher quality education with a better allocation of personnel and services, the problem is also receiving more students than what the university could absorb. We now have 6,000 core faculty members; this is a really high number that could allow us to open new faculties. This staffing is a load on our budget. If used well it would help push us forward. I may assign one of the ranking administrators to completely restructure the administrative system of the university in order to fix that. This also would include retraining and reassigning administrators to other locations. (Elmeshad, 2014)

Jordan University—the country's largest public university, with some 49,000 students—has 4,700 employees, including 1,600 university professors. According to a statement from its then president, Azmi Mahafzah, "Seventy-seven percent of university revenue goes to university employees. . . . This hampers progress within the university, which needs to develop its tools in various fields" (Fraij, 2017).

Jordan University was founded in 1962. Soon after, a dedicated tax to support it was introduced, apparently on transactions, that is, like a value added tax. Until about 1974 and the founding of Yarmouk University, Jordan University was the sole recipient of the tax revenues. At that point it was relatively well-funded. But Yarmouk, then Mutah in 1981, then Jordan University of Science and Technology in 1986 all took a cut of public funding (Mahafzah, interview, 2015).

Abdullah Ensour became Jordan's minister of higher education in 1994 and redesignated the tax. Only then did Jordan University and other universities draw directly on the annual state budget. The total allocation for universities was based on the level of revenue of the special tax in 1994, or about 50 million Jordanian dinars. The figure did not much evolve in ensuing years, forcing universities to use fees and auxiliary services to fill funding gaps. The allocation in 2015 was about 57 million Jordanian dinars to ten universities. Of necessity, they achieved substantial financial autonomy (Mahafzah, interview, 2015).

Jordan University is stuck with old tuition levels that, because of political sensitivity, cannot be raised. Newer universities started from a higher tuition base. Today Jordan University generates around 80 million Jordanian dinars in fees from 45,000 students. The operating budget is about 150 million Jordanian dinars, added to which is the Medical Center at about 100 million Jordanian dinars.

The university will try to generate 50 million Jordanian dinars (about $71 million at the 2015 exchange rate) in non-fee revenues annually. Two buildings have already been constructed for investment purposes in the northern area of the Amman campus. The university has the right to erect such buildings but will need the approval of the board of trustees and the government before proceeding farther. The investment buildings will hold shopping centers, supermarkets, car parks, cafeterias, offices, and other facilities. The fourth and fifth floors of one of the buildings house sixteen apartments of varying sizes, for rent (Faek, 2013d). Mahafzah's predecessor, Ekhleif Tawarneh, referred to Jordan University's outstanding debts of 57 million Jordanian dinars (more than the entire Jordanian higher education budget), and went through a list of projects designed to help service the debt: solar arrays to supply the university and sell power to the grid, a stem cell bank, an epidemiology center, and even a date-palm plantation aimed at exports (Malkawi, 2015). The goal was to balance the university budget by 2018. As of 2019 it is not clear that either objective has been achieved.

As we shall see below (page 253), tuition revenues are greater than government support in Jordan. All Jordanian universities are in quest of alternate revenue streams. Investments, like Jordan University's, are projected to generate income equivalent to nearly one-third of tuition revenue and about 20 percent above total government support for higher education. Meanwhile Gulf states provide a large portion of Jordan's public university capital budgets.

CAU in Marrakesh is planning a new 'eco-campus' at Tamansourt, capable of accommodating 60,000 students. Some faculty speculated that CAU might sell its high-priced Marrakesh property to finance Tamansourt. Although CAU has five campuses in southern Morocco, the great majority of students are in Marrakesh. The utilization rate of space at the main campus is now 180 percent (Miraoui, interview, 2018).

Tuition

Mohamed ElBaradei was director general of the International Atomic Energy Agency,[13] and in 2005 both he and the agency were awarded the Nobel prize for peace. He went on to become Egypt's vice president and resigned from that position in August 2013 because of the bloody repression of Muslim Brotherhood members in Cairo. In an interview prior to his resignation (Charbel, 2013), he recalled a meeting with Hosni Mubarak, then Egypt's president:

> I reminded him that Egypt would never rise again without education and that free education has problems. Our focus should be on quality not on quantity. And I said to him that even from the point of view of social justice, how could my son be educated for free while I am financially capable and why not ask me to share in the state's obligations? He said to me, "Don't go there; if we open the question of free education, the Egyptian people will rise in revolt," and he recalled the days of the 1977 riots. (Author's translation from the Arabic)

Of all the populist planks in the social contracts of the MENA, none has more emotive power than that of free education, including at the tertiary level. Since the 1980s and 1990s, various regimes have gingerly tried to pry that plank loose. Licensing by the state to private, sometimes for-profit, institutions has spread everywhere. Proliferating fees and selling basic services such as food, books, and lodging is another gambit. Partial tuition has crept in through parallel courses and distance learning. A very few countries, such as Jordan, charge tuition in all public IHLs. It is a matter of time before tuition of some sort is charged throughout the region.

But the path will be rocky. Commitments to free education have been made in constitutions and other basic documents.

In early 2018 Morocco's parliament heatedly debated introducing tuition fees. This provoked dismay among many Moroccans. Parliamentarians and teachers' syndicates objected to a proposed law that would require higher-income families to pay fees for high school and university. The law did not specify what the income threshold income would be. According to a news report, "A number of members of parliament from both the ruling coalition and opposition parties have threatened to vote against the move, pointing out that the proposed law prejudices the right of Moroccans to free education. The opponents of the bill also warn[ed] that the new legislation will lead to a serious decline in the quality of the country's educational system" (Rais, 2018).

We saw at the beginning of this chapter that Jordan has already fought and apparently won the battle to force public universities to rely on fees, tuition, and other revenue streams to cover the bulk of their expenses. That notwithstanding, university students have decried this evolution, so far to no avail (National Campaign for the Rights of Students, 2015). They call for strengthening university governance, ending parallel courses, and eliminating the quotas for the military, civil servants, teachers, tribes, the handicapped, and others that exempt close to 40 percent of all students from paying fees. It is estimated that only about 50 percent of students pay fees (Mahafza, interview, 2015).

University faculty are often of two minds regarding tuition. Their professional calling and values suggest that they should be the natural defenders of free education. At the same time, they often moonlight in private institutions that are tuition-dependent or they give private lessons (see above on Completion Rates, pages 239–42). If the public universities introduced tuition fees, professorial pay packets might actually rise.

In 2018, I met with a few seasoned faculty members at CAU (Aziz, 2018). They came from lower-income families of Morocco's High Atlas region. They identified strongly with the thousands of CAU students of similar background and income level. Yet they had concluded that the payment of some level of tuition is desirable, to attest to the value of higher education (see also Buckner, 2013).

It is argued elsewhere (for example, the UK) that when education is free and at the same time biased toward the better-off, the private returns to education are captured by the relatively privileged. Free tuition tends to skew returns to education even more than a combination of fees and loans. Put another way, free higher education confers a huge rent to those who have access to it. And the rich are better placed to seize those rents than the poor (Devarajan, 2016).[14]

A good that is free but scarce will generate a price, often through private lessons and tutoring. That reality may explain some survey results that show a willingness to pay fees among certain students. Jaramillo and Melonio (2011: 68) cite International Finance Corporation and Islamic Development Bank surveys that found that over one-third of surveyed young people would be willing to pay student fees if they felt it would improve their job prospects. That suggests that two-thirds would *not* be so willing.

Leaving aside Lebanon, only the Kingdom of Jordan and the Palestinian Authority have chosen to rely significantly on private contributions to finance public education. In the West Bank and Gaza, approximately 60 percent of universities' costs are covered by tuition fees, close to the 66 percent recorded in Jordan. In Jordan, tuition fees in public universities vary between $1,500 and $3,000 per year, that is, 45 to 90 percent of GDP per capita (2011: 46). Public contributions declined from 71 million Jordanian dinars in 2002 to 65 million in 2007.

In the fall of 2014, Egypt began to deliberate the first steps toward charging tuition. An advisory council on education and scientific research, established by President al-Sisi, drafted a policy to introduce scholarships that would only cover costs for students with an average grade of more than 70 percent. Students under that line would be required to pay partial tuition, while those with less than a 50 percent average would pay full tuition (Shams El-Din, 2015). The economic regressivity of this policy is clear.

The growth of private higher education is expanding the tuition-paying population rapidly, without the state reneging on its formal commitments. In Lebanon, where well over half the tertiary student body is in fee-paying, private institutions, the habit is decades, and in a few instances a century, old. We should expect to see more Arab countries following that model.

Parallel Courses

In the past two decades university leaders have resorted to various forms of course offerings, parallel to the official curriculum, in order to generate revenues for the university. These courses and degree programs may use distance learning or blended learning. They may supplement existing offerings (that is, the equivalent of in-house tutoring or private lessons) or be stand-alone courses and programs. They may target students who are struggling with the regular curriculum, who failed to gain entry to university, who have dropped out, or who are non-nationals. The common denominator is ability to pay (El Baradei, 2010; Hammoud, 2010).

Such courses and programs have become so widespread that one must surmise that academic leaders shared their experiences. As the example of Makerere University shows, the World Bank has endorsed them but with considerable ambivalence.

Instructors in parallel courses are recruited from the standing faculty, whether regular or adjunct, and the recruits, many of whom are nominally full-time in their current positions, are paid extra for their teaching time.

In order to justify fees for these courses, they may be offered in English or another foreign language, class size may be kept fairly low, and greater individual attention may be provided. In Egypt, such courses may cost $900 to $1,500 annually, as compared to the $40 in annual fees that 'regular' students would pay (Tarek, 2015). Since 2009, Cairo University has been developing a new campus, International Cairo University, which will offer joint degrees with foreign universities (among others, Nottingham in the UK and Georgia State in the US), teach mainly in English, and charge tuition ranging from $1,800 to $11,000 (at 2009 exchange rates, Cairo University, 2009: 41–42).

Syria, prior to the civil war that began in 2011, had essentially three fee rates. Regular students paid about 30 euros in nontuition fees, students in open or distance learning paid up to 500 euros, and students in parallel courses paid between 200 and 1,000 euros (European Commission, 2017). The open learning (ta'lim maftuh) courses were introduced prior to the civil war, targeting students suffering from low grades. Classes met only on weekends and were not considered to be on a par with other four-year bachelor's degree programs. Newly created applied programs such as media studies, translation, computer science, and insurance were on offer. Such programs reach about one-quarter of all enrolled students. Students are charged approximately $600 a year. In 2009–2010, fee-based, parallel courses enrolled 50,320 nationwide and 17,665 at Damascus University alone (Buckner, 2013; European Commission, 2017).

In Morocco, specific universities developed special diplomas and certificates. MVUS at one time offered fifty such specialized diplomas, accounting for 10 percent of total revenues. Continuing education also generated significant revenue (Mrabet, interview, 2013).

Jordan pioneered in parallel courses, first introducing them in 1994. They targeted students who did not score high on the high school exam and who could not pursue their preferred majors. Jordan University refused to go along, seeing the programs as 'unconstitutional.' But by 2000 it caved. The general rule was that no more than 30 percent of total students could be enrolled in parallel programs, but that norm was widely violated because the alterative—frustrated students and shrinking revenues—was even worse (Mahafza, interview, 2015). The proportion of parallel students is 55 percent of enrolled students at Mutah University, 60 percent at the Jordan University of Science and Technology, 40 percent at Jordan University, and 39 percent at the Hashemite University. According to a National Campaign for the Rights of Students study (2015), Jordan eventually froze admissions to over thirty competitive specializations, forcing students into fee-based parallel courses. The report claims Minister of Higher Education Labib al-Khadra stated that 70 percent of students were pushed into parallel programs.

A wealthy Jordanian student with an 85 percent score on the high school exam can go to parallel medical school, while a low-income student would have to score 97 percent to get into the regular medical school. Parallel fees could take from a third to half the average annual income of Jordanians (Kanaan, 2010; National Campaign for the Rights of Students, 2015; Fraij, 2017). "I wanted to study pharmacology, but I could not, due to my marks in *tawjihi*," said Amer Al-Masri, "and as I could not pay the fees of [the] parallel program I joined biology" (Guttenplan, 2014). In 2014, the pharmacology program at Jordan University cost $15,196 for five years, while the parallel program cost $27,353 for the five years. Biology, on the other hand, would cost just $4,829 for four years (Guttenplan, 2014).

Yemen has its own regressive parallel system. Some students with high qualifications are only charged $37 a year. Others with lesser qualifications are in a 'parallel system' and charged moderate fees, ranging from $1,500 for studying medicine to $210 for studies outside of science and engineering. Others with even lower qualifications are considered 'self-paying' and pay even higher fees (Darem, 2013).

Like private lessons and tutoring, parallel courses sap the formal, free-education system. Instructional time in some ways is zero-sum. What goes into parallel courses is taken out of regular offerings. The standard curriculum is further debased as resources shift to the parallel offerings. New facilities (in the case of Cairo University or CAU in Marrakesh, a new campus) may be built to accommodate the parallel programs while existing infrastructure is neglected.

Foreign Students

The Arab world misses out on most of the five million (or more) international students that are a financial boon to universities in Europe, North America, and Australia. More important, Arab universities attract relatively few Arab students from outside their borders. That is beginning to change, and the change is driven mainly by the search for new revenue streams.

According to data released by Egypt's Ministry of Higher Education, 41,000 foreign undergraduate students enrolled at Egyptian universities in the five years from 2012 to 2017. In the same period, there were 50,360 foreign students in master's degree and PhD programs. In 2010 there were only a few thousand such students (Farouk, 2017; Abd El-Galil, 2017a). Jordan and Morocco attracted similar numbers. In 2007, close to 25,000 foreign students were enrolled at Jordanian universities. Of this number 13,000 attended private universities and 6,686 were female. The majority of these students were Arab nationals. The relatively high number of foreigners (more than 10 percent of the total) is attributed to the reputation of Jordanian universities, the diversity of program offerings, and the modern yet conservative community, coupled with greater security and political stability than in other countries in the region (Kanaan, 2010).

Fees for foreign students in Egypt vary according to the subject of study and the university, and range from $5,000 to $9,000 a year, although the government intends to raise this to $12,000 a year. Foreign students generated $120 million in fees in 2017, according to the minister of higher education.

Adjuncts

The pressures in the MENA to resort to short-term, contractual teaching personnel to meet both steady-state and fluctuating enrollment levels are similar to those found in the US. The IHL obtains flexible service from broadly qualified instructors who can be dismissed at the end of their contract and who receive no health or retirement benefits. Most often they do not enjoy voting rights in faculty affairs. Some decades ago, so-called adjuncts might have represented at most a third of faculty FTEs in the US. Today the proportion is more like two-thirds. Tenure-track faculty make up the rest. They are the researchers whose reputations, promotions, and tenure depend on their research output (Kezar, Maxey, and Eaton, 2014).

William Massy (2003) outlined something he called the 'ratchet.' It is a curve graphing the trade-off between the quality of teaching and the quality of research. His unit of analysis was the US research university. Despite

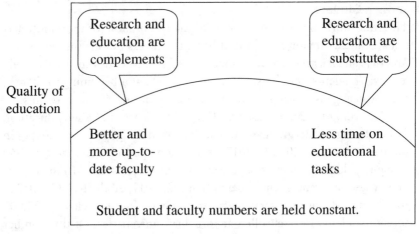

Figure 8.1. The Academic Ratchet
Source: Massy (2003: 97)

his long experience at Stanford, he saw such universities drifting inexorably rightward along the curve. To make that drift sustainable, research universities have had to resort to adjunct faculty to take up the slack left by tenured faculty whose time is given over predominantly to research (Figure 8.1).

All MENA IHLs, at least in their mission statements, aspire to institute joint production of education and research. There will surely be a few, such as KAUST, AUB, SUT, King Abdulaziz University, Khalifa University, Bilkent, Boğazici, and Middle East Technical University, which achieve it to some extent, but they will be in the minority. Finding the 'sweet spot' of the joint production of education and research is a distant challenge for most MENA universities

In the region, the driving force of what I call 'adjunctivitis' (the resort to short-term, contract instruction) is low academic salaries that create a reserve army of vagabond academics. Significant student dropout rates and admissions policies set by central authorities make annual enrollments unpredictable. IHL administrators have their reserves of adjuncts to meet teaching demand. This, for example, is the way Lebanese University handles fluctuating enrollments (Hassan Diab, email, 2018). Egypt's Ministry of Higher Education in 2010–2011 listed 40,511 full-time faculty members in the country's public universities, alongside 28,726 adjuncts. Similarly, Wail Benjelloun, in his plan for MVUA, emphasized the substantial role of *vacataires* (temporary instructors). MVA had 880 research professors and 330 *vacataires* or part-timers in 2009/10. In a SWOT (strengths, weaknesses, opportunities, threats) analysis in the same document Benjelloun identified reliance on part-timers as a major threat.

Corporate Actors

While it is mainly a private sector phenomenon, both public and private corporations have taken on direct funding of higher education. The major public sector actors are the OCP in Morocco, Saudi Aramco in Saudi Arabia, and Etisalat and Abu Dhabi National Oil Company in Abu Dhabi.

An early, and for some time unique, funding formula was invented by İhsan Doğramacı, a pediatrician and entrepreneur who founded Bilkent University in Ankara, Turkey, in 1984.[15] According to Ali Doğramacı, the son of the founder, Bilkent, Koç, and Sabanci Universities, all private, follow the same basic model (email, 2016). They benefit from the income of commercial companies owned by the corporate group. These companies are held by the respective families, which donate substantial amounts each year to education. Bilkent has been ranked as high as number 112 worldwide by the Times Higher Education ranking system.

Bilkent's companies, managed by professionals, are owned by Bilkent Holding, which in turn is owned by the university. The board of Bilkent Holding includes the university's rector and the vice rector for finance. "Success in the business world is never guaranteed," said Ali Doğramacı. "That actually was how my father convinced Vehbi Koç and Sakip Sabanci to establish universities. He said, 'Companies are likely not to last forever. Universities that you establish are more likely to carry your names into the future.'

"Bilkent's endowment includes the ownership of Bilkent Holding, income-generating real estate, and securities invested in Europe. These generate about a quarter of the annual income of the university. Another quarter comes from research grants. The remaining half is from tuition fees. . . . While Bilkent-owned companies are much smaller in size than Koç or Sabanci holdings, having the university as the sole owner and sole user of the funds compensates for the corporate size difference to some extent.

"Bilkent avoided leasing land from the Turkish state or enjoying it rent-free as happens in many countries. The Turkish state leases land for forty-nine years but there are strings attached. Most of the campuses of Koç and Sabanci are on land rented from the government at the start-up of the university. Since the founders do not own the deeds to the land, they cannot sell it for revenue-generating purposes."

Bilkent experimented with state-leased land in Erzurum (Eastern Anatolia). "Every time we build a new building [at our expense], the state says its their building. Given that we are using an additional building, they increase the rent! . . . So, we'd rather pay for the land when possible.

"My father's 'land' investments were made decades before building the university. Much of the land my father bought in the 1960s (about five million square meters) became the property of Bilkent University when he founded it. It was an endowment. Part of the land was used as the university campus. On other parts of the land Bilkent-owned companies built and sold residences, office buildings, and shopping centers. Land that my father had bought in the 1960s for $2 to $9 per square meter was decades later going for about $1,000 per square meter. Income generated was used to cover the initial capital costs of the university."

Lotteries

One of the most ingenious vehicles for generating revenues has been developed by Mexico's Monterrey Institute of Technology, a leading private IHL. The Monterrey Institute received initial funding through a group of businesses supporting the newly created university. It became clear that to become a long-term sustainable initiative, the Monterrey Institute would require other sources of support because of its lack of access to public funds. Beginning in 1947, the founders of the institute took advantage of a legal mechanism allowing not-for-profit organizations to conduct lotteries, supervised by the federal government, for the purpose of supporting social causes. The Monterrey Institute lottery (currently known as Sorteo Tec) eventually became one of the most important sources of funds for the institution's growth.

Currently, the institute conducts three editions of its national lottery annually, awarding $23 million in prizes and netting over $60 million a year. Sorteo Tec provides resources for scholarships and, more recently, for the establishment of endowed chairs, which have become key to supporting the research activities of the university (Marmolejo, 2011: 261–91). While the institute is private, there is no reason why such a mechanism could not be developed for public institutions as well.

Endowments

I posit that an endowment, especially if on the scale of Yale's or Harvard's, is the best bulwark of university autonomy. Certainly, endowment managers will be mightily concerned in the health of asset classes in which the endowment is invested, but simply by following best practice in spreading risk, the portfolio is unlikely to be exposed for more than 10 percent of market value in any one sector, let alone firm. Like public pension funds, university endowments are market-friendly and market-sensitive and thus 'capitalist tools.' They are also at the heart of university philanthropy, whereby programs, buildings, and professorships are endowed and named.[16]

We most frequently think of endowments as major sources of operational funding. Perniciously, they produce the Matthew effect—the rich get richer—because the bigger the endowment the more risk one can afford. Higher risk leads to higher returns so the distance between the rich and not-so-rich widens.

But endowments have another, critical function. If a university fails in whole or in part, the endowment is there to cover outstanding obligations—pay off debts, settle with tenured faculty, meet pension commitments, and so forth. In the final analysis, endowments fund liquidation. We do not think about that very often, as IHLs seldom fail, but AUB came very close in the early 1970s. I know of only a few closings in the MENA, mainly branch operations in the GCC that were very small at the time of closing and backed by the resources of 'mother' institutions in the US and elsewhere.

Endowments in the MENA are rare and so far confined to private institutions, although KAUST, a Saudi Arabian public institution, was inaugurated with an endowment of $10 billion. Legal frameworks are not yet in place, although Jordan's universities law of 2009, in Article 33, states, "A public university may establish funds for housing, saving, investment, donations, students and other funds related to the teaching staff and workers. Each fund (except donation and student funds) has a legal personality, whose regulations, purposes, management, membership, subscription, fees, liquidation and other relevant matters are subject to regulations issued therefor." In 2013, Lebanese University's president Adnan al-Sayyid Hussein stated his intent to establish an endowment (Hussein, 2013).

I suspect that, as a pillar of enhanced university autonomy, endowments stoke the suspicions of political leaders, wary of *any* form of civil society autonomy.

Issuing Bonds

Western IHLs often sell bonds to raise funds. For universities that charge tuition, bonds tend to be a fairly solid risk, above all when the demand for higher education is strong (inter alia, see Blum, 2014). Can bond sales be generalized? First, such sales presuppose an autonomous, corporate entity that can issue the bonds and be rated. Would any MENA public universities fit that bill? Second, MENA universities would have to have predictable and sizable revenue streams. None does and the state ultimately controls the purse strings. As we have seen, the state can be an unpredictable funder.

Incubation

Incubation led by universities may provide a public good for the macro-economy, but, given failure rates, not a significant source of revenues to universities. Every now and then there will be patentable blockbusters, generally in the biomedical field, that will yield huge returns to a handful of universities—Stanford, MIT, NYU, Northwestern—but they are the exception, not the rule. In the MENA, the most successful incubator has been Berytec, associated with the USJ in Beirut (see Chapter 7).

Conclusion

There are structural forces at work that are pushing financial and institutional arrangements in positive directions. The fiscal challenges of publicly funding a mass education system at all levels remain formidable. That means that private IHLs will become the default position for flagging state action. As the private educational sector grows, the issue of autonomy, financial and otherwise, for public IHLs will diminish in saliency. Private institutions already enjoy considerable autonomy: they answer to boards, charge tuition, and, in the case of for-profits, offer returns on investment. Some have constituted substantial endowments and others will do so. That model may feed back into the public sector as well.

With a more robust private sector presence, the public sector can concentrate on improving quality in the residual educational institutions. As we explored in Chapter 5 on governance, this may lead to greater differentiation among public IHLs, perhaps with the competition for resources hinging on performance. New flagships and new centers of excellence may emerge or the old ones may reassert themselves. There is a strong pro-public sector bias in the MENA and a great deal of suspicion of private undertakings.[17] Iran shares both, but private institutions enroll more than half of all Iranian students in higher education. Jordan in 2018 saw the private sector enroll 12 percent of all tertiary students. I do not see any going back on this gradual privatization. The questions are its extent and the speed of its spread.

Facing both public and private providers is the question of replicating the expensive bricks-and-mortar university. University infrastructure costs a lot to build and maintain. Distance learning and virtual campuses may seem to offer cheaper alternatives, but many experts, like William Massy, are skeptical. They see the issue of improved quality, and improved completion rates, being dealt with through improved teaching. To be sure, improved teaching may involve distance learning, flipped classrooms, and the like, but it is unlikely to be cheaper than existing practice.

The positive synergies that take place in the conventional university—between research and teaching, among faculty colleagues, and among students in their curricular and extracurricular lives—are conspicuously absent from the giant public universities of the MENA. There, absenteeism is rife, contact between overwhelmed faculty and students is rare, and student life is grossly underfunded and close to nonexistent. There is a very large sunk investment in existing infrastructure. Should that infrastructure be improved at great cost or sold off and the proceeds invested in new models of higher education?

With the growth of private education, it may become easier to align incentives in the public sector. A key move would be to bring personnel budgets out of the civil service and into the university so that university leaders have an incentive to match hiring to real teaching and research needs. Similarly, dropouts are today a cost to the system and to society but not so much to the university itself. Enhanced retention needs to be a critical piece of institutional performance evaluation. As we have noted repeatedly, 'enjoying' such responsibility will be relevant only if IHL leadership is operating in a competitive environment in which it wants to excel. That is not the case today.

Could these transformations occur in an authoritarian framework? Yes, although it would not be easy. If incumbent regimes did not initiate their own velvet revolutions through promoting private education, anything from the soft paternalism of Lee Kuan Yew's Singapore to the party-dominated hard order of China's Xi Jinping could accommodate a major transformation of public higher education in the MENA. Theoretically, the private sector has already won the battle for institutional autonomy, but in practice many private providers of higher education have wanted to make money, not trouble.

Asking how to feed the beast obliges us to focus on the deep philosophical divide that lies at the heart of various funding frameworks (see Salmi and Hauptman, 2006; Jaramillo and Melonio, 2011). Is it in the best interests of society, the taxpayer, and the student, among others, that good performance, however defined, be rewarded and by the same token mediocrity punished financially? If the answer is yes, then the implication is that, over time, elite institutions will separate themselves from the rest, becoming even stronger, while the rest may actually fall further behind relative to the elite or even in absolute terms.

Some find that process abhorrent, unethical, and unfair. They propose that all institutions be treated the same and that the funding not be based on performance, or at least not predominantly so.

It is possible to combine rankings with egalitarianism. Basic educational funding can be uniform across institutions while relative excellence guides the allocation of research funds or support for other targeted goals.[18] Whatever the solution, it should be the subject of public debate. Authoritarians are not good at that.

9

Living in the Beast:
Neither Ivory nor a Tower

The formal parameters of universities in the MENA depict an illusion. They are described as autonomous, founded on academic freedom, legally responsible, employing full-time faculty, and educating, for the most part, full-time students. Outside a few elite, mainly private, institutions, that is seldom the case. In practice, as we have seen, they lack autonomy, responsibility and authority are not aligned, they lack independent sources of revenue, their faculty is poorly paid and, of necessity, de facto part-time, and many students are similarly unmoored.

We will examine the economic incentive systems within universities that structure academic life. Some of those incentives have already been examined in Chapter 8. Similar to the prevailing legal endorsements of university autonomy throughout the MENA, the ideal of the full-time professor whose working life is exclusively devoted to research and teaching is built into teaching contracts. The ideal is seldom honored in practice.

The President
The previous chapter demonstrated that university presidents in the MENA are an enterprising lot. There is still a great deal of residual prestige in occupying that position, and in some instances it comes with the rank of minister. Appointment requires cabinet approval and an appointment decree from the head of state. The fate of many people lies in the hands of the president—tens of thousands of students, thousands of faculty members, and equal numbers of nonacademic employees. The president also oversees a large, even if inadequate, budget. The authority university

265

presidents have over budgets does not match their responsibility for student and employee welfare. The system determines resources while the institution determines responsibilities. Based on a limited sample of flagship universities (Table 9.1), it appears they are given little time to try to effect change.

Over time, the tendency seems to be shorter tenures. At the beginning, near-legendary figures like Rida Said at Damascus University, Ahmad Lutfi al-Sayyid at Cairo University, and Abdalatif Benabdaljelil at MVU each served for more than a decade. Perhaps the longest tenure of a 'founding' president was that of Fuad Afram al-Bustani at Lebanese University from 1953 to 1970. Abdusalam Majali served twice as president of Jordan University, in 1971–78 and in 1980–89, for a total of sixteen years. MVU has the longest average tenure of any of this small sample. Next comes King Abdulaziz University of Saudi Arabia, which is often ranked the number one university in the Arab world.[1]

With this very limited data, it would be hard to test the hypothesis that longer tenure would enhance institutional excellence. The president is an agent in the system. Long tenure measures the confidence the principals have in their agent. That confidence may be based on academic considerations involving the reputation and output of the university or on the

Table 9.1. Average Presidential Tenure, Select Universities, 2018*

University	Founding Date	No. of Presidents	Average Tenure: Years
Baghdad	1957	14	4.2
Cadi Ayyad	1978	4	10
Cairo	1925	25	3.7
Damascus	1923	20	4.7
Jordan University	1960	13	4.5
King Abdulaziz (Saudi Arabia)	1967	7	5.7
Lebanese University	1951	11	5.9
Mohammed V	1957	6	10

*Gathered from websites, except for Damascus University and MVU. Former President Hani Murtada supplied the information on Damascus University. It had three periods—1954–56, 1964–68, and 1971–73—for which no president is listed. The gaps were not used in the calculation of average years served. The former president of MVUS, Wail Benjelloun, supplied the information on MVU. Both Jordan and Morocco stipulate a presidential term of four years, renewable once.

ability of the president to keep the university quiet, or both. Confidence is essential to improvement unless it is founded exclusively on the ability to keep an unruly institution quiescent.

Anything less than five years in presidential leadership is probably insufficient to bring about any kind of structural reforms. The Jordanian and Moroccan systems limit presidents to an initial four-year term that can be renewed once. Perhaps four years is enough, but my own experience would suggest otherwise. And in two recent instances in Morocco, the minister of higher education terminated two presidents before they had completed their initial terms.

The puzzle is, why do presidents try as hard as they do? In virtually all instances, presidential salary is not an inducement. At the turn of the millennium, Hani Murtada, president of Damascus University, was paid $300 per month. When he subsequently became minister of education, his salary increased to $700 per month. However, as a clinical physician he could earn multiples of his salary through his clinical practice. It is true that university presidencies often confer ministerial status on the president so there is considerable prestige attached to them.

The solution to the puzzle appears to lie in self-esteem, a commitment to higher education, the challenge of reform 'in tight places,' and some role for public opinion and public scrutiny. I put this question to Azmi Mahafzah, a PhD in microbiology and for two years (2016–2018) president of Jordan University.[2] He built his career methodically and won each promotion. In June 2018 he was appointed minister of education (pre-university education). The following November, flash floods in the area of the Dead Sea caused the deaths of several Jordanian schoolchildren. Mahafzah submitted his resignation as minister.

Mahafzah answered my question about what motivates presidents in these words:

> To be frank, I never thought of this matter and I do not have a ready answer for it. However, I will try my best to provide you with an honest personal perspective on the issue. First, the position of a university president in Jordan is very prestigious, especially if it is of the caliber of the University of Jordan, and qualified academicians always compete fiercely for such position. Second, and since the tenure of a university president in Jordan is usually short, as you rightfully noticed, and his appointment can be easily terminated if he does not meet the satisfaction of the concerned authorit(y/ies)

he has no choice but to work very hard and exert his utmost efforts to perform up to expectations. These expectations, however, are never clearly defined or agreed upon in advance because this aspect is not usually given enough consideration in the process of selection among candidates. Moreover, it is rare that the new president is from the same university [no less] that he was part of the previous administration as vice president or at least a dean. Consequently, and under the assumption that he will serve for at least one term of four years, a president and his team start working on defining goals and objectives for their administration in the form of a strategic plan, with an action plan for implementation, which usually takes a minimum of six months. Also, the president of the university in Jordan, especially big universities such as such as UoJ and JUST [University of Jordan and Jordan University of Science and Technology], are under continuous scrutiny by the media, university staff, and the public. In such circumstances, a president must convince all parties that he is doing his utmost to lead the university successfully, which is judged by certain indicators in areas like academic and research achievements, budget deficit, university ranking and others. Without being highly motivated and creative, it would be unlikely for a president to meet success. From a personal point of view, motivation stems from the need for recognition and reward and is a reflection of self-esteem. Personally, I was totally preoccupied with university administrative affairs days and nights. I used to work for no less than twelve hours at campus for six days a week and continue at home until bedtime; even my dreams were about university affairs. I must admit that I did not have time to care for personal or family matters. (Email, 2018)

This summary challenged an assumption that I entertained: that there is little cost to a president punching the clock and shuffling papers, so long as his or her campus remains quiet and graduates students. It is not so simple. Abdallatif Miraoui returned to Morocco from a successful career in France in academia and consulting to run CAU. No doubt the prestige of the position, his self-pride, and the size of the challenge all played their part in his decision.

The office of university president defines a much more select and visible group. It may be, as in the case of Professor Mahafzah, a stepping stone to a cabinet position. Such recognition is ephemeral and is dwarfed by self-motivation.

Wail Benjelloun, former president of MVUA, had this reflection:

Moroccan university presidents in general have had a rich experience in teaching and research before taking on the presidency. I think the principal motivation of most is a desire to improve a system they believe can become better, according to a project which served as a basis for their initial selection for the post. Once in office, competition between universities also becomes a driving force. Finally, the desire to qualify for a second term through notable achievements may become a motivating factor for some. (Email, 2019)

Despite the fact that women students now outnumber men in most IHLs in the MENA, it is still very rare to find women in leadership positions, let alone presidencies, at Arab universities. A woman did head Egypt's SCU, but at the time of writing (2018) no woman headed an Egyptian public university. From 1992 to 2002, Syria's minister of higher education was Saliha Sanqar, a woman.

I do not have an explanation for this dearth of female leaders. By and large, women are better represented at the cabinet level or in national legislatures than they are in university leadership.

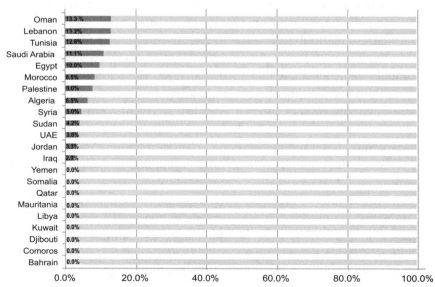

Figure 9.1. Percentage of University Presidents Who Are Women
Source: Al-Fanar Media/Info Times Survey, 2018

The Myth of the Full-time Professor

Outside the GCC, the average professorial salary does not afford a comfortable middle-class lifestyle, commensurate with a PhD or other advanced degree. Consequently, many if not most faculty members seek alternate sources of revenue to supplement their salaries. Adjuncts are legally part-time and may constitute as much as a third of the teaching corps. But full-time faculty, enjoying medical and retirement benefits and often the equivalent of tenure, must, like adjuncts, supplement their salaries by teaching in other institutions, consulting in the private sector, tutoring, marketing lecture notes, or maintaining private practices in medicine, law, or architecture.

As we have seen elsewhere, most MENA systems insist on the full-time faculty member and prohibit teaching personnel from earning revenue outside the institution except under highly circumscribed circumstances. The number of hours devoted to teaching elsewhere or consulting is 'strictly' limited to a certain number of hours per week or semester and only after review and approval by the department chair and the dean. Morocco, for example, allows twenty hours per month of teaching outside one's home institution (Benjelloun, interview, 2013). The reality, however, is different. Rahma Bourqia (2011: 14), herself a former president of a Moroccan university, offers an estimate of moonlighting: "Eighty-nine percent of teachers in private schools and institutes are adjuncts, coming for the most part from public universities. A study shows that 42 percent of instructors exercise another activity outside teaching in their home institution."

Across the Arab world, Hanafi and Arvanitis (2016: 51) estimate the total professoriate at 170,000 to 180,000, of whom about 55,000 may be double-counted because they are moonlighting and registered twice.

Outside employment, however, is vital to the functioning of the system. Officials, from ministers to presidents and deans, turn a blind eye to the practice, above all in that there is no systemic solution to low salaries. Mark Bray (2009) argues that trying to ban such tutoring is a fool's errand. Better to try to regulate it—for example, by forbidding public sector teachers to tutor their own students—than to outlaw it.

The severity of the problem varies, as one would expect, by country, discipline, and cost of living (particularly housing). Sometimes moonlighting is serial, as is the case for many Egyptian professors who go abroad to work for years at a time. If they are tenured, their position is kept open for them in their home institution. Their absences, it is important to note, break no rules.

Salaries

In Chapter 1, I talked about a putative golden age in the history of MENA universities that may be as much myth as reality. It was a time when the position of university professor held great prestige, a decent salary, and a comfortable middle-class lifestyle. It was self-contained. Now, it is just one of several career options and always in tension with other possibilities. It is doubtful that it would be a first choice for many well-educated Middle Easterners. The transformation in image is surely due to the great expansion in campuses and enrollments beginning in the 1970s, but I vividly remember Egyptian universities in the early 1970s as already being factories in which students and faculty were on a mindless treadmill. Ali al-Din Hilal Dessouki, who went on to become dean of the Faculty of Economics and Political Science at Cairo University, recalled his own experience as a young professor in the early 1970s (interview, 2013). His base academic salary was 45 Egyptian pounds per month. He gave supplementary lectures in a departmental institute for 7 Egyptian pounds per month and earned 60 Egyptian pounds per month at the Center for Political Studies at *al-Ahram* newspaper, Egypt's most prestigious daily. His rent at the time was 18 Egyptian pounds per month.

By that time, the model of the part-time professor was already established and critiqued. Matta Akrawi, writing in 1979, noted the dearth of qualified professors and the increasing reliance on "demonstrators *(mu'id)* and assistant teachers and the phenomenon of the 'traveling professor,' teaching in two or three universities and being compensated by all three" (1979: 57). Teaching quality and research, Akrawi lamented, were sacrificed.

Major, especially capital, cities in the Arab world are relatively expensive and even salaries of $2,000 a month would not provide a comfortable lifestyle (Ma al-Barid, interview, April 16, 1998). Faissal Aziz, a professor at CAU in Marrakesh, is single and finds his salary adequate to cover his needs, but that would not be the case were he married with children. In Khartoum, Sudan, a professor's salary might cover 30 percent of his real cost of living (Elnur, 1998: 314).

Ahmed Abdulaziz in the 1990s was a professor of law at Damascus University. According to the university's president at the time, Abd al-Ghani Ma al-Barid, average professorial salaries were around $200 per month. Abdulaziz recalled that teaching had taken on an industrial character. He started teaching in 1992 in the Faculty of Law. There were two thousand students, of whom only about three hundred ever attended classes. The rest survived on crib notes and professors' 'books,' an important source of revenue. When he graded exams, he could find no significant difference between those who attended classes and those who did not.

The habit of nonattendance is deeply engrained. It fosters collusion between faculty, students, and private providers of crib notes. Students sell slides and notes to private providers who charge 5 Syrian pounds per page. Some students are spending nearly $20 per month for crib notes. David Wheeler and Rasha Faek (2018) observed, "An outsider unused to this practice might believe that the students should simply attend the lectures themselves. But the practice has become engrained in university life even if many professors don't like it. 'The university isn't participating in this but can't prevent it,' said a professor." Given the logistical difficulties in commuting to the campus in wartime, one has the formula for chronic absenteeism.

Trends in faculty salaries vary substantially by country. Syria's plummeted. On the eve of the 2011 uprising, a full professor's salary could reach the equivalent of 1,500 euros per month. By 2017, that sum had declined to 350 euros (European Commission, 2017: 16). Two years later, faculty members from Damascus University reported average monthly salaries of $100 in public universities and noted that about 40 percent of credentialed faculty had migrated. Al-Samar (2018: 143) cites the exodus of eight hundred faculty members by 2016.

Egypt's academic salaries, by contrast, were going up. The Supreme Council of the Armed Forces doubled salaries after the 2011 uprisings. "After that time, each professor's salary starts at 1,200 to 2,000 Egyptian pounds [$150 to $250], before the addition of rewards and incentives that range between 1,500 and 8,000 Egyptian pounds [$190 to $1,000], depending on the faculty member's degree," said Aliya al-Mahdi, a professor at Cairo University's Faculty of Economics and Political Sciences. She felt that a salary less than $1,800 per month would be inappropriate for a senior professor (Abd El-Galil, 2015).[3]

For over a decade, from 2001 to 2013, salaries in Lebanese University were frozen. They were then doubled. The Ministry of Education reemphasized its total ban on unauthorized part-time teaching outside one's home institution (Mneimneh, interview, 2012). Prior to 2011–2012, monthly salaries ranged from $1,308 for the lowest ranks, to $3,320 for the middle ranks, to $4,650 for the most senior. After 2011–2012, the corresponding levels were $2,456, $4,650, and $5,600. The Ministry of Higher Education openly acknowledged that low salaries incentivized moonlighting, reduced faculty allegiance to Lebanese University, and led to low research output. The minister at the time, Hassan Diab, emphasized that the increase in faculty salaries was in a sense indexed to the salaries of the corps of Lebanon's magistrates, which had been raised in 2011 (Diab, 2013: 1086–87). At the time of the raise, the average teaching load for a regular faculty member *(ustadh mutafarragh)* was seventy-five hours per year. The raise required additional public funding of $47 million.

Jabeen Bhatti and Janelle Dumalaon (2014) place Syria, Morocco, and Yemen at the bottom of the regional salary scale in their partial (and I think unique) survey of academic salaries. The top salary in those three countries was about $30,000 per annum, while Lebanon, with its core of private universities, had top salaries of $90,000.[4] In Morocco in 2013, the highest professorial salary was $2,300 per month and the lowest was $1,170 (Mrabet, interview, 2013).

Jordanian universities are subject to uniform salaries for the university system. At Jordan University, faculty salaries in 2015 ranged from 1,500 to 3,000 Jordanian dinars per month, including bonuses from parallel courses. The top earners were receiving the equivalent of $45,000 per

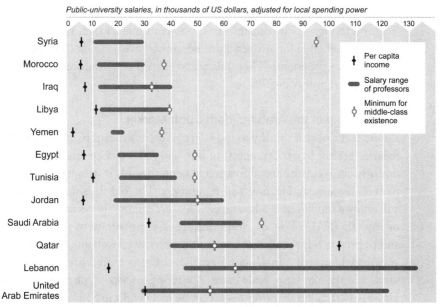

Figure 9.2. Arab Professors: Mostly Missing from the Middle Class
Source: ARA/Al-Fanar Media reporting, IMF, 2013 estimates. Copyright 2014: Al-Fanar Media.

year (Al-Zu'bi, interview, 2015). According to academic sources, this is not enough to live comfortably in Amman.

In Tunisia in about 2011, the average full professor's salary was $945 per month. Associate professors earned $845 and assistant professors earned $720 per month. Instructors earned about $680 per month. In 2011, for example, the University of Tunis employed 18,000 instructors (Labayd, 2017: 542–43).

Moonlighting is like other forms of corruption (the use of public office for private gain). All fixes seem to be temporary. When Georges Tohmé was president of Lebanese University in the 1980s (see Chapter 1), he saw faculty moonlighting as theft and used salary increases to try to thwart it. Three decades later, Hassan Diab tried the same thing. Might it not make better sense to assume the predominance of the part-time faculty member and build incentive and reward systems to reflect that reality?

Just as a professor's salary does not provide a comfortable middle-class standard of living, pension benefits are likewise inadequate. These may consist of lump-sum, end-of-service payments or in defined benefits. The retirement age is usually sixty to sixty-five. Unlike in the US, where tenured faculty may continue to work so long as they are physically and mentally capable of fulfilling their duties, the Middle Eastern professor faces the civil service statutory retirement age. In Egypt, that age is sixty. Tenured faculty, upon reaching sixty, may continue all their normal duties but are not eligible for any academic administrative position (such as dean, chair, or vice president). Their salary and any other perquisites remain the same (Gohar, interview, 2013).

Peculiarities of the Arab Academic Job Market

Public IHLs have no ability to use salary levels as a means to attract faculty. Salaries are set by governments, in line with civil service salaries, and are uniform across institutions. To attract talent, the only instruments available to IHL leaders are location and reputation. The old flagship universities still enjoy a reputational advantage.[5] They are almost always in major cities or capitals (KAUST is an exception), in close proximity to private IHLs and to private businesses that may hire university consultants. The salaries at Sohag University, in Upper Egypt, and Cairo University may be the same, but the similarity ends there. A senior professor of physics at Cairo University recalled that over his career he had taught in Saudi Arabia at six times his Cairo University salary and in Cairo consulted at Schlumberger Ltd. (oilfield services) at ten times.

There are all sorts of civil service rules that make it extremely difficult to move from one IHL to another. In Morocco, to recruit a faculty member or a member of the nonacademic staff takes on average two years: one year to get approval of a budget line and one year to advertise and recruit. Faculty and nonacademics remain state employees, so freedom of recruitment is highly constrained. The university cannot use its own resources to offer bonuses and incentives to academic and nonacademic personnel (Kleich Dray and Belcadi, 2008; Aziz, interview, 2018).

For over two decades I have reviewed postdoctoral grant applications for AFESD. It is striking to see typical academic career paths for Egyptian applicants. They complete their undergraduate education at one of the public universities. They complete their PhD either in the same university or abroad (but virtually never elsewhere in the Arab world). They are then hired by the same university where they did their undergraduate work. They will spend their career in that institution. It is a system of provincial silos.

Pre-civil war Syria offered a hiring system equally impervious to market forces. The selection procedure for academic staff with a PhD was mainly done via a public advertisement approved by the Ministry of Higher Education. In fact, the common procedure has been to appoint a large number of teaching assistants each year who are then sponsored by their institutions to prepare master's and PhDs in Syria or abroad. The contract for all positions is permanent until retirement, which is seventy for full professors (European Commission, 2017).

So far, lonely voices have called for universities to manage the academic hiring process (and, by extension, that of nonacademic staff as well). Amr Salama, the former president of Egypt's Helwan University and former minister of higher education, wanted to see presidencies, deanships, and faculty positions announced and advertised by the IHLs themselves. He advocated this when he was minister in 2004–2005. Salama cautioned that, as with promotions, one must assume a university has its own reputation at heart and that its leadership will have an incentive to enhance quality. So, advertising positions should take place in that spirit. Inside–outside committees should be formed to recruit for positions and to promote faculty. Salama's ideas went nowhere. Colleagues talked about scarce housing, pulling kids out of school, and so forth, ignoring the fact that it should be up to the individual faculty member to decide if a move is a good idea or not (interview, 2013).

There are regional or transnational academic markets in the MENA, but the logic of supply and demand is different from what one would find in the West. Supply is generated in the oil-poor, people-rich countries of the region, who export their PhDs to the oil-rich, people-poor countries of the GCC and, prior to 2011, to Libya. The main suppliers have been Egypt, Jordan, Palestine, and Sudan. It is important to note that there has always been a modest flow of academic political refugees, many from various branches of the Muslim Brotherhood, fleeing repression in Egypt, Syria, and elsewhere. The exchange is not one of talent for pay but rather one of compensating the importing countries for their lack of indigenous skills (in general see Plackett, 2019).

It was the oil-price surge after 1973 and the sudden and extraordinary wealth accruing to members of OAPEC that generated huge demand for skilled and educated white-collar emigrants, including schoolteachers and university professors. Egyptians seized the opportunity in large numbers. It is now an integral part of the Egyptian academic career. Once the faculty member has been awarded tenure (or its equivalent), s/he may seek employment abroad. The university rule stipulates that after five years' absence, the faculty member must return or lose her/his tenured position. Hani Gohar, director of Cairo University's Center for Quality Assurance, said that the rule is not applied and that there are exemptions that are routinely invoked (interview, 2013). The upshot is that at Cairo University in 2013, there were 10,323 regular faculty members, of whom about 2,000 were abroad. The university's president at that time, Hossam Kamel, estimated those abroad at 25 percent of the faculty (interview, 2013).

Absentees are not evenly spread across the university, but where the rate is high the result is a kind of actuarial donut. Departments are composed mostly of the non-tenured (and therefore vulnerable) junior faculty and the most senior and secure full professors. The middle stratum, which should be the most dynamic element, is abroad. The vulnerable are left to face the impregnable, leaving decision-making to the senior faculty.

After the fall from power of Hosni Mubarak in 2011, it was decided to use faculty elections for deanships for the first time since 1994. In the overwhelming majority of cases, incumbents were returned. A faculty member in the Faculty of Economics and Political Science noted that of fifty regular faculty members, eighteen were abroad. The remaining senior faculty tended to be approved by the regime's single party, the NDP. They preferred incumbents, and junior faculty went along. That said, the Faculty of Economics and Political Science at Cairo University elected Hala al-Said as dean. She was not an incumbent.

It appears that the turmoil unleashed in the Arab world in 2011 has motivated more faculty members to seek stability and higher incomes elsewhere. Over the period 2013–2016, 1,800 university professors left Tunisia, ironically the sole country to emerge successfully from the Arab uprisings (Jamel, 2017). In Morocco, because of relatively light teaching loads, some professors will meet all their obligations in a single semester and then go abroad to teach in the second semester (Benjelloun, interview, 2013).

Wealthy universities in the GCC, especially in Saudi Arabia, are chided or ridiculed for 'buying' their rankings by offering joint appointments to famous international scholars, including Nobel laureates. The GCC institutions seek to boost their international rankings while the professors receive hefty salaries and, perhaps, research support as well.

This, it seems to me, is simply a crude form of the bidding most successful institutions perform in trying to attract and retain talent. One might quibble that the crude version does not reflect a well-grounded institutional culture of creating knowledge, but the incorporation of international scholars, no matter how tenuous their links, may promote positive institutional change.

The Arab world, fittingly, boasts academic nomads. They are rare and therefore noteworthy. Erasmus, after whom the EU has named a program to encourage faculty movement among EU universities, would be proud of these intrepid voyagers. There is the Algerian mathematician who did his undergraduate work in Algeria and his PhD at Claude Bernard University in Lyon, France, then spent twenty years at Sana'a (Yemen) University, followed by five years at King Khalid University in Saudi Arabia and four years at Imam University, also in Saudi Arabia, and then finished up, presumably, at Msila University in Algeria.

A Mauritanian nuclear physicist did his undergraduate and MSc work at two Moroccan universities, doctoral work at Louvain, and a postdoc at Arhus in Denmark. He visited at Rennes and Luxembourg, taught at King Khalid University in Saudi Arabia and then at King Abdulaziz City for Science and Technology. He sought funding to go to the NASA Jet Propulsion Laboratory at Caltech.

Sudan produced a former professor of economics at the University of Gezira, Sudan; a former deputy director general of the Arab Planning Institute, Kuwait; and a former director of research at the Arab Center for Research and Policy Studies, Doha, Qatar.[6]

Supply and demand dynamics are at work within as well as between countries. Indeed, it is likely that faculty members would prefer, revenue being equal, to supplement their salaries through moonlighting at home than by emigrating. In Morocco, Cherkaoui (2011: 47) estimates that 22–35 percent of the arts and social science faculty nationwide exercise a second employment. That rises to 45 percent for law professors. Bourqia (2011) advances similar figures.

With the right skill set, such as that of the Egyptian professor of physics mentioned above, lucrative consulting gigs are possible. Faculty in the professions can and do run their own private businesses in law, medicine, architecture, and engineering. Burgeoning private-education sectors are happy to hire teaching staff from the public institutions. The private employer essentially hires contract labor without commitments to pensions and health insurance. In this way the public education sector, strapped for resources, subsidizes the private (inter alia, Bougroum and Ibourk, 2010). Note that the private employer is not interested in burnishing the reputation of his/her university or in enhancing the profile of the university's faculty. The moonlighter from the public sector is there to fill a hole, like any other adjunct.

For the less specialized, private lessons and tutoring are available. Translation is open to those with good language skills. Writing papers and coaching for exams for a fee is yet another possibility. Driving a cab or, today, an Uber may be more common than one would think.

As routinely occurs just about everywhere, some academics may see university employment as a track to high administrative office within the sector or as a stepping stone to high political office. This is especially the case in the several one-party autocracies of the MENA where being vetted by the party is a prerequisite for high administrative positions. The Ba'th party in both Iraq and Syria, the NDP in Mubarak's Egypt, and the Democratic Constitutional Rally in Ben Ali's Tunisia facilitated the merger of academic and political careers (inter alia, Labayd, 2017: 542).

The Incentive Structure for Promotion and Research

The same puzzle of what motivates university presidents to reform and innovate applies to faculty research. There is no major penalty for not doing it, or for going through the motions. Many expert observers, like Mohammed Cherkaoui and Adnan El-Amine, will stress the negative incentives to academic research, but there is solid evidence that an important minority (including Cherkaoui and El-Amine!) are highly productive, especially in light of inadequate labs and limited research funds. As noted above, for over twenty years I have reviewed applications for postdoctoral fellowships for AFESD. I have gone over hundreds of résumés for what are probably the best and the brightest in the Arab world. Most résumés read like their counterparts in the West or the Far East. The applicants tend to be concentrated in the STEM disciplines, perhaps because English is their working language, giving them a better chance to publish in prestigious English-language journals. For the more senior, they will have often occupied high academic leadership positions as departmental chairs and deans. Their productivity, while not widely shared, earned them institutional and peer respect. Self-motivation, professional pride, and peer respect probably drive them. The system may be malfunctioning, but it is providing good academic role models.

By and large, if the faculty member meets basic expectations in teaching, service, and research, s/he faces minimal risk of not being promoted, let alone dismissed. There is no way to reward outstanding performance in any of the three domains. It is truly a market for lemons, where the clock punchers will advance at about the same pace as the ambitious (confirmed for Turkey by Barblan et al., 2008, and for Morocco by Mrabet, interview, 2013). Writing on Tunisia, Boughazala et al. conclude:

> Faculty members' remuneration is almost totally independent of their effort and their performance; it depends on their position (from assistant to full professor) and also, but much less, on seniority. Remunerations and promotions are uniformly set for all institutions of the country. For example, an associate professor with a given experience in terms of years, is paid exactly the same salary in any institution (except for medical studies). Research and publications do not really matter except for recruitment and promotion. (2016: 8)

A dean at one of Morocco's oldest universities observed that the promotion system lacks rigor and incentives. "Two articles even in mediocre journals will get you to the *habilitation* [the review that certifies that a faculty member is competent to be a professor]. Eight years without doing anything will get you to the same place and the salary differences are minimal. You can apply endlessly for *habilitation*" (Anonymous).[7] One can normally reach full professor by age forty-eight. Research productivity would lop two years off that trajectory at most. Once one reaches the summit, salaries are uniform. Extra effort will not change that. While there is little incentive for research in Morocco, there is ample time. At the venerable university referred to above, average teaching time is eight hours per week.

Teaching loads at this university may be unusually light. A faculty member at a regional university reported to me that in his university "only 20 percent of faculty do real research. The others, in the swamped Faculties of Social Sciences, Economics, Law, and Letters merely go through the motions. One article every four years is enough to get by. All serious research is dependent on outside funding and foreign collaborations" (Anonymous). This professor spends most of his time writing grant proposals. Graduate students, he says, do the research. This means that most teaching is not based on the instructors' research. Professors, he alleges, download articles from the internet and teach from them.

Then there is the institutional culture that sees individual initiative as somehow pernicious. According to Bourqia (2011: 13), "The ranking hierarchy, which in principle is a hierarchy of experience and competence, is generally forced into retreat by a politically-correct egalitarianism that judges that all instructors are at the same level of competence."

An applicant for an AFESD postdoctoral fellowship from one of Jordan's five most prestigious universities wrote in his application: "The home university is dedicated for teaching. For example, I have to teach 3–4 courses every semester with more than 60 students per course. This situation leaves no time for professor [sic] to conduct research. Therefore, by residing in the host university and free [sic] myself for research, I will be able to perform well and conduct research that will have high impact."

At Lebanese University, promotion from assistant to associate professor generally comes after ten years' service. The candidate must offer one refereed journal article. Promotion to full professor requires five refereed journal articles. Lebanon is unusual in explicitly designating 25 percent of a salary to support research (El-Amine, 1997b: 594). "Research is considered an individual matter," notes El-Amine, "resting on the shoulders of the professor and at his expense or with external support—without the university knowing about it" (1997b: 590).

Egypt has a promotion framework that looks good on paper, but its application does not discriminate sufficiently among candidates. It is the SCU that orchestrates the process, not the university where the candidate is employed. As noted in Chapter 5 on governance, the Egyptian system seeks to thwart any drift toward institutional 'incest' and internal games of favoritism. The first step is for the full professors in the home department of the candidate to assess her/his service and performance. This assessment may count for 40 percent of the final evaluation. The departmental assessment is referred to a promotion committee constituted by the SCU. It in turn consults three referees who must be full professors in rank for at least five years and not from the candidate's institution. The referees focus on research. The committee, assisted by the three referees, then interviews the candidate. The final component is the assessment of the committee. Very few candidates fail to be promoted (Dessouki, interview, 2013).[8]

Egypt's incentive structure for research is deficient. Based on a May 2014 survey, 86 percent of Egyptian researchers believe that the institutional and legislative 'atmosphere' is not conducive to research and innovation (*Baseera* survey no. 536, December 14, 2014, emailed to author).

In North America, in particular, a basic component of the academic job market consists in those who are not promoted or are denied tenure. The promotion system works on the basis of 'up or out.' One result is that there is a built-in mechanism to redistribute talent from the more discriminating elite institutions to the less favored. Not everyone would agree that this redistribution is healthy, but whether it is or is not, it is mainly absent from the Arab world.

A key component of the research undertaking is the presence of PhD candidates in considerable numbers. As part of their preparation for the professoriate or for positions in the private sector, they must or should engage in advanced research under the supervision of the standing faculty. Their training thus becomes a critical component in the research output and quality of the regular faculty. But graduate and PhD education is developing slowly in the Arab world, although it is increasing fairly rapidly in Egypt as well as in Iran and Turkey. In 2009–2010, there were 28,000 doctoral candidates enrolled in Egyptian universities, compared to over 70,000 full-time professors. Without this element of graduate support, research, above all in the STEM fields, will suffer.

It is also no surprise that doctoral education will not privilege the STEM disciplines because of the costs involved and the skill sets required of candidates. Rather, we see the bulk of PhD candidates heading toward history, theology, Arabic language studies, and the humanities more generally. My anonymous Moroccan interlocutor pointed out that the country's early retirement scheme encouraged some of the best faculty to leave. They will be replaced by the burgeoning ranks of doctors of theology and Arabic. He called this "the mullahization of higher education." Many of them, he assured me, have no interest in research and are contemptuous of scientific methods. This gentleman is himself a historian.

Scholarly research often becomes an exercise in bean-counting, doing the minimum to meet promotion requirements. Placing articles in international refereed journals that almost always publish in languages other than Arabic means that applied research of direct relevance to the Arab world is sacrificed for more generic submissions (Hanafi, 2011; Hanafi and Arvanitis, 2016). In most countries there is no incentive to constitute research teams or interuniversity collaboration (Tunisia and Morocco are exceptions).

Bean-counting has spawned a new sector that supplies both students and faculty with ghost-written 'original' work. Commercial services sell products to students, and professors in the form of articles and dissertations: "In some cases, these organizations even arrange for articles to be published in science and research journals. Therefore, a large number of dissertations and research articles are not written by students and professors in the university but are instead produced by a trading firm" (Adib, 2014). The ghost writers come from the ranks of their clients.

All is not gloom. Tunisia has turned around its research enterprise since the early 2000s. It had been experiencing sluggish scientific production since the 1990s. It instituted a highly centralized funding system, based on core funding rather than competitive grant-making. The key is a national evaluation system managed by the Ministry of Research. An independent body, the National Evaluation Committee of Scientific Research Activities, established in 1996, evaluates public research organizations and research programs of private companies that benefit from public support. After 2008, the committee identified around 330 units and 250 laboratories as eligible for financing. Since its inception, scientific output has increased fourfold (Hanafi and Arvanitis, 2016: 145).

Morocco's Law No. 00-01 of 2000 moved the country in a direction similar to Tunisia's. It provided for "research collectivities that could be teams, laboratories, centers or networks." Some 896 collectivities had been recognized by 2006. In its Plan d'Urgence of 2008, Morocco endorsed a model that is plausible but controversial.

The plan states, "The attractiveness of the research profession is losing speed, due, notably, to the absence at the national level of a homogeneous statute of a dedicated researcher. Scientific research lacks resources, and the allocated budget, despite strong growth since 1998, has never exceeded 0.8% of GDP. The share of international cooperation, which has been active, represents only 3% of this budget" (Kingdom of Morocco, 2010?: 58).

Herein, Morocco aspires to the French model, especially that of the Centre National de la Recherche Scientifique (CNRS), of the dedicated researcher, totally or partially divorced from the teaching function. A tenet of what might be called the Humboldt model of education is to link teaching and research, thereby improving both, or so it is hoped.

Conclusion

By the time these lines appear in print, the Arab world may have over a thousand universities and ten million university-level students. Obviously, I have left out more than I have included about careers and experiences in public higher education. I have not analyzed the student experience except to the extent students are involved in politics (Chapter 3).

A central point is that the MENA university is founded on multiple myths. Foremost among them is the full-time faculty member. The myth is a direct result of the trilemma whereby educational systems seek to educate large numbers at reasonable cost but at the expense of quality. The inadequate higher education budgets result in low professorial pay, forcing the faculty to moonlight. Institutional loyalty, quality research, and attention to students are all sacrificed.

Some of the assumptions of what makes Western research universities tick are nonoperative in the Middle East. For students, the university is not a place of sustained interaction with faculty or other students. Such contacts are superficial and intermittent. The learning experience of daily contact and extracurricular activities (student organizations, clubs, sports) is stunted. Formal, in-class contact with professors is minimal except in the most elite faculties with selective admission.

Similarly, the kind of synergy between teaching and research that analysts like William Massy extol rarely occurs in the MENA because the research function is so underdeveloped. A Lebanese academic concluded that much of the teaching function at Lebanese University could be undertaken by high school teachers.

Not even the most senior academic leaders are paid anything near what their responsibilities entail. Often, theirs is a labor of love; their reward is the respect of their peers and the public more generally.

But there is a positive side to this. Those who lead, persist in their research efforts, and try to act as expert guides to their students do so out of love for the enterprise. They epitomize the academic ideal to an extent that is rare in better-funded systems.

Despite the presence of this devoted minority, it is probably time for MENA higher education to confront its myths and develop incentive structures that recognize and accept them. We shall look at ways in which this could be done in the final chapter.

Conclusion:
Gradual or Disruptive Change?

The MENA, along with much of the rest of the world, is trying to reinvent US and perhaps British higher education. The EU's Bologna process seeks standardization across European IHLs through their credit-hour, semester system and the 3–2–3-year sequence from high school through to the PhD. The GCC imports US and French 'branches.' KAUST seeks to be Caltech. The bricks-and-mortar university and the credit-hour system have proliferated around the world at a time when US higher education is under withering criticism for skyrocketing costs and reinforcement of socioeconomic privilege.

Cathy Davidson (2017), among many others,[1] has written a widely read critique of US higher education. She notes that the basics of the US model were assembled by Harvard's president, Charles Eliot (1869–1909). As a young man, Eliot studied Humboldt and other European reformers who designed the modern European research university. He introduced a model at Harvard using letter grades and curve grading, standardized tests, and one-size-fits-all credentialing. Davidson declares this model obsolete, indeed pernicious. She advocates "student-centered" learning, the antithesis of the prevailing "tyranny of selectivity" (2017: 49). Universities like Harvard publicize their rejection rate, which lies at the heart of institution-centered philosophies that build reputation on the basis of selectivity.

Davidson has good company in William Massy, Clayton Christensen, and Randy Bass, among others, who urge a pedagogic revolution at all levels of US education. Despite this growing chorus, the North American and European status quo exercises a massive gravitational pull, not only on the MENA but also on the rest of the world. Maybe the MENA should be thinking about jumping a stage, leaving Eliot and Harvard in the garbage bin of higher education history. There is little chance that will happen.

I advocate change, but what kind of change? Is it what Christensen calls sustaining or supportive innovation that helps the existing system to survive, if not prosper? Or is it disruptive innovation that emerges outside the system and makes the status quo increasingly unviable? My aim is to persuade university administrators and public policymakers that there are measures that can be taken that would measurably improve outcomes without destroying careers or so upsetting the distribution of resources that vested interests would bring any change to a halt. Most important, I cannot propose anything that would (obviously) threaten the political stability of a given political regime.

If, however, I enter into the logic of disruptive innovation, then administrators and policymakers are merely obstacles to be got around, not partners in change. My allies will be entrepreneurs who want to bring the disruptive innovation to market, or political revolutionaries who seek a new world. According to the theory of disruptive innovation this is always a market that is ill-defined or untested. It is a market in which existing educational institutions do not or cannot compete. Whatever my role, existing institutions are under threat and may not survive in their current form. Change that eliminates players is not reversible. That is why it is 'disruptive.'

It is hard to imagine a scenario in which I go to public policymakers and espouse change that would undermine existing structures, with all their mature patronage and power relations, in exchange for something that by its disruptive nature is unpredictable and destabilizing. But as cautious (cowardly?) as my approach may sound, disruptors are stalking the fields of higher education and they must be dealt with. I do not accept that disruptors are invisible or cloaked to their potential victims—in this case the entrenched public educational systems of the MENA. Reformers from inside or outside these systems must help shape the process of coping. Disruptive innovation need not be a train wreck.

The bodies of data and interpretations that I encountered throughout my research led me to the surprising (at least for me) conclusion that the state of higher education in the MENA is not as bad as it is often portrayed, and that 'crisis' is not an apt label. It all depends on the definition of mission and strategic goals. Let us take the paradigm of the 1950s and 1960s. Mass education, up to but not necessarily including higher education, was seen as a citizen's right and, simultaneously, as a step to correct the wrongs of colonialist elite education. The goal was to train the cadres necessary for the new, independent states. Lip service was paid to training citizens for the polities of the independent states, but that task was never taken seriously on a sustained basis. Prior to the structural adjustment crises of the 1970s and 1980s (continuing to the present time), training for the private sector was not a significant goal. The economic crises brought that goal to the forefront, but there was no effective policy response. Institutional and policy inertia had set in. It was that inertia that led to talk of a crisis.

The paradigmatic model fulfilled many of its tasks. The model was coherent, more inspired by France, republican Turkey, and the Soviet Union than by Anglo-Saxon examples. It was based on centralized, state-led systems applying uniform policies across all institutions, the professoriate, and student bodies.[2] IHLs were subordinate players in policymaking and in shaping their own destinies. The key players were heads of state, assisted by ministers of higher education and finance and Supreme Councils for Higher Education and Scientific Research. Competition among IHLs for students, faculty, and funding was not envisaged or encouraged. In the name of equity and fairness, one size was to fit all. It worked. Like any aging enterprise, it acquired barnacles with time, but that does not mean it was or is not viable, that it is not worth reforms designed to salvage it. The reforms have to be generated through the public-policy process.

What is the proper focus of public policy? There is a compelling logic to treating the 'system' as the relevant unit of policy analysis. It is one among a number of national systems that provide highly valued public goods to the citizenry. The public health system of clinics, hospitals, medical laboratories, and medical research centers seeks to improve the general health of all citizens. The police, prisons, and judicial corps seek to provide basic domestic security for all citizens (indeed, for anyone found physically within the nation's borders). The armed forces, intelligence services, and diplomatic corps provide regional and international security for the nation. In most countries these public goods are not devolved to federal or subnational units. They are financed and regulated nationally with oversight by the nation's legislature and executive authority. Given the importance of education, it is logical to group it among these other systems.

In this context, the reform effort must start from the premise that reforms cannot obviously weaken the stability of the political regime itself. Internal and external reformers may entertain notions of velvet revolutions whose first manifestations appear technocratic and innocuous. But the region's autocrats will see danger even where none exists, so structural reform by stealth will not long go undetected.

There are many reforms that can be accommodated by the existing paradigm. Let us not forget that Clark Kerr's 'system' for California was statewide and was built on a kind of institutional division of labor among elite research universities, state universities catering to a broader social stratum, and community colleges and vocational schools for the rest. MENA regimes could move in that direction. At least for the elite institutions, the resources for relative excellence might become available as well as the right to recruit faculty and select students. If the example of California is off-putting for some, contemporary China is clearly moving toward a tiered system of higher education.

Politically Non-threatening Reforms

Do not let excellence be the enemy of satisficing (Simon, 1947). Second or third best at an acceptable price may be a worthy goal. Gradual, incremental reform of repulsive regimes may be an unavoidable goal.

I assume that the reforms outlined below will be implemented at the level of the system. Any IHL in the system theoretically could introduce any one or all of these reforms, but few IHLs have the legal or administrative authority to do so. Individually or as a package, these reforms could transform MENA educational systems, making them stronger, more effective, and more responsive to societies' real needs. They do not require any significant political concessions. The closest they come to that is in implying that higher education must be responsive to the needs of the economy and of society, and that failure to deliver in this respect would reflect negatively on the nation's leaders.

Institute training in teaching for recent PhDs, adjuncts, and sitting faculty. This is spreading in the US and elsewhere, but I think not in the MENA— yet. As of 2019, Egypt's minister of education, Tarek Shawki, is taking steps in this direction at the K–12 level.

Make teaching a much more important part of performance evaluation (Pallas et al., 2017). When I started teaching in 1968 at the University of Michigan, I went to my first class without any coaching or instruction. How my course fit with other departmental offerings was not explicitly discussed. I recall no review of how our majors were advancing toward some sort of mastery of what we, the faculty, thought was essential. Ten years later I went through the same experience at Princeton. One should expect resistance from the faculty itself to raising the weight of appropriate teaching in promotion, but the political system should be indifferent. This reform bridges naturally to the following:

Enable teachers (even virtual, AI teachers) to recognize and accommodate different learning styles and aptitudes among their students.[3] This could be hugely disruptive in a pedagogical sense and would require very different teaching styles and practices than what prevails in the current model. Moves in this direction could provoke professional backlash, but they would not create threats to the political order unless teachers' unions tried to shut down the experiment. The interesting thing is that nearly everyone endorses this: those who want to reform the existing paradigm, such as Massy, and those who want to disrupt it if not replace it, like Christensen and Davidson.

Integrate policy focused on the transition from high school to IHL. Everywhere secondary-level students are ill-prepared for university. IHLs have to devote time and resources to remedial work or, worse, to giving students endless chances to repeat failed courses. Current administrative and policy barriers separate the two levels to the detriment of both (Kingdom of Morocco, 2018: 44, 87).

Institute competency-based education. This is a radical departure from the standard paradigm. The student self-paces him/herself, subject to periodic assessment of achievement until s/he is deemed to have mastered a subject or skill. While any subject or discipline could be incorporated in CBE, it seems best designed for sharply focused skill acquisition, probably among those already in the workplace who know what they need to make a new career move or to move up the ladder where they are (AAAS, 2017: 16). There is no reason why CBE could not be combined with more traditional pedagogic models.

Focus on graduation rates through remedial instruction and aptitude-centered learning. This follows naturally on the previous three reforms. It should contribute directly to enhanced employability of graduates and hence to reduced youth unemployment. It would reduce costs by lowering overstaffing but raise costs through more individual-focused, remedial instruction. Unfortunately, institutional costs will be frontloaded. Benefits will lag. Society will benefit more than the IHL itself.

Overhaul pedagogical assumptions. This is a question of resources—helping students overcome financial obstacles to pursuing their education—and of pedagogy. The standard formulas for imparting knowledge and delivering training must become much more interactive and tailored to the student's aptitudes and learning modes. It is potentially costly for the institution that provides the education but has a large and positive pay-off for society as a whole.

Indeed, it is not only those students who might drop out that need special attention, but all students. So pedagogical reform must be at the heart of repairing the status quo. Part of the reform package will surely be ICT-supported instruction and interaction. In some instances, this will save the system money, and, through remote learning, spare the student sometimes crippling travel and living expenses.

One gambit is the flipped classroom, where the lecture is accessed online and the class is built on discussion of the 'lecture.' Traditional roles of content delivery, coaching, and assessment, normally combined in the figure of the professor, may be separated, with each role requiring a different set of credentials or training.

A university in Ghana has flipped the university itself. At Achesi University, (private) students start with problem-solving, dealing with specific puzzles, then over time work from the problems and the cases to the study of the fundaments. The basic IHL sequence is stood on its head.

Explore where loans are most needed and guarantee them at negotiated interest rates and in light of students' socioeconomic status. Those who regard tertiary education as a near-pure private good will not be sympathetic, but those who regard it as a quasi-public good will want the taxpayer to help lower individual debt burdens in the name of social equity. Student loans assume that students are paying some fees. That represents more than tweaking the existing system (see page 297).

Recognize and accommodate the fact that many, if not most students and faculty members are part-time. Student expectations and faculty careers can be built around that fact. This is likely to be psychologically and materially disruptive, but, in essence, it is designed for people to accept reality. Just as some reforms will focus on students' learning modes, this reform will focus on the individual student's ability to move ahead and try to accommodate it. So, too, the part-time faculty member will be the focal point of hand-tailored contracts that accept multiple sources of income. The University of Maryland University College enrolls over 80,000 students. Ninety percent of its faculty is part-time, hired on contract. Most are 'scholar-practitioners,' and the institution's focus is on workforce development. Graduates are in the large majority very satisfied with the results. How the faculty feel is not reported (AAAS, 2017: 36).

Part-timers, adjuncts, and contract teachers should suffer from no stigma and be incorporated into departmental life with the right to vote on a broad, defined range of issues.[4]

Reduce credit requirements for degree completion. This means redefining what constitutes competency. It includes reducing the number of prerequisite courses to move from lower level to upper level. We can anticipate resistance from the professoriate/unions, as this may have implications for staff numbers. In the US the undergraduate degree usually takes four years, while in the LMD system of the EU it is three years. There is obviously something arbitrary in how we define time requirements. CBE would do away with that, but if old systems persist, then shortening the time to graduation would lower costs for the student and for the institution.

Review and simplify professional credentialing. This would help overcome artificial barriers to entry (recall the struggle over law instruction at Lebanese University in Chapter 1). Credentialing can often descend into professional protectionism rather than professional excellence.

Liberalize degree recognition and equivalency. It may include online education, open universities, and competency-based certificates. Again, resistance is to be expected from existing professional associations. It is simply a variant of the previous reform.

Facilitate, if not encourage, student and faculty mobility among public institutions. The aim would be to eventually develop a Bologna process for the Arab world. The goal here is to enhance the academic experience for both students and faculty. Note, however, that critics of existing systems want to move away from standardized programs and criteria, while that is at the heart of the Bologna process and the LMD. Maybe that tension will be healthy . . . .

Develop a regional autonomous Arab accreditation entity. If it is serious, it will cause political ripples, if not waves, so it may not be doable. There are public sacred cows and private cronies who will be appalled by the prospect. An international board would enhance the entity's credibility. If the accreditation board is itself credibly autonomous and honors best practice, it will help IHLs move in the same direction. The growing competition for foreign students should help (see pages 301–302). This innovation would increase the chances that best practice, established at the top-ranked universities, would spread to the rest.

Promote regional, peer-reviewed autonomous journals. It may help marginalize journals that reflect academic clubs and cronies *and* promote research that is of direct benefit to the region.

Promote Arab, regionwide professional academic associations. This may be easier to do across the region than for individual countries to promote their own professional associations. These associations could suggest standards for promotion in specific disciplines. They would reinforce the 'communities of practice' that link together isolated experts and academics and give support to other reform processes.

Some really bad guys (at the time of writing there are no female heads of state in the MENA) could survive all of these reforms, but citizens and society would benefit. Some of the reforms (such as CBE) would be pedagogically or institutionally disruptive.

Is Education a Public or a Private Good?

A public good is nonexcludable, meaning it will be enjoyed (or if a public bad, suffered) by everyone. It is also nonrivalrous, meaning that anyone's use of it does not reduce it for anyone else. Because a public good cannot be appropriated, private actors may have little incentive to provide it. Therefore, public authorities, using public resources, must provide the good. Universal primary education is a good example. There are few pure public goods, and education is not one of them. But nor is it, as Preston Cooper argues (2017), a pure private good. Those who benefit from education at any level do reap private rewards and, therefore, according to Cooper, the individual beneficiary should pay for it through tuition or loans or both. Cooper argues that the fact that society as a whole may benefit from the provision of this private good is not itself a public good but rather an externality. An externality is defined as the cost or benefit that affects a party who did not choose to incur that cost or benefit.

I find it hard to accept that argument, as do many others (Anomaly, 2018: 2). As was argued in Chapter 4, higher education provides all of society with the benefits of enhanced citizenship, a skilled professional workforce, and both basic and applied research. Those goods are nonexcludable and nonrivalrous, and in their absence, it would be hard to explain why taxpayers around the globe accept to pay for higher education.

K–12 education is a public good—one that must be consumed according to the law. This is not a market like that for automobiles or laptops, or software, or rides for hire. There are market-like aspects—such as public school systems adopting a specific, commercially marketed textbook—but that does not alter the fact that this educational market is defined by law, is dominated by quasi-monopolistic providers, and provides a public good. Unless I am missing something, disruptors will be private, seeking profit, and providing private goods.

The Trilemma Revisited

The Middle East is characterized by the possibility of a demographic dividend whereby the MENA dependency ratio maximizes the number of active members of the workforce—those paying taxes and funding education, retirement, and other social programs. But, as we have seen, the demographic dividend has not yet paid off. Too many MENA young people (perhaps 28–30 percent of relevant cohorts) are unemployed and part of the dependent population.

In democracies, citizens may indicate their relative preferences for tax-funded goods, such as public health, pensions, law and order, and education. In the US it is argued that since the halcyon period stretching from the GI Bill and the end of the Second World War to around 1978, when California's voters endorsed Proposition 13, placing severe limits on the state's capacity to tax property, public education has been seriously defunded. The quality leg of the trilemma stool was the victim. One response is to call upon voters to back initiatives to restore funding. But there is a reason why US states have reduced education funding: the need to fund Medicaid, repair aging infrastructure, and maintain overcrowded detention facilities has eaten into educational outlays. What, if anything, will give if educational outlays are to be restored?[5] The MENA may have a couple of decades before it faces this dilemma.

In the MENA, the main loser in the trilemma has been quality. Public systems underwent huge expansion and continue to expand more modestly today. Costs in terms of shares of GDP are high but not excessive. Quality, however, is poor and, in the eyes of many observers, declining (inter alia, Kingdom of Morocco, 2018). It is a moot question whether or not Middle East publics would vote to commit more public resources to education. The relative level of expenditure to GDP is already high.

Private Education

This could well be the most disruptive innovation of the last three decades and in the future. But private education will be disruptive in ways not envisaged by Christensen. It will not disrupt existing educational markets and business models in the public sector, so much as it *may* threaten political (big-P) arrangements.[6] That is because governance in the private sector is radically different from governance in the public sector.

I started this study a decade ago. At that time, private IHLs accounted for about 10 percent of total enrollments in the Arab world (Bhandari and El-Amine, 2011). By 2017 that proportion had risen to about 14 percent.

Tunisia is something of a bellwether with its French étatiste referents. The Tunisian private IHL sector grew from 1.1 percent of total enrollments in 2007–2008 to 9.4 percent in 2014–2015 (Boughazala et al., 2016: 5). Melonio and Mezouaghi (2015) list four main drivers of the spread of private education: declining quality of education in the public sector, the possibility to upgrade the skills of graduates, a focus on management training, and a response to local/parochial needs.

As Daniel Levy (Levy, forthcoming) has shown, globally, private higher education now accounts for about a third of all higher education enrollments. In absolute terms, global private higher education enrollments doubled in the first decade of the current century.

Let us recall that the financing of private education in the MENA today depends to some extent on its symbiotic relationship with the public sector. It hires public sector instructors as contract employees without pension rights and health insurance. To the extent these contractees do any research, it will be in the labs of their public, home institutions. Were that symbiosis to be curtailed or ended, the operating costs of private institutions would rise significantly. At the same time, the public sector cannot pay appropriate salaries to its teaching staff, so the private sector does it a favor by topping up salaries. In Morocco, experiments are underway to formalize that symbiosis through public–private partnerships (some of these experiments are reviewed in e4e, IDB, and IFC, 2011).

If Latin America and Iran serve as a model, over half of all MENA tertiary students may be in private institutions by 2040. This transition would follow a number of pathways. The private-university sector could capture all the high-quality education and serve a socioeconomic upper stratum. The lower strata would have to make do with the public institutions, which will be of low quality. One may well wonder if this is politically viable even in the medium term. The taxpayer will be called upon to fund gross inequity. It would shred the social contract beyond recognition.[7]

Or, the citizenry, either at the ballot box or otherwise, would show a preference for using public resources to maintain or enhance the quality of a few flagship public universities open to all with the appropriate academic qualifications. UNAM in Mexico is such an institution, as is SUT in Iran and the Middle East Technical University in Turkey.[8]

Finally, the MENA public may want to support a dominant public educational sector supported by direct and indirect subsidies not available to the private sector. The public sector in the MENA is still dominant, but the era of rapid expansion ended, with some exceptions like Morocco, two decades ago. Meanwhile private institutions have been proliferating. The fiscal crises faced by several states are not easing, so whatever public preferences may be, the state may not be able to respond.

Much of private higher education today is for-profit, of poor quality, and, as a part of crony capitalist networks, not politically challenging. Nor may it be more effective in preparing students for the private sector workplace (Assaad, Krafft, and Salehi-Isfahani, 2018). Nonetheless it enjoys considerable autonomy and its IHLs compete with one another for faculty, are more or less conscious of international rankings, and set their own pay scales and promotion systems in light of market conditions (Jaramillo et al., 2012: 32). It is hard to imagine that as the private sector expands, it will not bleed into the public system. It is also likely with time that the private institutions will try to enhance their quality, their research, and their international standing. What we see today may bear little resemblance to what we will see in a couple of decades. It is in that sense that the greatest change agent may lie in these new private institutions (see Ahmed, 2019). Their initial mission can be thoroughly recast, as has been the case of the SPC in Beirut (from evangelical Protestant to nondenominational secular). Specifically, one may anticipate that as the indigenous private IHLs sink roots, build quality, and increase their weight in society, they are likely to strengthen their autonomy and defend their academic prerogatives. One has only to look at Turkey's Bilkent, Koç, and Sabanci Universities to see the possibilities.

One of the many puzzles I have faced is why autocrats, sensitive to every real or imagined existential threat, would not only let the private sector into the education sphere but actually hold open the door. I have argued that the autocrats are obsessed by control. They go to great lengths to snuff out autonomy wherever it appears in civil society. Yet they have provided a legal framework and sometimes financial encouragement to private investors to take up the provision of education.

Part of the solution to the puzzle is down to the fact that they did not have much choice. The structural adjustment crises so shook public finances that alternative sources of funding education had to be found. Second, nearly all the MENA's autocrats were drifting into crony capitalism, and many of their cronies rightly saw higher education as a field where demand significantly exceeded supply. Indeed, public supply was going down. Third, presumably they felt they had nothing to fear from cronies.[9]

But it must have been clear that private providers would insist on a degree of autonomy never tolerated in the public sector. How would the autocrats and their agents know what was going on in these new entities? Many of the new players were or are likely to be purveyors of a religious mission at a time when most of the autocrats were aligned with the West. In the Turkish variant, we have seen the clash of two religious visions— those of Recep Tayyip Erdoğan and Fethullah Gülen—play out in multiple fields, including education. Erdoğan has been promoting private Islamic higher education to counter the Gülenists and to build support for his AKP. Turkey is also instructive in that the business moguls behind some of the private universities were either pillars of the political order (İhsan Doğramacı) or, in the interests of their businesses, carefully neutral.

The only lengthy experience any autocracy has had with private education has been in Egypt, where the AUC, founded in 1919, never posed any threat to Egyptian regimes. In fact, after the June War of 1967, when Egypt broke diplomatic relations with the US, the AUC was placed under Egyptian state sequestration. The example of AUB is not as relevant inasmuch as Lebanon has been an imperfect democracy at least since the Second World War. Indigenous private institutions are much more recent. They seem to reflect local clientelism or patronage. Islamic Azad University in Iran was founded by Hashemi Rafsanjani, a former president of the country and a close associate of Ayatollah Khomeini. In no way could Azad University be seen as a threat to the regime in Iran, and, in announcing its intention to open a branch in Syria, it could become an extension of Iran's soft power.

The gig economy may well prove a disruptor to the systems of private tutoring and fee-based cram schools that are common in the Middle East. Unemployed educated youth have the talent and the incentive to sell their skills as ghost writers and tutors, and there will surely be entrepreneurs who, like Uber, will capture them and market them. Christensen and colleagues (2008: 137) anticipate this. There is an Egyptian example up and running. Sayed Obaied launched Nafham (We Understand) in 2012. It markets educational videos and in 2015 reached 500,000 active users in Egypt, Algeria, Saudi Arabia, and Syria. It has a staff of twenty-five (Farahat, 2015). The private-lesson market in Egypt alone is worth $2–3 billion a year. This will attract private providers, as has been the case in Turkey for some time. Political authorities will have no problem with this. Public-university faculty will either have to join up with the new providers or lower their tutoring charges to compete with them.

Introduction of Fees in Public Universities

Even where some tuition is charged in the Arab world (such as Jordan), it is quite modest in relation to overall operating expenses. That is not the case in the private sector, where fees are substantial and, in some instances, generate a surplus, or profits, on operations. The introduction in public IHLs of parallel courses, offered for substantial fees, was designed to get around commitments to free or quasi-free public higher education.

One can sense the pressures building on entire systems and the educational units within them to introduce fees. This will surely happen in the coming years. Unlike the reforms discussed above, the introduction of fees will have potentially far-reaching political effects. It would be yet another nail in the coffin of old social-contract commitments. For such a step to be politically sustainable, it would require considerable improvement in the quality of the education provided and of the prospects for appropriate employment of graduates. That kind of accountability vanishes when education is free.

The Problematic Theory of Disruptive Innovation

Jules Ferry was minister of public instruction in France in the 1880s (the Third Republic) and the architect of France's secular, compulsory public school system. It was highly centralized and standardized. It is said that Ferry took great pride in the fact that on any school day he could look at his watch and know what was being taught at that exact moment everywhere in France. Such standardized systems became the hallmark of progress in Western societies. Less than a century later, in 1959, Clark Kerr introduced the California tiered system of higher education that for thirty years was the pride of the state. Now, such systems are widely criticized and questioned even as parts of the developing world clone them. What a pity it would be if, in a decade's time, these late adopters conclude they should have skipped this stage altogether. Disruptive innovators claim to offer that next stage.

Within the terms of reference laid down by Christensen, higher education in the Middle East is ripe for disruptive innovation. The current system only reaches about a third of its potential market, so there is a sea of nonconsumers available to disruptors. Relative to available resources, the current model is very expensive, and, as we have seen (Chapter 1), MENA countries in general devote more of their national resources to education than most of the rest of the world. So, if new providers can lower costs and still deliver an acceptable product, it could capture most of the nonconsumers. Moreover, Christensen predicts that once the established actors see the train coming down the track, they will invest in their existing business model, making it even more expensive and less competitive. The current model is not only expensive, it also fails to deliver employable graduates. Its pedagogy is flawed and outdated.

Taking Christensen's dominant logic, we should not expect large bureaucratic systems to anticipate, let alone adapt to, disruptive innovations out on the horizon. Indeed, it is in the nature of disruptive innovation that it is invisible to incumbent providers. They either do not see the threat or, following Christensen's S-curve analogy, belittle it when it is in the tail of the 'S.' Christensen and colleagues state categorically, "Organizations cannot naturally disrupt themselves" (2008: 75). So, if disruptive innovation ultimately holds the key to educational reform, there is no public policy lesson to be learned except that public authorities will not see the threat until it is too late.

Disruptors fly under the radar. They look for customers who are not being serviced by the existing system. Christensen provides many examples in the education field: provide online courses to supplement what can be feasibly offered in the public school, supplant private tutors, offer online advanced placement courses, and cater to homeschoolers (2008: 92). This is the foot-in-the-door phase. As disruptive innovation costs come down, incumbents try more and more sustaining reforms, raising their overall costs (think of public universities in the US) and further eroding their ability to compete with the disruptors. As the disruptors' offerings proliferate, costs come down and more consumers sign up. It is like the algae on the surface of a pond, doubling in extent every day. One day it covers an eighth, a day later a quarter, and two days later the entire surface. BAU never knew what hit it.

In his book on education (mainly K–12), Christensen and his co-authors realize that his paradigm creates a cul de sac that, insofar as education is concerned, they refuse to enter: the futility of reform and innovation if a disruptor is out there ready to eat your market. They hold out the possibility of incumbents (in this case the public system) seeing what needs to be done and going some of the distance of implementation.

They note, "Disrupting what actually happens in the classroom by instituting student-centric technologies is vital to customize learning for each individual student and to improve motivation for all" (2008: 214).

Initially it will be costly, but as the consumer market broadens and technologies are tested and refined, costs will come down. There is no way,

I believe, to square this vision with the claim above that organizations cannot naturally disrupt themselves, but as is often and wisely said in the Arab world, *ma'lish*.

Randy Bass zeroes in on student-centered learning as the focus for planned disruption. As he states, "by using the phrase 'disrupting ourselves' in this article's title, I am asserting that one key source of disruption in higher education is coming not from the outside but from our own practices, from the growing body of experiential modes of learning, moving from margin to center, and proving to be critical and powerful in the overall quality and meaning of the undergraduate experience" (2012: 1).

Bass focuses on the curriculum and its pedagogic assumptions. What he proposes is disruptive; it seeks to substitute a new paradigm for an old paradigm, using existing personnel and facilities. Disruptive technologies are not themselves disruptive but facilitate disruption. They could just as easily sustain paradigm-protecting reforms.

High schools have very different missions from IHLs. They are not much involved in the joint production of knowledge, and research. They take teaching very seriously and are consciously involved in debates over pedagogy and enhanced teaching. In my own experience as a university professor at both Michigan and Princeton I was entirely free to design my courses as I saw fit. I was given no tutorial in course design or delivery. There was no collective review or brainstorming about how our departmental offerings complemented or built on one another, or what linkages we saw among our offerings. All that is beginning to change in North American IHLs. Raising the profile of teaching at the tertiary level will be very disruptive. Isolated instances apart, it has not yet begun in the MENA.

Successful disruptors will offer a combination of two benefits: better instruction and lower cost. That either benefit would be provided is hotly contested. The bloom on online education has already begun to fade. In 2013 William Bowen saw online education as a solution to the higher education 'cost disease.' Other proponents warned the academy that "it is time for individual faculty to give up, cheerfully and not grudgingly, any claim to sole authority over teaching methods of all kinds." That is in exchange for an "important seat at a larger table" in discussions about online pedagogies, which they say hold largely untapped value (Flaherty, 2015). Almost as these lines appeared in print, they were called into question. MOOCs exploded, then imploded. Open universities faced questions of sustainability. The basic proposition of lower costs was challenged by empirical follow-up studies (McKenzie, 2017; Greenstein, 2019).

Even if there are no cost savings involved, online education might deliver an improved product based on a radically different pedagogy. The basic notion is to adapt teaching to the learning aptitudes of individual students. The Charles Eliot model assumes that all students are the same except in IQ. In fact, as Christensen argues, students fall into identifiable learning aptitude categories. He cites Howard Gardener, a psychologist at Harvard, who identified eight basic ways of learning or aptitudes that should be the basis for student-focused learning: linguistic, legal-mathematical, spatial, bodily-kinesthetic, musical, interpersonal, intrapersonal, and naturalist (Christensen et al., 2008: 26). Christensen and his colleagues ask the basic question: "Can the system of schooling designed to process groups of students in standardized ways in a monolithic instruction mode be adapted to handle differences in the way individual brains are wired for learning?" (2008: 35).

If aptitude-centered learning is the big disruptive innovation, Christensen, Davidson, and others may underestimate its implications. Universities must take over where the K–12 system left off, otherwise the transfer from grade school to university will be even more jolting than it is now, although the transition will be easier in community colleges or their equivalent than in four-year programs.

But what of the transition from university to work? The self-employed presumably can adapt their style of work to their aptitudes, which they will have identified long before. But what of employees, from sales managers to civil servants, indeed, to schoolteachers? Will work have to be designed to reflect the eight aptitudes or some other set? Maybe not only the way one learns one's new task will have to reflect the employee's aptitudes, but the task itself will have to be compatible with them. Perhaps the software will exist for this extension of aptitude-centered job assignment to the workplace, but if it does, it suggests that the underlying AI may be in place to do away with the employee altogether. That kind of disruptive innovation is surely coming down the track, but I am not qualified to comment on it.

A recent assessment (Goldrick and Goldrick, 2017) identified five disruptive technologies and how or where they will be applied:

- The internet of things, about which the authors have only vague ideas of application,
- Virtual augmented reality (applications in medical education),
- AI (student foci, mentoring, and guidance),
- Online learning (aims at Christensen's nonconsumers; the fully employed for example), and
- CBE (self-paced and individual (see pages 289–90)).

I believe the authors confound tools and content. CBE is a pedagogic innovation that could be delivered with ICT or by traditional methods. Augmented reality is a tool or vehicle for something else. The disruption comes if the 'something else' substitutes at lower cost and with similar if not superior results to the standard paradigm. In its study of the 'digital campus,' the *Chronicle of Higher Education* (2018) listed innovations, such as AI and enhanced reality, that are mainly supportive of existing practices, such as managing campus water, inquiries on financial aid, student advising, energy monitoring, and grading of written exams.

There is a major disruptive innovation underway in the US that conforms to the points made above. It is subsumed under the title of 'mega universities' and comprises, so far, the likes of Southern New Hampshire University, Maryland University College, Liberty University, Western Governors' University, Grand Canyon University, and Arizona State University. They each enroll between 60,000 and 95,000 'undergraduate' students. Their market is 30 million Americans in, or wanting to be in, the workforce, who began but did not complete a tertiary-level degree. Thirty million is a third more than the entire US university population (Gardner, 2019).

These new actors are spin-offs from established, more conventional IHLs. They are not-for-profit, so rewarding investors is not part of their mission. They rely on CBE to help their enrollees to get back into or climb higher in the job market. The students' average age is well above that of conventional undergraduates, although it is coming down. They engage in aggressive marketing and follow-up with students to counter the tendency of online enrollees to drop out before finishing their course. Distance learning is at the heart of their pedagogy, and they use part-time contractees to deliver their course material. Every element that has shaped their initial success is present in the MENA. Cairo University is as equipped as Coursera to jump into this market.

Playing in the International League

In the spirit of sustaining innovations with major structural implications, MENA countries will compete for a piece of the very large international student market. That market is, in 2019, on the order of five million international students, the bulk of whom pay some level of tuition. There are established players in this market, led by the US and Canada, Western Europe, China, and Australia. As of 2018, one million foreign students were in the US (Zong and Batalova, 2018). Egypt is looking to boost international enrollments from around 50,000 to 200,000 in the near future (Farouk, 2017 and Abdalgalil, 2017).

Similarly, Morocco's parastatal OCP is founding a university in Ben Guerir on donated land that will expand to 12,000 students, half of whom are to come from Sub-Saharan Africa. This university will be private (Sawahel, 2015).

The international market will be a tough one to break into, but for that very reason one that will demand structural changes in Middle East IHLs in order to compete. The obvious place to start is in the Arab region itself, where language barriers are minimal. To compete more broadly will require offering internationally recognized degrees and programs (hence the LMD in a number of Arab countries), upgrading physical facilities (dormitories, cafeterias, recreational facilities), and assuring the physical safety of foreign students. Distance learning would render these last two criteria less urgent, but not the first.

Responding to demand from both domestic students not served by existing systems and the international student market will be disruptors whose core competencies may be in distance learning and online pedagogies. What some call 'ed tech' is comprised of commercial firms mining big data, generated by millions of students (*Chronicle of Higher Education*, 2018). Rather than destroy incumbents, they may enter into partnerships with them. Nigel Thrift (2012), former vice chancellor of Warwick University, saw the trend some years ago: "Increasingly, conglomerates will rule the roost, made up out of universities that were formerly independent entities. These conglomerates will be public–private entities based on supplying performance-based contracts financed by government and on meeting demand from individual consumers who will have large arrays of information about quality variability available."

How Unique Is the Conventional University?

One of the main potential victims of disruptive innovation is the bricks-and-mortar IHL. These range from gritty urban campuses in scattered locales within cities to country-club-like facilities in rural areas or the suburbs at which many a Hollywood film has been shot. They are vulnerable because they are so costly to build and maintain. If reasonable cost is *primus inter pares* in the trilemma, then undermining this physical model is a good place to start.

Yet so many of those who work in or observe the academy are victims of its mystique. In many ways, it may have been the magic of place that attracted them to academia in the first place. Making matters more analytically difficult is the challenge of measuring the mystique and trying to quantify the benefits of disruption. I personally am not sure where I stand in the debate. I have benefited immensely from the traditional model (Princeton, Columbia, Michigan, Aix-en-Provence, AUB), but I do see that it may be to higher education what the mainframe was to the desktop computer.

Massy, like Christensen and Davidson, attacks the old paradigm, but he wants to transform it, not destroy it. The *sine qua non* for him is the joint production of research and education. It is the Humboldtian ideal, using the faculty to do both (not complicating the division of labor as disruptors tend to suggest). "I argue that this joint production is *the* major distinguishing feature of the traditional university," he says (Massy, 2016: 15). The magic of place for Massy lies in this joint production. Could it be carried out over the internet? Massy implies it would not be the same nor as good.

Then there is the literal coming together of experts and learners, of students of various backgrounds and aptitudes for whom the formal course of study may be no more important than the exposure to and interaction with a diverse faculty and student body. Could that happen online? Yes, but, again, probably not with the same quality.

At bricks-and-mortar IHLs, there are group projects and problem-solving within the formal curriculum, and community service and supervised internships off campus: "Significant student growth occurs when colleges provide structured opportunities for students from diverse backgrounds to learn and practice the skills and capacities needed to create real connection. This only happens when institutions leverage curricular and co-curricular activities that promote meaningful and sustained student dialogue and interaction" (AAAS, 2017: 14).

Many would argue that that dialogue and interaction can and will be carried out through online programs, but I read this passage to suggest strongly that students should be together literally, not virtually.

Some leaders, like NYU's former president, John Sexton, see the traditional model as generating huge positive externalities, especially in urban environments. Inspired, perhaps, by Richard Florida's 2005 book, Sexton has argued more than once that "what is going to be needed to make New York City great in 2050 is not just FIRE—finance, insurance, and real estate—but also ICE—the intellectual, the cultural, the educational" (Sexton, 2010). Central to this externality is the social and economic impact of the university on its environment, mainly in urban areas. Concentrating students, faculty, and staff with their individual and institutional buying power and impact on employment means the university may be at the heart of urban stabilization and renewal (Rodin, 2007). This is an externality in the sense that, outside of community service, it is not essential to the educational or research functions of the university itself. It is also not a pure public good, as it affects the well-being of city-dwellers but only indirectly the welfare of all taxpayers who support the institution. If it is a private institution, those paying tuition may wonder why they are called upon to provide this quasi-public good to the city as a whole.

Davidson (2017: 176) takes this a step further, claiming that universities subsidize private sector R&D, and that for every dollar in sponsored research-funding universities bring in, they lose, net, 24 cents. That puts in zero-sum terms what for most observers is a variable-sum, win-win partnership that creates innovation zones like Silicon Valley and Route 128 in Cambridge, Massachusetts (Mazzucato, 2015). Occasionally universities will incubate blockbuster innovations that become cash cows, through patents, for the university, but that is rare. If we then combine all these externalities, we could conclude that the taxpayer is getting a good deal. It is for that reason that both public and private not-for-profits receive public property at no cost and that many operations and properties are tax-free.

The problem with the magic-of-place and synergies arguments is that neither really applies to the Arab world, at least not to public institutions. They are huge, impersonal, largely nonresidential, and populated by part-time students and faculty, plus tens of thousands who already learn remotely. Their teaching is reputedly archaic, and they carry out little research (although that is changing). They do not have significant alumni associations, nor are they beneficiaries of significant private philanthropy. So, one could plausibly argue that they can safely ignore Massy's paradigmatic university without incurring any loss.

Missions Possible?

I return here to a thought experiment mentioned in the introduction to this book and in Chapter 7. A major innovative disruption would be to rewrite and apply the mission statements of all public IHLs. The goal would be to simplify missions and make them compatible with measurable, performance-based goals (the dread KPIs). In place of 'educating the nation's citizens,' 'creating and disseminating knowledge,' 'protecting the cultural and social heritage of the nation,' and 'contributing to strengthening the nation's economy,' we substitute a very different set of targets, progress toward which can be fairly unambiguously measured.

Let us imagine, as I have in earlier chapters, that the public IHLs' mission is reduced to three components: graduation rate, employment after graduation, and paying off student debt a certain number of years after graduation. Financing and the hiring of academic staff would be governed by the relative success of the IHL in achieving those goals.

This model would be driven by a very different value proposition than the bricks-and-mortar model of today. It would deal with mass education (quantity) at a reasonable cost and offer restricted quality. It would sacrifice the quality of life associated with a few MENA campuses, the training of citizens, the networking among classmates, and the extracurricular experiences that characterize 'good' universities. I have argued that those aspects of quality have long disappeared from the public IHLs of the Arab world, so a new model and mission might not be as disruptive as elsewhere. Finally, it would formally recognize the part-time nature of both faculty and students. While much of what I describe is offensive to me, I think new missions and new models badly need serious study and experimentation.

Desultory or Big Bang Reform?

The disruption of BAU in the MENA has taken place in two distinct phases with two distinct drivers. The first was the dismantling of the colonial order. Crisis was at its heart as new leaders sought to anchor their legitimacy by transformative change. It was exciting, uplifting for most participants, and enjoyed broad-based support. But it bore the seeds of its own undoing. In the second phase the crisis was depressing and delegitimizing, as what had generated the pride and euphoria in the first phase proved economically unsustainable in the second. Education lay and lies at the heart of both phases, both crises. I have argued that the current crisis is likely to produce educational reform. It will do so, as the current situation is seen as doubly crippling: it produces dangerously high levels of youth unemployment, and it risks squandering the 'demographic dividend' that may be the life vest of incumbent autocrats. But crisis-driven educational reform is likely to be slow, on the margins, and may well fail to correct perceived flaws. It is destabilizing but so is economic reform itself. To take a facile example, it is easier to nationalize the Suez Canal than to reform Egyptian higher education.

There are so many policy areas that cry out for change but offer a certain amount of political refuge to incumbent leaders. Swathes of their economies shelter in the informal sector, beyond the reach of the tax collector, but at least the informal sector provides employment to poorly educated youth. Never mind that it undermines public finances and requires indirect subsidies from the formal sector. The brain drain represents wasted public investment in human talent that will be deployed in some other country. But at least it gets rid of potential political troublemakers who would foment more Arab uprisings. Then there is the private sector itself. It was regarded as exploitative and possibly in league with colonial interests. It enjoyed little legitimacy until the era of prolonged structural adjustment. Then it had to be resuscitated, but the route taken was through cronyism rather than the organization of sectors through business associations and relatively open labor and capital markets. It is not the dynamic, innovative force that could begin to absorb educated MENA youth and contribute to R&D. To make it such a force would also require politically destabilizing reform.

Does it matter if one moves slowly, if one is moving in the right direction? No, if you can get away with it, but the twenty-first century is moving at an extraordinary pace and being left very far behind is a major risk (Lund et al., 2019). Higher education in the MENA is moving in the right direction, save in states devastated by civil war. With the region's current leadership, it is unlikely to pick up the pace. Radical political change, however, is no panacea. Tunisia, the one Arab political success to come out of the 2011 uprisings, has made no more progress in tackling its economic and educational reform challenges than its autocratic neighbors.

Crisis is not always a driver of policy change. Libya, Syria, Iraq, and Yemen are in the throes of civil war, invasion, Islamist terror, and physical destruction that constitute a crisis of near unimaginable proportions. It is, however, not at all clear that these crises will lead to a fundamental rethink of the way they have done business in politics, the economy, and education.

In Sum

Many of the sources cited in this concluding chapter do not focus on the Middle East. That fact underscores that the Arab world and the MENA are firmly situated in debates going on globally. The MENA has underperformed in all stages of education given the resources the region has flung at the problem, but the problem or problems are familiar to anyone, anywhere concerned with education. There is no Arab or MENA exceptionalism in that sense.

Having said that, I have tried to make the case that familiar problems combine in the MENA to produce if not a witches' brew then at least a very bitter soup that is distinctive. Education has become bound up to an unusual extent with the maintenance of autocracy and regime survival. It is not the only policy area of which that could be said. Above all, education is a cornerstone of structural adjustment and economic reform, both of which have a sorry history in the region.

Crisis, I am confident, is a critical driver of the reform process. In seeing higher education reform underway, one assumes that it is crisis-driven. That is probably true, but it is close to a tautology. Education reform is bound up in the greater crisis of fiscal and structural economic imbalances that overwhelm so many MENA economies and polities. It seems clear that higher education reform is no more difficult than grappling with the informal sector, converting the private sector from rent-seeking to innovation, or insulating the state apparatus from cronyism. In each reform sector there are powerful forces working to protect BAU. The menu of what is needed is daunting, and it is no surprise that I came to the conclusion that faced with a minefield, political leaders often opt to do as little as possible. If you are not moving, you won't step on a mine.

Every reform and innovation is at least two-edged. We have seen that with respect to university autonomy, shared governance, and tuition-free education for all. Reversing the brain drain may mean re-importing political trouble (follow China's efforts closely). Enhancing international rankings may mean adhering to standards over which the national political authorities have little control and that link local education communities of practice to external standard-setters. Some political control is sacrificed.

There is much fragmented reform that can be carried out within the current political context, and the likelihood is that a good deal of it will be. That is where both internal and external policy reformers will play a role. The question is whether or not such reforms will set in motion a process of broader structural reform. That is what many reformers hope, and what most political leaders viscerally fear.

Appendix to Chapter 1
GER Estimates for Select Arab Countries

Prem C. Saxena

A Brief Note on the Methodology

The present study uses the required data from the *World Population Prospects* 2012—the official population estimates and projections released by the Population Division of the Department of Economic and SocialAaffairs of the United Nations Secretariat, New York on June 13, 2013 (visit the website http://esa.un.org/wpp/unpp/panel_indicators.htm). To obtain the estimates of the projected populations in the tertiary education age group (18–24) years from 2010 to 2050, for the five selected Arab countries, namely, Egypt, Jordan, Lebanon, Morocco, and Syria, first the required projected populations in the age groups 10–14, 15–19, and 20–24 have been downloaded from the website for all the five countries at the five-year intervals. Applying the Karup-King's third-difference osculatory interpolation formula* and using the data of the three five-year age-groups, the population of age-group 15–19 is sub-divided into single years of ages. To obtain, the population of tertiary education age-group (18–24), the single year populations of ages 18 years and 19 years have been added to the population of the age group (20–24) years.; that is, P(18–24) = P(18) + (P19) + P(20–24). [* For details of Karup-King formula, see Shryock et al., 1980.]

Projection of GERs for Selected Five Countries for the Period 2010 to 2050

As a next step, after taking into consideration, the present and future socioeconomic, demographic, and political conditions, and the trends in the Gross Enrollment Ratios (GERs) for each of the five countries, three sets of assumptions of the future course of increase in GERs (Fast, Medium, and Slow) have been made for each of the study countries. All the three sets of assumptions for each of the five Arab countries are presented in Table A1.6. For projecting GERs, the modified exponential function has been used. It is an asymptotic growth curve used to describe a trend in which the amount of growth declines by a constant percentage and the curve approaches an upper limit, called the *asymptote*. The latter has the most important property, which does not allow the values to grow more than the upper limit. The upper limit is an asymptote, which means tangent to the curve at infinity. The curve will approach the upper limit and would come closer and closer to the value, but never quite equal it. Hypothetically, it will meet the upper limit only at infinity (and not at any finite value of t). The mathematical form of the curve is,

$$Yt = k + ab^t$$

where, Yt is the projected value at time t; 'k' is the asymptote to the curve, i.e., the upper limit of Yt, that could be approached very close to the upper value but will never attain the exact value at any finite value of t. The second parameter, 'a', is the value obtained by subtracting the asymptote 'k' from the trend value when 't' is zero. The third constant 'b' is the ratio between successive increments of growth (Croxton et al., 1973). For each of the three assumptions made and using the modified exponential curve discussed above, GERs have been projected from the year 2010 to 2050 at five-year intervals for the selected five Arab countries. The projected populations in the age group (18–24) years and of GERs for Egypt, Jordan, Lebanon, Morocco, and Syria are presented below in Tables A1.1 and A1.2 (a, b, and c), respectively.

Table A1.1. Projected Population (in Thousands) in the Age Group 18–24 in Selected Arab Countries from 2010–2050*

Year	Country				
	Egypt	Jordan	Lebanon	Morocco	Syria
2010	10,915	880	602	4,329	3,104
2015	10,427	1,000	706	4,262	2,911
2020	10,638	936	519	3,923	3,582
2025	11,267	1,029	443	3,776	3,620
2030	12,343	1,219	401	4,158	3,573
2035	12,735	1,299	434	4,829	3,619
2040	12,615	1,251	440	4,499	3,736
2045	12,336	1,176	418	4,186	3,846
2050	12,249	1,165	385	3,959	3,787

*The population in 18–24-year age group for selected Arab countries have been obtained by adding the single year populations in ages 18 and 19 years (found earlier) of a particular country with the respective population of the 20–24-year age group of the country.

That is, the required population in the 18–24-year age group is obtained as, $P(18–24) = P(18) + P(19) + P(20–24)$.

Table A1.2a. Projected GERs (in %) for Egypt and Jordan under Fast, Medium, and Slow Increase in GERs from 2010 to 2050

Year	Observed	GERs (in %) for EGYPT		
		Projected GERs under Assumption		
		I	II	III
		k = 55.0 a = - 22.6 b = 0.758	k = 50.0 a = -17.6 b = 0.716	k = 45.0 a = -12.6 b = 0.745
1980	15.5	--	--	--
1985	17.6	--	--	--
1990	13.7	--	--	--
1995	N.A.	--	--	--
2000	N.A.	--	--	--
2005	30.8	--	--	--
2010	32.4	32.4	32.4	32.4
2015	--	37.8	37.4	35.6
2020	--	42.0	41.0	38.0
2025	--	45.2	43.5	39.8
2030	--	47.5	45.4	41.1
2035	--	49.3	46.7	42.1
2040	--	50.7	47.6	42.8
2045	--	51.7	48.3	43.4
2050	----	52.5	48.8	43.8

Year	Observed	GERs (in %) for JORDAN		
		Projected GERs under Assumption		
		I	**II**	**III**
		k = 55.0 a = -17.3 b = 0.723	k = 50.0 a = - 12.3 b = 0.699	k = 45.0 a = - 7.3 b = 0.585
1980	14.8	--	--	--
1985	20.3	--	--	--
1990	20.4	--	--	--
1995	18.6	--	--	--
2000	N.A,	--	--	--
2005	38.2	--	--	--
2010	37.7	37.7	37.7	37.7
2015	--	42.5	41.4	40.7
2020	--	45.9	44.0	42.5
2025	--	48.5	45.8	43.5
2030	--	50.3	47.1	44.2
2035	--	51.6	47.9	44.5
2040	--	52.5	48.6	44.7
2045	--	53.2	49.0	44.8
2050	----	53.7	49.3	44.9

0 – 37.8 = 4.2 The Ratio is: 0.7
Third Increment = 45.2 – 42.0 = 3.2 The Ratio is: 0.7

Table A1.2b. Projected GERs (in %) for Lebanon and Morocco under Fast, Medium, and Slow Increase in GERs from 2010 to 2050

Year	Observed	GERs (in %) for LEBANON		
		Projected GERs under Assumption		
		I	II	III
		k = 70 a = - 16.0 b = 0.739	k = 65 a = - 11.0 b = 0.659	k = 60 a = - 6.0 b = 0.789
1980	30.6	--	--	--
1985	24.0	--	--	--
1990	--	--	--	--
1995	--	--	--	--
2000	33.9	--	--	--
2005	44.0	--	--	--
2010	54.0	54.0	54.0	54.0
2015	--	58.2	57.7	55.3
2020	--	61.3	60.2	56.3
2025	--	63.5	61.8	57.1
2030	--	65.2	62.9	57.7
2035	--	66.5	63.6	58.2
2040	--	67.4	64.1	58.6
2045	--	68.1	64.4	58.9
2050	----	68.6	64.6	59.1

Year	Observed	GERs (in %) for MOROCCO		
		Projected GERs under Assumption		
		I	II	III
		k = 45 a = - 30.2 b = 0.568	k = 40 a = - 25.2 b = 0.536	k = 35 a = - 20.2 b = 0.451
1980	--	--	--	--
1985	--	--	--	--
1990	10.9	--	--	--
1995	11.3	--	--	--
2000	9.5	--	--	--
2005	11.4	--	--	--
2010	14.8	14.8	14.8	14.8
2015	--	27.8	26.5	25.9
2020	--	35.3	32.8	30.9
2025	--	39.5	36.1	33.1
2030	--	41.9	37.9	34.2
2035	--	43.2	38.9	34.6
2040	--	44.0	39.4	34.8
2045	--	44.4	39.7	34.9
2050	----	44.7	39.8	34.98

Table A1.2c. Projected GERs (in %) for Syria under Fast, Medium, and Slow Increase in GERs from 2010 to 2050

Year	Observed	GERs (in %) for SYRIA		
		Projected GERs under Assumption		
		I	II	III
		k = 40 a = - 24.0 b = 0.589	k = 35 a = - 19.0 b = 0.599	k = 30 a = - 14.0 b = 0.607
1980	14.1	--	--	--
1985	17.1	--	--	--
1990	18.0	--	--	--
1995	14,8	--	--	--
2000	16.0*	--	--	--
2005	16.0*	--	--	--
2010	16.0*	16.0	16.0	16.0
2015	--	25.9	23.6	21.5
2020	--	31.7	28.2	24.8
2025	--	35.1	30.9	26.9
2030	--	37.1	32.5	28,1
2035	--	38.3	33.5	28.8
2040	--	39.0	34.1	29.3
2045	--	39.4	34.5	29.6
2050	----	39.7	34.7	29.7

* Average of GERs observed for years 1980, 1985, 1990, and 1995.

Finally, the above projected estimates of the GERs have been applied to the corresponding projected populations of the 18–24-year age group computed earlier (given in A1.1 above) to yield the estimates of the enrollments of college-going populations for each of the five study countries from 2010 to 2050 at five-year intervals. The estimated college going populations have been presented below in Tables A1.3, A1.4, and A1.5 under the assumptions of Fast, Medium, and Slow increase of GERs (Assumptions I, II, and III), respectively.

Table A1.3. Estimated College-going Population in Tertiary Age Group 18–24 for Selected Arab Countries under Assumption–I (Fast Increase in GERs)

Year	Egypt	Jordan	Lebanon	Morocco	Syria
2010 (Base)	3,536,460	331,760	325,080	640,692	496,640
2015	3,941,406	425,000	410,892	1,184,836	753,949
2020	4,467,960	429,624	318,147	1,384,819	1,135,494
2025	5,092,684	499,065	281,305	1,491,520	1,270,620
2030	5,862,925	613,157	261,452	1,742,202	1,325,583
2035	6,278,355	670,284	288,610	2,086,128	1,386,077
2040	6,395,805	656,775	296,560	1,979,560	1,457,040
2045	6,377,712	625,632	284,658	1,858,584	1,515,324
2050	6,430,725	625,605	264,110	1,769,673	1,503,439

Table A1.4. Estimated College-going Population in Tertiary Age Group 18–24 for Selected Arab Countries under Assumption–II (Medium Increase in GERs) (In Absolute Numbers)

Year	Egypt	Jordan	Lebanon	Morocco	Syria
2010 (Base)	3,536,460	331,760	325,080	640,692	496,640
2015	3,899,698	414,000	407,362	1,129,430	686,996
2020	4,361,580	411,840	312,438	1,286,744	1,010,124
2025	4,901,145	471,282	273,774	1,363,136	1,118,580
2030	5,603,722	574,149	252,229	1,575,882	1,161,225
2035	5,947,245	622,221	276,024	1,878,481	1,212,365
2040	6,004,740	607,986	282,040	1,772,606	1,273,976
2045	5,958,288	576,240	269,192	1,661,842	1,326,870
2050	5,977,512	574,345	248,710	1,575,682	1,314,089

Table A1.5. Estimated College-going Population in Tertiary Age Group 18–24 for Selected Arab Countries under Assumption–III (Slow Increase in GERs) (In Absolute Numbers)

Year	Egypt	Jordan	Lebanon	Morocco	Syria
2010 (Base)	3,536,460	331,760	325,080	640,692	496,640
2015	3,712,012	407,000	390,418	1103,858	625,865
2020	4,042,440	397,800	292,197	1,212,207	888,336
2025	4,484,266	447,615	252,953	1,249,856	973,780
2030	5,072,973	538,798	231,377	1,422,036	1,004,013
2035	5,361,435	578,055	252,588	1,670,834	1,042,272
2040	5,399,220	559,197	257,840	1,565,652	1,094,648
2045	5,353,824	526,848	246,202	1,460,914	1,138,416
2050	5,365,062	523,085	227,535	1,384,858	1,124,739

It is proposed to obtain the estimates of Gross Enrollment Ratios (GERs) during the period 2010–2050 under the following three sets of assumptions concerning increase in the GERs:

Table A1.6. Consolidated Table of Three Sets of Assumptions Concerning Increase in GERs

Country	Assumption–I (Fast) GER Would Increase* from Base Year (2010) End Year (2050) Value to Value	Assumption–II (Medium) GER Would Increase* from Base Year (2010) End Year (2050) Value to Value	Assumption–III (Slow) GER Would Increase* from Base Year (2010) End Year (2050) Value to Value
Egypt	32.4% 55.0%	32.4% 50.0%	32.4% 45.0%
Jordan	37.7% 55.0%	37.7% 50.0%	37.7% 45.0%
Lebanon	54.4% 70.0%	54.4% 65.0%	54.4% 60.0%
Morocco	14.8% 45.0%	14.8% 40.0%	14.8% 35.0%
Syria	16.0% 40.0%	16.0% 35.0%	16.0% 30.0%

Note: GERs are assumed to increase following modified exponential law of growth.

References

Croxton, Frederick E., Dudley J. Cowden, and Sidney Klein. 1973. *Applied General Statistics*, 3rd ed. Chapter 13. New Delhi: Prentice-Hall of India Private Limited.

Shryock, Henry, Jacob S. Siegel & Associates. 1980. *The Methods and Materials of Demography*, [Fourth Printing (rev.)]. Washington DC: U.S. department of Commerce, Bureau of the Census.

United Nations (200), World Population Prospects 2012—The 2010 Revision, Vol. II: Population Database, Department of Economic and Social Affairs, Population Division, New York, U.S.A. [http://esa.un.org/wpp/unpp/panel_indicators.htm].

Interviews

Abdulaziz, Ahmed, former professor of law, Damascus University; former director general, Syrian Investment Authority; former governor, Hama Province (May 4, 2013, Kuwait City).

Abou Dounia, Mohammed, assistant professor of molecular biology, Princeton University (Princeton, October 24, 2014).

El-Amine, Adnan, professor of education, Lebanese University; former head, Lebanese Association of Educational Studies (November 7, 2012, and July 30, 2015, Beirut).

al-Arabi, Nabil, secretary-general, League of Arab States; former foreign minister, Egypt (February 26, 2014, Abu Dhabi).

Aziz, Faissal, professor, Centre National d'Etude et de Recherche sur l'Eau et l'Energie (CNEREE), CAU (March 6, 2018, Marrakesh).

al-Azm, Sadiq Jalal, retired professor of philosophy, Damascus University (d. 2016) (December 8, 2013, Princeton).

Benhadda, Abderrahim, dean of the Faculté des Lettres et Sciences Humaines, MVA (October 24, 2013, Rabat).

Benjelloun, Wail, president, MVUA (October 23, 2013, Rabat).

Bhandari, Rajika, deputy vice-president of research and evaluation, International Institute of Education (June 19, 2013, New York).

Bitar, Khalil, former dean of arts and sciences, AUB (November 8, 2012, Beirut).

Blackton, John, former USAID official (December 13–14, 2012, email exchanges).

Buckner, Elizabeth, PhD candidate, Stanford University (September 26, 2013, telephone conversation).

Cherkaoui, Mohammed, Moroccan professor of sociology and a director of research at the French CNRS (October 30, 2013, Casablanca).

Choucri, Nazli, professor of political science, MIT, and Fred Moavenzadeh, president, Masdar Institute (Abu Dhabi), MIT (August 14, 2012, MIT, Cambridge, MA).

Conway, Gordon, former vice chancellor, Sussex University; former president, Rockefeller Foundation (June 24, 2015, London).

Daoudi, Lahcen, minister of higher education, Kingdom of Morocco (October 28, 2013, Rabat).

Dessouki, Ali al-Din Hilal, former minister of youth and sports, Egypt; former secretary-general, Supreme Council of Universities, Egypt; former dean, Faculty of Politics and International Relations, Cairo University (February 23, March 9, and May 14, 2013, Cairo).

Dewachi, Omar, graduate, Baghdad University; member, Faculty of Health Science, AUB; professor in anthropology, Rutgers University (December 13, 2013, Princeton).

Diab, Hassan, former minister of education and higher education, Lebanon (March 19, 2012, April 13, 2013, and March 10, 2016, Beirut).

Doğramacı, Ali, president, Bilkent University (September 30, 2016, email exchange).

Elkarmi, Fawwaz, assistant secretary-general for scientific and technological affairs, Higher Council for Science and Technology, Jordan (August 5, 2015, Amman).

Ergüder, Üstün, former rector, Bosphorus University (April 25, 2014, Istanbul).

Ezzat, Heba, assistant professor of political science, Cairo University (April 28, 2013, Cairo).

Fergany, Nader, former professor of biostatistics, Cairo University (February 24, 2013, Cairo).

Gall, Norman, director, Fernand Braudel Institute of World Economics, Brazil (December 16, 2012, email exchange).

Gohar, Hani, director, Center for Quality Assurance, Cairo University (April 28, 2013, Cairo).

Hanafi, Sari, chair of sociology, anthropology, and media studies, AUB (January 28, 2016, Beirut).

Hatem, Ashraf, secretary-general, Supreme Council of Universities, Egypt (April 29, 2013, Cairo).

Hindi, Khalil, former president, Birzeit University, Palestine (March 10, 2016, Beirut).

Hussein, Adnan al-Sayyid, president, Lebanese University (November 9, 2012, Beirut).

Ibrahim, Ali, president, Central Management Services Authority, Ministry of Finance, Egypt (May 18, 2014, Cairo, assisted by Fatma al-Ashmawy).

Jaber, Yassine, member of parliament, Lebanon (April 11, 2014, Beirut).

Jammal, Ahmad, director general, Ministry of Education, Lebanon (April 13, 2013, March 3, 2014, and July 30, 2015, Beirut).

Kabbani, Nader, Syrian economist, senior fellow with the Brookings Global Economy and Development Program (November 14, 2012, Doha).

Kamel, Hossam, president, Cairo University (March 10, 2013, Cairo).

Kankanhalli, Mohan, vice provost of graduate education, NUS (May 25, 2015, Singapore).

Kapur, Devesh, director, Center for Advanced Study of India, University of Pennsylvania (January 18, 2013, email exchange).

Kassim-Lakha, Shamsh, chair, Pakistan Higher Education Council; former vice chancellor, Agha Khan University (November 14, 2012, Doha).

Khalil, Mohammed, graduate of Damascus University; professor of Arabic, NYU Abu Dhabi (February 10, 2013, Abu Dhabi).

Levy, Daniel, director, Program for Research on Private Higher Education; distinguished professor, Syracuse University (January 9, 2013, email exchange).

Ma al-Barid, Abd al-Ghani, president, Damascus University (April 16, 1998, Damascus).

Mahafzah, Azmi, president, Jordan University; former vice president of scientific faculties, Jordan University (August 5, 2015, Amman, August 10, 2015, email exchange, and November 4, 2016, Beirut).

Mahbubani, Kishore, dean, Lee Kwan Yew School of Public Policy, NUS (May 25, 2015, Singapore).

Makouk, Khalid, advisor for agriculture and the environment, CNRS-L (November 5, 2013, Beirut).

Marmolejo, Francisco, former lead, Tertiary Education Global Solutions Group, World Bank (January 26, 2016, Beirut).

Mas'ad, Mustafa, minister of higher education, Egypt (April 29, 2013, Cairo).

Miraoui, Abdallatif, president, CAU (March 5, 2018, Marrakesh).

Mneimneh, Ali, dean, Faculty of Sciences, Lebanese University (November 6, 2012, Beirut).

Mrabet, Radouane, president, MVUS (October 23, 2013, Rabat).

Mrad, Fouad, executive director, ESCWA Technology Center (July 28, 2015, Amman).

Al-Mulki, Nael, Jordan University (August 5, 2015, Amman).

Mullinix, Joseph, deputy president of administration, NUS (May 25, 2015, Singapore).

Murtada, Hani, former president, Damascus University; former minister of higher education, Syria (April 14, 2014, Beirut).

Nasser, Gaber Gad, president, Cairo University (February 16, 2014, Cairo).

Nawara, Gamal, secretary-general, Council of Private Universities, Egypt (April 29, 2013, Cairo).

Ouaattar, Said, director, Institut Agronomique et Vétérinaire Hassan II (September 22, 2014, Lisbon).

Ouaouicha, Driss, president, Al Akhawayn University (October 24, 2013, Rabat).

Prasad, Ajith, senior director, Office of Resource Planning, NUS (May 25, 2015, Singapore).

Rashid, Youssef, deputy secretary-general, Supreme Council of Universities, Egypt (March 9, 2014, Cairo).

Regragui, Fakhita, head of quality assurance, MVUA (October 23, 2013, Rabat).

Sabra, Wafic, former student, Lebanese University; director, Center for Advanced Mathematical Sciences, AUB (March 19, 2013, Beirut).

Salama, Amr Ezzat, former president, Helwan University; former minister of education, Egypt (May 18, 2013, Cairo).

Salehi-Isfahani, Djavad, professor of economics, Virginia Tech University (August 1, 2014, email exchange).

Salmi, Jamil, former World Bank senior expert on education (September 1, 2012, email exchange).

Al-Sayyid, Mustapha, chair of the department of political science, Cairo University (May 19, 2013, Cairo).

Schwartzman, Simon, senior researcher, Instituto de Estudos do Trabalho e Sociedade, Brazil (December 17, 2012, email exchange).

Soliman, Khalid, Quality Assurance Center, Cairo University (April 28, 2013, Cairo).

Tohmé, Georges, former president, Lebanese University; president, CNRS-L (November 5, 2013, Beirut).

Yeo, Philip, chair of SPRING Singapore, Economic Development Innovations Singapore (May 25, 2015, Singapore).

Zahlan, Antoine (Tony), former professor of physics, AUB; expert on science in the Arab world (April 15, 2013, Beirut).

Al-Zu'bi, Bashir, president, Higher Education Accreditation Commission, Jordan (August 5, 2015, Amman, Jordan).

Zurbuchen, Mary, director for Asia and Russia, Ford Foundation (June 19, 2013, telephone conversation).

Notes

Preface

1   Lisa Anderson is a distinguished political scientist, former dean of Columbia's School of International and Public Affairs, and former provost and then president of the American University in Cairo.

2   In economics, a public good is a good that is both nonexcludable and nonrivalrous in that individuals cannot be effectively excluded from its use and use by one individual does not reduce availability to others.

Introduction

1   The editors and authors who contribute to Diwan, Malik, and Atiyas (2019) on crony capitalism hypothesize that market reforms in the 1990s drove autocrats to recruit private sector actors who were offered special rent-generating privileges in exchange for accepting some neoliberal reforms and for political loyalty. There is no *direct* evidence to sustain this plausible conjecture.

2   In another essay I identified significant change in national water policy in Saudi Arabia, Jordan, and Morocco (coincidentally, I think, all monarchies) in the absence of any systemic crisis (Waterbury, 2013).

3   Writing about Damascus University, al-Samar (2018: 126) describes its multiple missions: "Those in charge defined the university's mission ('duties'), fifty years after its founding, as follows: inscribing truths in the Arabic language; teaching science; preparing professionals among the *ulama* and the workers; scientific research; the spread of public culture; the orientation of students towards high standards. Could it (the university) undertake these duties?"

4   Rankings will be discussed throughout the text. Here, I cite only one, the QS
     World Rankings of eight hundred universities for 2016. QS uses four basic
     variables in its index: academic reputation (4 percent); employer reputation
     (20 percent); student–faculty ratio (20 percent); citations per faculty member
     (as per Scopus) (20 percent). The highest-ranked universities in the geo-
     graphic Middle East are Hebrew University at 148 and Technion University
     at 198 (both in Israel), and King Fahd University of Petroleum and Minerals
     at 199 (in Saudi Arabia). In general, see Hazelkorn, 2015 and 2008.

5   Kenneth Pollack (2019) has written a lengthy study of Arab military under-
     performance and the long-established track record of punching well below
     their weight. His main explanatory variable is culture combined with the
     educational system.

6   One of the notable exceptions was Khartoum University, where student
     demonstrations in 1964 led to the collapse of the military dictatorship of
     General Ibrahim Abboud (see Chapter 3 on politics and the university).
     Sana'a University was the seat of Yemen's short-lived uprising in 2011.

7   The chronic problem of educated-youth unemployment was exacerbated
     by these same economic reforms, although they were not the cause. Public
     employment dried up, and a university education was not suitable prepara-
     tion for work in the informal sector or in the formal private sector.

8   In Algeria and Sudan, the protest movements led to the ouster of the
     respective heads of state, Abdelaziz Bouteflika and Omar Bashir, but not, at
     the time of writing, to the end of military rule.

9   See the video "Mosul University Liberated."

1. Orders of Magnitude

1   My former colleague at AUB, Prem Saxena, who went on to the Aba Gaware
     Chair of Social Sciences at the Tata Institute of Social Sciences in Mumbai,
     India, was my indispensable guide to some of the analysis in this chapter. His
     country-by-country forecasting of GERs is in the appendix to this chapter
     (see page 309). He is in no way responsible for my interpretation of the data.

2   All such projections are hazardous, as small changes in fertility at the begin-
     ning of a period may have large numerical consequences at the end of a
     period, say, a quarter of a century.

3   The transition to lower rates is not always smooth. Egypt bounced back up
     to three live births per female at the time of the Arab uprisings, then fell
     back to 2.8 shortly thereafter. The overall trend is down. Iran, despite its
     Islamist and sometimes pro-natalist regime, has been below replacement for
     some time.

4 The most explicit example of this is Tunisia, which in 2017 began to freeze public employment and began lay-offs that aimed to reach 50,000 by 2020. These measures were taken in the context of an IMF loan. Egypt is trying to shrink its civil service from six to four million (*Al-Araby Al-Jadeed*, 2018).

5 The parameters of educational systems in the MENA, and sometimes their deficiencies, are analyzed in Bashshur (1997; 2004), World Bank (2008), Fergany (2000), and UNDP and AFESD (2003).

6 The explosion is of long date. In 1953 there were only thirteen public and private universities in the Arab world.

7 In 1995–96, Egypt admitted three times as many students as in 1991–92, while the faculty grew by 13 percent. At Ain Shams this yielded student-to-teacher ratios of 366:1 in commerce, 234:1 in law, and 104:1 in arts. Ratios of 15:1 and 30:1, respectively, were registered in medicine and engineering (Bashshur, 2004: 19).

8 The University of Mosul was under ISIS occupation for about two years, then partially destroyed in the 'liberation' of Mosul in 2017.

9 I am grateful to Talal El Hourani and Daniel Ejov of UNESCO for helping me understand the Turkish GERs.

10 A reflection of the difficulty of obtaining hard data comes in UNESCO (2009), which relegates dropouts to just one box, "Staying at University" (2009: 45).

11 Sylke Schnepf (2014) examines European dropout rates, which are around 20 percent on average, and concludes that about 40 percent of dropouts complete a tertiary degree sometime during their working lives.

12 Wastage may be even greater in the primary and high school levels. Tunisia reputedly has one of the better K–12 systems in the Arab world, but its youth unemployment rates and its dropout rates are as high as in other Arab countries. Out of one million K–12 students, 130,000 drop out each year. Seventy percent are male, and they are concentrated in ages thirteen to seventeen. The bulk of the dropouts are from lower-income families or the poor (Al-Militi, 2015).

13 In the early 2000s, when I was president of AUB, a faculty-rich institution, our instructor-to-student ratio was about 1:13.

14 Cadi Ayyad University in Marrakesh, Morocco, saw its total enrollments rise from 29,000 in 2011 to 102,000 in 2018. Its corps of professors did not grow at all, so that the student-to-teacher ratio rose to 68:1.

15 In the US and in US-inspired institutions the unit of accounting for faculty is the full-time equivalent (FTE). It is a formula to convert part-time hires into the equivalent of one fully employed faculty member.

16 Abdallatif Miraoui, the president of CAU, gave me the figure of 9,200 Moroccan dirhams per capita as the outlay at CAU. This is equivalent to about $920 per student.

17 Because the bulk of current expenditures go to salaries for faculty and staff, we can assume that these per capita differences reflect different salary levels in the countries mentioned.

18 In one Arab country of which I had direct experience, the minister of education was the founder of a private university, and a couple of dozen other universities were licensed during his tenure.

19 In the early 1960s, when Yemen became an Arab socialist republic, a joke making the rounds was that Egypt's Ministry of Education received an urgent appeal to send the Yemeni republic schoolteachers "in the name of the Arab nation and socialist transformation." Egypt did so, and some months later the Ministry received another appeal: "In the name of the Arab nation and socialist transformation, please send students."

2. The Modern Flagship Universities of the Arab World

1 Some areas escaped direct European control after the First World War. Iran was subject to Russian and British 'spheres of influence,' the Ottoman Empire was dismembered, leaving Anatolia as the core of the Turkish Republic, and what are today Saudi Arabia and Yemen were left to their own devices.

2 A partial exception to this generalization are the madrasas of Qom in Iran and Najaf in Iraq. Both have been active and dynamic centers for the formation of Shi'i religious leaders in Iran and Iraq. Ayatollah Khomeini and virtually all the political leaders of the Islamic Republic were educated between Qom and Najaf. The same cannot be said for the political impact of graduates of Egypt's al-Azhar.

3 Late in the preparation of this manuscript, a book exploring the history of ten Arab public universities was published (ACRPS, 2018). The ten universities are Cairo, Damascus, Lebanese, Khartoum, Jordan, Sana'a, Sultan Qaboos (Oman), Tunis, Libya, and Kuwait. Each case study covers governance, student life, and movements, faculty, and academic affairs. Mohammed V University of Morocco was not covered, but Yaqtin (2017) does so in a different ACRPS collection. I have incorporated findings from both studies in this chapter.

4 The detail I provide on the four universities reflects the available literature. Cairo University is the best documented of the four.

5 The university at its inception had two main advisory committees, one for administration and internal affairs and the other for fundraising. How little has changed since in terms of trustee oversight.

6   It is also said that his refusal to authorize honorary degrees for some palace favorites contributed to his dismissal.

7   In 1958, at the peak of President Gamal Abd al-Nasser's popularity in the Arab world, Alexandria University established a branch in Beirut, Lebanon, called the Beirut Arab University. One of its most famous graduates was Rafic Hariri, a wealthy businessman and Lebanese prime minister who was assassinated in February 2005.

8   That did not apply to the American University in Cairo, which by its charter had to maintain a certain percentage of US nationals among its faculty.

9   Galal Amin, a professor of economics at both Cairo University and the American University in Cairo, recalled his conversation in the mid-1980s with Hilmy Murad, a professor of public finance at Cairo University. Murad commented on a conference on "Reforming Education in Egypt" in the mid-1980s, noting, "They don't need to hold a conference to reform education. If they opened any drawer in any office in the Ministry of Education they would find enough memos and proposals to fix all the flaws in Egyptian education, if only they were implemented." The chairman of the conference was Ahmad Fathi Sorour, the minister of education who in 1990 became speaker of the People's Assembly, serving until the overthrow of Mubarak in 2011. Amin, not one to hold back, quipped that Sorour proved himself "highly competent at ruining education in Egypt" (2013: 146).

10 The principal leaders on the MIT side were Professor of Political Science Nazli Choucri and Professor of Engineering Fred Moavenzadeh. Professor Moavenzadeh, a few decades later, in 2012, went on to head the Masdar Institute of Science and Technology in Abu Dhabi.

11 Mughaith (2018: 54) estimates that for several years, up to 1987, Cairo University supplied the executive seventy-six ministers and fifteen governors.

12 An excellent study of third-party leverage in Egypt is to be found in Ikram (2018).

13 I am grateful to Ali al-Din Hillal Dessouki for his insights on Egyptian higher education. He served as the dean of the Faculty of Politics and International Relations at Cairo University, secretary-general of the SCU, and minister of youth and sports.

14 The separation of Syria and Lebanon meant that the Syrian Protestant College in Lebanon had to change its name, which it did, to the American University of Beirut.

15 Medicine is, perhaps, as many see it, the most difficult discipline to teach in Arabic. Yet in 1919 the Arab Medical Institute was reopened in Damascus after a committee passed a draft law comprising twelve articles,

one of which provided that teaching be conducted in Arabic. The Faculty of Medicine then produced a thesaurus of medical terms in Arabic, consisting of 14,534 terms. This dictionary was critically reviewed by the president of the Arabic Academy and professor of endocrinology at the Faculty of Medicine at the time. Recommended amendments and additions were then compiled in a large volume containing 1,102 pages and published in 1983. Eventually, the Unified (Arabic) Medical Dictionary was compiled in cooperation with the World Health Organization (WHO) regional office. During the period 1970–91, the Faculty of Medicine at Damascus University graduated 1,442 specialists, all of whom had studied medicine and pursued graduate studies in Arabic (UNDP and AFESD, 2003: Box 9.6).

16 For example, France had annexed Algeria to the French Republic in 1848. The University of Algiers was not founded until 1909. In 1961, on the eve of independence, the University of Algiers student body was only 11 percent 'native' (Mohammed and Brahim, 2010). Tunisia offers a similar story (Labayd, 2017: 517–46).

17 In the otherwise informative survey of higher education in Syria (European Commission, 2017), I could find no mention of the Ba'th Party as it relates to university governance, curriculum, promotions, appointments, and other factors. Third parties are inclined to overlook awkward truths.

18 I am grateful to Tara Mahfoud, formerly of the Issam Fares Institute of AUB, for her synopsis of Law No. 6. Note that Hani Murtada, quoted extensively, had completed his public career as Damascus University president and minister of higher education by the time this law was enacted.

19 We explore returns to education in Chapter 6 on reform and Chapter 7 on innovation. The reference here is to private returns, meaning what additional years of education bring by way of higher earnings compared to those without such education.

20 El-Amine (2018) bemoans the state of Lebanese University records. There are no archives. Georges Tohmé is the only president to have written his memoirs. Each new administration belittles or ignores its predecessor.

21 Shahine (2011: 86) portrays Bustani as a stalking horse for the Jesuits, who wanted no expansion of the university. Rather, Shahine alleges, Bustani saw it as training high school teachers, not competing with USJ or AUB.

22 In 1994 the Hadath campus received funding from AFESD ($75 million), the Saudi Development Fund ($25 million), and the Islamic Development Fund ($18 million). Oman put in $12.5 million for a medical faculty.

23 By 2015 total enrollments at the Beirut Arab University had reached 16,000. Although sponsored by a public university in Egypt, it is treated as a private institution in Lebanon.

24 This was not an idle fear. Nasser swamped the Lawyers Syndicate in Egypt with legions of freshly minted, mass-produced lawyers. The result was the subordination of the syndicate to the Nasserist agenda (see Moore, 1980).

25 Lebanon has state-directed intelligence services, led by military intelligence (*deuxième bureau*). From 1976, and until probably today, Syrian intelligence was thick on the ground, including around universities. In addition, a number of militias and confessional organizations, most prominent among them, Hezbollah, had and have their own intelligence wings.

26 In an interview (2013), Georges Tohmé insisted to me that the proliferation of Lebanese University subunits did not exacerbate confessional problems, at least not on his watch.

27 Adnan al-Sayyid Hussein was minister of state in the government of Prime Minister Saad Hariri. He was initially considered an independent, a minister reserved for the president of the republic, Michel Suleiman. However, when Hezbollah ministers resigned from the government, Hussein resigned too. The government fell. Hussein's reward was apparently the presidency of Lebanese University. In an interview with me (2012), he claimed to detest confessionalism and described himself as *laique*, a French term that could be translated as 'militantly secular.'

28 El-Amine (2018: 181) has a jaundiced view of Tohmé's tenure, suggesting that he intentionally ignored the university council.

29 Even AUB opened a campus, the Off-Campus Program, in East Beirut, nominally to serve students who could not risk travel to West Beirut, where the main campus is located. The program was 'captured' by the Phalange, a Christian faction led at the time by Bashir Gemayel, who became president of the republic and then was assassinated in 1982. A few years later the trustees of AUB closed the program.

30 The Lebanese lira is pegged to the US dollar at the rate of 1,506 lira per dollar. That rate has prevailed since the mid-1990s. In 2019/20 the lira sharply devalued in the midst of economic crisis.

31 Public outlays on education as a percentage of GDP are relatively low in Lebanon, but that is because private outlays are so high. In combination, Lebanon is a leader in educational outlays (see Chapter 8 on financing education).

32 At the time, Ben Barka was a leader of the left wing of the dominant Istiqlal Party. He and others broke away from Istiqlal in 1959 to found the

National Union of Popular Forces. In the fall of 1965, Ben Barka was kidnapped in France and presumably killed.

3. Politics and the University

1   Rustum Ghazali, Syria's *gauleiter* in Lebanon until 2005, took a PhD in history from Lebanese University, supervised by Professor Hassan Hallaq—who, it is alleged, actually wrote his thesis. "Half of Lebanon's political elite attended his defense," notes Husseini (2012: 19). Michael Young (2010: 75) has a less damning account of this.

2   The World Development Report 2018 (World Bank, 2017) is devoted to education and learning outcomes. Chapter 10 is entitled "Unhealthy Politics Drives Misalignments." The unhealthy politics are of the small-p variety: patronage, misappropriation of funds, catering to key interests such as teachers' unions. The entire report carefully avoids big-P politics that involve regime survival.

3   Springborg (2018) illustrates this obsessive concern with autonomy and intergroup links in his analysis of the deep state in Egypt.

4   The riots saw twenty-one students killed, seven hundred injured, and a thousand jailed (Springborg, 2018: 64).

5   The formal regulations for Syrian universities are contained in Law No. 6 of 2006, the Law for the Regulation of Universities in Syria.

6   Alan George (2003) notes that students protested Hafez al-Assad's seizure of power in 1970. Students were killed in Aleppo in 1979 when they marched on *mukhabarat* headquarters.

7   Hisham Matar (2006) makes the same point of widespread complicity in the maintenance of autocracy. He writes of Qadhafi's Libya.

8   In general, see Chapter 6 in UNDP and AFESD (2016).

9   Batatu (1999: 270) observed that from the outset, the Ba'th regime targeted students disproportionately. In the period 1976–81 they outnumbered other classes of prisoners, such as schoolteachers and professionals, three to one.

10   See https://en.wikipedia.org/wiki/Hisham_Ben_Ghalbon.

11   The coup took place on September 12, 1980, when Jimmy Carter was president of the United States. Turkey was and is a member of the North Atlantic Treaty Organization. Carter failed to condemn the coup.

12   The Turkish Academy of Sciences was founded in 1993. In 2011, one-third of its members resigned in protest of a new policy introduced by Erdoğan and the AKP to expand membership from 140 to 300, with a hundred appointed by the president of the republic, a hundred by the YÖK, and the rest by sitting members (Alberts, 2011b: 1801).

In 2013 six academics were given long prison sentences for plotting against the state in an alleged military conspiracy known as Ergenekon. Ironically, one of those sentenced was Kemal Gürüz, former chairman of the YÖK from 1997 to 2003 (Bohannon, 2013). The Ergenekon conspiracy was eventually dismissed by Erdoğan as a fabrication of his former ally and now nemesis, Fethullah Gülen.

13 This is a variant on a theme prevalent in the Mashriq, close to the war zone with Israel, summarized in the slogan "no voice higher than that of the battle" *(la sawt fawq al-maʿraka)*. The obverse of this was that students and other activists could always go into the streets to denounce Israel or defend Palestinian rights. That was the substitute for direct confrontation with the regimes. President Sadat proclaimed 1971 a "decisive year" in Egypt's war with Israel. When 1971 came and went without any progress, students demonstrated, accusing Sadat of having lengthened the year beyond twelve months.

14 One of those Syrians is today a religious advisor to Mohammed bin Zayed, crown prince of Abu Dhabi ('Ida, 2013).

15 The exact cause of Hussein being removed from the deanship is not entirely clear. He had written a controversial book on pre-Islamic poetry (1926) that provoked Egypt's Islamic establishment. It is also said he refused the order of the minister of education to confer honorary degrees on some of the latter's favorites. The confusion weds big-P and small-p politics. Taha Hussein subsequently became minister of education in 1950. He died in 1973.

16 Dunne and Hamzawy (2019) provide a history of politically-driven-out migration in Egypt and current efforts on the part of the authorities to monitor the political diaspora.

17 In sharp contrast with this movement of individual faculty members is the fact of severely stunted research collaboration among Arab universities. Out of all collaborative research in the Arab world in 2005, only 5 percent involved intra-Arab collaborative research (Zahlan, 2012: 86; Lamine, 2010).

18 The main exception to this assessment is probably Saudi Arabia's King Fahd University of Petroleum Mines, which combines large-scale education with research related to the petroleum sector. Closer to the enclave model is Saudi Arabia's King Abdullah University of Science and Technology (KAUST), devoted entirely to graduate education and advanced research.

19 Daqu (2017) relies on survey data.

20 Ryan (1998) presents a useful case study of Jordan.

4. Excellence in Higher Education: Enabler and Enabled

1   Academic freedom is the right to teach or learn freely without unreasonable interference from authority or fear of reprisal.

2   For a survey of academic freedom, see Scholars at Risk Network (2015; 2017). In Diani (2017), a portion of the text is devoted to university autonomy and academic freedom in the Arab world. In ACRPS (2018), dealing with ten Arab public universities, there is a section on academic freedom for each university.

3   The United States, like Turkey, considers the PKK to be a terrorist organization.

4   Throttling academic dissent is ubiquitous in the region, including in the well-financed, seemingly stable countries of the GCC. In 2017 the UAE sentenced Nasser bin Ghaith, an academic economist, to ten years in prison. He was convicted of "communicating with secret organizations linked to the Muslim Brotherhood, by creating accounts on social media and publishing photos and articles that are offensive to the state's symbols and values, its internal and foreign policies and its relations with an Arab state" (Lindsey, 2017).

5   A particularly notorious case following the coup against the government of Mohammed Morsi involves Professor Emad Shahin, accused of espionage and treason, tried in absentia, and condemned to death along with 120 others. Most were associated with the Muslim Brotherhood, one was already dead, and another had been in prison for nineteen years. Mohammed Morsi himself died in prison in June 2019.

6   An inconvenient fact, noted by Diwan (2012b), is that over the decade prior to the uprisings, as university enrollments grew exponentially, the Arab world became less democratic and more repressive—its exceptionalism was intensified. GERs are not the same as average years of schooling, the base measure Glaeser et al. (2007) use, but there is no obvious reason that rising GERs would be associated with *declining* levels of democratic practice. Similarly, with respect to the United States, Bok (2017) notes that as more Americans acquire tertiary education, voting rates and political participation decline.

7   In partial support of Glaeser et al. (2007) are the findings on 'civic engagement.' UNDP and AFESD (2016: 60) shows a correlation between levels of education and levels of civic engagement.

8   Daqu (2017) suggests that the autocratic, nonanalytic style of Arab higher education effectively erodes any tendency for its products to seek more democratic institutions.

9   Abu Bakr Baghdadi, who established the Islamic State in Raqqa, Syria, and proclaimed himself caliph in 2014 in Mosul, Iraq, took a PhD in Qur'anic Studies at Saddam University in Baghdad.

10 Chong and Gradstein (2015), as already noted, found that years of schooling correlated with democratic preferences, regardless of the degree of democracy manifest in the polities from which the respondents came.

11 Khouri (2015) writes in the spirit of Warren with respect to the Arab world: "Nasser set the precedent for military rule and severe controls on the flow of information and knowledge, arguably the two greatest constraints on human and national development in the Arab world since 1952."

12 It was only after writing this chapter that I came across the remarkable study of Simon Ings (2016).

13 Hanafi and Arvanitis (2016b) examine this 'broken triangle' in depth.

14 Altbach and Salmi (2011) devote a book to case studies of some of the most important success stories, several in democracies (South Korea, India, Mexico) and some in autocracies (China, Singapore, Russia). They cover Pohang University of Science and Technology, National University of Singapore, University of Malaysia, Mexico's Monterrey Institute of Technology, Russia's Higher School of Economics, the Hong Kong University of Science and Technology, Shanghai Jiao Tong University, India's Institutes of Technology, Nigeria's Ibadan University, and the Chilean university system. There are no MENA cases in this study. The editors stress autonomy as a major factor in explaining excellence but otherwise do not pay much attention to political context. The main point is that enabling environments vary enormously.

15 There is no Nobel Prize in mathematics. The Fields Medal is considered the equivalent.

16 Money has led to big gains in the quality of Saudi universities, including KAUST. Foreign scholars with big reputations and a list of achievements realized elsewhere are handsomely compensated to enter into joint appointments between their 'home' institutions and a Saudi university. The latter lists them as faculty, and they are counted as such by the major ranking organizations (McPhedran, 2013). This takes the meaning of enclave to another, virtual, level.

17 When Zewail received an honorary doctorate at AUB in June 2005, he told me that Mubarak and his people confused money with innovation. They thought, he said, that once the money was invested, the innovation would follow, not understanding the human dynamics of creativity in academic settings.

18 In 1958 the People's Republic of China established a top-secret nuclear and satellite R&D facility. At its peak 17,000 'researchers' worked there. The Soviet Union assisted China, but in 1960 it suspended its assistance. China tested its first device in 1964 (*Science*, 2015).

19 Kapur and Perry (2015) make an interesting comparison between India, a democracy since 1947, and China, a communist autocracy since 1949, in terms of educational quality. In most respects authoritarian China is the clear winner. Democratic politics and patronage in India have had profoundly negative effects on educational quality.

20 In 2013–2016, Tsinghua University was right behind MIT in production of the top one percent most highly cited papers in maths and computing. Tsinghua may overtake MIT in five years in this respect. In 2006–2009, Tsinghua was sixty-sixth in this ranking (*The Economist*, 2018c).

5. Governance: Why Does It Matter?

1 The Center for Mediterranean Integration (CMI) has devised a governance scorecard for universities in its region. Its most recent iteration concludes, "The preliminary findings of the second version of the UGSC (University Governance Score Card) show significant developments in tertiary education governance practices in comparison to the previous version, particularly in the areas of participation of stakeholders in decision-making, evidence-informed management, and formal mission- and goal-setting and monitoring. Yet, not much progress has been achieved under 'accountability,' which points to the need for increased attention to this policy area" (CMI, 2016: 23).

2 For private institutions, a crucial function of the endowment is to cover, in whole or in part, the costs of liquidating the university—meeting outstanding obligations, pension and tenure commitments, and so forth—in the event of bankruptcy. Public universities may rely on the resources of public authorities to backstop them.

3 An outstanding example is that of the Pohang University of Science and Technology in South Korea, founded by the private Pohang Steel Company in the 1980s and now ranked among the top thirty STEM universities in the world (Rhee, 2011).

6. Reform in Tight Places

1 The status quo and BAU are not the same. BAU refers to process, the prevailing way of doing things, while the status quo refers to a situation or a *rapport de forces*.

2 UNESCO (2009) finds evidence of some progress in the decade 1998 to 2008, but that progress was mainly quantitative, measured by the ratio of tertiary-level students per hundred thousand inhabitants and the absolute number of universities (see Chapter 1).

3   In 2011 I was an advisor on higher education to the Executive Affairs
     Council of Abu Dhabi. I recently reviewed the non-compete clauses and
     information restrictions in my contract. They are very restrictive and have a
     long time-horizon.

4   By way of example, see Dreisback (2017) on the introduction of e-govern-
     ment reforms in Tunisia, and Elmes (2016) on Tawfik Jelassi, who became
     minister of higher education and scientific research following the ouster of
     Ben Ali and who undertook a range of structural reforms in education.

5   They of course focus also on policies *after* they are made, such as removing
     long-standing consumer and fuel subsidies. From the MENA itself there
     are a few studies that seek to influence policymaking in its early stages.
     One is a diagnostic history of Turkish higher education (Barbalan, Ergüder,
     and Gürüz, 2008). Two of the authors are former university rectors, one
     running a policy institute and the other the head of the YÖK. They want
     to move from a bureaucratic mode to a more evaluative mode, and from a
     bureaucratic model to an entrepreneurial model. They see globalization as
     an opportunity not a threat. The other study, by Mahmood and Slimane
     (2018), prescribes ways to insulate public policy from capture by economic
     interests.

6   This paragraph is built on surmise and reading backward from results to
     causes.

7   Rahman (2015) got the ear of Pervez Musharraf, who had seized power
     in Pakistan: "As the Federal Minister of Science and Technology in 2001,
     I persuaded the government to increase the development budget for sci-
     ence by about 6,000 percent. The abolishing of the University Grants
     Commission and the establishment of the Higher Education Commission
     in 2002 as a powerful new national body on higher education that was
     headed by a person with the status of a Federal Minister and which
     reported directly to the Prime Minister of Pakistan marked a new chapter
     in the history of higher education in Pakistan." Mohammed Cherkaoui, one
     of Morocco's leading social scientists, lamented the misaligned incentive
     system and low research output in Morocco's higher education system and
     concluded that only the king could bludgeon through reforms to address
     the situation (interview, 2013).

8   Salmi (2002) lists major World Bank loans for higher education over
     the period 1990–2000. For a somewhat triumphalist study of reforms at
     Makerere University in Kampala, Uganda, see World Bank (1999).

9   Libya, Algeria, Syria, Spain, Turkey, Cyprus, and the Balkan states are *not*
     members of the CMI.

10   Ikram (2006: 96) shows that where you sit provides a very different perception of leverage. During the crisis of 1976–77 in Egypt, Minister of Planning Mahmood al-Imam saw the IFIs as providing Egypt with a button while expecting Egypt to come up with a coat to sew it on.

11   The most recent iterations in the chain of educational reform documents are Kingdom of Morocco (2015a; 2018) prepared by the Supreme Council of Education.

12   Most assessments find these councils as underperforming due mainly to the absenteeism of the non-university members.

13   See, http://projects.worldbank.org/P117838/
first-education-development-policy-loan?lang=en.

14   Mrabi (2013) shows that over the period 2007–2013 new hires in the civil service far outnumbered retirees: 128,986 new hires versus around 50,000 retirements. About 35 percent of all new hires were in education of all levels, which is to be expected for a sector in full expansion.

15   Article 5 of Morocco's 2011 constitution makes Amazigh an official national language.

16   Special recognition on this subject is owed to the Economic Research Forum and the several working papers authored by Ragui Assaad, Caroline Krafft, and other collaborators.

17   The unemployment rate in Jordan reached 18.7 percent in the fourth quarter of 2018. It was 24.5 percent among university graduates. Of the unemployed, 52 percent have high school degrees or above (al-Dibissiya, 2019).

18   Bishop (2011) notes that in advanced economies, early in the millennium, "35–40% of surveyed employers indicated that they had trouble finding qualified hires. The fields that had inadequate supply are all what universities purportedly produce: technicians, sales reps, skilled trades persons, engineers, management, ICT staff, etc."

19   Assaad and Krafft (2016a: 11) show that after age thirty-five, employment rates drop significantly. Assaad, Krafft, and Salehi-Isfahani (2018) show that waithood in Egypt and Jordan has declined to nine months and seven months, respectively.

20   RORE are typically reported as percentages. For example, a value of 5 percent implies that a worker with an additional year of schooling earns that much more than an otherwise identical worker who has one year less education.

21   The deliberate promotion of brain drain is not lost on the informed public. Mohammed Si Bashir (2018), an Algerian university professor, wrote about the phenomenon, noting the stifling of innovation in Algeria. He cited three

Algerian scientists who had achieved fame abroad, including Elias Zerhouni, who became the head of the National Institute of Health in the United States.

22 See http://www.kafd.jo/en/program/darb. I am grateful to Rasha Faek for alerting me to DARB.

23 In Egypt, 80 percent of tertiary graduates are in the humanities/social sciences, while in South Korea and Iran it is more like 40 percent. Tunisia is around 50 percent (Melonio and Mezouaghi, 2015).

24 The EBRD MENA enterprise survey was conducted in 2013 and 2014 in eight middle-income economies in the region: Djibouti, Egypt, Jordan, Lebanon, Morocco, Tunisia, the West Bank and Gaza, and Yemen. Surveyed firms employed at least five employees, operating in manufacturing or service sectors. Six thousand firms were surveyed, while 100-percent publicly owned firms were excluded.

25 In Egypt the tourism sector employs four million people, making it one of the country's largest employment sectors (Alrawi and Kamel, 2019).

26 See http://www.aroqa.org. It was joined by the Arab Network for Quality Assurance in Higher Education. Its membership is so far restricted to Kuwait, Qatar, Sudan, Yemen, and Palestine.

27 Regional accreditation is likely to be a tough sell. Public universities resist accreditation even by domestic agencies that are likely to be lenient. Private institutions are more likely to seek accreditation abroad, especially in the United States (Lindsey, 2011a).

28 The Qatar Foundation made grants to institutions outside Qatar contingent on joint research with Qatar University or other institutions in Qatar's Education City.

7. Innovation and Critical Linkages

1 In March 2018, Mark Zuckerberg was confronted with the data breach of Cambridge Analytica and its use of Facebook personal data to influence, allegedly, the 2016 US elections. Zuckerberg told CNN that he had never imagined in 2004, when Facebook was starting up, that interference in elections was a charge he might face in twelve years' time . . . or ever. If the originator of the innovation can't anticipate its fallout, who can?

2 Another dynamic Moroccan university leader is Omar Halli, president of Agadir University (80,000 students). He is trying to promote and categorize applied research, such as exploring the medicinal properties of local natural products like argan oil (see Plackett, 2014). Cairo University's president, Mohamed Elkosht, has a similar vision, coupled with combining scientific method with Islamic values (Wirtschafter, 2017).

3   Clayton Christensen and his co-authors (2008: 26) invoke the Harvard psychologist Howard Gardner, who identified eight basic learning modes: linguistic, logical-mathematic, spatial, bodily-kinesthetic, musical, interpersonal, intrapersonal, and naturalist.

4   'Flipped classroom' is an instructional strategy and a type of blended learning that reverses the traditional learning environment by delivering instructional content, often online, outside the classroom. It moves activities, including those that may have traditionally been considered homework, into the classroom. In a flipped classroom, students watch online lectures, collaborate in online discussions, or carry out research at home and engage in concepts in the classroom with the guidance of a mentor.

5   It may be that other reforms and innovations in higher education will be as important as 'soft skills.' They involve the negative effects of social media and their supporting technology. Faculty encounter the phenomenon of 'digital distraction,' where capturing a student's attention is a mountainous challenge. There are also the emotional pathologies associated with social media of isolation and loneliness that fuel digital distraction and impede the learning process, however it is designed.

6   University of California Davis, the American Association of Collegiate Registrars and Admissions Officers, and AUB are helping to develop a digital platform called the Article 26 Backpack, targeted at school-age Syrian refugees. It enables them to constitute and store personal files and evidence of academic credentials that can be shared with universities (see Watenpaugh, 2018). The Ford Foundation and Open Society Foundation have supported the project, named after Article 26 of the 1948 Universal Declaration of Human Rights.

7   In this subsection I have relied on Galal and Kanaan (2010), Jaramillo and Melonio (2011), and Salmi and Hauptman (2011).

8   Bond (Bond et al., 2014?), looking ahead optimistically after 2011, sees Egypt's R&D heading in these directions, but with the ICT sector being the most dynamic.

9   I list here some examples of what might be called an R&D virtuous circle. Norwick Mills, a small, specialized textiles plant in New Hampshire, is joining with the US Department of Defense and research universities, including MIT, and fifty other companies in a $320 million project to produce smart textiles, using blends of advanced synthetic materials and embedded with sensors to make the battlefield uniforms of the future (Lohr, 2016). The German industrial giant BASF invests $2.2 billion in R&D annually and employs about ten thousand in research. It generates about a thousand patents a year. It works with six hundred universities, research firms, and companies and has its own venture

capital company (*The Economist*, 2016a). Alexandria University, the second-largest (after Cairo University) and third-oldest (after al-Azhar University and Cairo University) higher education institution in Egypt, is in an administrative district with the same name that is home to 40 percent of Egypt's industries. It functions as a chief research hotbed for local companies, which often do not have their own R&D operations (Lynch, 2013).

10　Note that my reasoning here reflects the trap mentioned at the outset of this chapter, that we read back from results to find plausible causes, and that if crisis is assumed to be a driver of change, then all changes are by definition the result of crisis.

11　It is significant that one of Egypt's most prominent private sector businessmen, Samih Sawiris, made a gift of 100 million Egyptian pounds to Zewail City (Wikipedia).

12　Salmi (2002: 39) early on noted the presumed cost-saving that online education could deliver. Open University UK spent about a third of what a conventional British university would expend to educate a graduate.

13　There are forty-six partners in the initiative, including the British Council, Cisco Systems, Computer Associates, Corning Cable Systems, Dell, Fastlink, France Telecom, Hewlett Packard, Intel, the Krach Family Foundation, Microsoft, the Jordanian Ministry of Education, the Jordanian Ministry of ICT, RazorView, USAID, the US–Middle East Partnership Initiative, and the WEF.

14　Kuwait, Lebanon, Jordan, Saudi Arabia, Egypt, Bahrain, Oman, and Sudan. I am grateful to Imad Baalbaki, Arab Open University board member, for background information on the university (email, 2017).

15　University President Miraoui did say to me that unless Moroccan public universities became 'smart' universities they would be displaced by the private sector, with negative consequences for social equity.

16　By 2017 KUSTAR merged with the Masdar Institute and the Petroleum Institute, both of Abu Dhabi, to make it one of the three top research universities in the Arab World.

17　See https://www.darpa.mil.

8. Feeding the Beast: Financing Tertiary Education

1　Cairo University's president, Gaber Gad Nasser, told me that the SCU played no significant role in financial planning (interview, 2014).

2　In Morocco, two directions in the Ministry of Finance can make life miserable for university leaders: the *Direction des Etablissements* and the *Direction du Budget*. For example, they must sign off on any contract work with third parties or on the importation of lab equipment and materials (Mrabi, 2013).

3   In 2006, MVUA had 18,000 students *en licence* (bachelor's degree), of whom 4,634 graduated. If enrollments were evenly spread over three years, class size should be 6,000. One can impute a dropout rate of 1,366 spread over three years but probably front-loaded (Kingdom of Morocco, 2007).

4   The growth of private, often for-profit institutions means that dropouts from the public system can usually find a home. But their new home will charge them significant tuition, so those who continue their education are from the wealthier strata of society.

5   A faculty member at Cairo University commented, "Annual salaries are only a thing in the US and Jane Austen."

6   TÜBITAK, under the AKP government since 2002, has been accused of deliberately discouraging any research having to do with the theory of evolution. It is inevitable that such funds will reflect the political outlook of the authorities that control them.

7   In 2011 when I was working in Abu Dhabi, I heard from a Gulf national student that one time in his student career, an expatriate Arab teacher entered the classroom at the beginning of the semester, wrote his telephone number on the blackboard, and read a newspaper for the rest of the class session. The message was clear: call this number for private lessons.

8   As we examined further in Chapter 3, tutoring centers became embroiled in Turkish politics. Fethullah Gülen, who became a bitter rival of Recep Tayyip Erdoğan, and the Gülenist movement, owned thousands of tutoring centers *(ders hane)*. After the attempted coup of the summer of 2016, Erdoğan accused them of fomenting political dissidence and began to shut them down.

9   Sayed Obaied in Egypt launched Nafham (We Understand) in 2012. It targets Egypt, Saudi Arabia, Algeria, and Syria and has 500,000 active users. It has a staff of about twenty-five and relies on educational videos that it develops (Farahat, 2015). One should expect many variants on this theme.

10 I have no direct evidence that parallel courses in the Arab world were leveraged by the World Bank.

11 By comparison, in 2008 the operating budget of AUB was about $225 million for some seven thousand students and also covering a hospital with four hundred beds.

12 Cairo, Ain Shams, and Alexandria Universities all enjoy the advantages of location and reputation. The other public universities cannot yet hope to rival them.

13 ElBaradei graduated from the Law Faculty of Cairo University in 1962. His father was also a lawyer and at one time president of the Egyptian Bar Association.

14 Latin America once again may signal where the MENA is headed. In the early 1990s Argentina authorized public universities to charge tuition. Tuition was introduced at UNAM in Mexico in 1999, instigating strikes (De Moura Castro and Levy, 2000: 74).

15 In Chapter 2 I reviewed some of the seminal founding figures in Arab higher education, like Ahmad Lutfi al-Sayyid and Wafiq Said. İhsan Doğramacı (1915–2010) was of equal stature. His father had been an Ottoman governor in what is today northern Iraq. Doğramacı was born and raised in Erbil and attended the International College in Beirut. He had already had a noted career in medicine, business, and higher education when, in 1981, he was made the founding president of the YÖK. He occupied the presidency until 1992. The YÖK was in part an instrument of the military regime that came to power by coup in 1980 and supervised purges of leftists in Turkish academia (see Chapter 3). He also chaired the board of trustees of the WHO.

16 In 2008, then French president Nicolas Sarkozy introduced legislation named Travail, Emploi, Pouvoir d'Achat (TEPA) that included tax exemptions of up to 60 percent on gifts to foundations. The *grandes écoles*, elite professional schools like the ENA, Polytechnique, and Hautes Etudes Commerciales (HEC) began fundraising efforts to build endowments that could guarantee an annual source of revenue. The *grandes écoles* relied on their networks of successful graduates, many of whom had gone on to senior positions in large public and private enterprises. Giving in support of financial aid was a powerful draw. Public universities tried to emulate the *grandes écoles* but did not have the same level of alumni loyalty and ran into the basic reaction, "I paid my taxes which support the universities, that is enough." For that reason, philanthropy and endowments have remained financially marginal to most French universities. For example, Université Paris-Dauphiné raised only 10 million euros in ten years (De Triornot, 2018).

17 In their sample of nine thousand Arab youth, Gertel and Hexel (2018: 251–53) found that 53 to 90 percent, according to the country, supported greater state action in their everyday lives and viewed privatization of education negatively.

18 Khalil Hindi, former president of Birzeit, made just such a recommendation for Palestinian universities (interview, 2016).

9. Living in the Beast: Neither Ivory nor a Tower

1 By way of comparison, Charles Eliot became president of Harvard in 1869 at the age of thirty-five and retired in 1909. In the region, the founding president of the SPC, which became AUB, was Daniel Bliss in 1862. He stepped down in 1902.

2　Azmi Mahafzah obtained his MD in 1977 from Damascus University and earned his PhD in microbiology and immunology in 1984 from AUB. He then joined the Faculty of Medicine of Jordan University as an assistant professor of microbiology and immunology before pursuing postdoctoral training in virology at Yale University's Medical School. Mahafzah has been working as a faculty member at Jordan University since 1984, during which period he has served as the chairman of the Department of Pathology, Microbiology, and Forensic Medicine, the director of the Department of Laboratory Medicine at the Jordan University Hospital, the vice dean of the Faculty of Medicine, and the dean of the Faculty of Medicine since October 28, 2010. Mahafzah is a member of several scientific societies and committees at the national and regional levels. His research interests include diagnosis of infectious diseases, nosocomial infections, and the epidemiology of infectious diseases.

3　Contrast a professor's salary with that of a police officer. In 2013 a police commander earned $90 per month and a police lieutenant colonel $141 (Aclimandos, 2016: 183). At the public steel plant, Helwan Iron and Steel, the average monthly wage in 2013 was about $1,100, more or less the equivalent of a full professor's salary (Kamil, 2014). In this comparison, the aggrieved party is surely the police officer.

4　All such estimates are perilous. At AUB in the early 2000s a number of faculty members earned over $100,000, and clinical medical faculty could earn far more, although they had to generate most of their salary from patient fees.

5　The flagships, as we have noted elsewhere, may be living on borrowed time. The Times Higher Education 2019 rankings for the Arab world show AUB dropping to number six, MVU falling behind CAU, Jordan University of Science and Technology coming ahead of Jordan University, and Suez Canal, Benha, and others ahead of Cairo and Alexandria Universities.

6　These three cases were extracted from applications for research fellowships awarded by AFESD.

7　My reaction to this critique was to share my interlocutor's dismay, but then I thought, is this system so bad? Only those who are really committed to research will do it. This raises the odds in favor of original research and avoids reams of pro forma rubbish.

8　Boughazala et al. (2016: 14) note that Tunisia, like Egypt, handles academic promotions at the national rather than the university level.

Conclusion: Gradual or Disruptive Change?

1　Inter alia, Arum and Roksa (2011), Ginsberg (2011), and Rawlings (2014).

2　In my study of public enterprise in Egypt, India, Mexico, and Turkey, I found that Egypt adhered more closely to a Weberian meritocracy in its recruitment and promotion of senior management than the other three. Training, experience, and performance determined one's professional status. The Nasserist educational system must surely have had a role in this (Waterbury, 1993). In contrast, Assaad, Krafft, and Salehi-Isfahani (2018: 970) conclude that "access to formal jobs in Egypt is nepotistic."

3　Pallas et al. (2017: 1) refer to this as "pedagogical content knowledge."

4　Such a system might make tenure obsolete, but if it persists then the old rule that only those of equal or superior rank may vote in tenure cases should hold.

5　State educational funding is not only structural (aging populations) but also cyclical. The crash of 2008 battered finances in many US states, but beginning around 2015, several states significantly increased spending on higher education.

6　Christensen anticipates resistance to *any* reform or innovation from change-resistant faculty or entrenched teacher unions, but he does not see the political system itself as a problem.

7　It is worth noting that in the United States, with its bedrock allegiance to private markets, nearly 80 percent of all enrollments in two-year and four-year institutions are in public IHLs (AAAS, 2017: 2).

8　As usual, the GCC must be treated separately. Many of its universities are quasi-public, like the American University of Sharjah or NYU Abu Dhabi. Some are fully public like Al Ain University, Qatar University, and the University of Sharjah. For the foreseeable future the GCC will have the resources to maintain high-quality, public flagship universities.

9　I put the puzzle to Daniel Levy, who commented, "You suggest . . . that authoritarian regimes don't have much to fear from private higher education. That too is basically correct. It's certainly true of the non-elite bulk. In Latin America, the issue of the boundaries of permissible opposition to authoritarian rule arose more from freestanding private research centers, which I thus made the topic of my 1996 *Building the Third Sector*. Whether in general among universities authoritarian regimes . . . have had more to fear from private universities or public universities is an open question, I'd guess with varied answers by setting" (email, 2018).

References

Not all of these references are cited in the text, but all of them have contributed to my understanding of the questions covered in this book.

AAAS (American Academy of Arts and Sciences). 2017. *The Future of Undergraduate Education*. Cambridge, MA: Commission on the Future of Undergraduate Education.

_____. 2016. *Public Research Universities: Understanding the Financial Model*. Cambridge, MA: Lincoln Project.

_____. 2015. *Public Research Universities: Changes in State Funding*. Cambridge, MA: Lincoln Project.

'Abbas, Ra'uf. 2008. "Qadiyyat istiqlal al-jami'at." In *al-Jami'a al-misriya wa-l-mujtama': mi'at 'am min al-nidal al-jami'i, 1908–2008*, edited by Ra'uf 'Abbas, 75–105. Cairo: Jama'at al-'Amal min Ajl Istiqlal al-Jami'a (9 Maris).

Abd El-Galil, Tarek. 2018. "Rising Fees Make Students Quit Master's Degrees in Egypt." *Al-Fanar Media*, March 27.

_____. 2017a. "Egyptian Universities See Boom in Foreign Students." *Al-Fanar Media*, February 7.

_____. 2017b. "Participation in Student Activities Drops in Egypt." *Al-Fanar Media*, May 23.

_____. 2017c. "Egypt Plans Radical Change in Measuring High-School Success." *Al-Fanar Media*, August 22.

_____. 2015. "Egyptian Finance Ministry Gives Professors a Pay Cut." *Al-Fanar Media*, November 9.

Abd al-Razzaq, Adnan. 2018. "Tadahwur al-jami'at al-suriya." *Al-Araby Al-Jadeed*, August 3.

Abdalla, Ahmed. 1985. *The Student Movement and National Politics in Egypt, 1923–1973*. London: Al Saqi Books.

Abdel Salam, Mohamed. 2017. "In Egypt, Harsh Measures against Academic Freedom Persist." *Al-Fanar Media*, May 29.

Abdessalam, Taher. 2010. "Financing Higher Education in Tunisia." In *Financing Higher Education in Arab Countries*, edited by Ahmed Galal and Taher Kanaan, 117–38. Economic Research Forum Policy Research Report, no. 34.

_____. 1997. *Biens publics avec exclusion: allocations efficaces, production décentralisée*. Monographies d'Econométrie. Paris: CNRS éditions.

Abdul Nabi, Msaddak. 2015. "Why Tunisia Is the Top Supplier of Students to the Islamic State." *Al-Fanar Media*, July 8.

Abe, Nicola. 2012. "Open Sesame: Joint Regional Project Creates Extraordinary New Science Research Hub." *Egypt Independent*, December 17.

Abou-Setta, Amal. 2015. "Expensive Education Equals Social Injustice." *Al-Fanar Media*, February 10.

_____. 2014. "In Egypt, the Failure of Privatizing Education." *Al-Fanar Media*, June 2.

Abu Farha, Saba. 2015. "Jordanian Higher Education Flunks a National Test." *Al-Fanar Media*, February 20.

Abul-Ghar, Mohammed. 2005. "Ma bayn al-khutut al-hamra': al-hurriyat al-akadimiya fi al-jami'at al-misriya." *Weghat nazar* 7 (80).

Abu-Orabi, Sultan T. 2014. "Scientific Research and Higher Education in the Arab World." PowerPoint presentation.

Aclimandos, Tewfiq. 2016. "Between Collapse and Professionalism: Police Reform in Egypt." In *Building the Rule of Law in the Arab World*, edited by Eva Bellin and Heidi Lane, 173–88. Boulder, CO: Lynne Reinner.

ACRPS (Arab Center for Research and Policy Studies). 2018. *Siyar 'ashar jami'at hukumiya 'arabiya*, prepared by Adnan El-Amine. Beirut: Arab Center for Research and Policy Studies.

Adib, Muhammad Jawad. 2014. "The Paradox of Higher Education in Iran." *AI Monitor*, Iran Pulse, February 20.

Adib-Moghaddam, Arshin. 2016. "World Insight: Iran after the

Sanctions, And What It Means for Higher Education." Times Higher Education World University Rankings, January 22.

Al Adwan, Mustafa. 2013. "Higher Education Situation in the Arab World: Jordan as an Example." PowerPoint presentation.

Ahmed, Adamu A. 2019. "The New Generation of Indigenous Private Universities." *University World News*, June 29.

Ait Mous, Fadma, and Driss Ksikes. 2014. *Le métier d'intellectuel: Dialogues avec quinze penseurs du Maroc*. Casablanca: Les Presses de l'Université Citoyenne.

Akrawi, Matta. 1979. "Changing Patterns of Higher Education in the Middle East." In *The Liberal Arts and the Future of Higher Education in the Middle East*, 39–67. Beirut: American University of Beirut Press.

Alami, Aida. 2013. "Morocco's King Criticizes the Country's Education." *Al-Fanar Media*, August 28.

Alashloo, Fariborz, Pavel Castka, and John Sharp. 2005. "Towards Understanding the Impeders of Strategy Implementation in Higher Education (HE): A Case of HE Institutes in Iran." *Quality Assurance in Education* 13 (2): 132–47.

Alayan, Aya. 2014. "Why Aren't Jordanian Children in School?" *Al-Fanar Media*, December 3.

Alberts, Bruce. 2011a. "The New Egypt." Editorial, *Science* 332, no. 6029 (29 April): 513.

_____. 2011b. "Turkey and Science Academies." Editorial, *Science* 333, no. 6051 (30 September): 1801.

'Allam, Muna. 2013. "Misr: waqa'i' ihmal al-ta'lim al-jami'i wa-l-bahth al-'ilmi." *al-Safir*, October 31.

Alrawi, Mustafa, and Deena Kamel. 2019. "Egypt Sees Tourism Sector Offering a Job for Every Household." *The National*, December 4.

Altbach, Philip G. 2011. "The Past, Present, and Future of the Research University." In *The Road to Academic Excellence: The Making of World-class Research Universities*, edited by Philip Altbach and Jamil Salmi, 11–32. Washington, DC: World Bank.

_____. 2007. "Academic Freedom in a Global Context: 21st Century Challenges." *NEA Almanac of Higher Education*, 49–57, http://www.nea.org/assets/img/PubAlmanac/ALM_07_05.pdf

Altbach, Philip G., and Jamil Salmi, eds. 2011. *The Road to Academic Excellence: The Making of World-class Research Universities*. Washington, DC: World Bank.

Amin, Galal. 2013. *Whatever Happened to the Egyptian Revolution?* Translated by Jonathan Wright. Cairo: American University in Cairo Press.

Amin, Magdi, Ragui Assaad, Nazar al-Baharna, Kemal Dervis, Raj M. Desai, Navtej S. Dhillon, Ahmed Galal, Hafez Ghanem, Carol Graham, and Daniel Kaufmann. 2012. *After the Spring: Economic Transitions in the Arab World*. Oxford: Oxford University Press.

El-Amine, Adnan. 2018. "al-Jami'at al-lubnaniya taht wat'a: al-tahawwulat al-siyasiya." In *Siyar 'ashar jami'at hukumiya 'arabiya*, prepared by Adnan El-Amine, 147–206. Beirut: Arab Center for Research and Policy Studies.

———. 2017. "Wasawis al-bahth al-tarbawi fi al-jami'at al-'arabiya." In *al-Jami'at wa-l-bahth al-'ilmi fi al-'alam al-'arabi*, coordinated by Murad Diani, 255–88. Beirut: Arab Center for Research and Policy Studies.

———. 2014. "al-Mas'uliya al-madaniya li-l-jami'a." *Majallat al-difa' al-watani*, no. 90, 54–55.

———. 2013. "Jami'at al-qarya, jami'at al jama'a." *al-Mudun*, April 2.

———. 2009a. *Financing and Administrative Autonomy (Istiqlaliya) in Higher Education*. Beirut: Arab Thought Foundation. (in Arabic)

———. 2009b. "Orbits of Arab Universities." *al-Mudun*. (in Arabic)

———. 1997a. "al-Hayakil al-tanzimiya li-l-jami'at." In *al-Ta'lim al-'ali fi Lubnan*, edited by Adnan El-Amine, 167–209. Beirut: al-Hay'a al-Lubnaniya li-l-'Ulum al-Tarbawiya.

———. 1997b. "Qadaya al-ta'lim al-'ali fi Lubnan wa-afaqihi." In *al-Ta'lim al-'ali fi Lubnan*, edited by Adnan El-Amine, 559–638. Beirut: al-Hay'a al-Lubnaniya li-l-'Ulum al-Tarbawiya.

———, ed. 1997c. *al-Ta'lim al-'ali fi Lubnan*. Beirut: al-Hay'a al-Lubnaniya li-l-'Ulum al-Tarbawiya.

El-Amine, Adnan, Ahmed Baydoun, Antoine Haddad, Melhem Shaoul, and Khalil Nour Eddine. 1999. *Qadaya al-jami'a al-lubnaniya wa-islahiha*. Beirut: al-Hay'a al-Lubnaniya li-l-'Ulum al-Tarbawiya.

El-Amine, Adnan, and Muhammad Faour. 1998. *al-Tullab al-jami'iyyun fi Lubnan wa ittijahatuhum: irth al-inqisamat*. Beirut: al-Hay'a al-Lubnaniya li-l-'Ulum al-Tarbawiya. (in Arabic; English and French summaries of chapters).

Anderson, Lisa. 2012. "Too Much Information? Political Science, the University, and the Public Sphere." *Perspectives on Politics* 10 (2): 385–96.

Anomaly, Jonathan. 2018. "Public Goods and Education." In *Philosophy and Public Policy*, edited by Andrew I. Cohen, 105–20. London: Rowman and Littlefield.

El-Araby, Ashraf. 2010. "Comparative Assessment of Higher Education Financing in Six Arab Countries." In *Financing Higher Education in Arab Countries*, edited by Ahmed Galal and Taher Kanaan, 1–10. Economic Research Forum Policy Research Report, no. 34.

Al-Araby Al-Jadeed. 2018. "Misr: istibdal al-ta'yin fi al-hukuma bi-nizam ta'aqudat mu'aqqat." November 4.

Arum, Richard, and Josipa Roksa. 2011. *Academically Adrift: Limited Learning on College Campuses.* Chicago, IL: University of Chicago Press.

Ashdown, Nick. 2016. "Turkish Teachers Missing as School Year Begins." *The Media Line*, September 27, https://themedialine.org/news/turkish-teachers-missing-school-year-begins/

Ashour, Omar. 2012. "From Bad Cop to Good Cop: The Challenges of Security Sector Reform in Egypt." Brookings Doha Center–Stanford Project on Arab Transitions, Paper Series No. 3.

Assaad, Ragui. 1997. "The Effects of Public Sector Hiring and Compensation Policies on the Egyptian Labor Market." *World Bank Economic Review* 11 (1): 85–118.

Assaad, Ragui, and Ghada Barsoum. 2009. "Rising Expectations and Diminishing Opportunities for Egypt's Youth." In *Generation in Waiting: The Unfulfilled Promise of Young People in the Middle East*, edited by Navtej Dhillon and Tarik Yousef, 67–94. Washington, DC: Brookings Institution Press.

Assaad, Ragui, Samir Ghazouani, and Caroline Krafft. 2017. "The Composition of Labor Supply and Unemployment in Tunisia." Economic Research Forum Working Paper, no. 1150.

Assaad, Ragui, and Caroline Krafft. 2016a. "Labor Market Dynamics and Youth Unemployment in the Middle East and North Africa: Evidence from Egypt, Jordan and Tunisia." Economic Research Forum Working Paper, no. 993.

———. 2016b. "Comparative Analysis of Higher Education Processes in Egypt, Jordan and Tunisia: An Examination of Pedagogy, Accountability and Perceptions of Quality." Economic Research Forum Working Paper, no. 1069.

Assaad, Ragui, Caroline Krafft, and Djavad Salehi-Isfahani. 2018. "Does the Type of Higher Education Affect Labor Market Outcomes? Evidence from Egypt and Jordan." *Higher Education* 75 (6): 945–95.

Assaad, Ragui, Caroline Krafft, and Colette Salemi. 2019. "Socioeconomic Status and the Changing Nature of School-to-Work Transitions in Egypt, Jordan and Tunisia." Economic Research Forum Working Paper, no. 1287, February.

Assaad, Ragui, Caroline Krafft, and Shaimaa Yassin. 2018. "Job Creation or Labor Absorption? An Analysis of Private Sector Job Growth in Egypt." Economic Research Forum Working Paper, no. 1237, October.

Association for Freedom of Thought and Expression. 2010. "Hukm al-Mahkama al-Idariya al-'Ulya fi qadiyyat al-haras al-jami'i", http://www.afteegypt.org/academic_freedom/2010/10/26/177-afteegypt.html

Assouad, Lydia. 2018. "Is the Middle East the World's Most Unequal Region?" Economic Research Forum Policy Portal, March 27.

Aubin, Eugène. 1906. *Morocco of To-day*. London: J.M. Dent & Co.

Ayan, Robert. 2010. "Higher Education Creates Higher Expectations in Jordan: Combating the Loss of the Kingdom's Intellectual Wealth." In *Innovation through Education: Building the Knowledge Economy in the Middle East*, edited by Daniel Obst and Daniel Kirk, 27–42. New York: International Institute of Education and American Institute for Foreign Study.

al-Azmeh, Aziz. 2003. *Constantine Zurayk: 'Arabiyyun li-l-qarn al-'ishrin*. Beirut: Mu'assasat al-Dirasat al-Filastiniya.

Badran, Adnan. 2017. "Indicators of Institutional and Program Ranking of Universities in the Arab Region." Arab Academy of Sciences conference, "Major Challenges Facing Higher Education in the Arab World: Quality Assurance and Relevance," Beirut, November 10–11. Paper abstract.

El Baggari, Yasmine. 2013. "Implications of Morocco's Bifurcated Educational System." *Jadaliyya*, December 2.

Balán, Jorge, ed. 2013. *Latin America's New Knowledge Economy: Higher Education, Government and International Collaboration*. New York: International Institute of Education and American Institute for Foreign Study.

Bali, Maha. 2014. "Another Step Forward for Arab MOOCs." *Al-Fanar Media*, February 23.

Bannayan, Haif, Juliana Guaqueta, Osama Obeidat, Harry Anthony Patrinos, and Emilio Porta. 2012. "The Jordan Education Initiative: A Multi-stakeholder Partnership Model to Support Education Reform." World Bank Human Development Network Education Team Policy Research Working Paper 6079.

El Baradei, Mona. 2010. "Access, Equity and Competitiveness: The Case of Higher Education in Egypt." In *Towards an Arab Higher Education Space: International Challenges and Societal Responsibilities*, edited by Bechir Lamine, 159–85. Cairo: Arab Regional Conference on Higher Education.

Barakat, Halim. 1977. *Lebanon in Strife: Student Preludes to Civil War*. Austin, TX: University of Texas Press.

Barakat, Sultan, and Sansom Milton. 2015. "Houses of Wisdom Matter: The Responsibility to Protect and Rebuild Higher Education in the Arab World." Brookings Doha Center Policy Briefing, July.

Barbalan, Andris, Üstün Ergüder, and Kemal Gürüz. 2008. *Higher Education in Turkey: Institutional Autonomy and Responsibility in a Modernising Society— Policy Recommendations in a Historical Perspective*. Bologna: Observatory for Fundamental University Values and Rights, Bononia University Press.

Barsoum, Ghada. 2012. "No Jobs and Bad Jobs." *Cairo Review*, November 18.

Bashshur, Munir. 2004. *Higher Education in the Arab States*. Beirut: UNESCO Regional Bureau.

_____. 1997. "al-Ta'lim al-'ali fi Lubnan fi al-masar al-tarikhi." In *al-Ta'lim al-'ali fi Lubnan*, edited by Adnan El-Amine, 15–94. Beirut: al-Hay'a al-Lubnaniya li-l-'Ulum al-Tarbawiya.

Basken, Paul. 2016. "Election Casts Spotlight on an Unusual For-profit with Global Ambitions." *Chronicle of Higher Education*, September 23.

Bass, Randy. 2012. "Disrupting Ourselves: The Problem of Learning in Higher Education." *EDUCAUSE Review* 47 (2): 1–14.

Batatu, Hanna. 1999. *Syria's Peasantry: The Descendants of Its Lesser Rural Notables and Its Politics*. Princeton, NJ: Princeton University Press.

Baum, Sandy, and Michael McPherson. 2011. "Is Education a Public Good or a Private Good?" *Chronicle of Higher Education*, January 18.

Belghazi, Taieb, ed. 1997. *The Idea of the University*. Rabat: Faculty of Letters and Human Sciences, University Mohammed V Agdal.

Bellin, Eva, and Heidi Lane, eds. 2016. *Building the Rule of Law in the Arab World*. Boulder, CO: Lynne Reinner.

Bellin, William. 2015. *The Islamic Republic of Iran: Its Educational System and Methods of Evaluation*. Milwaukee, WI: Educational Credentials Evaluators.

Ben Hafaiedh, Abdel Wahab. 2010. "On Building an Academic Space for the Arab Region: The Possible, the Probable and the Hoped For." In *Towards an Arab Higher Education Space: International Challenges and Societal Responsibilities*, edited by Bechir Lamine, 93–111. Cairo: Arab Regional Conference on Higher Education.

Ben Hamida, Nadia. 2012. "Is Over-education a Temporary Phenomenon? The Case of Tunisian Higher Education Graduates." Paper presented at Workshop on the Social-economic Situation of Middle East Youth on the Eve of the Arab Spring, held by Silatech and the Middle East Youth Initiative at the American University of Beirut, Beirut, December 8–9.

Benjelloun, Wail. 2010?. "Training Tomorrow's Leaders Today: Strategic Plan of Mohammed V University Agdal 2011–14." Unpublished paper, Rabat.

_____. 2008. "The Knowledge-based Economy: Challenges for the Moroccan University." *Prospectives Universitaires*, no. 1, 177–81.

_____. 1997. "Quality in Higher Education." In *The Idea of the University*, edited by Taieb Belghazi, 115–21. Rabat: Faculty of Letters and Human Sciences, University Mohammed V Agdal.

Berdahl, Robert. 1983. "Co-ordinating Structures: The UGC and US State Coordinating Agencies." In *The Structure and Governance of Higher Education*, edited by Michael Shattock, 68–107. Surrey, UK: Society for Research into Higher Education.

Bergquist, Kyle, Carsten Fink, and Julio Raffo. 2017. "Identifying and Ranking the World's Largest Clusters of Inventive Activity." In *Global Innovation Index*. Fontainebleau: INSEAD.

Bhandari, Rajika, and Adnan El-Amine. 2011. *Classifying Higher Education Institutions in the Middle East and North Africa: A Pilot Study*. New York: Institute for International Education.

Bhattacharjee, Yudhijit. 2012. "Prominent Turkish Academic Who Advocated Secular Reforms Arrested." *Science* 337, no. 6090 (July 3): 23.

_____. 2011. "Saudi Universities Offer Cash in Exchange for Academic Prestige." *Science* 334, no. 6061 (December 7): 1344–45.

Bhatti, Jabeen, and Janelle Dumalaon. 2014. "A Survey of Public University Professors' Pay." *Al-Fanar Media*, January 11.

Bildu Ali, Ismail. 2013. "The Muslim Brethren in the Service of the Palace." *Zaman* (Morocco), October, 6–16.

Birdsall, Nancy. 1999. "Putting Education to Work in Egypt." *Carnegie Endowment for International Peace*, August 25.

Birgenau, Robert. 2015. "The Lincoln Project: Excellence and Access in Public Higher Education." *Bulletin of the American Academy of Arts and Sciences*, Winter, 26–28.

Bishai, Linda. 2008. "Sudanese Universities as Sites of Social Transformation." United States Institute of Peace Special Report 203.

Bishop, Matthew. 2011. "The Great Mismatch." Special Report: The Future of Jobs, *The Economist*, September 10.

Bitar, Khalil. 2013. "The Development of a Scientific Culture in the Arab/Islamic World." Unpublished manuscript.

Blanchard, Kathryn. 2016. "Trigger Warnings: Not the Greatest Threat to Higher Education." *Chronicle of Higher Education*, January 8.

Blaydes, Lisa. 2018. *State of Repression: Iraq under Saddam Hussein*. Princeton, NJ: Princeton University Press.

Blum, Patrick. 2014. "In Britain, Universities Are Turning to Capital Markets." *New York Times*, May 26.

Boehnke, Kevin. 2016. "Selling Out Science?" *Science* 354, no. 6314 (November 17): 934.

Bohannon John. 2013. "Grim Day for Turkish Science as Six Academics Get Long Prison Terms." 2013. *Science* 341, no. 6146 (August 9): 603–604.

Bok, Derek. 2017. "The Crisis of Civic Education." *Chronicle of Higher Education*, October 1.

_____. 2013. "The Ambiguous Role of Money in Higher Education." *Chronicle of Higher Education*, August 12.

Boland, Colleen. 2012. "Where They Are Now: Higher Education in Today's Iraq." *Your Middle East*, October 12.

Bollag, Burton. 2016. "Turkish Crackdown on Dissent Muzzles Professors." *Al-Fanar Media*, March 23.

Bond, Michael, Heba Maram, Asmaa Soliman, and Riham Khattab. 2014?. *Science and Innovation in Egypt*. London: British Council, International Development Research Centre, Organization of Islamic Countries, Nature, Qatar Foundation, Biblioteca Alexandrina, and the Royal Society.

Bou Hassan, Ahmad. 1997. "Questions around the Moroccan University: The University and the State." In *The Idea of the University*, edited by Taieb Belghazi, 13–24. Rabat: Faculty of Letters and Human Sciences, University Mohammed V Agdal. (in Arabic)

Boudarbat, Brahim, and Aziz Ajbilou. 2009. "Moroccan Youth in an Era of Volatile Growth, Urbanization and Poverty." In *Generation in Waiting: The Unfulfilled Promise of Young People in the Middle East*, edited by Navtej Dhillon and Tarik Yousef, 166–88. Washington, DC: Brookings Institution Press.

Boughazala, Mongi, Samir Ghazouani, and Abdelwahab Ben Hafaidh. 2016. "Aligning Incentives for Reforming Higher Education in Tunisia." Economic Research Forum Working Paper, no. 1031.

Bougroum, Mohammed, and Aomar Ibourk. 2010. "Financing Higher Education in Morocco." In *Financing Higher Education in Arab Countries*, edited by Ahmed Galal and Taher Kanaan, 86–102. Economic Research Forum Policy Research Report, no. 34.

Bourdieu, Pierre, and Jean-Claude Passeron. 1970. *La reproduction: Éléments pour une théorie du système d'enseignement*. Paris: Éditions de Minuit.

Bourguignon, François, and Thierry Verdier. 2000. "Oligarchy, Democracy, Inequality and Growth." *Journal of Development Economics*, no. 62, 285–313.

Bourqia, Rahma. 2011. *Vers une sociologie de l'université Marocaine*. Rabat: Conseil Supérieur de l'Education.

Bowen, William. 2013. *Higher Education in the Digital Age*. Princeton, NJ: Princeton University Press.

Bowen, William, and Eugene Tobin. 2015. *Locus of Authority: The Evolution of Faculty Roles in the Governance of Higher Education*. Princeton, NJ: Princeton University Press.

Braune, Ines, and Achim Rohde. 2015. "Arab Higher Education and Research: An Interview with Sari Hanafi." *Middle East Topics and Arguments* 4:138–44.

Bray, Mark. 2009. *Confronting the Shadow Education System: What Government Policies for What Private Tutoring?* Paris: UNESCO International Institute for Educational Planning.

Brown, Jessie, and Martin Kurzweil. 2017. *The Complex Universe of Alternative Postsecondary Credentials and Pathways*. Cambridge, MA: American Academy of Arts and Sciences.

Brown, Nathan, and Mayss Al Alami. 2017. "A Walk on the Wild Side? Egypt's Education Minister, Tariq Shawqi, May Be Showing More Initiative than Is Good for Him." Washington, DC: Carnegie Middle East Center.

Brown, William O. 2001. "Faculty Participation in University Governance and the Effects on University Performance." *Journal of Economic Behavior and Organization* 44 (2): 129–43.

Brummer, Alex. 2017. "Thorny Task of Creating a Truly Shared Society." *Jewish News*, November 23.

Buckner, Elizabeth. 2013. "The Seeds of Discontent: Examining Youth Perceptions of Higher Education in Syria." *Comparative Education* 49 (4): 440–63.

———. 2011. "The Role of Higher Education in the Arab State and Society: Recent Reform Patterns." *Comparative and International Higher Education* 3:21–26.

Buckner, Elizabeth, and Khuloud Saba. 2010. "Syria's Next Generation: Youth Un/employment, Education, and Exclusion." *Contemporary Middle Eastern Issues* 3 (2): 86–98.

Bollag, Burton. 2000. "Arab Public-Opinion Survey Finds Widespread Dissatisfaction with Education", *Al-Fanar Media*, January 29.

Çağaptay, Soner. 2017. *The New Sultan: Erdo an and the Crisis of Modern Turkey*. London: I.B. Tauris.

Cairo University. 2009. "al-Khitta al-istratijiya li-Jami'at al-Qahira: 2010–2015."

Camau, Michel, and Vincent Geisser. 2003. *Le syndrome autoritaire: politique en Tunisie de Bourguiba à Ben Ali*. Paris: Presses de Sciences Po.

Cammack, Perry, Michele Dunne, Amr Hamzawy, Marc Lynch, Marwan Muasher, Yezid Sayigh, and Maha Yahya. 2017. *Arab Fractures: Citizens, States, and Social Contracts*. Washington, DC: Carnegie Endowment for International Peace.

Cammett, Melani, and Nisreen Salti. 2018. "Popular Grievances in the Arab Region: Evaluating Explanations for Discontent in the Lead-up to the Uprisings." *Middle East Development Journal* 10 (1): 64–96.

Campante, Filipe, and David Chor. 2012. "Why Was the Arab World Poised for Revolution? Schooling, Economic Opportunities, and the Arab Spring." *Journal of Economic Perspectives* 26 (2): 167–88.

Carlson, Scott. 2016. "When College Was a Public Good." *Chronicle of Higher Education*, November 27.

Carpenter, Jennifer. 2014. "Job Change Lands Egyptian Scientist in Legal Battle." *Science* 344, no. 6185 (May 16): 681–683.

CAU (Cadi Ayyad University). 2017. "Stratégie UCA: 2017–2019." Unpublished paper, Marrakesh.

Chaaban, Jad. 2015. "The Corporatization of Higher Education in Lebanon." Corporatization of Education Conference, American University of Beirut, December 2.

Chaney, Eric. 2015. "Religion and the Rise and Fall of Islamic Science." Working Paper, Department of Economics, Harvard University.

Chaney, Eric, George Akerloff, and Lisa Blaydes. 2012. "Democratic Change in the Arab World, Past and Present," *Brookings Papers on Economic Activity*, Spring, 363–414.

Chapman, David W., and Suzanne L. Miric. 2009. "Education Quality in the Middle East." *International Review of Education* 55 (4): 311–44.

Charbel, Ghassan. 2013. Interview with Mohamed ElBaradei. *al-Hayat*, June 19.

Chauffour, Jean-Pierre. 2017. *Morocco 2040: Emerging by Investing in Intangible Capital*. Washington, DC: World Bank.

Chedati, Brahim. 2009. *Financement et coût en education au Maroc*. Kingdom of Morocco, Conseil Supérieur de l'Enseignement, Rabat, October, http://search.shamaa.org/FullRecord?ID=62961

Cherkaoui, Mohammed. 2011. *Crise de l'université: Le nouvel esprit académique et la sécularisation de la production intellectuelle*. Paris: Librairie Droz.

Chomiak, Laryssa. 2014. "Architecture of Resistance in Tunisia." In *Taking to the Streets: The Transformation of Arab Activism*, edited by Lina Khatib and Ellen Lust, 11–51. Baltimore, MD: Johns Hopkins University Press.

Chong, Alberto, and Mark Gradstein. 2015. "On Education and Democratic Preferences." *Economics and Politics* 27 (3): 362–88.

Christensen, Clayton. 1997. *Innovator's Dilemma: Why New Technologies Cause Great Firms to Fail*. Cambridge, MA: Harvard Business Review.

Christensen, Clayton, Curtis W. Johnson, and Michael B. Horn. 2008. *Disrupting Class: How Disruptive Innovation Will Change the Way the World Learns*. New York: McGraw Hill.

Chronicle of Higher Education. 2018. "The Digital Campus." Special issue, April 8.

Chuan, Tan Chorh. 2016. "Asia University Rankings 2016: The Pillars of National University of Singapore's success." *Times Higher Education*, June 20.

Cinali, Gina. 2016. "What Good Governance Is . . . and What It Is NOT." PowerPoint presentation. World Bank-CMI MENA Tertiary Education Conference, Algiers, June 1.

Clément, Jean-François. 1995. "Les effets sociaux du programme d'ajustement structurel marocain." *Politique étrangère*, no. 4, 1003–13.

CMI (Center for Mediterranean Integration). 2016. *Annual Report*. Marseille: Center for Mediterranean Integration.

Cole, Jonathan R. 2009. *The Great American University: Its Rise to Preeminence, Its Indispensable National Role; Why It Must be Protected*. New York: Public Affairs.

Coleman, James, ed. 1965. *Education and Political Development*. Princeton, NJ: Princeton University Press.

Collins, Jim. 2001. *Good to Great: Why Some Companies Make the Leap and Others Don't*. New York: Random House.

Commins, David. 2015. *Islam in Saudi Arabia*. Ithaca, NY: Cornell University Press.

Connelly, John, and Michael Grüttner, eds. 2005. *Universities under Dictatorship*. University Park, PA: Pennsylvania State University Press.

Cook, James Bradley. 2000. "Egypt's National Education Debate." *Comparative Education* 36 (4): 477–90.

Cooper, Preston. 2017. "If Higher Education Were a Public Good . . . ." *Forbes*, August 18.

Cristillo, Lou, Amaney Jamal, and Nader Said. 2009. "Preliminary Results: National Study of Undergraduate Teaching in Palestine." In National Study of Undergraduate Teaching in Palestine. Presented at An-Najah University, Nablus, July 23–24.

Daily Beast. 2008. "The Star Students of the Islamic Republic," August 8.

Daily Star. 2014. "An Open Letter to Ban Ki-moon on the Fate of Mosul's Christians," August 8.

Daqu, 'Amir Mahdi. 2017. "al-'Ilaqa bayn al-ta'lim al-jami'i wa-l-dimuqratiya fi al-watan al-'arabi." In *al-Jami'at wa-l-bahth al-'ilmi fi al-'alam al-'arabi*, coordinated by Murad Diani, 353–87. Beirut: Arab Center for Research and Policy Studies.

Darem, Faisal. 2013. "Yemen's Largest University Is Shut Down." *Al-Fanar Media*, October 14.

Davidson, Cathy. 2017. *The New Education: How to Revolutionize the University to Prepare Students for a World in Flux*. New York: Basic Books.

De Bellaigue, Christopher. 2016. "Turkey Chooses Erdogan." *New York Review of Books*, August 6.

———. 2015. "Dreams of Islamic Liberalism." *New York Review of Books*, June 4.

De Moura Castro, Claudio, and Daniel C. Levy. 2000. *Myth, Reality and Reform: Higher Education Policy in Latin America*. Washington, DC: Inter-American Development Bank and Johns Hopkins University Press.

De Triornot, Adrien. 2018. "Fondations: Les grandes écoles mènent le bal." *Le Monde*, January 10.

DeMillo, Richard. 2015. *Revolution in Higher Education: How a Small Band of Innovators Will Make College Accessible and Affordable*. Cambridge, MA: Massachusetts Institute of Technology Press.

Devarajan, Shanta. 2016. "The Paradox of Higher Education in MENA." Brookings Institution, June 27.

Devran, Peter B. 2016. "Ahmed H. Zewail (1946–2016)." *Science* 353, no. 6304 (September 9): 1103.

Dhillon, Navtej, and Tarik Yousef, eds. 2009. *Generation in Waiting: The Unfulfilled Promise of Young People in the Middle East*. Washington, DC: Brookings Institution Press.

Diab, Hassan. 2013. *'Ala tariq al-hadatha: khitta inqadhiya, mashari' wa-munjazat wazarat al-tarbiya wa-l-ta'lim al-'ali*. Beirut: Wazarat al-Tarbiya wa-l-Ta'lim al-'Ali fi al-Jumhuriya al-Lubnaniya.

"Dialogue avec Abdallah Laroui: Subjectivité d'un rationaliste." 2014. In *Le métier d'intellectuel: Dialogues avec quinze penseurs du Maroc*, edited by Fadma Ait Mous and Driss Ksikes, 59–87. Casablanca: Les Presses de l'Université Citoyenne.

Diani, Murad, coordinator. 2017. *al-Jami'at wa-l-bahth al-'ilmi fi al-'alam al-'arabi*. Beirut: Arab Center for Research and Policy Studies.

al-Dibissiya, Zayd. 2019. "Musakkinat al-shari': al-hukuma al-urduniya tuwajih al-batala bi-liqa'at ma' al-shabab." *Al-Araby Al-Jadeed*, March 9, 10–11.

Dinçşahin, Şakir. 2015. *The State and Intellectuals in Turkey: The Life and Times of Niyazi Berkes, 1908–1988*. New York: Lexington Books.

Diwan, Ishac. 2017. "Low Social and Political Returns to Education in the Arab World." The Forum: Economic Research Forum Policy Portal, December 26.

———. 2016. "Low Social and Political Returns to Education in the Arab World." Economic Research Forum Policy Brief, no. 17, August.

———. 2012a. "Liberals, Islamists, and the Role of the Middle Class in the Demise of the Arab Autocracies." *Harvard Journal of Middle Eastern Policy and Politics*, 31–54.

———. 2012b. "Understanding Revolution in the Middle East: The Central Role of the Middle Class." Economic Research Forum Working Paper, no. 726, November.

Diwan, Ishac, Adeel Malik, and Izak Atiyas, eds. 2019. *Crony Capitalism in the Middle East: Business and Politics from Liberalization to the Arab Spring*. Oxford and New York: Oxford University Press.

Diwan, Ishac, and Irina Vartanova. 2018. "Does Education Indoctrinate? The Effect of Education on Political Preferences in Democracies and Autocracies." Economic Research Forum Working Paper, no. 1178, April.

Dowling, Dame Ann. 2015. *Dowling Review of Business–University Research Collaboration*. Royal Academy of Engineering, July, https://www.raeng.org.uk/publications/reports/the-dowling-review-of-business-university-research

Dreisback, Tristan. 2017. "For the People: Tunisia Embraces Open Government, 2011–2016." *Innovations for Successful Societies*, Princeton University, May, https://successfulsocieties.princeton.edu/.

Dubai School of Government. 2013. *Arab Social Media Report*, 5th ed., June. Dubai: Dubai School of Government.

Duchatelle, Vanessa, Marc Gurgand, and Adrien Lorenceau. 2015. "Part Four: Financing Higher Education—A Review of the Economic Literature." In *Financing Higher Education in the Mediterranean Region: The Case of Egypt, Lebanon and Tunisia*, edited by Thomas Melonio and Mihoub Mezouaghi, 145–95. Paris: Agence Française de Développement.

Dudley, Renee, Steve Stecklow, Alexandra Harney, and Irene Jay Liu. 2016. "Special Report: College Board Gave SAT Exams That It Knew Had Leaked." *Reuters*, March 28.

Duncan, Emma. 2015. "Universities: Excellence v. Equity," "Special Report: Excellence v. Equity, *The Economist*, March 28.

Dunne, Michele, and Amr Hamzawy. 2019. *Egypt's Political Exiles: Going Anywhere but Home*. Washington, DC: Carnegie Endowment for International Peace.

Dyer, Paul. 2009. "Youth Exclusion and the Transition to Adulthood in the MENA." PowerPoint presentation. Studying Youth in the Arab World, Issam Fares Institute, American University of Beirut, January 13–14.

e4e (Education for Employment), IDB (Islamic Development Bank), and IFC (International Finance Corporation). 2011. *Educating for Employment: Realizing Arab Youth Potential*. April.

EBRD (European Bank for Reconstruction and Development), EIB (European Investment Bank), and IBRD (International Bank for Reconstruction and Development/World Bank). 2016. *What's Holding Back the Private Sector in MENA? Lessons from the Enterprise Survey.*

The Economist. 2019a. "The Great Experiment: Can China Become a Scientific Superpower?," January 12, 69–73.

_____. 2019b. "The Twilight of the Bureaucrats: Millions of Retiring Arab Civil Servants Need Not Be Replaced," March 30, 54.

_____. 2018a. "Expanding Higher Education: Time to End the Academic Arms Race," February 3, 16.

_____. 2018b. "The Knowledge Factory: All Must Have Degrees," February 3, 56–57.

_____. 2018c. "Seizing the Laurels: Tsinghua University May Soon Top the World League in Science Research," November 17, 65–66.

_____. 2018d. "Special Report: Spain," July 28, 3–12.

_____. 2017. "Erdogan v Darwin: The Decline of Turkish Schools," September 30, 35.

_____. 2016a. "BASF: Chemical Reaction: How the World's Largest Chemical Company Brews Innovation," September 15.

_____. 2016b. "Free Exchange: Tales from Silicon Wadi," June 4, 76.

_____. 2016c. "French Manufacturers in Morocco: Factories in the Sun," June 4, 67–68.

_____. 2016d. "Higher Education: Flying High," June 25, 54–55.

_____. 2016e. "Open, Sesame: A Particle Accelerator in the Middle East," December 24, 112–13.

_____. 2016f. "Schrödinger's Panda," June 4, 77–79.

_____. 2015a. "Arab Bureaucracies: Aiwa (Yes) Minister," November 14.

_____. 2015b. "Education in South Korea: The Crème de la Cram," September 19.

_____. 2015c. "Low-cost Private Schools: Learning Unleashed," August 1, 17–20.

_____. 2014. "Higher Education: Is College Worth It?," April 5, 40–41.

_____. 2013a. "Higher Education: The Attack of the MOOCs," July 20.

_____. 2013b. "Islam and Science: The Road to Renewal," January 26.

Education Reform Initiative. 2013. "Do Private Tutoring Centers Provide Equality of Opportunity and Quality of Education?" November 26, Istanbul, http://en.egitimreformugirisimi.org/wp-content/uploads/2017/03/Do_Private_Tutoring_Centers_Provide_Equa.pdf

Egypt, Ministère de l'Instruction Publique. 1921. *Rapport final de la Commission de l'Université*. Cairo: Imprimérie Nationale.

Egypt, Ministry of Education. 2007?. *al-Khitta al-istratijiya al-qawmiya li-islah al-ta'lim qabl al-jami'i fi Misr, 2007/08–2011/12*. Cairo: Ministry of Education.

Egypt, Ministry of Higher Education. 2004. *The Quality Assurance and Accreditation Handbook for Higher Education in Egypt*. Cairo: Ministry of Higher Education.

Egyptian Center for the Advancement of Science, Technology and Innovation. 2014. "Science, Technology and Innovation in Egypt: Status Brief." June, Cairo, https://www.kooperation-international.de/fileadmin/redaktion/doc/AEgypten_wpdm_ECASTI_Report.pdf

Elbadawi, Ibrahim, and Samir Makdisi, eds. 2017. *Democratic Transitions in the Arab World*. Cambridge: Cambridge University Press.

Elbadawy, Asmaa. 2014. *Education in Egypt: Improvements in Attainment, Problems with Quality and Inequality*. Economic Research Forum Working Paper, no. 854.

Elbadawy, Asmaa, Ragui Assaad, Dennis Ahlburg, and Deborah Levison. 2007. "Private and Group Tutoring in Egypt: Where is the Gender Inequality?" Economic Research Forum Working Paper, no. 429, October.

Elgayar, Aisha, and Edward Fox. 2018. "Crown Prince Pushes Change in Saudi Higher Education." *Al-Fanar Media*, July 19.

Elhaj, Faten. 2013. "Lebanon: The University as Exporter of Graduates." *Al-Akhbar English*, June 19.

Elmes, John. 2016. "The Scholar Given a Year to Save Tunisia." *Times Higher Education*, September 15.

Elmeshad, Mohammed. 2014. "A Conversation with the New President of Menoufia University." *Al-Fanar Media*, October 28.

Elnur, Ibrahim. 1998. "al-Ta'lim al-'ali: min al-safwa ila al-a'dad al-kabira, ba'd awjuh al-istidama wa-l-muwa'ama." In *Mudawalat mu'tamar waqi' wa mustaqbal al-ta'lim al-'ali fi al-Sudan*, edited by Mohammed al-Amin Ahmad al-Tum, 293–337.

Enserink, Martin. 2016. "Peace of Mind: A Young Palestinian Neuroscientist Hopes to Create a Research Oasis in the West Bank that Transcends Politics." *Science* 352, no. 6290 (June 3): 1158–61.

El Erian, Mohamed. 2015. "America's Education Bubble." *Arab News*, November 10.

ESCWA (United Nations Economic and Social Commission for West Asia). 2014. *The Broken Cycle: Universities, Research and Society in the Arab Region—Proposals for Change*. Beirut: ESCWA.

————. 2012. "Employment and Education: Repairing the Broken Link." *ESCWA Social Development Division Bulletin* 4 (1).

ESCWA (United Nations Economic and Social Commission for West Asia) and UNDP (United Nations Development Programme). 2002. *Education: Women and Men in the Arab Countries*. Beirut: ESCWA.

European Commission. 2017. *Syria: Overview of the Higher Education System*. Brussels: European Union.

Faek, Rasha. 2017. "A Regional Survey: How Arab Countries Regulate Quality in Higher Education." *Al-Fanar Media*, September 12.

————. 2016. "The End of Sanctions Opens Iran's Academic Gates." *Al-Fanar Media*, August 26.

————. 2013a. "A Conversation with the World Bank's Higher Ed Leader." *Al-Fanar Media*, July 4.

————. 2013b. "New Portal Will Help Bring MOOCs to the Arab World." *Al-Fanar Media*, December 7.

_____. 2013c. "Paralyzing Strike in Lebanese Public Education Ends." *Al-Fanar Media*, March 19.

_____. 2013d. "University of Jordan Seeks Independence through Investment." *Al-Fanar Media*, October 28.

Fahim, Yasmine, and Noha Sami. 2010. "Access to and Equity in Financing Higher Education in Egypt." In *Financing Higher Education in Arab Countries*, edited by Ahmed Galal and Taher Kanaan, 11–28. Economic Research Forum Policy Research Report, no. 34.

Fahmi, Georges, and Hamza Medded. 2015. "Market for Jihad: Radicalization in Tunisia." Carnegie Middle East Center Report, October 15.

Fakhsh, Mahmud. 1977. "The Climate of Education for Development in Egypt: The Socio-Economic Role of University Graduates." *Middle Eastern Studies* 13, no. 2 (May): 229–40.

Al-Fanar Media. 2014."The Economic Struggle of Public-University Professors," January 13.

Faour, Mohammed. 2013. "A Review of Citizenship Education in Arab Nations." Carnegie Middle East Center Paper, May.

_____. 2012. "Religious Education and Pluralism in Egypt and Tunisia." Carnegie Middle East Center Paper, August.

_____. 2007. "Religion, Demography and Politics in Lebanon." *Middle Eastern Studies* 43 (6): 909–21.

Faour, Mohammed, and Marwan Muasher. 2011. "Education for Citizenship in the Arab World: Key to the Future." Carnegie Middle East Center Paper, October.

Farahat, Mostafa. 2015. "Crowdsourced Videos Plug Gap in Arab World." *Financial Times*, November 3.

Farouk, Menna. 2017. "Egyptian Universities Want More Foreign Students." *Al-Fanar Media*, April 19.

Farrag, Iman. 2010. "Directions of Educational Reform in Egypt." In *Educational Reform in the Middle East*, edited by Samira 'Ulayan, Sirhan Duwaib, and Akim Ruda, 109–24. Amman: Dar al-Shorouk.

Fergany, Nader. 2009. "Educational Reform Can Empower Youth in Arab Countries and Help Build Human Development." UNESCO 2009/ED/EFA/MRT/PI/05.

_____. 2000. *Arab Higher Education and Development: An Overview*. Cairo: AlMishkat Center for Research.

Fingleton, Eamonn. 2013. "America the Innovative?" *New York Times*, March 31.

Fischer, Karen. 2016. "When Everyone Goes to College: A Lesson from South Korea." *Chronicle of Higher Education*, May 1.

_____. 2013. "A College Degree Sorts Job Applicants, but Employers Wish It Meant More." *Chronicle of Higher Education*, March 4.

_____. 2009. "Academics Propose Ways to Rebuild Iraqi Higher Education." *Chronicle of Higher Education*, March 16.

Flaherty, Colleen. 2015. "Locus of Authority." *Inside Higher Ed*, January 5.

Florida, Richard. 2005. *Cities and the Creative Class*. New York: Routledge.

Foley, Tom. 2014. "The 'Job Market' That Is Not One." *Chronicle of Higher Education*, December 15.

Foreign Affairs. 2015. "Africa Calling: A Conversation with Mo Ibrahim." *Foreign Affairs* 94 (1): 24–30.

Fox, Edward. 2019. "In a Fractious Region, a New Physics Facility Fosters Collaboration." *Al-Fanar Media*, January 24.

Fox, Michael-David. 2005. "Russian Universities across the 1917 Divide." In *Universities under Dictatorship*, edited by John Connelly and Michael Grüttner, 15–43. University Park, PA: Pennsylvania State University Press.

Fraij, Mohammad. 2017. "Rising Tuition in Jordan Highlights Flawed University Finances." *Al-Fanar Media*, August 13.

Freiha, Nimr Mansour. 2010. "Educational Reform in the Arab World." In *Educational Reform in the Middle East*, edited by Samira 'Ulayan, Sirhan Duwaib, and Akim Ruda, 16–51. Amman: Dar al-Shorouk.

Friedson, Michael. 2015. "Court Nullifies Erdogan's Attempt to Stifle Opponent's Educational Program." *The Media Line*, July 14.

Galal, Ahmed. 2003. "Social Expenditure and the Poor in Egypt." European Centre for Electoral Support Working Paper, no. 89.

Galal, Ahmed, and Taher Kanaan, eds. 2010. *Financing Higher Education in Arab Countries*. Economic Research Forum Policy Research Report, no. 34, July.

Gall, Carlotta. 2019. "Turks Voting with Their Feet." *New York Times*, January 5–6.

Gambetta, Diego, and Steffen Hertog. 2016. *Engineers of Jihad: The Curious Connection between Violent Extremism and Education*. Princeton, NJ: Princeton University Press.

Gardner, Lee. 2019. "The Rise of the Mega-University." *Chronicle of Higher Education*, February 18.

Geer, Benjamin. 2013. "Autonomy and Symbolic Capital in an Academic Social Movement: The March 9 Group in Egypt." *European Journal of Turkish Studies* 17, https://journals.openedition.org/ejts/4780

George, Alan. 2003. *Syria: Neither Bread nor Freedom*. London: Zed Books.

Gertel, Jörg, and Ralf Hexel. eds. 2018. *Coping with Uncertainty: Youth in the Middle East and North Africa*. London: Saqi Books.

Ghabra, Shafeeq, with Margreet Arnold. 2007. "Studying the American Way: An Assessment of American-style Higher Education in Arab Countries." Washington Institute for Near East Policy, Policy Focus 71, June.

El-Ghali, Hana, Qianyi Chen, and John Yeager. 2010. "Strategic Planning in Higher Education in the Middle East: The Case of the Non-Gulf Countries." In *Innovation through Education: Building the Knowledge Economy in the Middle East*, edited by Daniel Obst and Daniel Kirk, 43–60. New York: International Institute of Education and American Institute for Foreign Study.

El-Ghobashy, Mona. 2016. "Dissidence and Deference among Egyptian Judges." *Middle East Report*, no. 279, Summer, 12–19.

Ginsberg, Benjamin. 2011. *The Fall of the Faculty: The Rise of the All-Administrative University and Why it Matters*. Oxford: Oxford University Press.

Glaeser, Edward, Giacomo Ponzetto, and Andrei Shleifer. 2007. "Why Does Democracy Need Education?" *Journal of Economic Growth* 12:77–99.

Glossary of Education Reform. 2014. "Competency-based Learning," https://www.edglossary.org/.

Goldin, Claudia, and Lawrence Katz. 2009. *The Race between Education and Technology*. Cambridge, MA: Belknap Press of Harvard University Press.

Goldrick, Leigh M., and Thomas Goldrick. 2017. "The Top Five Disruptive Technologies in Higher Education." *eCampus News*, June 5.

Golkar, Saeid. 2015. *Captive Society: The Basij Militia and Social Control in Iran*. New York: Woodrow Wilson Center Press and Columbia University Press.

Goujon, Anne, and Bilal Barakat. 2010. "Future Demographic Changes in the Arab World." Emirates Center for Strategic Studies and Research Occasional Paper 75.

Greenstein, Daniel. 2019. "The Future of Undergraduate Education: Will Differences Across Sectors Exacerbate Inequality?" *Daedalus* 148, no. 4 (Fall): 108–37.

Grüttner, John. 2005a. "German Universities under the Swastika." In *Universities under Dictatorship*, edited by John Connelly and Michael Grüttner, 75–111. University Park, PA: Pennsylvania State University Press.

_____. 2005b. "Concluding Reflections." In *Universities under Dictatorship*, edited by John Connelly and Michael Grüttner, 283–95. University Park, PA: Pennsylvania State University Press.

Guessoum, Nidhal, and Athar Osama, eds. 2015. *Report of Zakri Task Force on Science at Universities of the Muslim World*. London: Muslim World Science Initiative.

Gutmann, Amy. 1999. *Democratic Education*. Princeton, NJ: Princeton University Press.

Guttenplan, D.D. 2014. "Who Should Pay for Education?" *Al-Fanar Media*, June 5.

Gyögy, Pétri. 2005. "The Communist Idea of the University: An Essay Inspired by the Hungarian Experience." In *Universities under Dictatorship*, edited by John Connelly and Michael Grüttner, 140–66. University Park, PA: Pennsylvania State University Press.

Haas, Peter. 1992. "Introduction: Epistemic Communities and International Policy Coordination." *International Organization* 46 (1): 1–35.

El-Haddad, Amirah, and May Gadallah. 2018. "The Informalization of the Egyptian Economy, 1998–2012: A Factor in Growing Wage Inequality." Economic Research Forum Working Paper, no. 1210, June.

Hajji, Siham. 2008. "Management universitaire à l'épreuve de la réforme." *Prospectives Universitaires*, no. 1, 127–36.

Hakim, Danny. 2016. "Scientists Loved and Loathed by an Agrochemical Giant." *New York Times*, December 31.

Hamamou, Sabah. 2017. "Arab Universities and MOOCs: Cautious Cooperation." *Al-Fanar Media*, March 7.

Hamdan, Sara. 2011. "Arab Spring Spawns Interest in Improving Quality of Higher Education." *New York Times*, November 6.

Hameesh, BenSalem. 1997. "Whither the University?" In *The Idea of the University*, edited by Taieb Belghazi, 37–42. Rabat: Faculty of Letters and Human Sciences, University Mohammed V Agdal. (in Arabic)

Hammoud, Rafica. 2010. "Admission Policies and Procedures in Arab Universities." In *Towards an Arab Higher Education Space: International Challenges and Societal Responsibilities*, edited by Bechir Lamine, 69–83. Cairo: Arab Regional Conference on Higher Education.

Hanafi, Sari. 2011. "University Systems in the Arab East: Publish Globally and Perish Locally vs Publish Locally and Perish Globally." *Current Sociology* 59 (3): 291–309.

Hanafi, Sari, and Rigas Arvanitis. 2016a. "Practicing Research in Lebanon: Institutions and Institutionalization." In *Knowledge Production in the Arab World: The Impossible Promise*, 170–206. New York: Routledge.

———. 2016b. *Knowledge Production in the Arab World: The Impossible Promise*. New York: Routledge.

Handoussa, Heba, and Zafiris Tzannatos. 2002. *Employment Creation and Social Protection in the Middle East and North Africa*. New York: World Bank and the Economic Research Forum, American University in Cairo Press.

Harris, Kevin. 2014. "The Sociologist Has Left the Building." *Middle East Report* 270, Spring, 47.

Hartmann, Sarah. 2008. "The Informal Market of Education in Egypt: Private Tutoring and Its Implications." Institute for Ethnology and African Studies, Gutenberg University, Working Paper 88.

Haskel, Jonathan, and Stian Westlake. 2018. *Capitalism without Capital: The Rise of the Intangible Economy*. Princeton, NJ: Princeton University Press.

El-Hassan, Karma. 2016. "Trends in Higher Education in MENA Region." PowerPoint presentation. MENA Tertiary Education Conference: Trends in Higher Education in MENA, Algiers, June 2.

_____. 2012. "Quality Assurance in Higher Education in Arab Region." OECD Education, September 28.

Hayat, Rim. 2015. "Algeria Moves to Halt the Tutoring Trade." *Al-Fanar Media*, February 3.

Hazelkorn, Ellen. 2015. *Rankings and the Reshaping of Higher Education: The Battle for World Class Excellence*. New York: Palgrave Macmillan.

_____. 2008. "Learning to Live with Leagues Tables and Ranking: The Experience of Institutional Leaders." *Higher Education Policy* 21 (2): 193–216.

Hebel, Sara. 2014. "From Public Good to Private Good: How Higher Education Got to a Tipping Point." *Chronicle of Higher Education*, March 2.

Hirschman, Albert O. 1970. *Exit, Voice, and Loyalty: Responses to Decline in Firms, Organizations, and States*. Cambridge, MA: Harvard University Press.

Holmes, Amy, and Sahar Aziz. 2019. "Egypt's Lost Academic Freedom." Carnegie Endowment for International Peace, January 24.

Al-Hroub, Anies. 2014. "Quality Issues in Education Programs in Arab Universities: A Synthesis of Case Studies." In *Qadaya al-naw'iya fi mu'assasat al-ta'lim al-'ali fi al-buldan al-'arabiya*, edited by Adnan El-Amine, 55–76. Beirut: al-Hay'a al-Lubnaniya li-l-'Ulum al-Tarbawiya

Hubble, Sue, David Foster, and Paul Bolton. 2016. "Higher Education and Research Bill 2016 [Bill No 004 of 2016-17]." Briefing Paper, House of Commons Library, No. 7608, June 8.

Human Rights Watch. 2005. *Reading between the 'Red Lines': The Repression of Academic Freedom in Egyptian Universities*, June 8, hwr. org.

Hurtado, Maria Elena. 2015. "Only Three Out of Ten University Students Graduate." *University World News*, no. 364, April 24.

Hussein, Adnan al-Sayyid. 2013. "Awda' al-Jami'a al-Lubnaniya la tastaqim illa bi-tashkil majlisiha." *Al-Safir*, March 18.

_____. 2012. *Development Strategy for the Lebanese University* (English, French, and Arabic). Beirut: Lebanese University.

Husseini, Rola. 2012. *Pax Syriana: Elite Politics in Post-war Lebanon.* Syracuse, NY: Syracuse University Press.

Hvistendahl, Mara. 2013. "Foreigners Run Afoul of China's Tightening Secrecy Rules." *Science* 339, no. 6118 (January 25): 384–85.

_____. 2012. "China's Push in Tissue Engineering." *Science* 338, no. 6109 (November 16): 900–902.

Hymans, Jacques. 2012a. *Achieving Nuclear Ambitions: Scientists, Politicians and Proliferation.* Cambridge: Cambridge University Press.

_____. 2012b. "Botching the Bomb: While Nuclear Weapons Programs Often Fail on Their Own—and Why Iran's Might Too." *Foreign Affairs* 91, no. 3 (May–June): 44–53.

'Ida, Mohammed Ahmad. 2013. "In This Manner Did the Syrian Ulema Arrange Moroccan Religious Affairs." *Akhbar al-youm* (Morocco), October 26–27, 6–7. (in Arabic)

Ikram, Khalid. 2018. *The Political Economy of Reforms in Egypt: Issues and Policymaking since 1952.* Cairo: American University in Cairo Press.

_____. 2006. *The Egyptian Economy, 1952–2000.* New York: Routledge.

Ings, Simon. 2016. *Stalin and the Scientists: A History of Triumph and Tragedy, 1915–1953.* London and New York: Faber and Faber.

INSEAD. 2017. *Global Innovation Index*, https://www. globalinnovationindex.org/Home.

International Institute of Education (IIE). 2015. "Reinventing Academic Ties: Opportunities for U.S.–Iran Higher Education Cooperation." International Institute of Education's Center for International Partnerships Briefing Paper, August.

Iskandar, Shawkat. 2014. "Jami'at Zewail tastati'u wad' Misr 'ala kharitat al-taqniyat al-mutaqaddima." *al-Hayat*, May 17.

'Issa, Najib. 1997. "Ba'd al-jawanib al-maliya li-l-ta'lim al-'ali." In *al-Ta'lim al-'ali fi Lubnan*, edited by Adnan El-Amine, 211–29. Beirut: Beirut: al-Hay'a al-Lubnaniya li-l-'Ulum al-Tarbawiya.

Jacobs, Andrew. 2013. "As China Moves to Lower Professor's Profile, Colleges Are Seeking to Raise Theirs." *New York Times*, October 15.

Jamel, Ibtessim. 2017. "Tunisian Professors Flee the Country for Better Salaries." *Al-Fanar Media*, July 28.

Jaramillo, Adriana, and Thomas Melonio, eds. 2011. *Breaking Even or Breaking Through: Reaching Financial Sustainability while Providing High Quality Standards in Higher Education in the Middle East and North Africa.* Washington, DC: World Bank.

Jaramillo, Adriana, Juan Manuel Moreno, Axel Demenet, Hafedh Zaafrane, and Odile Monet. 2012. *Universities through the Looking Glass: Benchmarking University Governance to Enable Higher Education Modernization in MENA.* Washinton, DC: World Bank.

Jilali, Makram. 2008. "Quelques éléments de réflexion sur la profession et le statut des enseignants-chercheurs." *Perspectives Universitaires*, no. 1, 119–23.

Johnstone, D-B. 1998. "The Financing and Management of Higher Education: A Status Report on Worldwide Reforms." Presentation. UNESCO World Conference on Higher Education, October 5–9, Paris.

Juha, Shafiq, and Helen Khal. 2004. *Darwin and the Crisis of 1882 in the Medical Deptartment: And the First Student Protest in the Arab World in the Syrian Protestant College.* Beirut: American University of Beirut Press.

Jump, Paul. 2014. "Secondary Affiliations Lift King Abdulaziz University in Rankings." *Times Higher Education*, July 17.

Kaaouachi, Abdelali. 2010. "L'évaluation dans le système d'enseignement supérieur au Maroc: Bilan des réalisations, limites et principaux defies." In *Towards an Arab Higher Education Space: International Challenges and Societal Responsibilities*, edited by Bechir Lamine, 409–22. Cairo: Arab Regional Conference on Higher Education.

Kabbani, Nader. 2019. "Youth Unemployment in the Middle East and North Africa: Revisiting and Reframing the Challenge." Brookings Doha Center Policy Briefing, February.

Kabbani, Nader, and Noura Kamel. 2009. "Tapping into the Economic Potential of Young Syrians during a Time of Transition." In *Generation in Waiting: The Unfulfilled Promise of Young People in the Middle East*, edited by Navtej Dhillon and Tarik Yousef, 189–210. Washington, DC: Brookings Institution Press.

Kabbani, Nader, and Siba Salloum. 2010. "Financing Higher Education in Syria." In *Financing Higher Education in Arab Countries*, edited by Ahmed Galal and Taher Kanaan, 103–16. Economic Research Forum Policy Research Report, no. 34.

Kadivar, Mohammed Ali. 2014. "The Battle over Higher Education in Iran." *Middle East Report*, February 20.

Kamil, Hamdi. 2014. "17 alf muhandis yatanafasun 'ala 769 wazifa bi-l-rayy." 2014. *Masress*, March 26.

Kamil, Husam. 2008. "Kalimat al-ustadh al-duktur Husam Kamil, ra'is Jami'at al-Qahira." December 21. From the office of Husam Kamil.

Kanaan, Taher, in collaboration with Mamdouh Al-Salamat and May Hanania. 2010. "Financing Higher Education in Jordan." In *Financing Higher Education in Arab Countries*, edited by Ahmed Galal and Taher Kanaan, 29–47. Economic Research Forum Policy Research Report, no. 34.

Kandil, Hazem. 2014. *Inside the Brotherhood*. Cambridge: Polity Press.

Kapur, Devesh. 2012. "India: Unleashing Potential in Innovation and Creativity." *EastAsiaForum*, April 5, 1–3.

———. 2011. "Addressing the Trilemma of Higher Education." *Seminar*, no. 617, January, 87–92.

———. 2010. "Indian Higher Education." In *American Universities in a Global Market*, edited by Charles Clotfelter, 305–34. Chicago, IL: University of Chicago Press.

Kapur, Devesh, and Elizabeth Perry. 2015. "Higher Education Reform in China and India: The Role of the State." Harvard–Yenching Institute Working Papers, January.

Kaya, Muzaffer. 2018. "Turkey's Purge of Critical Academia." *Middle East Report*, no. 288, Fall, 25–28.

Kelderman, Eric. 2016. "Unshared Governance: New Pressures Threaten the Faculty's Role in Leadership." *Chronicle of Higher Education*, February 29.

Kelly, Cristina Bonasegna. 2013. "Argentina at the Top—For Its Dropout Rate!" *Inside Higher Ed*, August 5.

Kenbib, Mohammed. 1997. "A propos d'une letter du Sultan Moulay Abderrahmane relative à l'enseignement." In *The Idea of the University*, edited by Taieb Belghazi, 205–17. Rabat: Faculty of Letters and Human Sciences, University Mohammed V Agdal.

Kerr, Malcolm. 1965. "Egypt." In *Education and Political Development*, edited by James Coleman, 169–94. Princeton, NJ: Princeton University Press.

Kezar, Adrianna, Daniel Maxey, and Judith Eaton. 2014. "An Examination of the Changing Faculty: Ensuring Institutional Quality and Achieving Desired Student Learning Outcomes." Council for Higher Education Accreditation Occasional Paper.

Khairy, Amina. 2016. Matat al-madrasa wa 'ash 'al-sintar' bi-qarar al-talib wa-waliyy al-amr." *al-Hayat*, August 22.

Khalil, Osamah. 2016. *America's Dream Palace: Middle East Expertise and the Rise of the National Security State*. Cambridge, MA: Harvard University Press.

Khan, Mohammed Naeem. 2012. "Pakistan's Higher Education Miracle." *Saudi Gazette*, August 14.

Khatri, Sadia. 2014. "Do Human Evolution and Islam Conflict in the Classroom?" *Al-Fanar Media*, March 24.

Khouri, Rami G. 2015. "President Sisi's Very Bad Year." *Al-Jazeera*, July 6.

King, Mary-Claire. 2012. "The Scientist as World Citizen." *Science* 338, no. 6107 (November 2): 581.

Kingdom of Jordan. 2015?. *Education for Prosperity: Delivering Results—A National Strategy for Human Resource Development 2016–2025*. Amman: n.p.

Kingdom of Jordan, National Economic and Social Council. 2017?. *Financial Status of Government Universities in Jordan (Status and Solutions)*. Amman: National Economic and Social Council.

Kingdom of Morocco. 2018. *l'Enseignement supérieur au Maroc: Efficacité, efficience, et défis du système universitaire à accès ouvert*. Rabat: Conseil Supérieur de l'Education, de la Formation, et de la Recherche Scientifique.

_____. 2015a. *Pour une École de l'Équité, de la Qualité, et de la Promotion: Vision Stratégique de la Réforme 2015–30*. Rabat: Conseil Supérieur de l'Education, de la Formation, et de la Recherche Scientifique.

_____. 2015b. *Opinion of the Council re: Draft Law for Changing and Completing Law 01-00 with respect to Higher Education*. Rabat: Conseil Supérieur de l'Education, de la Formation, et de la Recherche Scientifique.

_____. 2013a. *Faculty of Letters and Human Sciences: Achievements, 2009–12: End of Service Report of Dean Abderrahim Ben Hadda*. Rabat: Mohammed V University Agdal. (in Arabic)

_____. 2013b. *Les Structures de recherche de l' Université Mohammed V-Agdal*. Rabat: Mohammed V University Agdal.

_____. 2013c. "Plan for the Evolution of the Faculty of Literature and Human Sciences, 2013–2016." Abderrahim Ben Hadda, Ministry of Higher Education, Scientific Research and Training of Cadres, Rabat.

——. 2010? *Report Synthesizing the Ermergency Plan (Plan d'Urgence)*. Rabat: Ministry of Higher Education, Scientific Research and Training of Cadres.

_____. 2008. *Evaluation institutionelle externe de l'Universite Mohammed V Agdal*. February. Rabat: Mohammed V Agdal.

_____. 2007. *Evaluation institutionelle interne de l'université Mohammmed V-Agdal*. June. Rabat: Mohammed V Agdal.

_____. 2000. "Dahir N. 1-00-199 19 mai 2000 Portant Promulgation de la Loi N. 01-100 Portant Orgainization de l'Enseignement Supérieur." *Bulletin Officiel*, no. 4800, 393.

_____. 1999?. "Charte nationale d'education et formation." Commission Spéciale Education Formation, Rabat.

Kingdom of Morocco, Ministry of National Education, Higher Education and Training of Scientific Research Personnel. 2019. *Rapport de Synthèse du Programme d'Urgence, 2009–2012*. Rabat: Ministry of National Education, Higher Education and Training of Scientific Research Personnel.

Kiwan, Fadya. 1997. "al-Shu'un al-wazifiya li-l-hay'a al-ta'limiya." In *al-Ta'lim al-'ali fi Lubnan*, edited by Adnan El-Amine, 395–425. Beirut: al-Hay'a al-Lubnaniya li-l-'Ulum al-Tarbawiya

Kleich Dray, Mina, and Said Belcadi. 2008. "l'Université marocaine en processus d'autonomisation." Kingdom of Morocco, Conseil Supérieur de l'Ensignement, February.

Kolster, Jacob, and Nono Matondo-Fundai. 2012. *Jobs, Justice and the Arab Spring: Inclusive Growth in North Africa*. Abidjan: African Development Bank.

Kornai, Janos. 1981. "Some Properties of the Eastern European Growth Pattern." *World Development* 9 (9–10): 965–70.

Koropeckyi, Sophia, Chris Lafakis, and Adam Ozimek. 2017. *The Economic Impact of Increasing College Completion*. Cambridge, MA: American Academy of Arts and Sciences.

Krafft, Caroline, and Halimat Alawode. 2016. "Inequality of Opportunity in Higher Education in the Middle East and North Africa." Economic Research Forum Working Paper, no. 1056, October.

Krafft, Caroline, and Ragui Assaad. 2015. "Promoting Successful Transitions to Employment for Egyptian Youth." Economic Research Forum Policy Perspective 15, April.

_____. 2014. "Why the Unemployment Rate Is a Misleading Indicator of Labor Market Health in Egypt." Economic Research Forum Policy Perspective 14, June.

Kroenig, Matthew. 2014. *A Time to Attack: The Looming Iranian Nuclear Threat*. New York: Palgrave Macmillan.

Krupnick, Matt. 2014. "MOOCs in the Developing World—Pros and Cons." *University World News*, no. 326, June 27.

Kupferschmidt, Kai. 2012. "Poor but Smart." *Science* 338, no. 6108 (November 9): 738–39.

Kuran, Timur. 2016. "Legal Roots of Authoritarian Rule in the Middle East: Civic Legacies of the Islamic Waqf." *American Journal of Comparative Law* 64 (2): 419–54.

_____. 2011. *The Long Divergence: How Islamic Law Held back the Middle East*. Princeton, NJ: Princeton University Press.

Labayd, Salim. 2017. "Tahawwulat al-jami'a al-tunisiya: tajarib al-islah wa-wad' al-mudarris al-bahith." In *al-Jami'at wa-l-bahth al-'ilmi fi al-'alam al-'arabi*, coordinated by Murad Diani, 517–46. Beirut: Arab Center for Research and Policy Studies.

Labi, Aisha. 2014. "Iran Signals Support for Greater Freedom in Academe." *Chronicle of Higher Education*, June 2.

_____. 2008. "Iran's Million Student Alternative." *Chronicle of Higher Education*, August 15.

Lamine, Bechir, ed. 2010. *Towards an Arab Higher Education Space: International Challenges and Societal Responsibilities*. Cairo: Arab Regional Conference on Higher Education.

Lamont, Michèle, and Anna Sun. 2012. "How China's Elite Universities Will Have to Change." *Chronicle of Higher Education*, December 10.

Law, John. 2014. "Can Libya's Universities Lead the Country to Stability?" *Voices Magazine*, June 4.

Lawler, Andrew. 2011. "A New Day for Egyptian Science?" Science 333, no. 6040 (July 15): 278–84.

Lebanese University. n.d. *Dalil al-jami'at al-lubnaniya: al-qawanin wa-l-anzima al-idariya wa-l-maliya*. Beirut: LU Publications.

——. 2010. *Hukumat al-mufaraqat*, principal author, Ali al-Musawi. Beirut: Lebanese University.

_____. 2003. *al-Taqyim al-dhati fi al-jami'at al-lubnaniya 2002–2003*. Beirut: Lebanese University.

Lee, Byung Gwon. 2016. "Kist at 50, Beyond the Miracle." *Science* 351, no. 6276 (February 26): 895.

Lepore, Jill. 2014. "The Disruption Machine: What the Gospel by Innovation Gets Wrong." *New Yorker*, June 23.

Levine, Arthur. 2015. "Time Is Right for Colleges to Shift from Assembly-line Education." *Chronicle of Higher Education*, September 14.

Levy, Daniel. Forthcoming. "Chapter 1: Discovering the World's Private Sector." In *A World of Private Higher Education*.

Lindsey, Ursula. 2018. "Education in Morocco: A Plea for a Middle Way." *Al-Fanar Media*, April 6.

_____. 2017. "UAE Jails Economist: The Silence is Deafening." *Al-Fanar Media*, April 5.

_____. 2014. "A New Generation of Arab Innovation." *Chronicle of Higher Education*, April 7.

_____. 2013a. "The March 9 Movement Faces New Challenges." *Al-Fanar Media*, February 14.

_____. 2013b. "After Centuries of Stagnation Science is Making a Comeback in the Islamic World." *Chronicle of Higher Education*, April 1.

_____. 2011a. "Information Gap Hinders Coordination and Reform among Arab Universities." *Chronicle of Higher Education*, December 13.

_____. 2011b. "Bigger Private Sector Role Recommended for the Middle East." *Chronicle of Higher Education*, April 14.

_____. 2010a. "In Morocco, Visions of a Silicon Valley Campus." *Chronicle of Higher Education*, August 16.

_____. 2010b. "Saudi Arabia's Education Reforms Emphasize Training for Jobs." *Chronicle of Higher Education*, October 3.

Lohr, Steve. 2016. "American Textiles Gain an Edge with Technology." *New York Times*, April 2–3.

Longuenesse, Elisabeth. 2007. *Professions et société au Proche-Orient: Déclin des elites, crises des classes moyennes*. Rennes: Presses Universitaires de Rennes.

Lund, Susan, Jane Manyika, and Michael Spence. 2019. "The Global Economy's Next Winners." *Foreign Affairs* 98, no. 4 (July–August): 121–30.

Lynch, Sarah. 2015a. "Turkey's Foundation Universities: Model for the Region?" *Al-Fanar Media*, January 13.

_____. 2015b. "Calculating the Cost of a 'Free' Education." *Al-Fanar Media*, February 1.

_____. 2013. "University of Alexandria Seeks to Become a Pocket of Excellence." *Al-Fanar Media*, November 18.

Lyons, Kristen, Jeremy Tager, and Louise Sales. 2016. "Letter from the Editors: Introduction to the Special Issue" in "Challenging the Privatised University." Special issue, *Australian Universities' Review* 58 (2): 3–4.

Mahbubani, Kishore, and Larry Summers. 2016. "The Fusion of Civilizations." *Foreign Affairs* 95, no. 3 (May–June): 126–35.

Mahmoud, Mohamed. 2013a. "Egyptian Court Supports Universities' Independence." *Al-Fanar Media*, April 5.

_____. 2013b. "New Egyptian Government Gives Academics a Strong Role." *Al-Fanar Media*, August 4.

Mahmood, Syed Akhtar, and Meriam Ait Ali Slimane. 2018. *Privilege-resistant Policies in the Middle East and North Africa: Measurement and Operational Implications*. Washington, DC: World Bank.

Majeed, Sawsan. 2010. "Impact of Crises on Scientific and Research Activities of Faculty Members: A Comparative Study (Iraq and Jordan)." In *Towards an Arab Higher Education Space: International Challenges and Societal Responsibilities*, edited by Bechir Lamine, 63–76. Cairo: Arab Regional Conference on Higher Education.

Malkawi, Khetam. 2015. "UN Expanding Role beyond Academia, Encouraging Volunteerism—Tarawneh." *Jordan Times*, July 26, http://www.jordantimes.com/news/local/uj-expanding-role-beyond-academia-encouraging-volunteerism-%E2%80%94-tarawneh

Maloney, Suzanne. 2015. *Iran's Political Economy since the Revolution*. Cambridge: Cambridge University Press.

Mansour, Muhammad. 2013. "Egyptian Academics Arrested in the Crackdown on the Muslim Brotherhood." *Al-Fanar Media*, November 11.

Mansouri, Brahim. 2009. "What Determines Production and Utilization of Research for Development? The Case of the Moroccan Ministry of Finance." Presentation. Seventh Globelics Conference, Dakar, October 6–8.

Marmolejo, Francisco. 2011. "The Long Road toward Excellence in Mexico: The Monterrey Institute of Technology." In *The Road to Academic Excellence: The Making of World-class Research Universities*, edited by Philip G. Altbach and Jamil Salmi, 261–91. Washington, DC: World Bank.

al-Marouni, al-Makki. 1996. *al-Islah al-ta'limi bi-l-Maghrib, 1956–1994*. Faculty of Arts and Human Sciences, MVU. Casablanca: al-Matba'a al-Jadida.

Masri, Safwan. 2017. *Tunisia: An Arab Anomaly*. New York: Columbia University Press.

Massialas, Byron, and Samir Ahmad Jarrar. 1991. *Arab Education in Transition: A Source Book*. New York: Garland Publishing.

Massy, William. 2016. *Reengineering the University*. Baltimore, MD: Johns Hopkins University Press.

———. 2003. *Honoring the Trust: Quality and Cost Containment in Higher Education*. Boston, MA: Anker Publishing.

Matar, Hisham. 2006. *In the Country of Men*. New York: Penguin.

Mazzucato, Mariana. 2015. "The Innovative State." *Foreign Affairs* 94 (1): 61–68.

MBRF (Mohammed Bin Rashid Al Maktoum Foundation) and UNDP (United Nations Development Programme). 2014. *Arab Knowledge Report 2014: Youth and the Localisation of Knowledge*. Dubai: UNDP, Regional Bureau for Arab States.

—— 2009. *Arab Knowledge Report 2009: Towards Productive Intercommunication for Knowledge*. Dubai: UNDP, Regional Bureau for Arab States.

Mckenzie, Lindsay. 2017. "Cost of Online Education May Be Higher than We Think, Study Suggests." *Chronicle of Higher Education*, February 27.

McPhedran, Charles. 2013. "How Saudi Universities Rose in the Global Rankings." *Al-Fanar Media*, October 15.

MEED (Middle East Economic Digest). 2011. "Middle East Fails to Make the Grade." Special Report on Rankings, no. 48, December 2–8.

Mellouk, Mohamed. 1997. "A propos de la qualité de l'enseignement supérieur: Quelques eléments d'appréciation." In *The Idea of the University*, edited by Taieb Belghazi, 77–83. Rabat: Faculty of Letters and Human Sciences, University Mohammed V Agdal.

Melonio, Thomas, and Mihoub Mezouaghi. 2015. *Financing Higher Education in the Mediterranean Region: The Case of Egypt, Lebanon and Tunisia*. Paris: Agence Française de Développement.

Menashri, David. 1992. *Education and the Making of Modern Iran*. Ithaca, NY: Cornell University Press.

Merrouni, Mekki. 1997. "l'Université et le paradigme de l'efficacité." In *The Idea of the University*, edited by Taieb Belghazi, 85–99. Rabat: Faculty of Letters and Human Sciences, University Mohammed V Agdal.

Mervis, Jeffrey. 2009. "The Big Gamble in the Saudi Desert." *Science* 326, no. 5951 (October 16): 354–57.

MESA (Middle East Studies Association). 2017. "Academic Freedom Committee Statement on Turkey." March 30.

Mezue, Bryan, Clayton Christensen, and Derik van Bever. 2015. "The Power of Market Creation." *Foreign Affairs* 94 (1): 69–76.

El-Mikawy, Noha, Mohamed Mohieddin, and Sarah El Ashmaouy. 2017. "Egypt: The Protracted Transition from Authoritarianism to Democracy and Social Justice." In *Democratic Transitions in the Arab World*, edited by Ibrahim Elbadawi and Samir Makdisi, 133–83. Cambridge: Cambridge University Press.

Al-Militi, Munawwar. 2015. "Tunisian Institutions Turn Thousands Each Year to the Streets." *Al-'Arab* (London), December 5. (in Arabic)

al-Minawi, Mahmoud Fawzi. 2007. *Jami'at al-Qahira fi 'idiha al-mi'awiya*. Cairo: al-Maktaba al-Akadimiya.

Mitchell, Joshua. 2013. *Tocqueville in Arabia: Dilemmas in a Democratic Age*. Chicago, IL: University of Chicago Press.

Mohammed, Meziane, and Mahi Brahim. 2010. "The LMD Higher Education System in the Maghreb Countries: The Example of Algeria." In *Towards an Arab Higher Education Space: International Challenges and Societal Responsibilities*, edited by Bechir Lamine, 267–80. Beirut: UNESCO Regional Bureau for Education in the Arab States.

Mokhtari, Najib. 1997. "The Cult of Excellence and the Idea(l) of the University." In *The Idea of the University*, edited by Taieb Belghazi, 101–14. Rabat: Faculty of Letters and Human Sciences, University Mohammed V Agdal. (in Arabic)

Momani, Basma. 2018. "Egypt's IMF Program: Assessing the Political Economy Challenges." Brookings Doha Report, January 30.

Moore, Clement Henry. 1980. *Images of Development: Egyptian Engineers in Search of Industry*. Cambridge, MA: Massachusetts Institute of Technology Press.

Moroccan Coalition for Education for All, the National Federation of Student–Parent Associations, and others. 2014. Parallel report submitted to the UN Committee on Economic and Social Rights and Cultural Rights in the 55th Session, 3.

Moroccan World News. 2017. "58 percent of Moroccan Students Enrolled in Universities Do Not Graduate," https://www.moroccoworldnews. com/2017/05/216662/moroccan-students-enrolled-universities-graduate/

Mossalem, Mohammed. 2015. *The IMF in the Arab World: Lessons Unlearnt*. London: Breton Woods Project.

"Mosul University Liberated." 2017. Video available at https://www.thenational.ae/world/inside-mosul-university-after-its-liberation-from-isil-video-1.89144.

Moudden, Abdelhay. 1997. "The Moroccan University and Post-modernism." In *The Idea of the University*, edited by Taieb Belghazi, 241–45. Rabat: Faculty of Letters and Human Sciences, University Mohammed V Agdal.

Mrabi, Mohamed Ali. 2013. "Projet de budget 2014: La masse salariale creuse le gouffre." *L'Economiste*, October 23, 4–5.

Msaddaq, Abdul Nabi. 2015. "Why Tunisia Is the Top Supplier of Students to the Islamic State." *Al-Fanar Media*, July 8.

Muasher, Marwan. 2014. *The Second Arab Awakening*. New Haven, CT: Yale University Press.

Mughaith, Kamal. 2018. "Jami'at al-Qahira: tarikh wa sira." In *Siyar 'ashar jami'at hukumiya 'arabiya*, prepared by Adnan El-Amine, 25–88. Beirut: Arab Center for Research and Policy Studies.

Mukherjee, Hena, and Poh Kam Wong. 2011. "The National University of Singapore and the University of Malaya: Common Roots and Different Paths." In *The Road to Academic Excellence: The Making of World-class Research Universities*, edited by Philip G. Altbach and Jamil Salmi, 129–65. Washington, DC: World Bank.

NACUBO (National Association of College and University Business Officers). 2002. *Explaining College Costs: NACUBO'S Methodology for Identifying the Costs of Delivering Undergraduate Education*. Washington, DC: NACUBO.

Nahas, Charbel. 2010. "Finance and Political Economy of Higher Education in Lebanon." In *Financing Higher Education in Arab Countries*, edited by Ahmed Galal and Taher Kanaan, 49–86. Economic Research Forum Policy Research Report, no. 34.

———. 2009. "Financing Higher Education in Lebanon." Economic Research Forum, April.

National Campaign for the Rights of Students. 2015. *Higher Education Strategy: Privatization of Public (Rasmi) Universities, Raising Fees in Parallel and Competitive Programs*. Amman: Studies Committee.

Naufal, Diane. 2009. "Do Educational Outcomes in Lebanese Universities Differ Based on the Academic Model?" *Education, Business and Society: Contemporary Middle Eastern Issues* 2 (1): 6–19.

Neaime, Simon. 2017. "Lebanon's Challenge of Fiscal Sustainability." Economic Research Forum Policy Portal, November 14.

Nizam, Jawad. 1997. "Simat al-hay'a al-ta'limiya." In *al-Ta'lim al-'ali fi Lubnan*, edited by Adnan El-Amine, 427–93. Beirut: al-Hay'a al-Lubnaniya li-l-'Ulum al-Tarbawiya.

Obst, Daniel, and Daniel Kirk, eds. 2010. *Innovation through Education: Building the Knowledge Economy in the Middle East.* New York: International Institute of Education and American Institute for Foreign Study.

OECD (Organisation for Economic Co-operation and Development). 2010. "Singapore: Rapid Improvement Followed by Strong Performance." In *Strong Performers and Successful Reformers in Education: Lessons from PISA for the United States*, 159–76. OECD Publishing, http://dx.doi.org/10.1787/9789264096660-en

Oubenal, Mohamed. 2019. "The Role of Finance and Banks in Moroccan Cronyism." In *Crony Capitalsim in the Middle East: Business and Politics from Liberalization to the Arab Spring*, edited by Ishac Diwan, Adeel Malik, and Izak Atiyas, 309–29. Oxford and New York: Oxford University Press.

Overbye, Dennis. 2017. "A Light for Science, and Cooperation, in the Middle East." *New York Times*, May 8.

Najjar, Fauzi M. 2000. "Islamic Fundamentalism and the Intellectuals: The Case of Nasr Hamid Abu Zayd." *British Journal of Middle Eastern Studies* 27 (2): 177–200.

Normile, Dennis. 2012. "Flocking to Asia for a Shot at Greatness." *Science* 337, no. 6099 (September 7): 1162–66.

Pallas, Aaron, Anna Neumann, and Corbin Campbell. 2017. *Policies and Practices to Support Undergraduate Teaching Improvement.* Cambridge, MA: American Academy of Arts and Sciences.

Parry, Marc. 2015. "Can Robert Putnam Save the American Dream?" *Chronicle of Higher Education*, March 12.

Parry, Marc, Kelly Field, and Beckie Supiano. 2013. "The Gates Effect." *Chronicle of Higher Education Special Report*, July 14.

Patel, Vimal. 2014. "Most Ph.D.'s in STEM Fields Work Outside of Academe, Analysis Finds." *Chronicle of Higher Education*, April 1.

Pettit, Emma. 2016. "Turkey's Education Board Tells 1,577 University Deans to Resign." *Chronicle of Higher Education*, July 19.

Plackett, Benjamin. 2019. "Most Arab-World Researchers Want to Leave, a New Survey Finds." *Al-Fanar Media*, December 3.

_____. 2018. "Behind the Numbers: Arab Women in Research." *Al-Fanar Media*, August 6.

_____. 2016. "How to Break the Informal Ban on Studying Evolution." *Al-Fanar Media*, April 7.

_____. 2014. "A Conversation with Morocco's Pushiest President." *Al-Fanar Media*, July 12.

Pollack, Kenneth M. 2019. *Armies of Sand: The Past, Present and Future of Arab Military Effectiveness*. Oxford: Oxford University Press.

Portnoi, Laura, Val Rust, and Sylvia Bagley, eds. 2010. *Higher Education, Policy, and the Global Competition Phenomenon*. New York: Palgrave Macmillan.

Press, William. 2013. "What's So Special about Science (and How Much Should We Spend on It)?" *Science* 342, no. 6160 (November 15): 817–22.

Prewitt, Kenneth. 2013. "Is Any Science Safe?" *Science* 340, no. 6132 (May 3): 525.

Przeworski, Adam, and Fernando Limongi. 1997. "Modernization: Theories and Facts," *World Politics* 49:155–83.

Qamaas, Mustafa. 2018. "al-Maghrib yatabanna khitta li-tawfir 1.2 milyun wazifa jadida." *Al-Araby Al-Jadeed*, April 27.

Qing Hui Wang, Qi Wang, and Nian Cai Liu. 2011. "Building World-class Universities in China: Shanghai Jiao Tong University." In *The Road to Academic Excellence: The Making of World-class Research Universities*, edited by Philip G. Altbach and Jamil Salmi, 33–104. Washington, DC: World Bank.

Qiu, Jane. 2017. "China Bets Big on Big Facilities." *Science* 353, no. 6306 (September 23): 1353.

QS Asia News Network. 2017. "Vision 2030: Saudi Arabia Shifts from Oil to Higher Education." *QS*, December 19.

Rafiq, Abd al-Karim. 2004. *Tarikh al-jami'a al-'arabiya: al bidaya wa-l-numuw, 1901–1946*. Damascus: Maktabat Nubil.

Rahman, Atta-ur. 2015. *Building a Knowledge Economy: Imperative for Socioeconomic Development*. Lahore: Institute for Policy Reforms.

Rais, Oumnia. 2018. "Morocco Tuition Fee Law Sparks Anger." *Al-Jazeera*, January 18.

Rajabany, Intissar, and Lihi Ben Shitrit. 2014. "Activism and Civil War in Libya." In *Taking to the Streets: The Transformation of Arab Activism*, edited by Lina Khatib and Ellen Lust, 76–108. Baltimore, MD: John Hopkins University Press.

Ramirez, Francisco. 2010. "Accounting for Excellence: Transforming Universities into Organizational Actors." In *Higher Education, Policy, and the Global Competition Phenomenon*, edited by Laura Portnoi, Val Rust, and Sylvia Bagley, 43–58. New York: Palgrave Macmillan.

Rawlings, Hunter. 2014. "Universities on the Defensive." *Princeton Alumni Weekly*, April 2, 28–31.

Rea, Jeannie. 2016. "Critiquing Neoliberalism in Australian Universities" in "Challenging the Privatised University." Special issue, *Australian Universities' Review* 58 (2): 9–14.

Reich, Justin, and José A. Ruipérez-Valiente. 2019. "The MOOC Pivot: What Happened to Disruptive Transformation of Education?" *Science* 363, no. 6423 (January 11): 130–31.

Reid, Donald. 1990. *Cairo University and the Making of Modern Egypt*. Cambridge: Cambridge University Press.

Reisz, Matthew. 2015. "The Palestinian Academy: Pressing Concerns and Future Prospects." *Times Higher Education*, March 26.

Republic of Lebanon and CNRS-L (National Council for Scientific Research, Lebanon). 2011?. *Five Years Report: 2007–2011*. Beirut: CNRS-L

———. 2006. Science, Technology and Innovation Policy for Lebanon. Beirut: CNRS-L.

Republic of Lebanon Ministry of Education and Higher Education and Tempus. 2010?. *The Lebanese Higher Education System: A Short Description*. Beirut: Ministry of Education and Higher Education.

Reynolds, Nancy. 2013. "Building the Past: Rockscapes and the Aswan High Dam in Egypt." In *Water on Sand: Environmental Histories of the Middle East*, edited by Alain Mikhail, 181–205. Oxford: Oxford University Press.

Rhee, Byung Shil. 2011. "A World-class Research University on the Periphery: The Pohang University of Science and Technology, the Republic of Korea." In *The Road to Academic Excellence: The Making of World-class Research Universities*, edited by Philip G. Altbach and Jamil Salmi, 101–28. Washington, DC: World Bank.

Richards, Alan. 1992. "Higher Education in Egypt." Policy Research Working Paper 862, Population and Human Resources Department, World Bank.

Rizk, Reham. 2016. "Returns to Education: An Updated Comparison from Arab Countries." Economic Research Forum Working Paper, no. 986, April.

Rizk, Reham, and Hala Abou-Ali. 2016. "Out of Pocket Education Expenditure and Household Budget: Evidence from Arab Countries," *Economic Research Forum Working Paper*, no. 996, May.

Rodin, Judith. 2007. *The University and Urban Revival: Out of the Ivory Tower and into the Streets*. Philadelphia, PA: University of Pennsylvania Press.

Rougier, Eric. 2016. "'Fire in Cairo': Authoritarian–Redistributive Social Contracts, Structural Change, and the Arab Spring." *World Development* 78:148–71.

Russo, Jonathan. 2018. "The Man Who Hopes to Bring Peace to the Middle East by Solving Sky-high Unemployment." *Observer*, April 10.

Ryan, Curtis. 1998. "Peace, Bread and Riots: Jordan and the International Monetary Fund." *Middle East Policy* 6, no. 2 (October): 54–66.

Sabry, Manar. 2009. "Funding Policy and Higher Education in Arab Countries." *Journal of Comparative and International Higher Education* 1:11–12.

Said, Rushdi. 2000. *Rihlat 'umr: tharwat Misr bayna 'Abd al-Nasir wa-l-Sadat*. Cairo: Dar al-Hilal.

Salamé, Ramzi. 2010. "Career Path of Higher Education Teaching Personnel in the Arab States and the Quality Challenges." In *Towards an Arab Higher Education Space: International Challenges and Societal Responsibilities*, edited by Bechir Lamine, 319–46. Cairo: Arab Regional Conference on Higher Education.

Saleh, Mohammed. 2015. "Management of Oil Revenue in the Rentier Economies: A Case Study in Libya." Henley Business School, Reading University.

Salehi-Isfahani, Djavad. 2009. "Education and Earnings: A Comparative Study of Returns to Schooling in Egypt, Iran, and Turkey." Economic Research Forum Working Paper, no. 504, September.

_____. 2005. "Human Resources in Iran: Potentials and Challenges." *Iranian Studies* 38 (1): 117–47.

Salehi-Isfahani, Djavad, and Daniel Egel. 2009. "Beyond Statism: Toward a New Social Contract for Iranian Youth." In *Generation in Waiting: The Unfulfilled Promise of Young People in the Middle East*, edited by Navtej Dhillon and Tarik Yousef, 39–66. Washington, DC: Brookings Institution Press.

Salisbury, Peter. 2011. "Educating the Future Labor Force." *Middle East Economic Digest* 48, December 2–8.

Salmi, Jamil. 2011. "The Road to Academic Excellence: Lessons of Experience." In *The Road to Academic Excellence: The Making of World-class Research Universities*, edited by Philip G. Altbach and Jamil Salmi, 323–40. Washington, DC: World Bank.

_____. 2009. *The Challenge of Establishing World Class Universities*. Washington, DC: World Bank.

_____. 2002. *Constructing Knowledge Societies: New Challenges for Tertiary Education*. Washington, DC: World Bank.

Salmi, Jamil, and Authur Hauptman. 2006. "Innovations in Tertiary Education Financing." World Bank Education Paper 4, September.

al-Samar, 'Ammar. 2018. "al-Jami'a al-suriya: 'Jami'at Dimashq,' jami'a hukumiya fi al-'alam al-'arabi." In *Siyar 'ashar jami'at hukumiya 'arabiya*, prepared by Adnan El-Amine, 91–146. Beirut: Arab Center for Research and Policy Studies.

Saoud, Mohamed. 2014. "Teaching of the Amazigh Language in Moroccan Universities: Benefits and Challenges." *Morocco World News*, July 12.

Sassoon, Joseph. 2012. *Saddam Hussein's Ba'th Party: Inside an Authoritarian Regime*. Cambridge: Cambridge University Press.

Sawahel, Wagdy. 2015. "Regional Hub Planned to Lure African and Arab Students." *University World News*, no. 352, January 30.

_____. 2014. "New Arab Platform for MOOCs Launched." *University World News*, no. 322, May 30.

_____. 2011. "North Africa: Social Anger Prompts Universities Reform." *University World News*, no. 73, March 13.

Saxena, Prem. 2013. *Demographic Profile of the Arab Countries: Analysis of the Ageing Phenomenon*. Beirut: Economic and Social Commission for Western Asia.

Sayed Ahmad, Amira. 2017. "Egypt Debates Introducing Electronic Text Books." *Al-Fanar Media*, May 5.

Sayigh, Yezid. 2019. *Owners of the Republic: An Anatomy of Egypt's Military Economy*. Washington DC: Carnegie Endowment for International Peace.

Schnepf, Sylke. 2014. "Do Tertiary Dropout Students Really Not Succeed in European Labour Markets?" Discussion Paper No. 8015, Institute for the Study of Labor.

Scholars at Risk Network. 2017. *Free to Think: Report of the Scholars at Risk Academic Freedom Monitoring Project*, https://www.scholarsatrisk.org/.

_____. 2015. *Free to Think: Report of the Scholars at Risk Academic Freedom Monitoring Project*, https://www.scholarsatrisk.org/.

Schramm, Carl. 2008. "Reinvigorating Universities in an Entrepreneurial Age." In *The Globalization of Higher Education*, edited by Luc Weber and James Duderstadt,. 15–26. London: Economica.

Science. 2016. "German Ivy League Gets Boost." *Science* 352, no. 6285 (April 29): 498–500.

_____. 2015. "Unveiling China's Nuclear Past." News this Week, *Science* vol. 350, no. 6256, October 2, https://science.sciencemag.org/content/350/6256/news-summaries

_____. 2011. "Competition, Tough Standards, Bring New Vigor to Saudi Science." *Science* 333, no. 6042 (July 29): 536.

Serageldin, Ismail. 2008. "Science in Muslim Countries." *Science* 321, no. 5890 (August 8): 745.

Service, Robert. 2016. "Founder's Death Unsettles Egypt's Science City." *Science* 353, no. 6300 (August 12): 632–33.

Sexton, John. 2010. "The Global Network University." Press release from the office of the president, NYU, New York, December 5.

Shahine, Emile. 2011. *al-Jami'a al-lubnaniya: thamrat nidal al-tullab wa-l-asatidha*. Beirut: Dar al-Farabi.

Shahla, Zina. 2018. "Syrian Higher Education Faces a Long Recovery." *Al-Fanar Media*, May 2.

Shams El Din, Mai. 2015. "Dropping the Right to Free Education?" *Al-Fanar Media*, March 11.

Sharabi, Hisham. 1988. *Neo-patriarchy: A Theory of Distorted Change in Arab Society*. Oxford: Oxford University Press.

Al-Sharqi, Mohammed. 2016. "Morocco Supports Development and Investment in Africa." *al-Hayat*, August 22. (in Arabic)

Shavarini, Mitra. 2005. "The Feminisation of Iranian Higher Education." *International Review of Education* 51 (4): 329–47.

al-Shayi', Khalid. 2016. "Su'udiyyat yahmilna shahadat 'ala waraq." *Al-Araby Al-Jadeed*, January 9.

Shepard, Stuart, and James Agresti. 2018. "Government Spending on Education Is Higher than Ever. And for What?" *Foundation for Economic Education*, March 1.

Shepland, Greg. 2016. "The Perils and Pitfalls of Scholarly Research in the Arab World." *Arab Digest*, December 4.

Shibeika, Alaa. 2014. "A Sudanese Student Watches a University Grow Dark." *Al-Fanar Media*, August 4.

Si Bashir, Mohammed. 2018. "'An i'aqat al-taghyir fi al-Jaza'ir." *Al-Araby Al-Jadeed*, July 11.

Siira, Katerina, and Thomas Hill. 2016. "The University of Mosul Could Show the Way in Post-war Reconstruction." *Al-Fanar Media*, November 13.

Silverstein, Paul, and David Crawford. 2004. "Amazigh Activism and the Moroccan State." *Middle East Report* no. 233, Winter, 44–48.

Simon, Herbert. 1947. *Administrative Behavior: a Study in Decision-making Processes in Administrative Organization*. New York: MacMillan.

Solomon, Jay. 2016. *The Iran Wars*. New York: Random House.

Spaulding, Seth, Klaus Bahr, Vinayagum Chinapah, and Nader Fergany. 1996. *Review and Assessment of Reform of Basic Education in Egypt*. Paris: United Nations Economic and Social Council.

Springborg, Robert. 2018. *Egypt*. Cambridge, UK, and Medford, MA: Polity Press.

Starr, Steven. 2012. *Revolt in Syria: Eye Witness to the Uprising*. New York: Columbia University Press.

Stern, Lord Nicholas. 2016. *Building on Success and Learning from Experience: An Independent Review of the Research Excellence Framework*. London: Department for Business, Energy and Industrial Strategy.

Stiffler, Douglas. 2005. "Resistance to Sovietization of Higher Education in China." In *Universities under Dictatorship*, edited by John Connelly and Michael Grüttner, 213–43. University Park, PA: Pennsylvania State University Press.

Stone, Richard. 2016. "Iranian Sun: A Fusion Research Program Nurtured in Isolation Could Blossom as Iran Joins the ITER Megaproject." *Science* 353, no. 6304 (September 9): 1083–87.

———. 2015. "Unsanctioned Science." *Science* 349, no. 6252 (September 4): 1038–43.

Stripling, Jack. 2016. "Obama's Legacy: An Unlikely Hawk on Higher Ed." *Chronicle of Higher Education*, September 25.

Taha, Rana. 2012. "Nile University Case Resolved." *Daily News Egypt*, November 18.

Tan, Tony. 2007. "Strategies for Emerging Universities and University Systems: A Case Study of Singapore." Sixth Glion Colloquium, Glion, June 16–20.

Tansel, Aysit. 2013. "Supplementary Education in Turkey: Recent Developments and Future Prospects." Economic Research Forum Working Paper, no. 822, December.

Tarek, Rania. 2015. "English Courses a 'Cash Cow,' Cairo University Students Say." *Al-Fanar Media*, October 12.

Tareq, Hassan. 2015. "Governance Authorities in the Moroccan Constitution: Governance or Democracy?" In *Science Education in Universities in the Islamic World*, edited by Nidhal Guessoum and Athar Osama, 94–98. Report of Zakri Task Force on Science at Universities of the Muslim World, London and Islamabad.

El Tayeb, Mustafa. 2015. "Science Education in Universities in the Arab World." In Nidhal Guessoum and Athar Osama, eds., *Science at the Universities of the Muslim World*, 94–98. London, Islamabad: Muslim World Science Initiative.

Tohmé, Georges. N.d. "al-Jami'a al-lubnaniya fi sanawat al-harb bayn 1975 wa 1988." Unpublished manuscript.

Thomas, Kathrin. 2018. "Civic Engagement in the Middle East and North Africa." *Arab Barometer –Wave IV Topic Report*, https://www.arabbarometer.org/wp-content/uploads/PublicOpinion_CivicEngagement_MiddleEast_NorthAfrica_2018.pdf

Thrift, Nigel. 2012. "The Future of Big Ed." *Chronicle of Higher Education*, December 6.

Tignor, Robert. 2010. *Egypt: A Short History*. Princeton, NJ: Princeton University Press.

Times Higher Education. 2015. "World University Rankings 2015–2016 Methodology." September 24, https://www.timeshighereducation.com/news/ranking-methodology-2016.

Tolba, Mustafa. 2006. "Interview." *Magazine of Higher Education*, October, 7–11. (in Arabic)

Trager, Eric. 2016. *Arab Fall: How the Muslim Brotherhood Won and Lost Egypt in 891 Days*. Washington, DC: Georgetown University Press.

Turk, James. 2015. "A Chance to Get Science Right." *Science* 350, no. 6257 (October 9): 139.

Tzannatos, Zafiris. 2016. "Employment and Rates of Return to Education in Arab Countries Gender and Public Sector Perspectives." Economic Research Forum Policy Brief, no. 13, June.

———. 2011. "Labour Demand and Social Dialogue: Two Binding Constraints for Creating Decent Employment and Ensuring Effective Utilization of Human Resources in the Arab Region?" Expert Group Meeting on Addressing Unemployment and Underemployment in the Islamic Development Bank Member Countries, Islamic Development Bank, May.

Tzannatos, Zafiris, Ishac Diwan, and Joanna Abdel Ahad. 2016. "Rates of Return to Education in Twenty-two Arab Countries: An Update and Comparison between the MENA and the Rest of the World." Economic Research Forum Working Paper, no. 1007, May.

'Ulayan, Samira, Sirhan Duwaib, and Akim Ruda. eds. 2010. *Educational Reform in the Middle East*. Amman: Dar al-Shorouk.

UNDP (United Nations Development Programme) and AFESD (Arab Fund for Economic and Social Development). 2016. *Arab Human Development Report 2016: Towards Freedom in the Arab World*. New York: United Nations Development Programme.

_____. 2005. *Arab Human Development Report 2005: Towards Freedom in the Arab World*. New York: United Nations Development Programme.

_____. 2003. *Arab Human Development Report 2003: Building a Knowledge Society*. New York: United Nations Development Programme.

UNESCO (United Nations Educational, Scientific and Cultural Organization) Regional Bureau for Education in the Arab States. 2009. *A Decade of Higher Education in the Arab States: Achievements and Challenges*. Beirut: UNESCO Regional Bureau for Education in the Arab States.

USAID (United States Agency for International Development). N.d. "Evaluation of the Technological Planning Program Cairo University/MIT." AID Contract NE-C-1291, scanned document, Cairo.

_____. 1980. "Evaluation of the Technological Planning Program Cairo University/MIT." AID Contract NE-C-1291, scanned document, Cairo.

Uthman, Magid. 2015. *Fairness and Justice in the Adherence of Different Social Strata to Higher Education*. Cairo: Population Council.

Van Diesel, Arthur, and Khalid Abu-Ismail. 2019. "MENA Generation 2030: Prospects for a Demographic Dividend." *ERF: The Forum Policy Portal*, April 17.

Veale, Laurene. 2015a. "A Mixed Bag of Scientific Commitment." *MIT Technology Review*, Arab Edition, February 8.

_____. 2015b. "Falling Behind." *MIT Technology Review*, Arab Edition, January 21.

_____. 2015c. "What Is Being Done about the State of Science in the Arab World." *MIT Technology Review*, February 10.

Vermeren, Pierre. 2002. *Ecole, élite et pouvoir au Maroc et en Tunisie au XXe siècle*. Rabat: Alizés.

Vietor, Richard, and Hilary White. 2014. "Singapore's 'Mid-life Crisis'?" Harvard Business School, N2-714-039 (revised).

Vogel, Gretchen. 2016. "Good Grades for Germany's Project to Build an Ivy League." *Science* 351, no. 6273 (February 5): 545.

Voyvoda, Ebru, and Erinç Yeldan. 2012. "On Applied Endogenous Growth Model with Human and Knowledge Capital Accumulation for the Turkish Economy." Economic Research Forum Working Paper, no. 707, September.

Watenpaugh, Keith David. 2018. "A 'Backpack' Helps Refugee Students Store and Share Credentials." *Al-Fanar Media*, March 29.

Waterbury, John. 2017a. "al-Jami'at al-hukumiya al-mustaqbaliya wa tahadiyyat tatwir al-ta'lim al-'ali fi al-'alam al-'arabi." In *al-Jami'at wa-l-bahth al-'ilmi fi al-'alam al-'arabi*, coordinated by Murad Diani, 33–47. Beirut: Arab Center for Research and Policy Studies.

_____. 2017b. "Water and Water Supply in the MENA." In *Water, Energy and Food Sustainability in the Middle East: The Sustainability Triangle*, edited by Adnan Badran, Sohail Murad, Elias Baydoun, and Nuhad Daghir, 57–84. New York: Springer.

_____. 2013. "The Political Economy of Climate Change in the Arab World." In *Arab Human Development Report*. New York: United Nations Development Programme.

_____. 1993. *Exposed to Innumerable Delusions: Public Enterprise and State Power in Egypt, India, Mexico and Turkey*. Cambridge: Cambridge University Press.

Weber, Luc, and James Duderstadt, eds. 2008. *The Globalization of Higher Education*. London: Economica.

Weise, Michelle, and Clayton M. Christensen. 2014. *Hire Education: Mastery, Modularization, and the Workforce Revolution*. Boston: Clayton Christensen Institute for Disruptive Innovation.

Wheeler, David, and Rasha Faek. 2018. "The Frustrating Lives of Syria's Future Leaders." *Al-Fanar Media*, November 15.

White, Jenny. 2012. *Muslim Nationalism and the New Turks*. Princeton, NJ: Princeton University Press.

Wickham, Carrie Rosefsky. 2013. *The Muslim Brotherhood: Evolution of an Islamist Movemement*. Princeton, Oxford: Princeton University Press.

Wildavsky, Ben. 2010. *The Great Brain Race: How Global Universities Are Reshaping the World*. Princeton, NJ: Princeton University Press.

Wirtschafter, Jacob. 2017. "Meet Cairo University's New President." *The National*, November 5.

Wirtschafter, Jacob, and Mina Nader. 2017. "Cairo University President Leaves Legacy of Stability." *Al-Fanar Media*, June 28.

World Bank. 2017. *Learning to Realize Education's Promise*. Washington, DC: World Bank.

_____. 2016. "Public Employment and Governance in MENA, Middle East and North Africa." Report No. ACS18501.

_____. 2011. "Striving for Better Jobs: The Challenge of Informality in the Middle East and North Africa Region." MENA Knowledge and Learning Quick Notes Series 49, no. 4 (December).

_____. 2008. *The Road Not Traveled: Education Reform in the Middle East and North Africa*. Washington, DC: World Bank.

_____. 1999. "Financing Higher Education in Africa: Makerere—The Quiet Revolution." Findings, Africa Region, no. 143, September.

World Bank and CMI (Center for Mediterranean Integration). 2013. *Benchmarking Governance as a Tool for Promoting Change: 100 Universities in the MENA Paving the Way*. Washington, DC: World Bank.

_____. 2012. *Universities through the Looking Glass: Benchmarking University Governance to Enable Higher Education Modernization in MENA*. Washington, DC: World Bank.

World Bank and OECD (Organisation for Economic Co-operation and Development). 2010. *Reviews of National Policies for Education: Higher Education in Egypt*. Paris: OECD.

Yahia, Mohammed, and Declan Butler. 2015. "Science in Turmoil: After the Arab Spring." *Nature*, April 29, 604–607.

Yaqtin, Said. 2017. "Dirasat halat jami'at Muhammad al-Khamis." In *al-Jami'at wa-l-bahth al-'ilmi fi al-'alam al-'arabi*, coordinated by Murad Diani, 67–118. Beirut: Arab Center for Research and Policy Studies.

Younes, Nidal. 2015. "Higher Education Council and the Issue of Self-Interest." *Jordan Times*, July 27.

Young, Michael. 2010. *The Ghosts of Martyrs Square*. New York: Simon and Schuster.

Yousef, Tarik M. 2004. "Development, Growth and Policy Reform in the Middle East and North Africa since 1950." *Journal of Economic Perspectives* 18 (3): 91–116.

Zahlan, A.B. 2012. *Science, Development and Sovereignty in the Arab World*. New York: Palgrave Macmillan.

Zakaria, Fareed. 2015. *In Defense of a Liberal Education*. New York: W.W. Norton.

Zand, Hossein, and Omaima Karrar. 2010. "Quality Assurance and a Bologna-type Process in the Arab World." In *Towards an Arab Higher Education Space: International Challenges and Societal Responsibilities*, edited by Bechir Lamine, 389–99. Cairo: Arab Regional Conference on Higher Education.

Zawya. 2014. "Arab Education Needs Unified Funding Efforts," November 13.

Zeghal, Malika. 1996. *Les oulémas d'al-Azhar dans l'Égypte contemporaine.* Paris: Presses de Sciences Po.

Zewail, Ahmed. 2002. *Voyage through Time: Walks of Life to the Nobel Prize.* Cairo: American University in Cairo Press.

Zong, Jie, and Jeanne Batalova. 2018. "International Students in the United States", migrationpolicy.org, May 9.

Index

Ecole Supérieure de Literature (Syria) 75

Greece 14, 47*t*, 48
Gülen, Fethullah 117, 130
Gutmann, Amy 128, 129, 131, 133

Hashemite University (Jordan) 107, 256
Hassan II of Morocco 97, 102, 116, 119
Hezbollah (Lebanon) 22, 50, 87
humanities and social sciences: enroll-
    ment in 38; graduate studies in 281;
    teaching of soft skills 209. *See also*
    STEM (science, technology, engi-
    neering, and mathematics)
Hussein, Kamal al-Din 63–64
Hussein, Saddam 16, 113, 114, 135, 148
Hussein, Taha 55, 58, 60, 61, 62
Hymans, Jacques 147–48

ICT (information and communications
    technology) 225–26. *See also* innova-
    tion; online education
IFIs (international financial institu-
    tions): and education reform 17;
    International Monetary Fund (IMF)
    6; World Bank 178, 180, 187*f*, 199,
    247; World Bank Group 183, 186–88.
    See also donor and NGO community;
    structural adjustment programs
IHLs (institutions of higher learning):
    in Egypt 64, 67, 123; governance
    of, centralized 164. *See also* research
    institutes; *specific institutions*
IMF (International Monetary Fund) 6.
    See also IFIs (international financial
    institutions); structural adjustment
    programs
infrastructure of education: cost of 214;
    damage to 183; disruptive changes
    in debated 302–304; investment in 5;
    need for physical universities 19–20,
    229, 263. *See also* financing tertiary
    education; innovation, disruptive;
    online education
innovation: overview 205–207, 228*t*,
    230–31; non-threatening 231; and
    policymaking 1–4; versus reform
    177–78; sustaining 2, 226, 230,
    286. *See also* innovation, disruptive;

innovation, inward-looking; innovation, outward-looking; Politics, big-P
(regime survival); politics, small-p
(games of influence and patronage);
reform
————, DISRUPTIVE: in infrastructure of
education 20, 229, 302–304; military
research 229–30; new corporate
actors 228; private education as 202,
207, 293–96; theory of 2–3, 20–21,
226–28, 297–301. *See also* innovation;
innovation, inward-looking; innovation, outward-looking; reform
————, INWARD-LOOKING: definition
205–206; CAU innovations 208–209;
ESCWA recommendations 208; incentive systems 213–14; new financial
models 214–16; pedagogy 209–13,
226. *See also* innovation; innovation,
disruptive; innovation, outward-
looking; reform
————, OUTWARD-LOOKING: overview
205–207; ICT (information and
communications technology) 225–26;
innovation hubs 223–24; quality of
business–university relations 221*t*;
R&D (research and development)
216–23, 220*t*, 221*t*. *See also* innovation; innovation, disruptive; innovation, inward-looking; R&D (research
and development); reform; research
institutes
Institut Supérieur de Technologie
(Morocco) 100
International Cairo University 255. *See
also* Cairo University (previously
Egyptian University, then Fuad I
University)
international education market 202, 257,
301–302
Iran: control of universities 110, 111,
114–15, 135–36, 142; enrollments in
tertiary institutions 27, 28*t*; examination results and careers 10; GER
(Gross Enrollment Ratio) 29*t*, 31–32;
Iranian Light Source Facility (syn-
chrotron) 144–45; nuclear research

performance, institutional 21, 230, 263–64, 304–305. *See also* innovation, disruptive; quality assurance reforms; reform

Petroleum Institute (UAE) 145, 228

PKK (Kurdish Workers' Party) (Turkey) 130

policy and policymaking: drivers of 3–4, 15–17; drivers of change, crisis as 15–16, 180, 182–83; drivers of change, donors and NGOs 17, 181, 182, 183–84; and education reform 17–19; and innovation 1–4; opaqueness of 180–81. *See also* governance; innovation; Politics, big-P (regime survival); politics, small-p (games of influence and patronage); reform

Politics, big-P (regime survival): overview 15, 105; activism in universities 117–22; ambivalence of autocratic regimes 111–13; autonomy of universities 173–75; control of civil society 109–11; *mukhabarat* (secret police) in universities 113–15; repression 115–17; social contract 108–109, 123–24. *See also* governance; policy and policymaking; politics, small-p (games of influence and patronage); social contract

politics, confessional 87–88, 106

politics, small-p (games of influence and patronage) 105–108. *See also* governance; policy and policymaking; Politics, big-P (regime survival)

private lessons 244–46

private tertiary education: birth of in economic crisis 6, 16, 26, 51–52, 236; corporate universities 172; as disruptive innovation 207, 293–96; in Egypt 27t, 49; in Iran 49, 52, 262; in Jordan 27t, 49, 262; in Lebanon 84; in Morocco 102; and need for student loans 242–43; number of universities 27t; political favors in growth of 173–74; quality of 49; and reform movements 203; in Syria 79, 80–81; in Turkey 259–60; use of adjunct faculty 278

professional associations 108, 121. *See also* communities of practice

public good, tertiary education as: argument against 21, 226–27, 292; argument for 136–37; dropouts as loss to society 241; and equity 152, 163, 215, 233–34. *See also* social contract

Qadhafi, Muammar 116, 134–35

Qarawiyyin University (Morocco) 54–55, 95–96, 119

Qatar: Cornell Weil Medical College 161; mediation by 87; per student expenditures 238; R&D investment by 219; universities and institutes in 145

quality assurance reforms 185, 199–201. *See also* innovation; performance, institutional; reform

al-Quds University (East Jerusalem) 107

Queen Rania Foundation (Jordan) 213, 225

R&D (research and development): and employment 222; expenditures worldwide 13, 218–20, 220t; failure of 7; funding, competitive 244; funding, innovative 213–15; incentive systems for 278–83; incubation 224, 262; and innovation 216–23; private sector investment in 197, 217–20; stimulation of 222–23. *See also* economic incentive systems; financing tertiary education, corporate actors; innovation; research institutes; research universities

Rabat School of Governance and Economics (EGE) (Morocco) 102

reform: overview 177–78, 202–203; cost of neglecting 153–54; dilemma of reform within autocracies 17–21, 184–85; in governance 179, 190–91; gradual versus disruptive 19–21, 305–306; versus innovation 177–78; for job market mismatch 179; jobs mismatch, destabilizing effect of 195–99, 197f, 198f; jobs mismatch, size of problem 191–95; Morocco and third-parties 185–90; non-threatening

economic crises 124; free education in 163, 252–54; in Kuwait 145; and public sector jobs 194; and regime survival 108–109. *See also* Politics, big-P (regime survival); public good, tertiary education as

social sciences: perceived as threat 148–50; teaching of soft skills 209

SOEs (state-owned enterprises) 11–12, 228. *See also* economy, public sector; financing tertiary education, corporate actors; politics, small-p (games of influence and patronage)

South Korea: class bias in 14; GER (Gross Enrollment Ratio) 28; massification of tertiary education 13; Pohang University 172; private lessons in 244; public expenditures on tertiary education 41*t*; R&D investment by 219; STEM studies in 38; unemployment and labor participation rates 47*t*. *See also* East Asia

Soviet Bloc 64–65, 89, 174

Soviet Union 142, 143

SPC (Syrian Protestant College, later AUB) (Lebanon) 56, 72, 73, 84, 295. *See also* AUB (American University of Beirut)

STEM (science, technology, engineering, and mathematics): bias toward 148–51; brain drain in 122; corporate universities 172; enrollment in 38; private sector investment in 197; in proposed reform model 21. *See also* financing tertiary education, corporate actors; humanities and social sciences; R&D (research and development); research institutes

Strait of Gibraltar 167

structural adjustment programs: effects of, generally 19; and expenditures on tertiary education 41–44; in Morocco 186–88; and reform attempts 71; and rise of private tertiary education 6, 16, 26, 51–52, 236

student activism: in Algeria 109; in Egypt 64, 109–10, 112, 115; in Lebanon 85; in MENA region 124, 158; in Morocco 97; in North Africa 108; outside MENA region 109; as political testing ground 108; in Sudan 109; in Syria 75, 78, 112

Sudan: under al-Bashir 111; civil service employment in 39; enrollments in tertiary institutions 27, 27*t*, 28*t*, 236; faculty members 37, 37*t*; faculty salaries in 271; GER (Gross Enrollment Ratio) 29*t*, 33; National Islamic Front 108; student protests in 109, 118, 124. *See also* education statistics

Suez Canal University (Egypt) 62, 66

Supreme Council for Education, Training, and Scientific Research (Morocco) 102

Supreme Council of Science (Egypt) 67. *See also* SCU (Supreme Council of Universities) (Egypt)

Supreme Councils 166–67, 235. *See also* Council for Higher Education (Syria); governance; SCU (Supreme Council of Universities) (Egypt); YÖK (Council of Higher Education) (Turkey)

SUT (Sharif University of Technology) (Iran) 115, 144

Syria: attitudes toward education 9–10, 11; Ba'th Party control of universities 113; civil service employment in 83; civil war 79; Council for Higher Education 82–83; cronyism in 196–97; educational policies 5; examination results and careers 10; faculty recruitment in 275; faculty salaries in 271–72, 273, 273*t*; as failed state 22; GER (Gross Enrollment Ratio) 29*t*, 30, 32; GER (Gross Enrollment Ratio), projected 316*t*, 318*t*; infrastructure destruction 183; language of instruction 74, 75; *mukhabarat* (secret police) in 78, 112, 113; online education in 213; Ottomans and tertiary education 72–73; parallel courses and opening learning 255; political turmoil 76, 77; private tertiary education

79, 80–81; public expenditures on tertiary education 41*t*, 42; quality assurance reforms 200; refugees from in MENA 24; secondary education 80; selection of Lebanese University's leadership 91; student activism in 112, 118; unemployment rates 83; use of Muslim student groups 118. *See also* Damascus University (previously Syrian University); education statistics; Syrian universities

Syrian Medical Association 74

Syrian universities 78–81. *See also* Damascus University (previously Syrian University); Syria

Syrian University (later Damascus University). *See* Damascus University (previously Syrian University)

Syrian University Medical Institute 74

Taiwan 38. *See also* East Asia

Technological Training Program (Egypt) 70–71

Tempus 92, 184

Texas A&M, Doha campus 238

Tishreen University (Syria) 79, 80

Tohmé, Georges 85, 88, 89–90, 168, 274

Tolba, Mostafa 67

trilemma of tertiary education (quantity, quality, cost) 5, 13–14, 43, 159, 283, 293. *See also* education statistics: expenditures; financing tertiary education; governance; innovation; jobs mismatch; massification of tertiary education; online education; reform; unemployment

TÜBITAK (Scientific and Technological Research Council) (Turkey) 244

Tunisia: attitudes toward education 9; civics education in 135, 151; civil service employment in 40; education excellence under Ben Ali 151; enrollments in tertiary institutions 27, 27*t*, 28*t*; faculty members 37, 37*t*; faculty salaries in 273*t*, 274; funding of research 244; funding of tertiary education 236; GER (Gross Enrollment Ratio)

29*t*, 32; Jasmine Revolution 110; Neo Destour Party 113; promotion system in 279; public expenditures on education 44; public expenditures on tertiary education 41*t*, 42, 43*t*; quality assurance reforms 200; R&D investment by 219; research funding 214, 217–18, 282; STEM students in extremist organizations 122; student activism 108, 118; unemployment rates 47*t*, 48, 51. *See also* education statistics

Turkey: academic freedom 130–31, 136; civil service and university education 53; civil service employment in 40; corporate universities 172; enrollments in tertiary institutions 27, 27*t*, 28*t*; GER (Gross Enrollment Ratio) 29*t*, 33, 33*t*; governance of universities 169; introduction of Latin alphabet in 111–12; out-migration 121; population of 24; private lessons in 245, 246; private tertiary education 259–60; public expenditures on education 43*t*, 44; public expenditures on tertiary education 239; religious instruction 136; repression in 116–17; risk of democratic tyranny in 128; Sesame (Synchrotron-light for Experimental Science and Applications in the Middle East) 146–47; unemployment rates 192. *See also* education statistics

UAE (United Arab Emirates): faculty members 50; graduates 34; non-national students in 50, 145; universities and institutes in 145, 228. *See also* education statistics

UAR (United Arab Republic) 76, 109–10

UNAM (Universidad Nacional Autónoma de México) 169, 174, 294

unemployment: among educated 9, 14, 16, 48, 122, 132, 179, 182; and education expenditures 51–52; and Gross Enrollment Ratios (GERs) 30; and jobs mismatch 46–48, 61, 163; and labor participation 47*t*; as long-term